FAIRY TAIL
100 YEARS QUEST

5

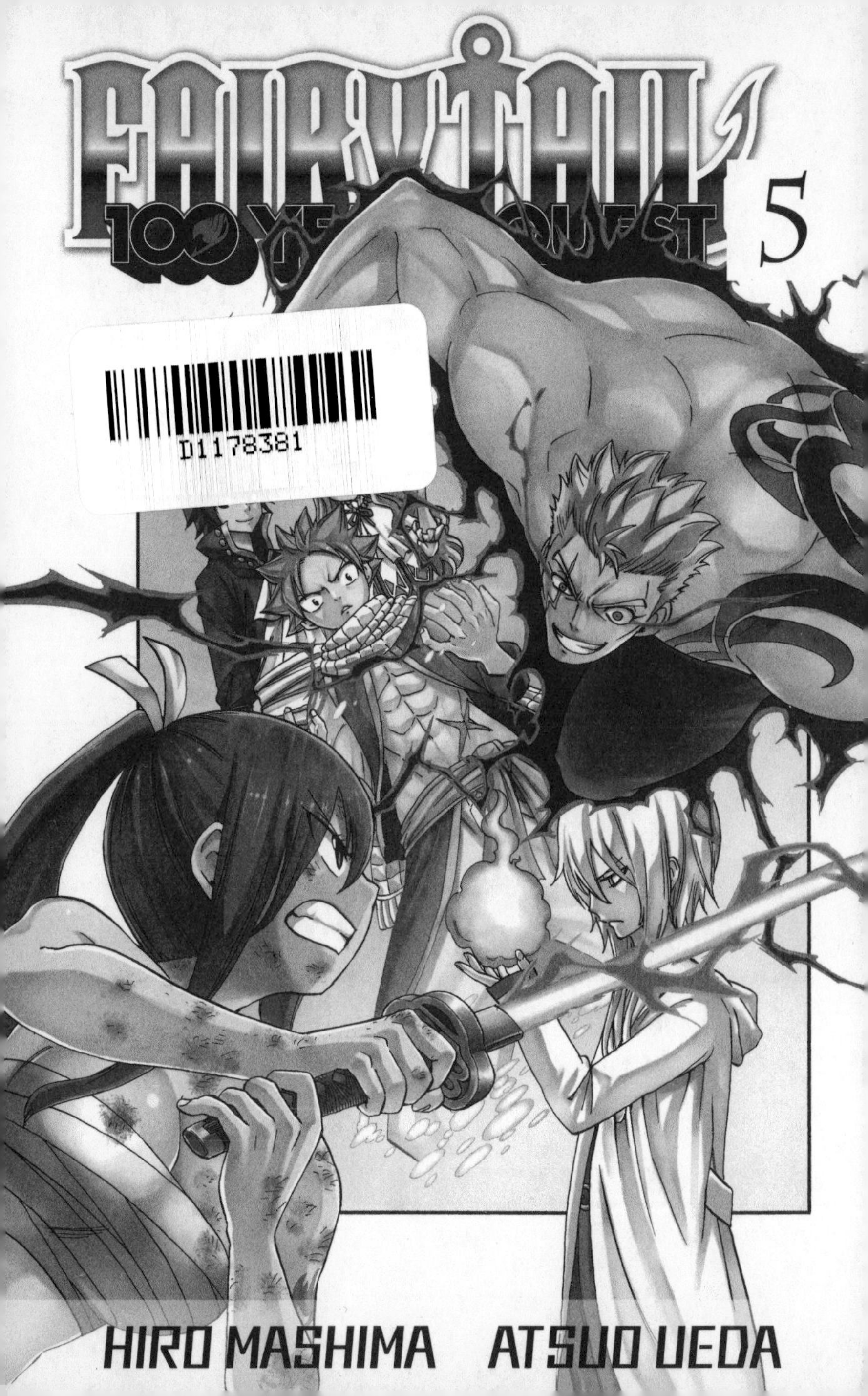

HIRO MASHIMA ATSUO UEDA

FAIRY TAIL 100 YEARS QUEST

CONTENTS

FAIRY TAIL 100 YEARS QUEST

Chapter 37: Beta Heaven

DANGER
FAIRY TAIL

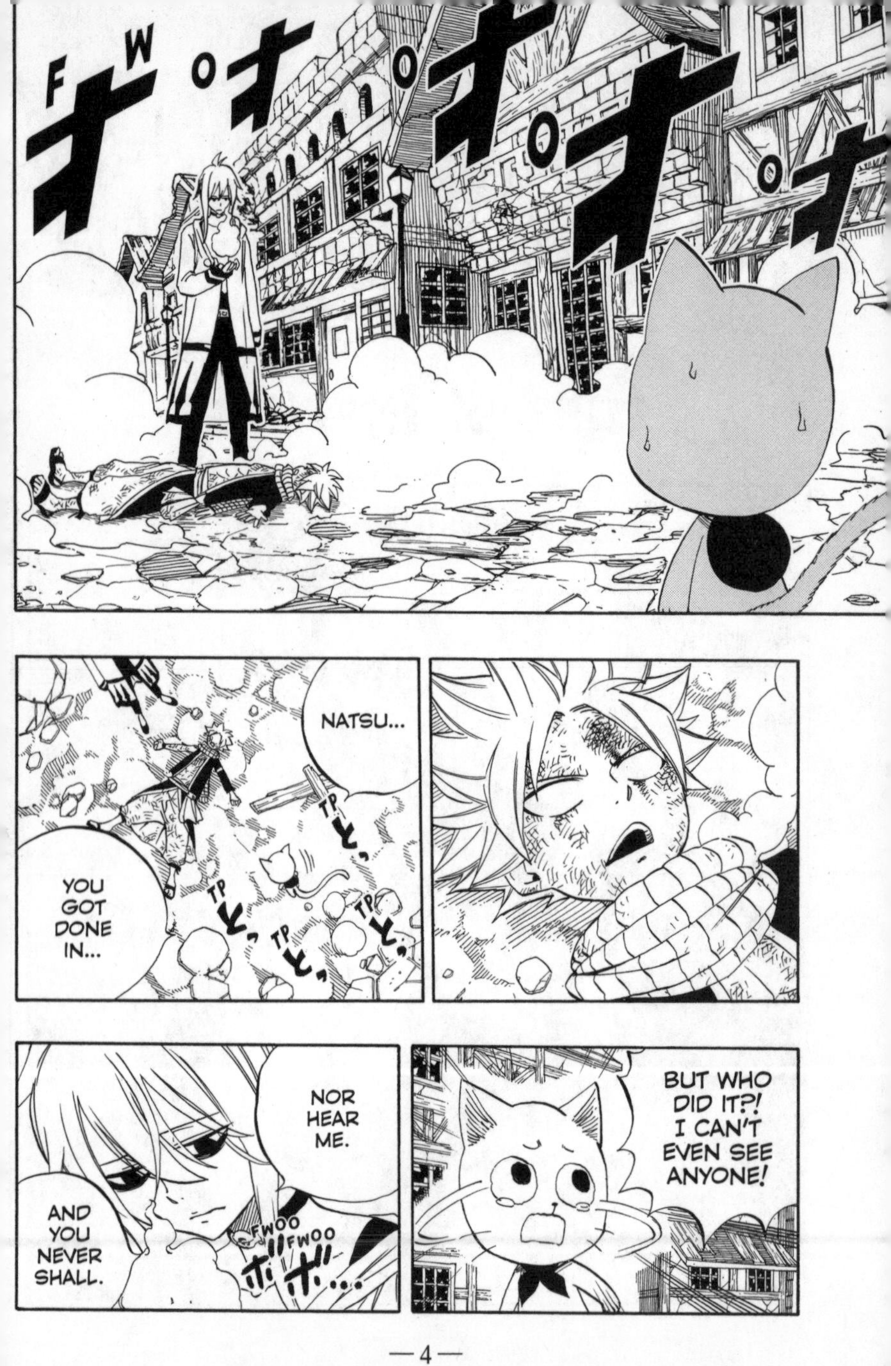
FWO
NATSU...
TP
TP
TP
TP
YOU GOT DONE IN...
BUT WHO DID IT?! I CAN'T EVEN SEE ANYONE!
NOR HEAR ME.
FWOO FWOO
AND YOU NEVER SHALL.

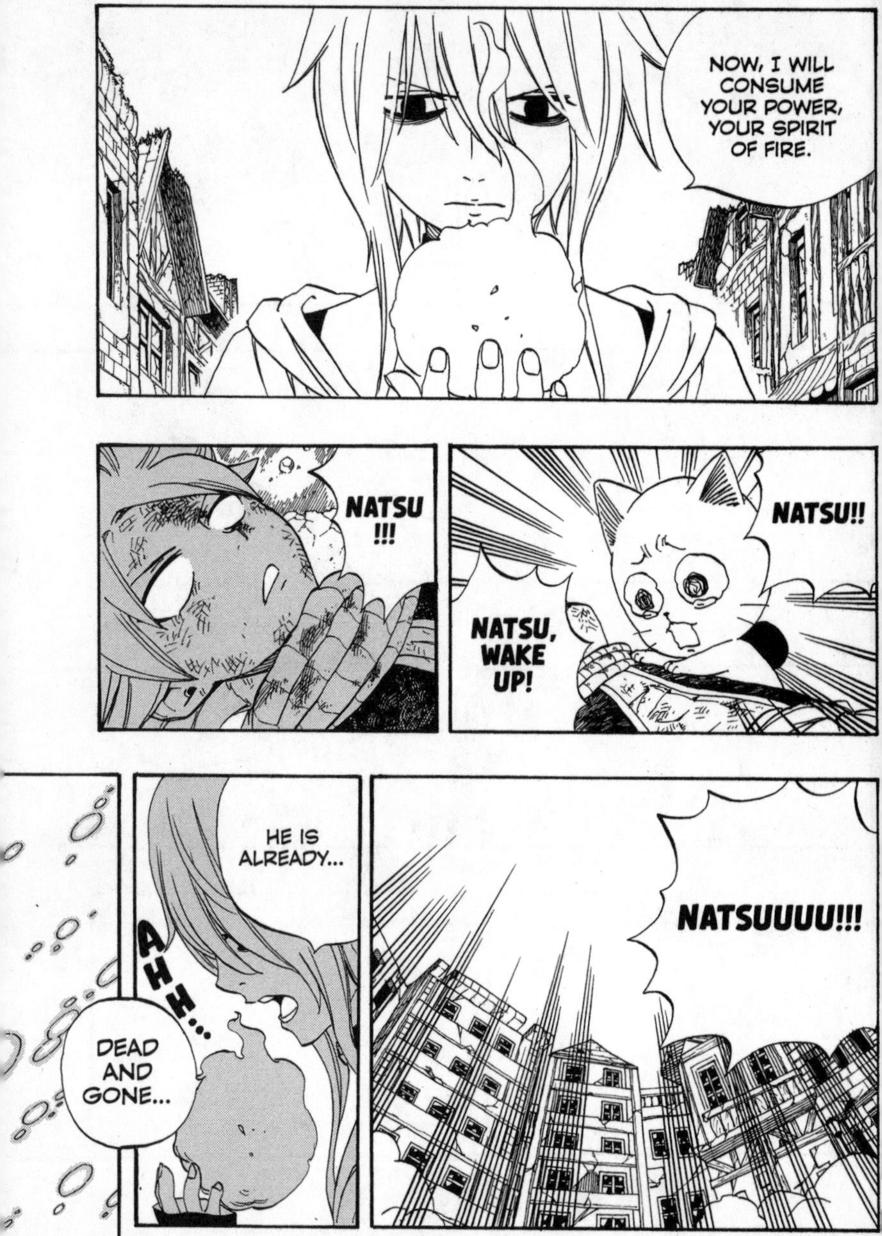
NOW, I WILL CONSUME YOUR POWER, YOUR SPIRIT OF FIRE.
NATSU!!
NATSU, WAKE UP!
NATSU !!!
NATSUUUU!!!
HE IS ALREADY...
AHH...
DEAD AND GONE...

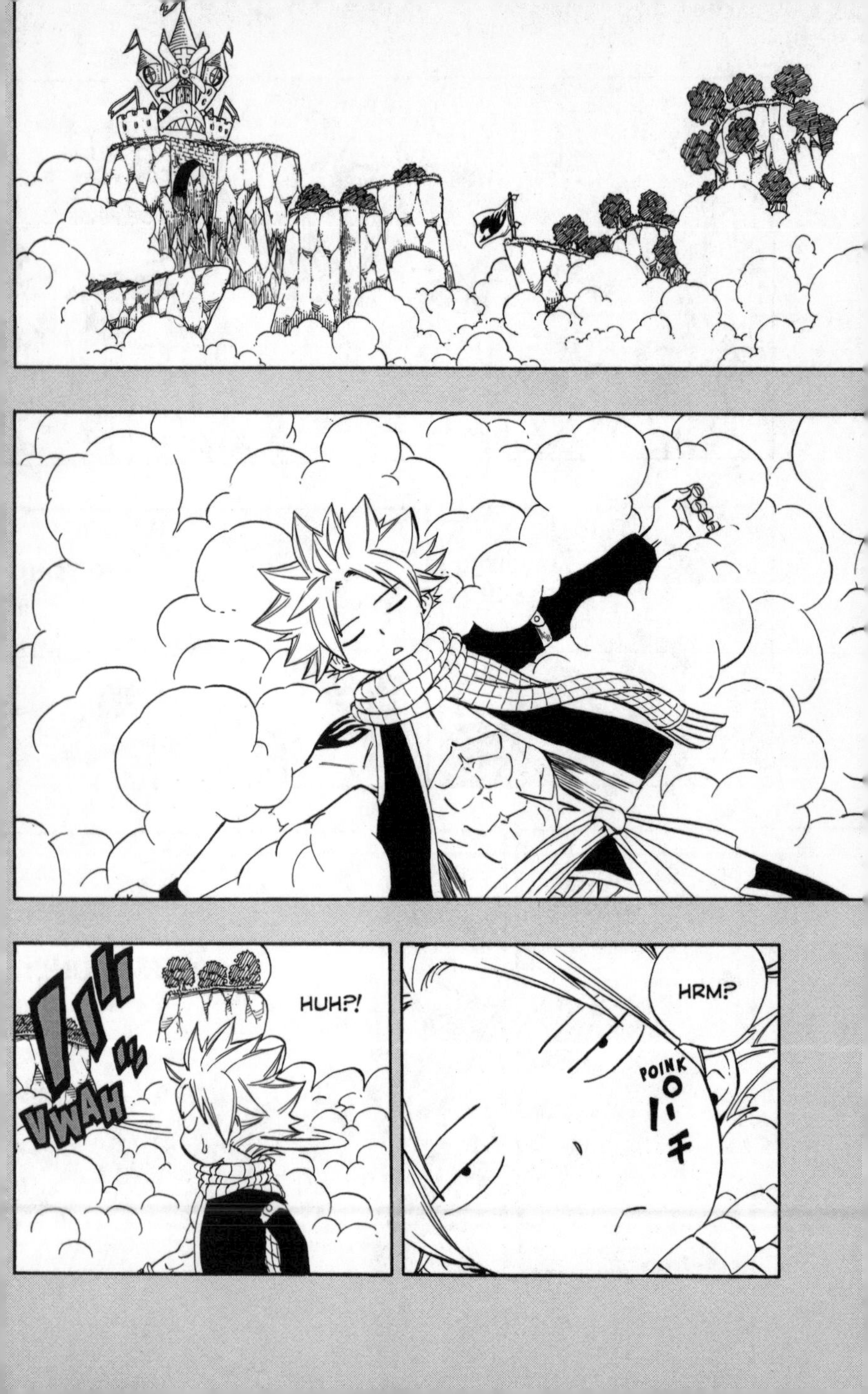
HRM?
POINK
パチ
HUH?!
VWAH

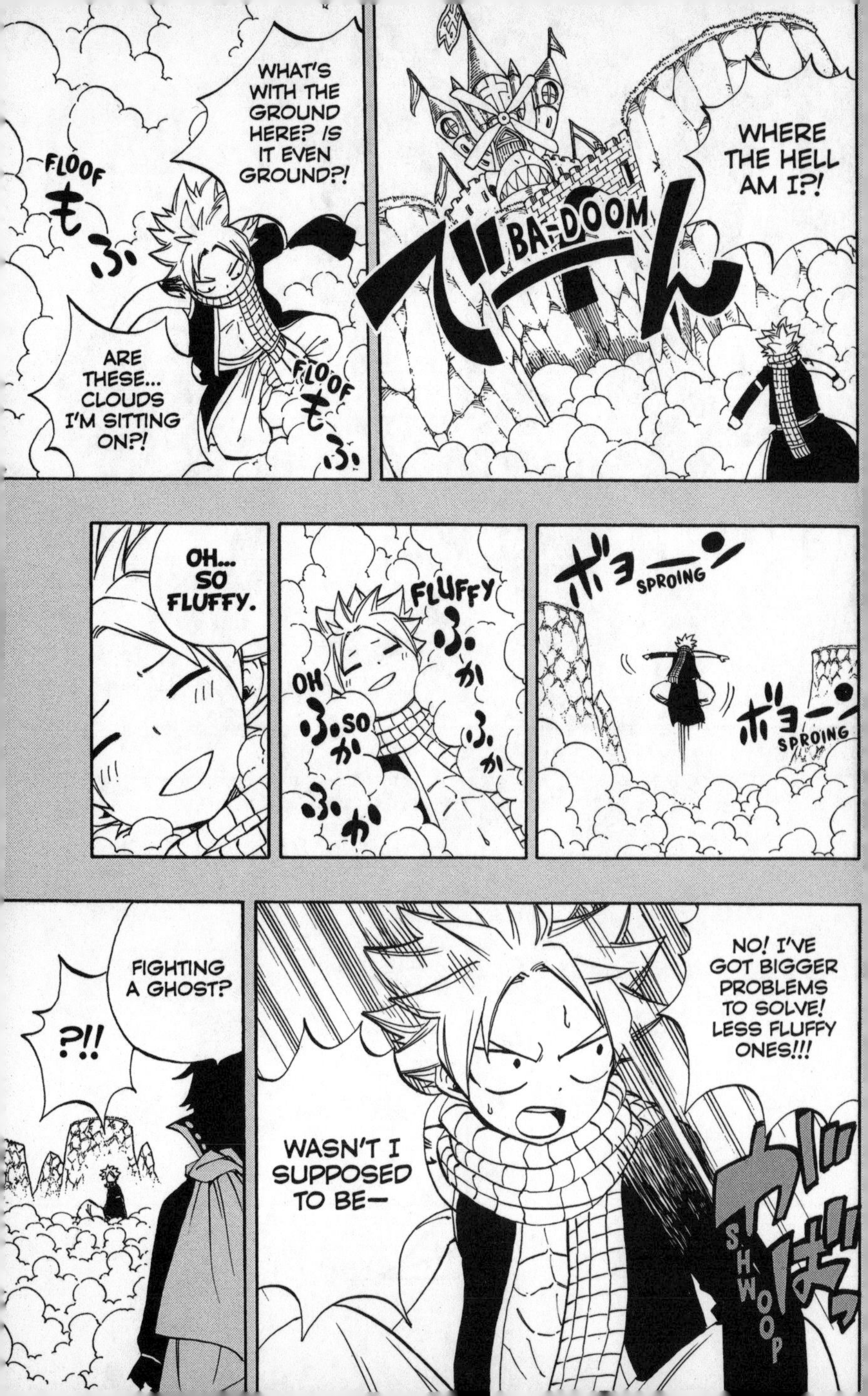
WHERE THE HELL AM I?!
BA-DOOM
WHAT'S WITH THE GROUND HERE? IS IT EVEN GROUND?!
FLOOF
もふ
ARE THESE... CLOUDS I'M SITTING ON?!
FLOOF
もふ
ボヨーン
SPROING
ボヨーン
SPROING
FLUFFY
ふかふか
OH SO
ふかふか
OH... SO FLUFFY.
NO! I'VE GOT BIGGER PROBLEMS TO SOLVE! LESS FLUFFY ONES!!!
WASN'T I SUPPOSED TO BE—
SHWOOP
FIGHTING A GHOST?
?!!

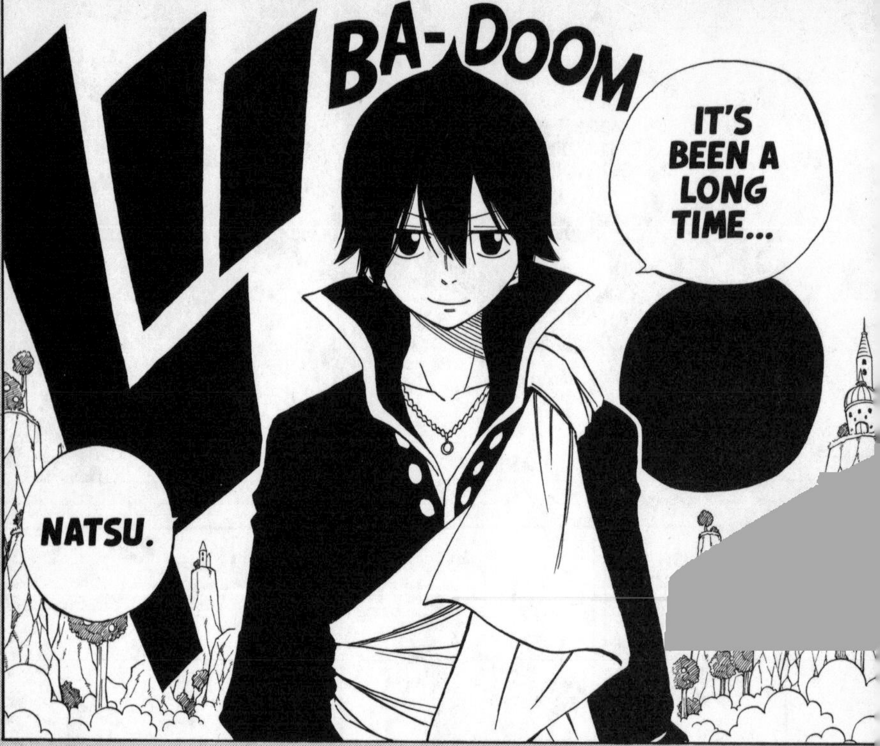
BA-DOOM
IT'S BEEN A LONG TIME...
NATSU.
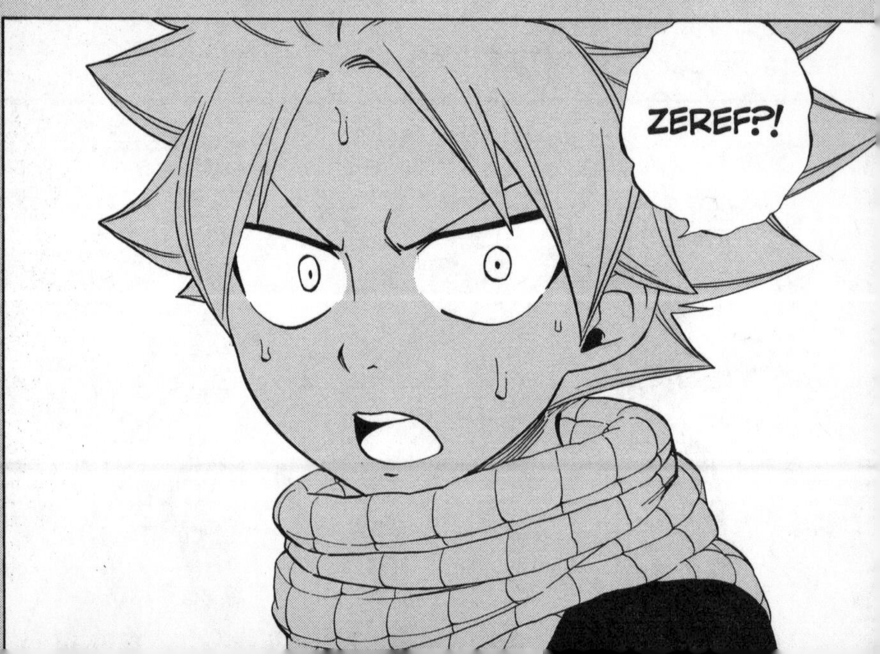
ZEREF?!

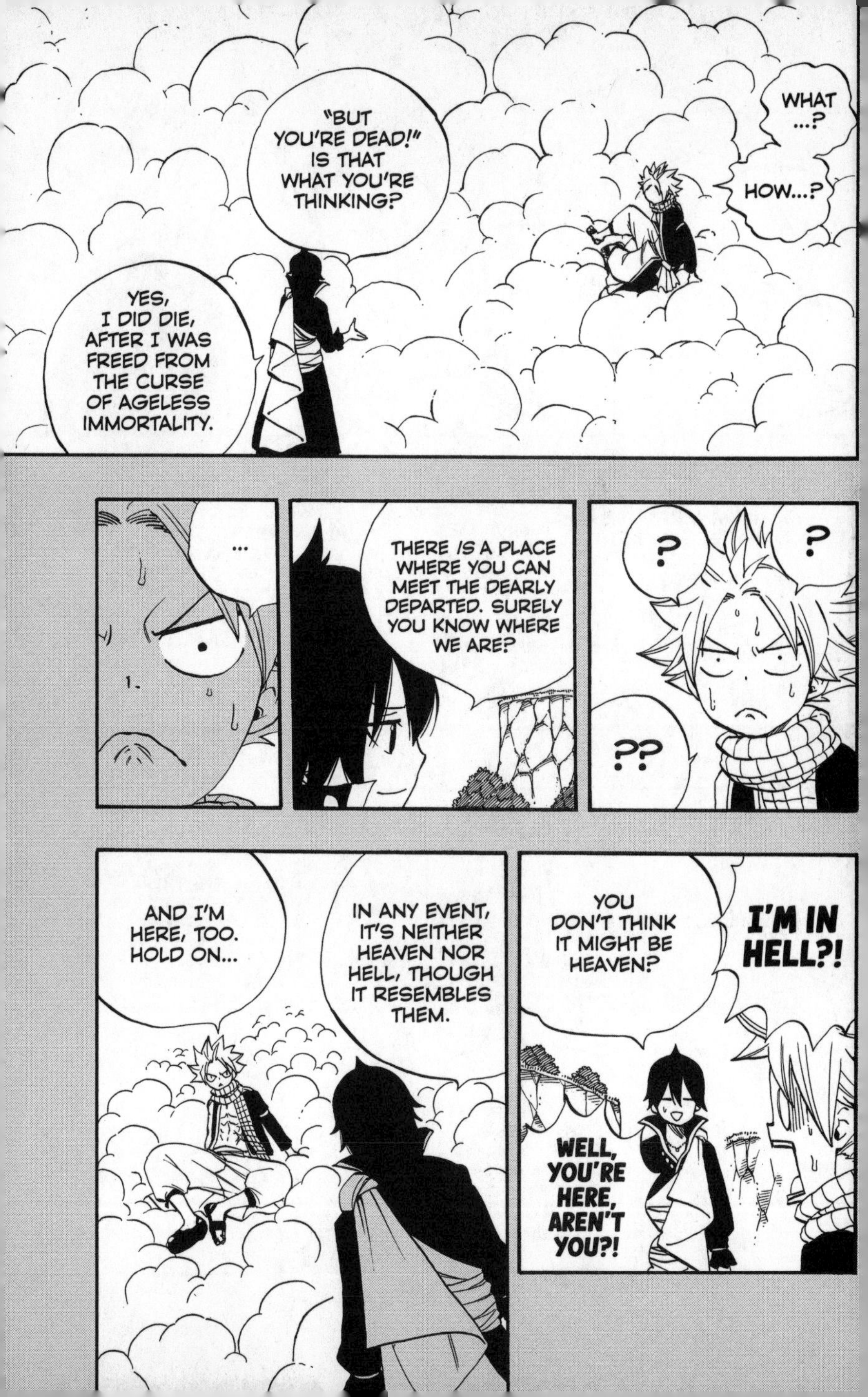
WHAT ...?
HOW...?
"BUT YOU'RE DEAD!" IS THAT WHAT YOU'RE THINKING?
YES, I DID DIE, AFTER I WAS FREED FROM THE CURSE OF AGELESS IMMORTALITY.
?
?
??
THERE IS A PLACE WHERE YOU CAN MEET THE DEARLY DEPARTED. SURELY YOU KNOW WHERE WE ARE?
...
I'M IN HELL?!
YOU DON'T THINK IT MIGHT BE HEAVEN?
WELL, YOU'RE HERE, AREN'T YOU?!
IN ANY EVENT, IT'S NEITHER HEAVEN NOR HELL, THOUGH IT RESEMBLES THEM.
AND I'M HERE, TOO. HOLD ON...

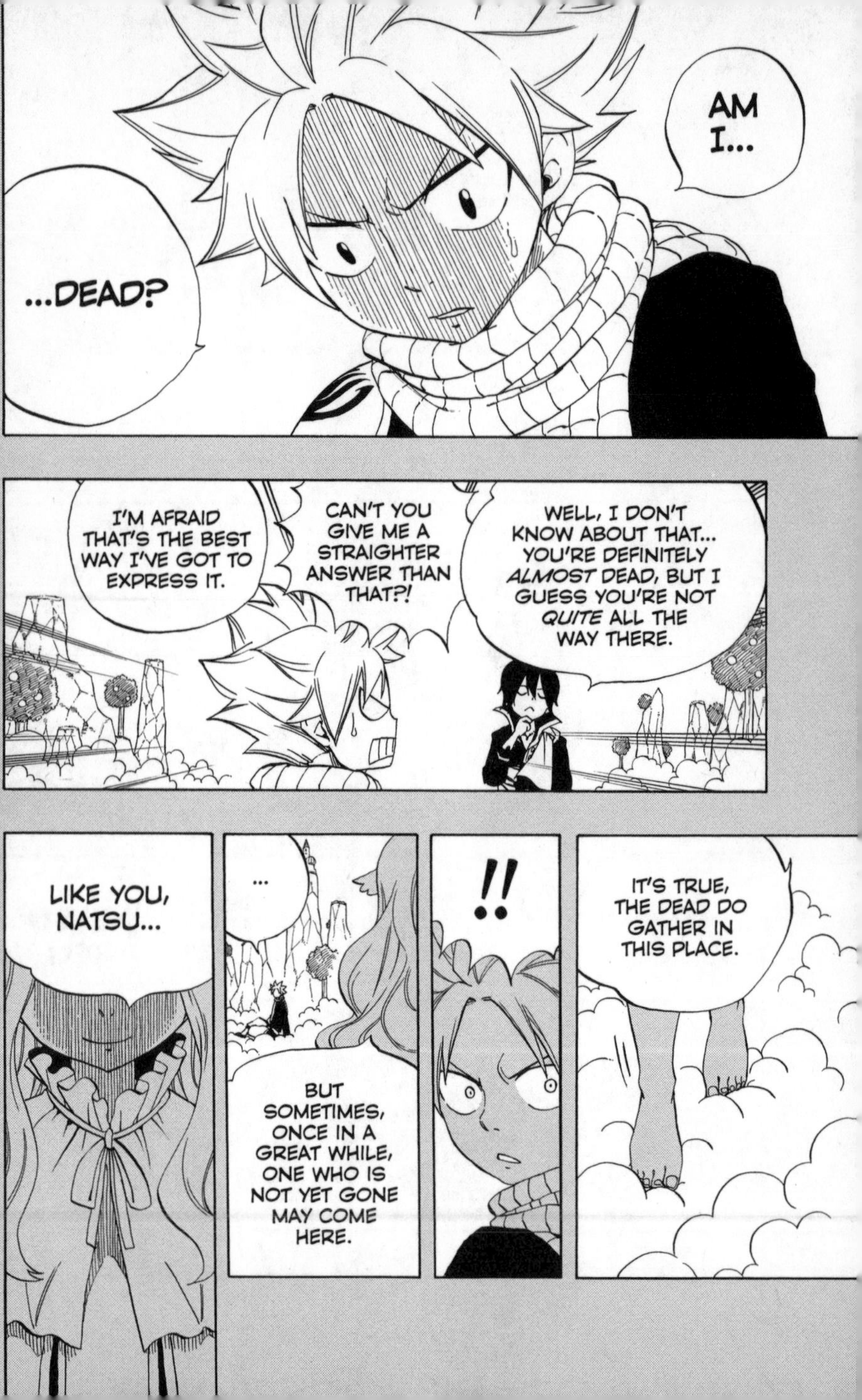
AM I...
...DEAD?
WELL, I DON'T KNOW ABOUT THAT... YOU'RE DEFINITELY *ALMOST* DEAD, BUT I GUESS YOU'RE NOT *QUITE* ALL THE WAY THERE.
CAN'T YOU GIVE ME A STRAIGHTER ANSWER THAN THAT?!
I'M AFRAID THAT'S THE BEST WAY I'VE GOT TO EXPRESS IT.
IT'S TRUE, THE DEAD DO GATHER IN THIS PLACE.
!!
...
BUT SOMETIMES, ONCE IN A GREAT WHILE, ONE WHO IS NOT YET GONE MAY COME HERE.
LIKE YOU, NATSU...

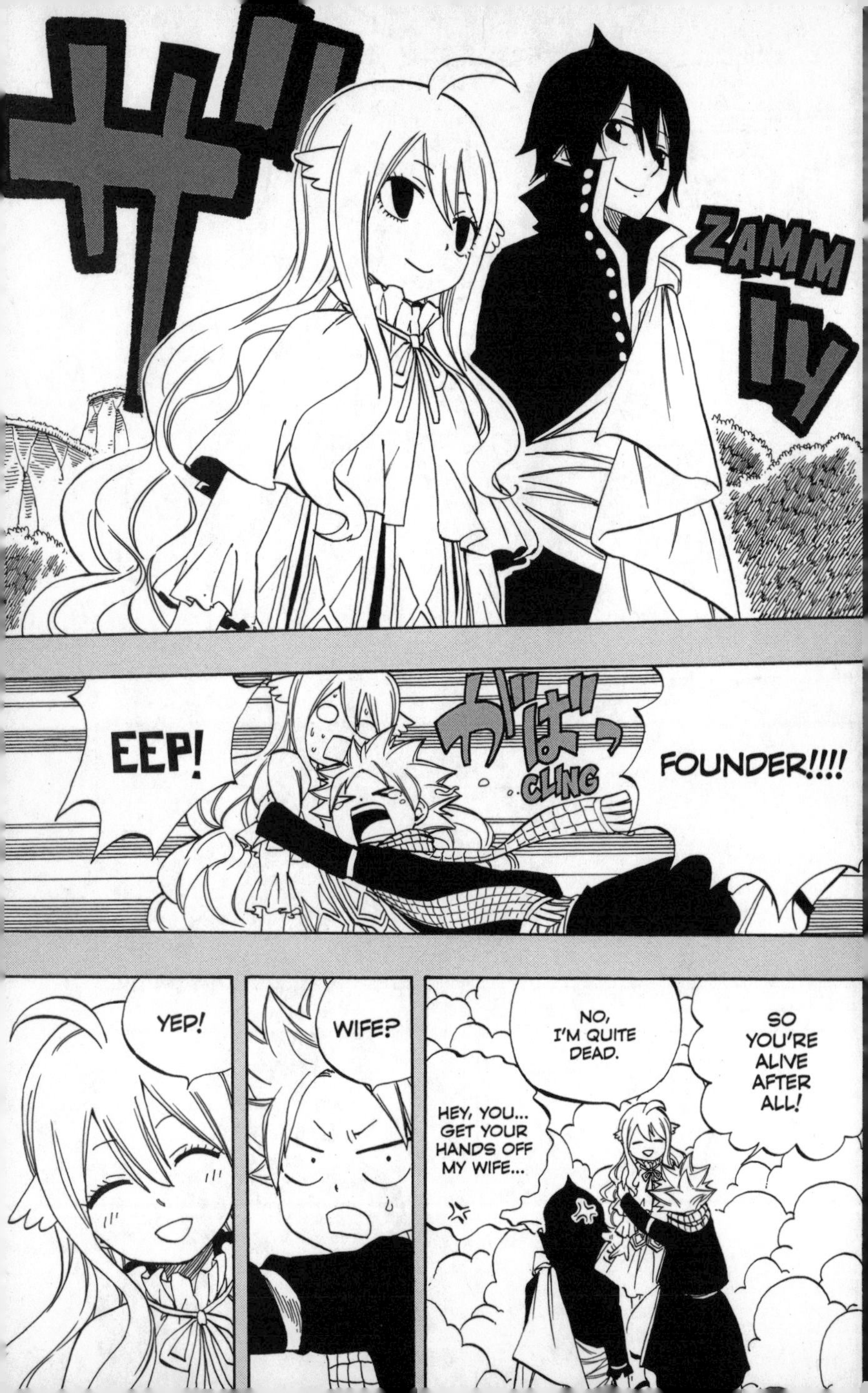

ZAMM
IY
FOUNDER!!!!
わばっ
CLING
EEP!
SO YOU'RE ALIVE AFTER ALL!
NO, I'M QUITE DEAD.
HEY, YOU... GET YOUR HANDS OFF MY WIFE...
WIFE?
YEP!

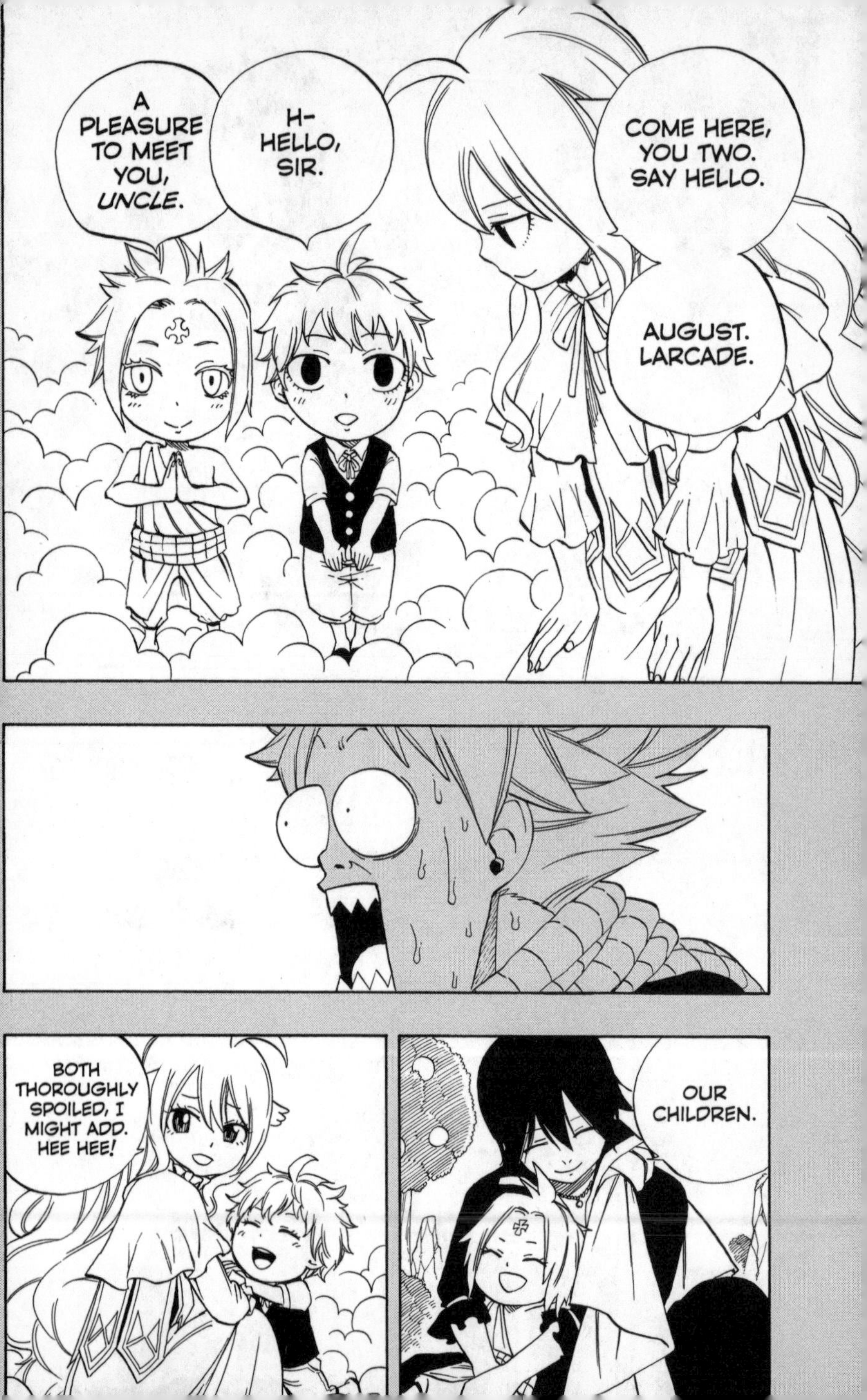
COME HERE, YOU TWO. SAY HELLO.
AUGUST. LARCADE.
H-HELLO, SIR.
A PLEASURE TO MEET YOU, *UNCLE*.
OUR CHILDREN.
BOTH THOROUGHLY SPOILED, I MIGHT ADD. HEE HEE!

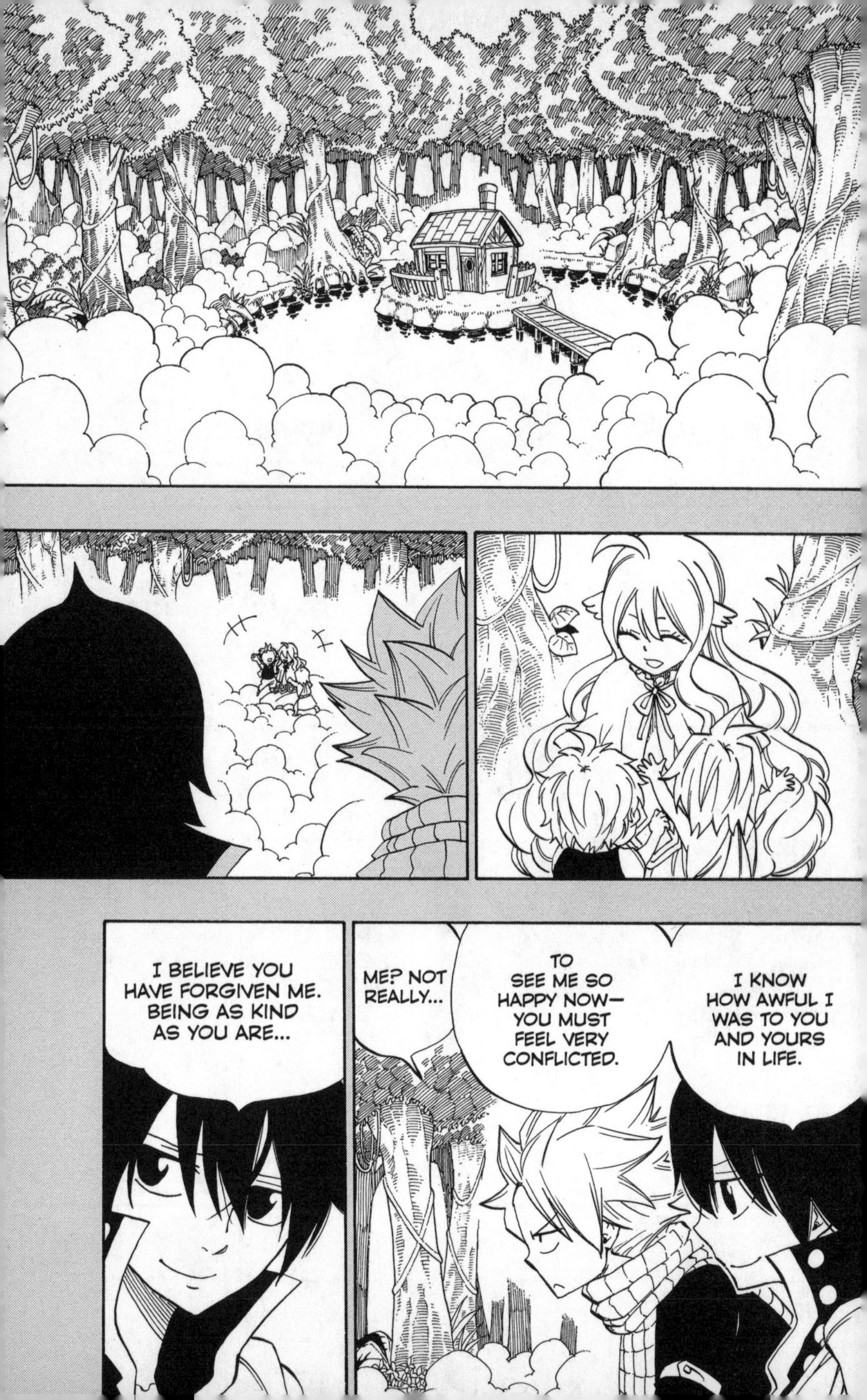
I KNOW HOW AWFUL I WAS TO YOU AND YOURS IN LIFE.
TO SEE ME SO HAPPY NOW— YOU MUST FEEL VERY CONFLICTED.
ME? NOT REALLY...
I BELIEVE YOU HAVE FORGIVEN ME. BEING AS KIND AS YOU ARE...

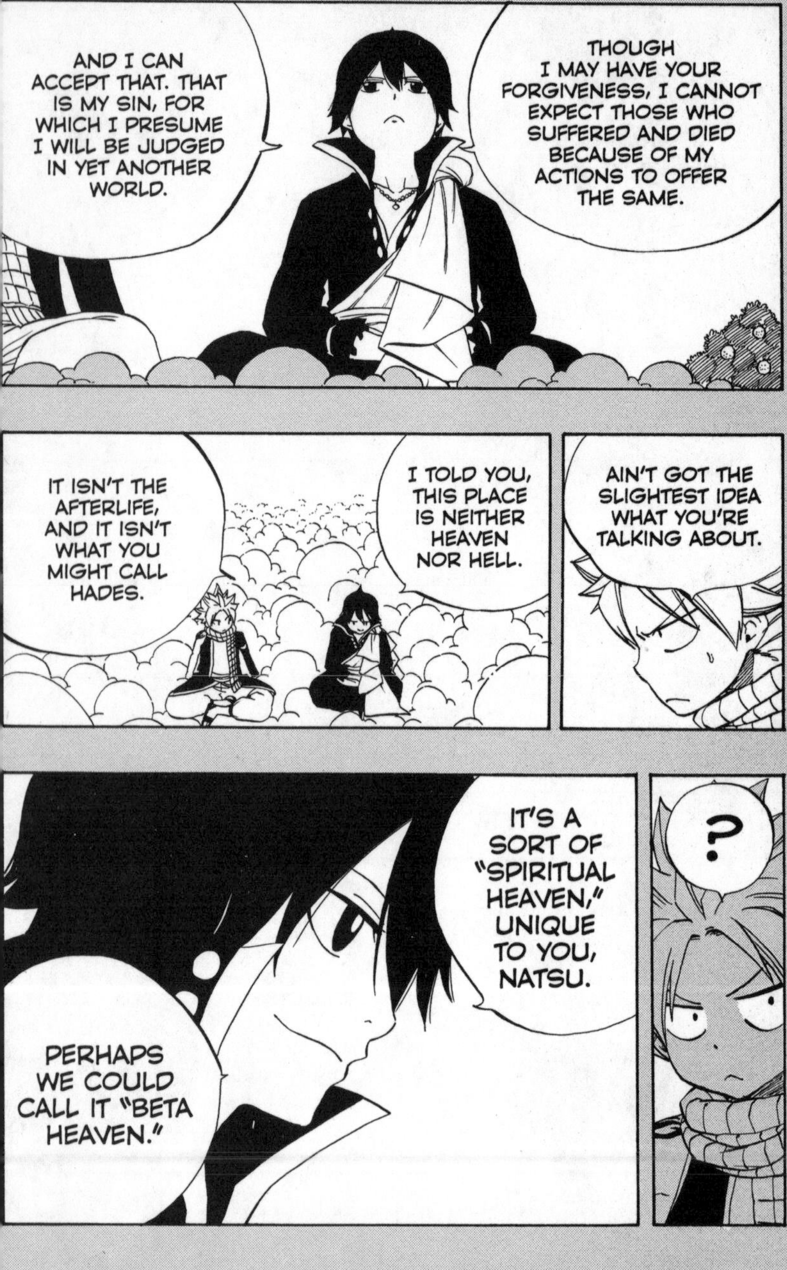
THOUGH I MAY HAVE YOUR FORGIVENESS, I CANNOT EXPECT THOSE WHO SUFFERED AND DIED BECAUSE OF MY ACTIONS TO OFFER THE SAME.
AND I CAN ACCEPT THAT. THAT IS MY SIN, FOR WHICH I PRESUME I WILL BE JUDGED IN YET ANOTHER WORLD.
AIN'T GOT THE SLIGHTEST IDEA WHAT YOU'RE TALKING ABOUT.
I TOLD YOU, THIS PLACE IS NEITHER HEAVEN NOR HELL.
IT ISN'T THE AFTERLIFE, AND IT ISN'T WHAT YOU MIGHT CALL HADES.
?
IT'S A SORT OF "SPIRITUAL HEAVEN," UNIQUE TO YOU, NATSU.
PERHAPS WE COULD CALL IT "BETA HEAVEN."

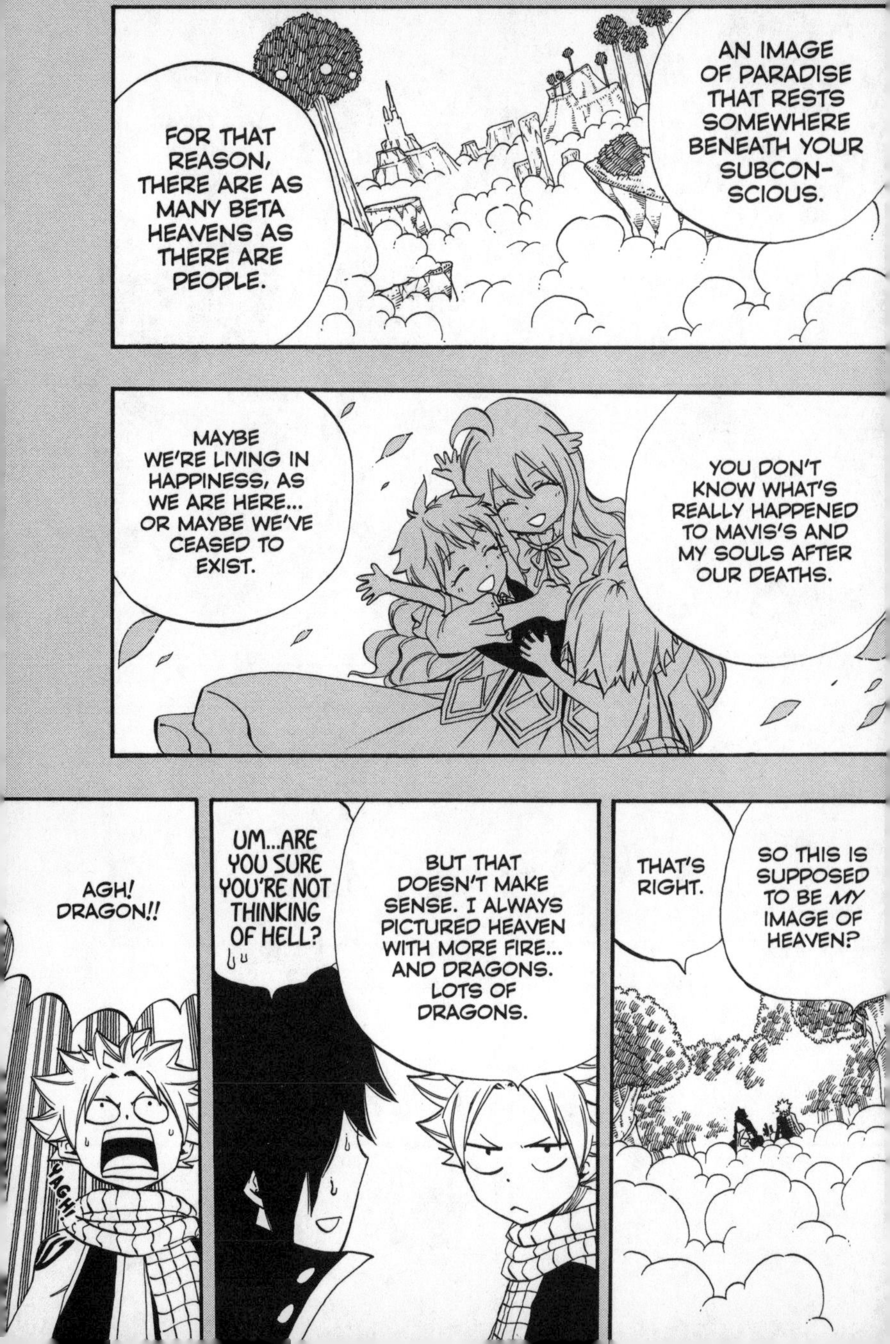
AN IMAGE OF PARADISE THAT RESTS SOMEWHERE BENEATH YOUR SUBCONSCIOUS.
FOR THAT REASON, THERE ARE AS MANY BETA HEAVENS AS THERE ARE PEOPLE.
YOU DON'T KNOW WHAT'S REALLY HAPPENED TO MAVIS'S AND MY SOULS AFTER OUR DEATHS.
MAYBE WE'RE LIVING IN HAPPINESS, AS WE ARE HERE... OR MAYBE WE'VE CEASED TO EXIST.
SO THIS IS SUPPOSED TO BE *MY* IMAGE OF HEAVEN?
THAT'S RIGHT.
BUT THAT DOESN'T MAKE SENSE. I ALWAYS PICTURED HEAVEN WITH MORE FIRE... AND DRAGONS. LOTS OF DRAGONS.
UM...ARE YOU SURE YOU'RE NOT THINKING OF HELL?
AGH! DRAGON!!
YAGH!

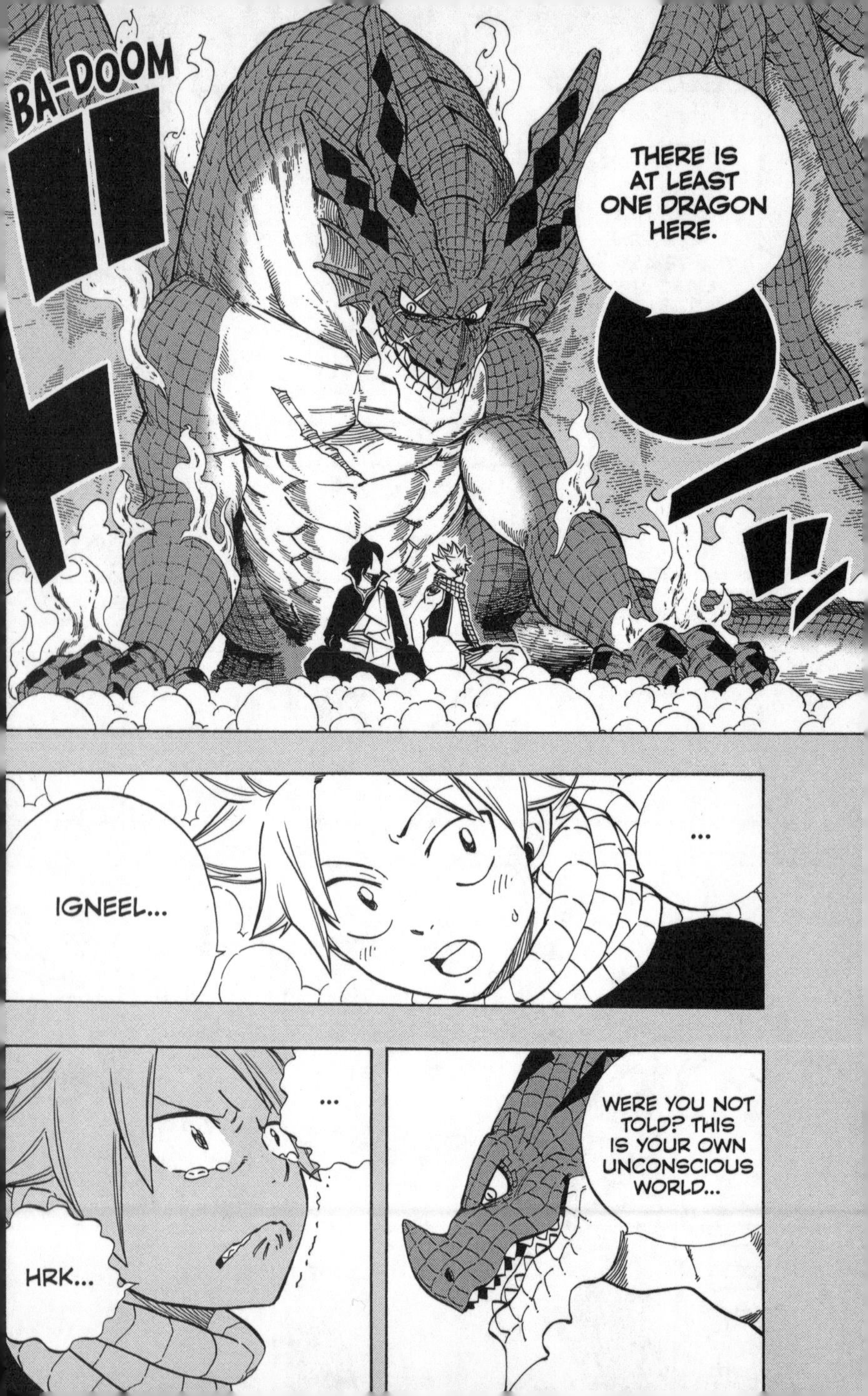
THERE IS AT LEAST ONE DRAGON HERE.
BA-DOOM
...
IGNEEL...
WERE YOU NOT TOLD? THIS IS YOUR OWN UNCONSCIOUS WORLD...
...
HRK...

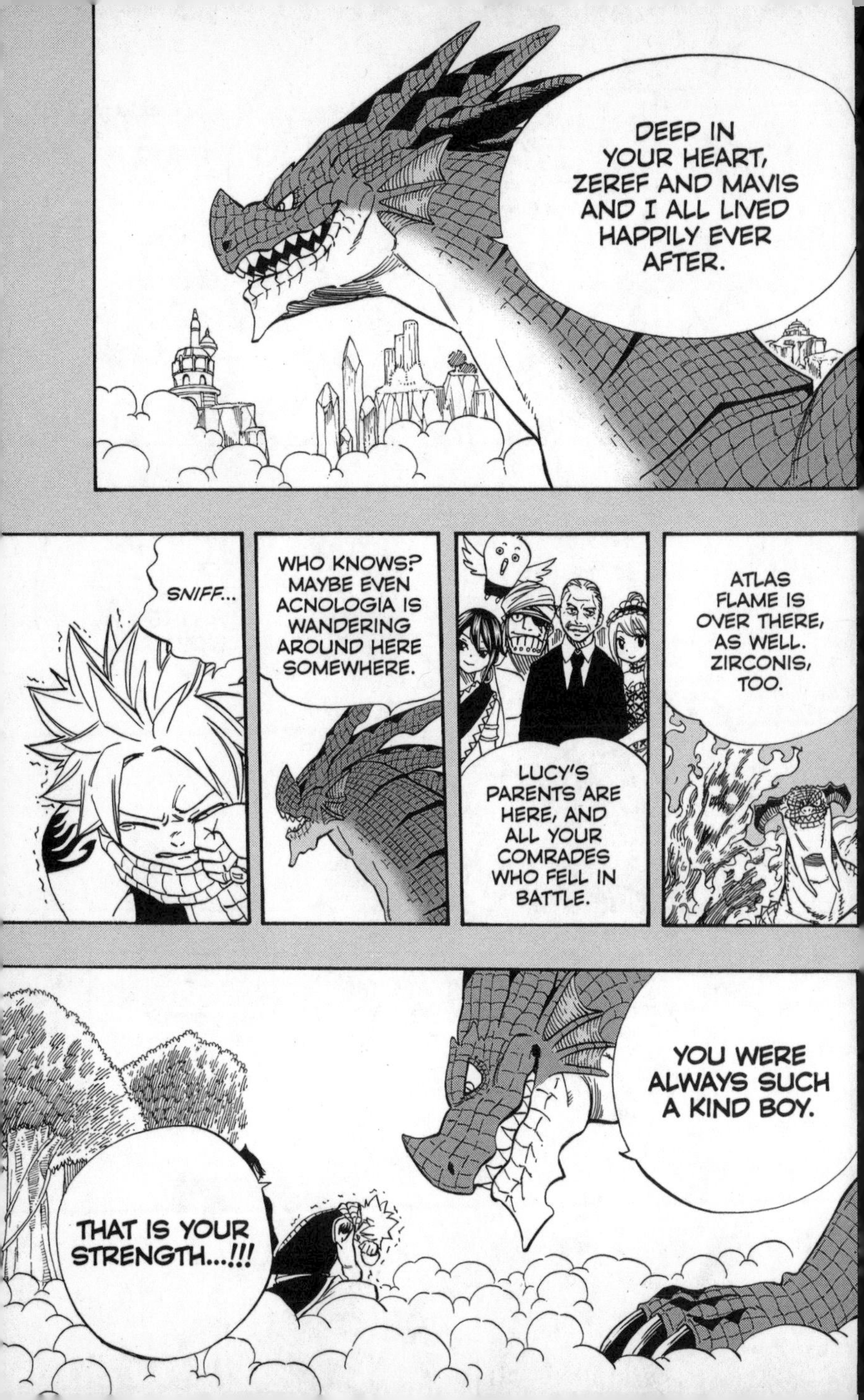
DEEP IN YOUR HEART, ZEREF AND MAVIS AND I ALL LIVED HAPPILY EVER AFTER.
ATLAS FLAME IS OVER THERE, AS WELL. ZIRCONIS, TOO.
LUCY'S PARENTS ARE HERE, AND ALL YOUR COMRADES WHO FELL IN BATTLE.
WHO KNOWS? MAYBE EVEN ACNOLOGIA IS WANDERING AROUND HERE SOMEWHERE.
SNIFF...
YOU WERE ALWAYS SUCH A KIND BOY.
THAT IS YOUR STRENGTH...!!!

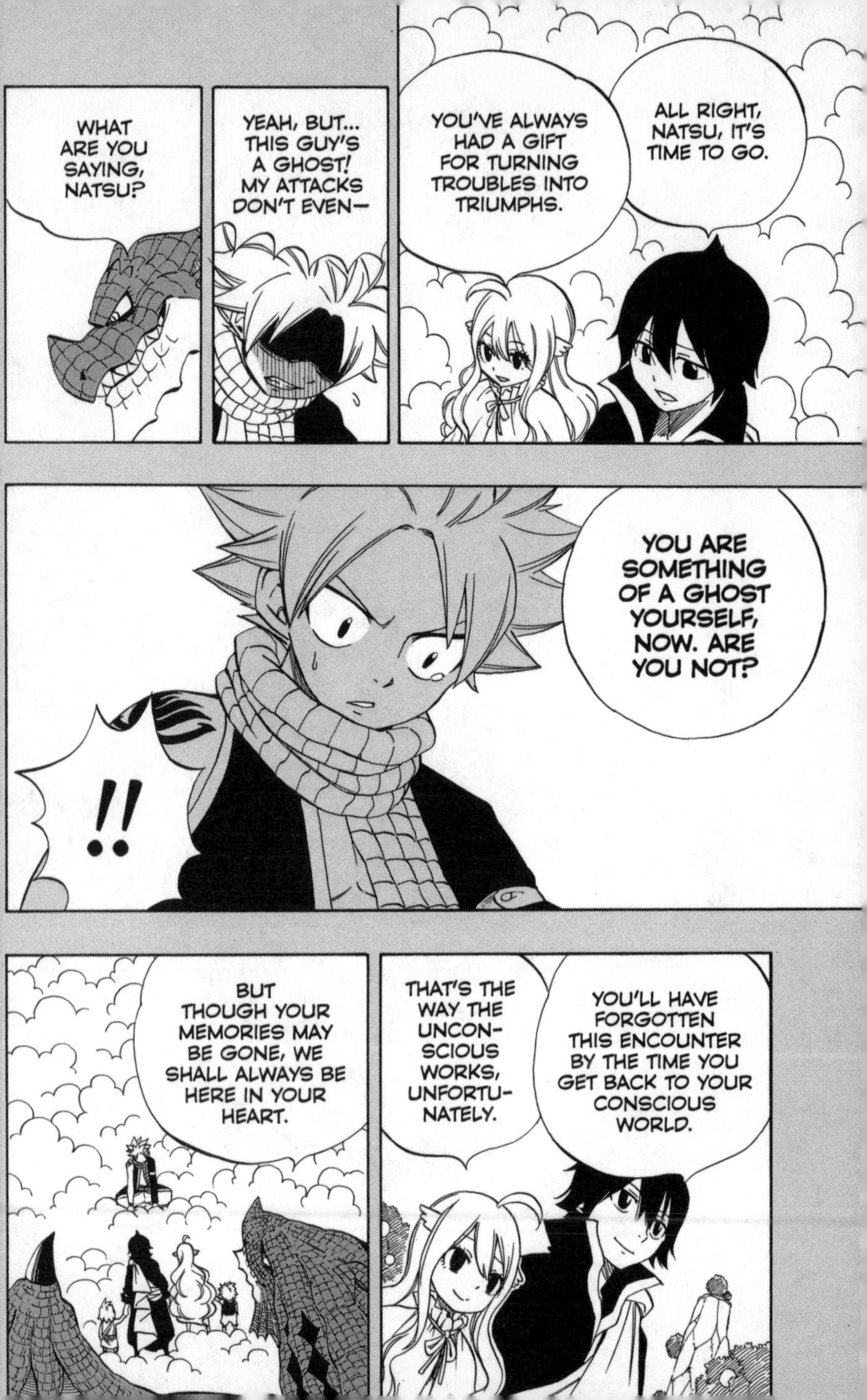
ALL RIGHT, NATSU, IT'S TIME TO GO.
YOU'VE ALWAYS HAD A GIFT FOR TURNING TROUBLES INTO TRIUMPHS.
YEAH, BUT... THIS GUY'S A GHOST! MY ATTACKS DON'T EVEN—
WHAT ARE YOU SAYING, NATSU?
YOU ARE SOMETHING OF A GHOST YOURSELF, NOW. ARE YOU NOT?
!!
YOU'LL HAVE FORGOTTEN THIS ENCOUNTER BY THE TIME YOU GET BACK TO YOUR CONSCIOUS WORLD.
THAT'S THE WAY THE UNCON-SCIOUS WORKS, UNFORTU-NATELY.
BUT THOUGH YOUR MEMORIES MAY BE GONE, WE SHALL ALWAYS BE HERE IN YOUR HEART.

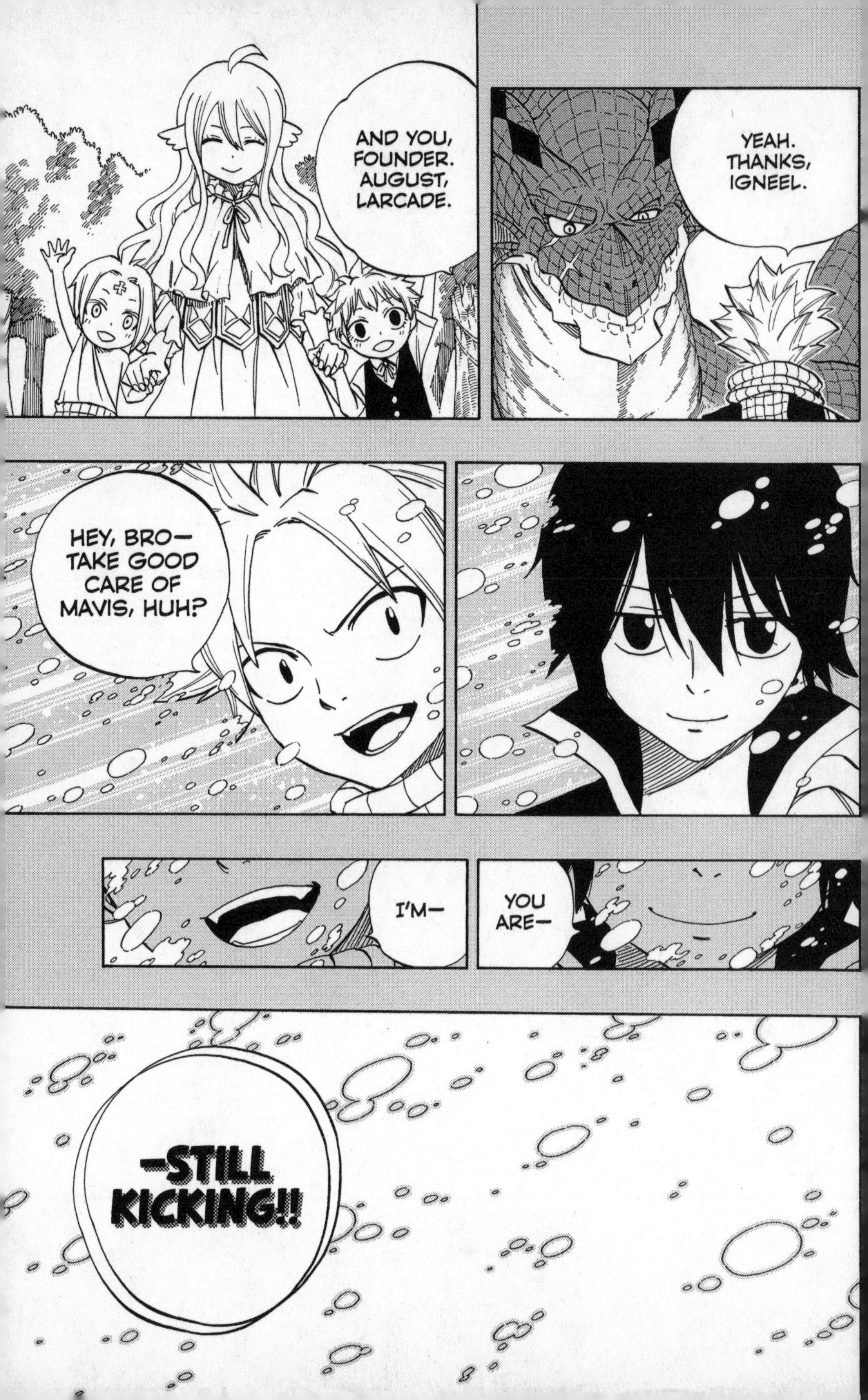
YEAH. THANKS, IGNEEL.
AND YOU, FOUNDER. AUGUST, LARCADE.
HEY, BRO— TAKE GOOD CARE OF MAVIS, HUH?
YOU ARE—
I'M—
—STILL KICKING!!

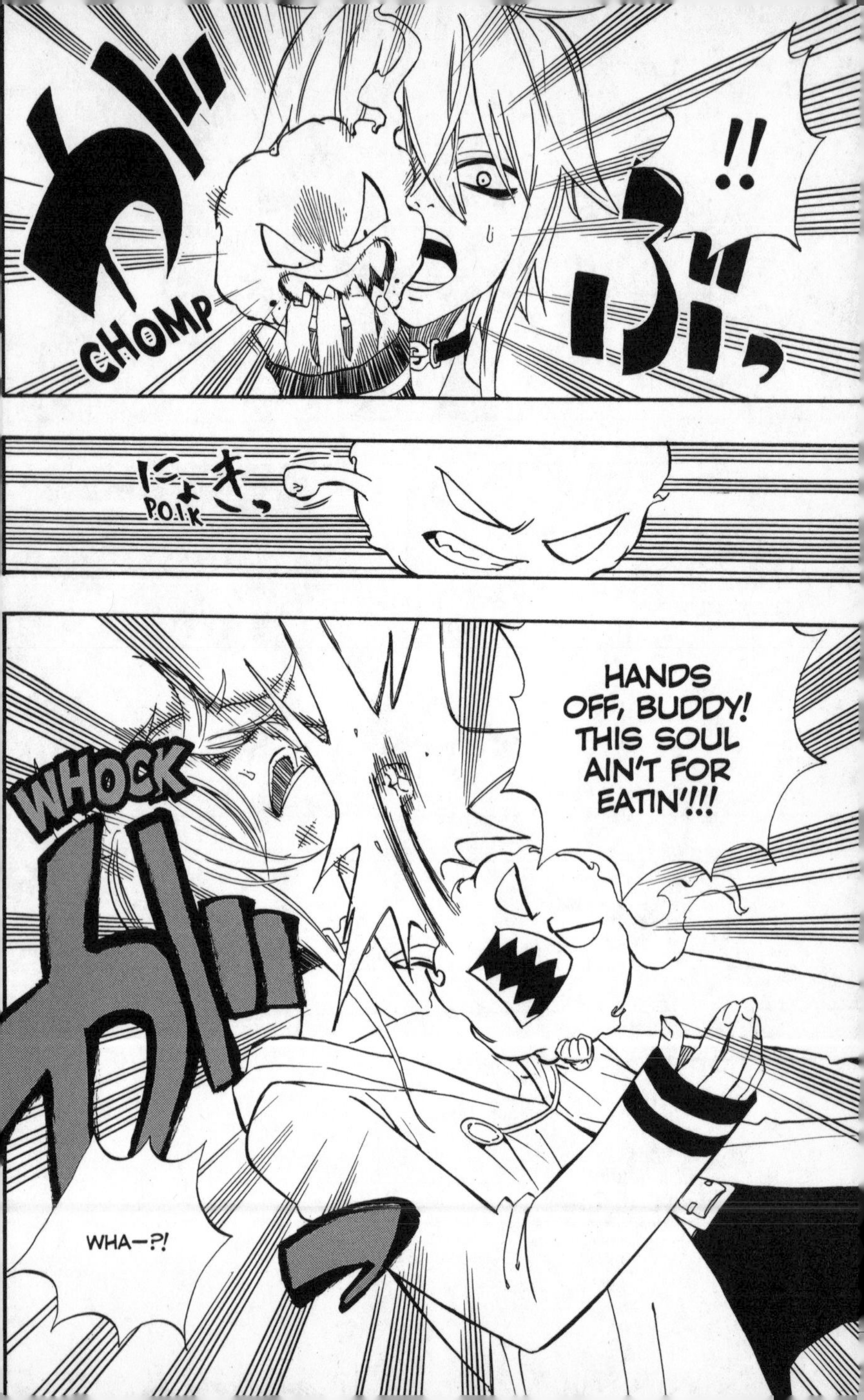
!!
CHOMP
にょきっ
POIK
HANDS OFF, BUDDY! THIS SOUL AIN'T FOR EATIN'!!!
WHOCK
WHA—?!

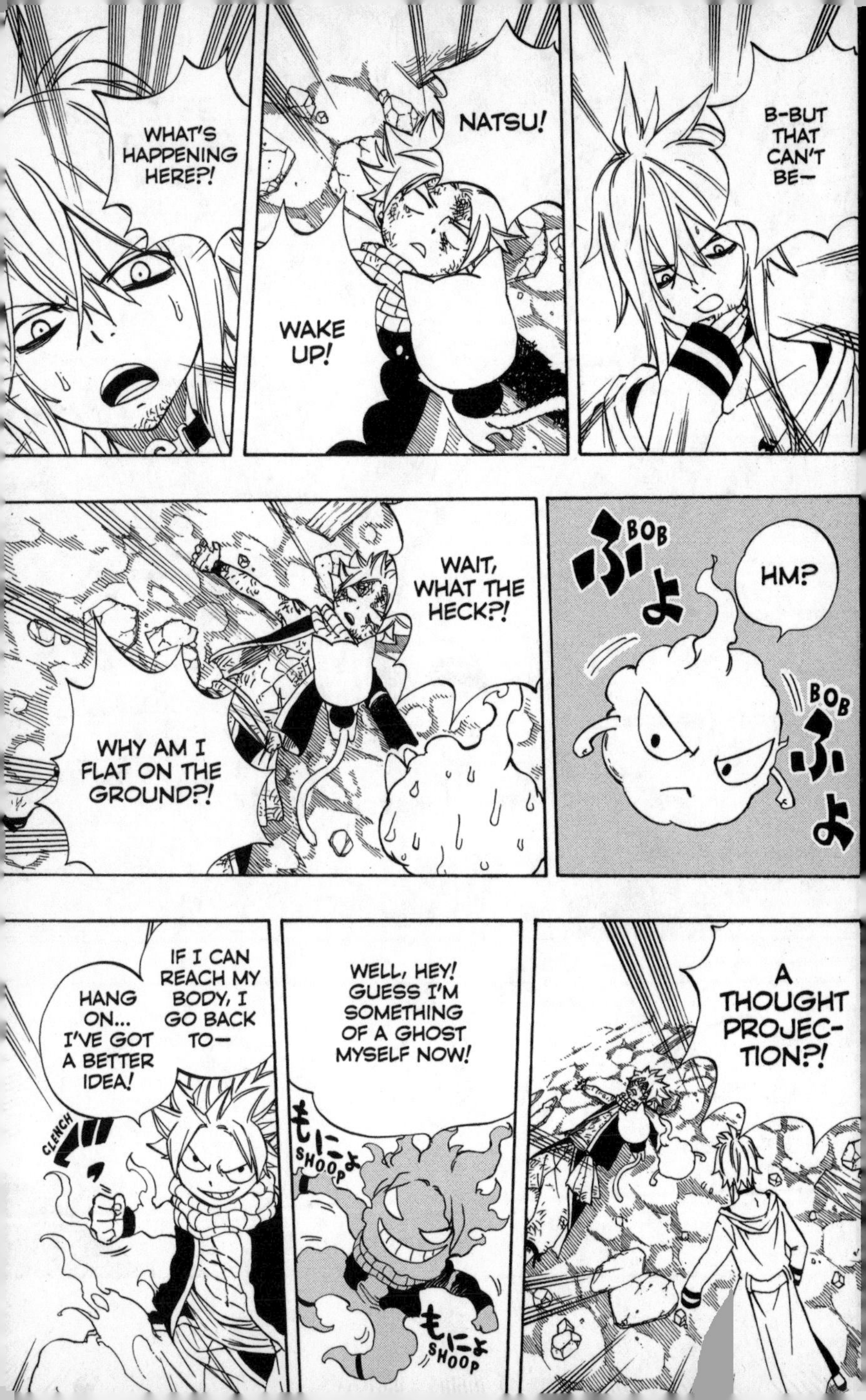
B-BUT THAT CAN'T BE—
NATSU!
WAKE UP!
WHAT'S HAPPENING HERE?!
ふよ BOB
HM?
ふよ BOB
WAIT, WHAT THE HECK?!
WHY AM I FLAT ON THE GROUND?!
A THOUGHT PROJECTION?!
WELL, HEY! GUESS I'M SOMETHING OF A GHOST MYSELF NOW!
もにょ SHOOP
もにょ SHOOP
IF I CAN REACH MY BODY, I GO BACK TO—
HANG ON... I'VE GOT A BETTER IDEA!
CLENCH

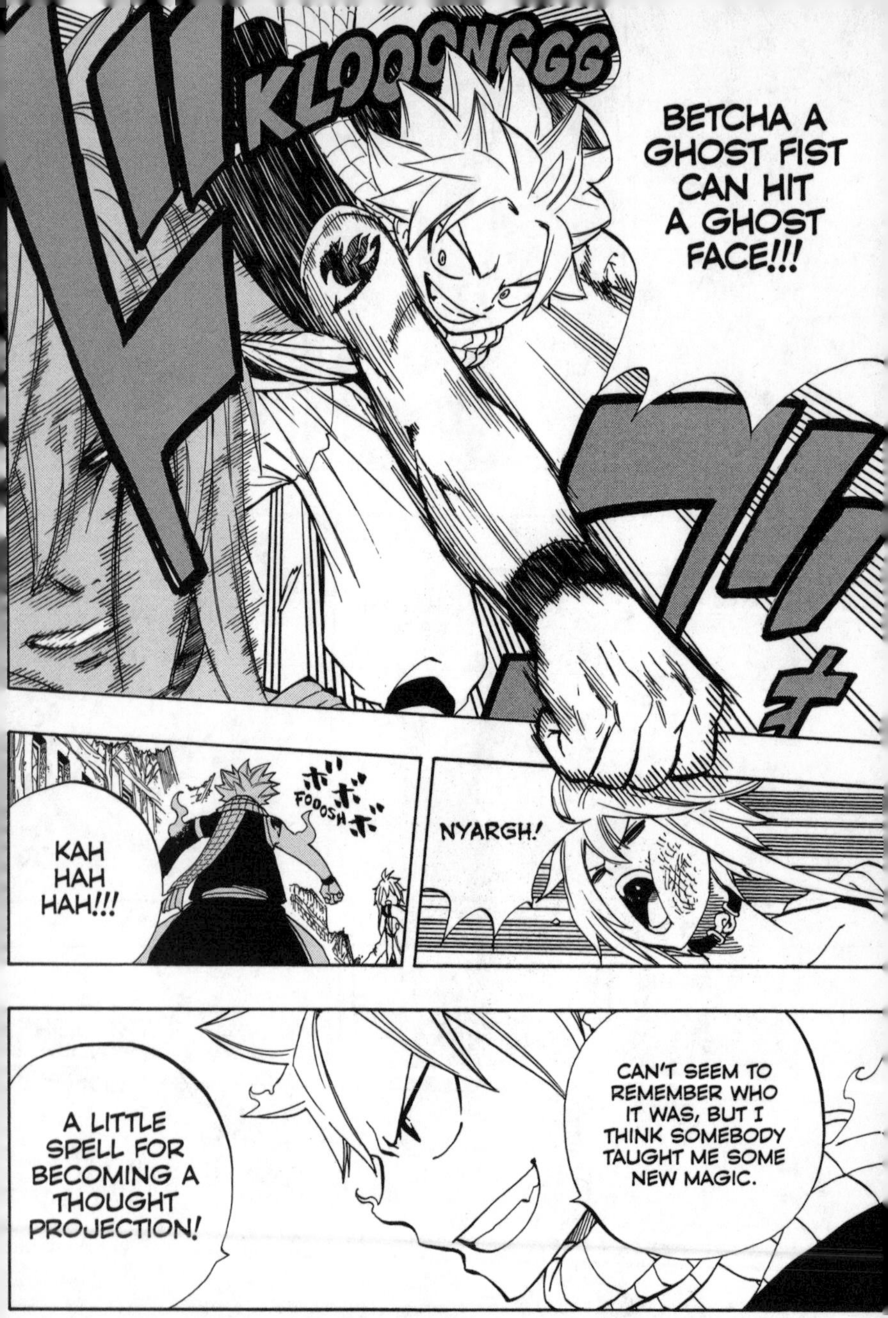
KLOOONGGG
BETCHA A GHOST FIST CAN HIT A GHOST FACE!!!
NYARGH!
FOOOSH
KAH HAH HAH!!!
CAN'T SEEM TO REMEMBER WHO IT WAS, BUT I THINK SOMEBODY TAUGHT ME SOME NEW MAGIC.
A LITTLE SPELL FOR BECOMING A THOUGHT PROJECTION!

FAIRY TAIL 100 YEARS QUEST

Chapter 38: Synchro Rate

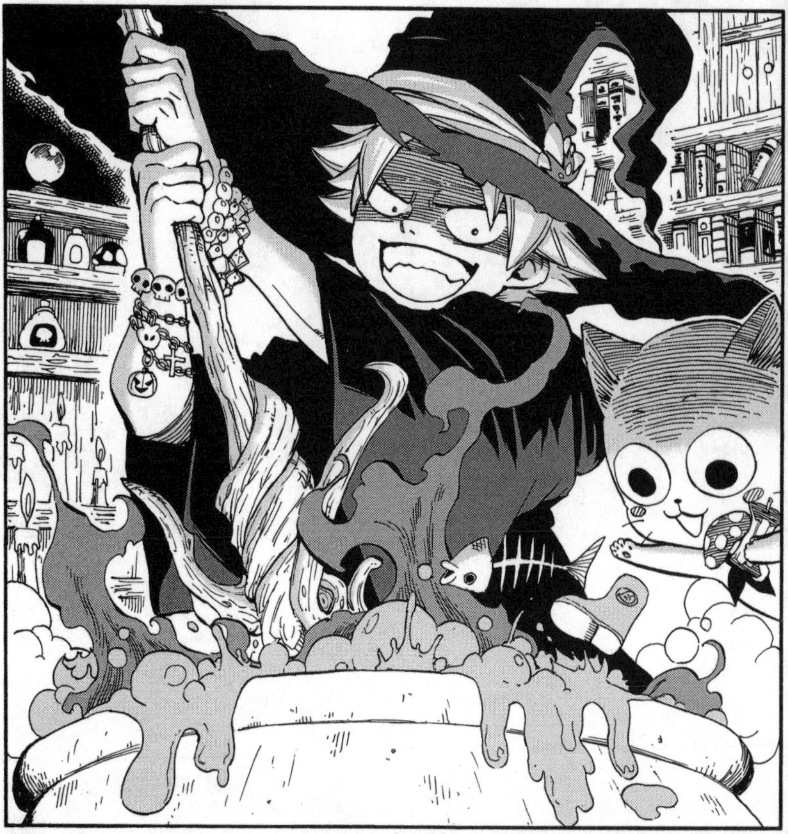

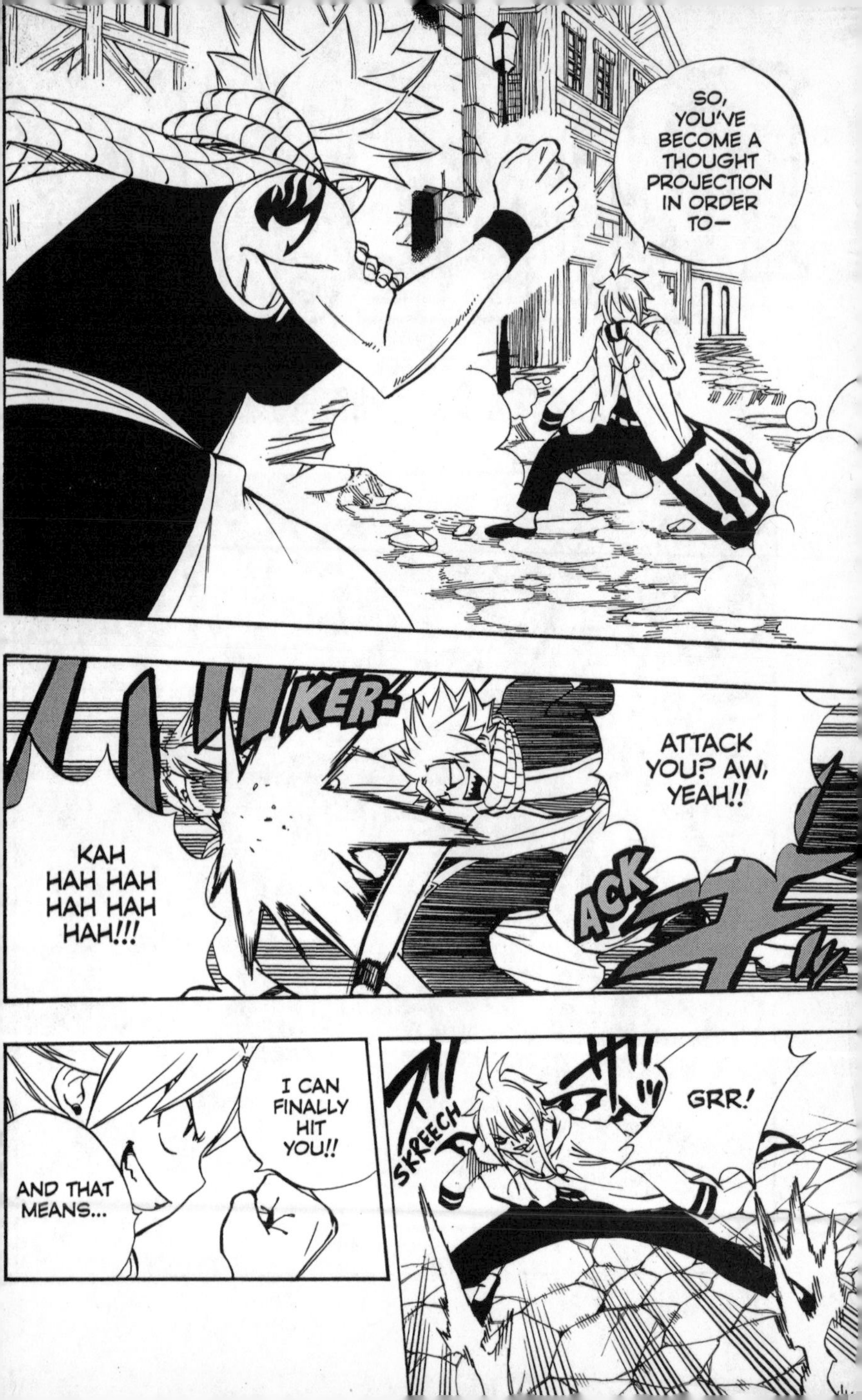
SO, YOU'VE BECOME A THOUGHT PROJECTION IN ORDER TO—
ATTACK YOU? AW, YEAH!!
KER-
ACK
KAH HAH HAH HAH HAH HAH!!!
GRR!
SKREECH
I CAN FINALLY HIT YOU!!
AND THAT MEANS...

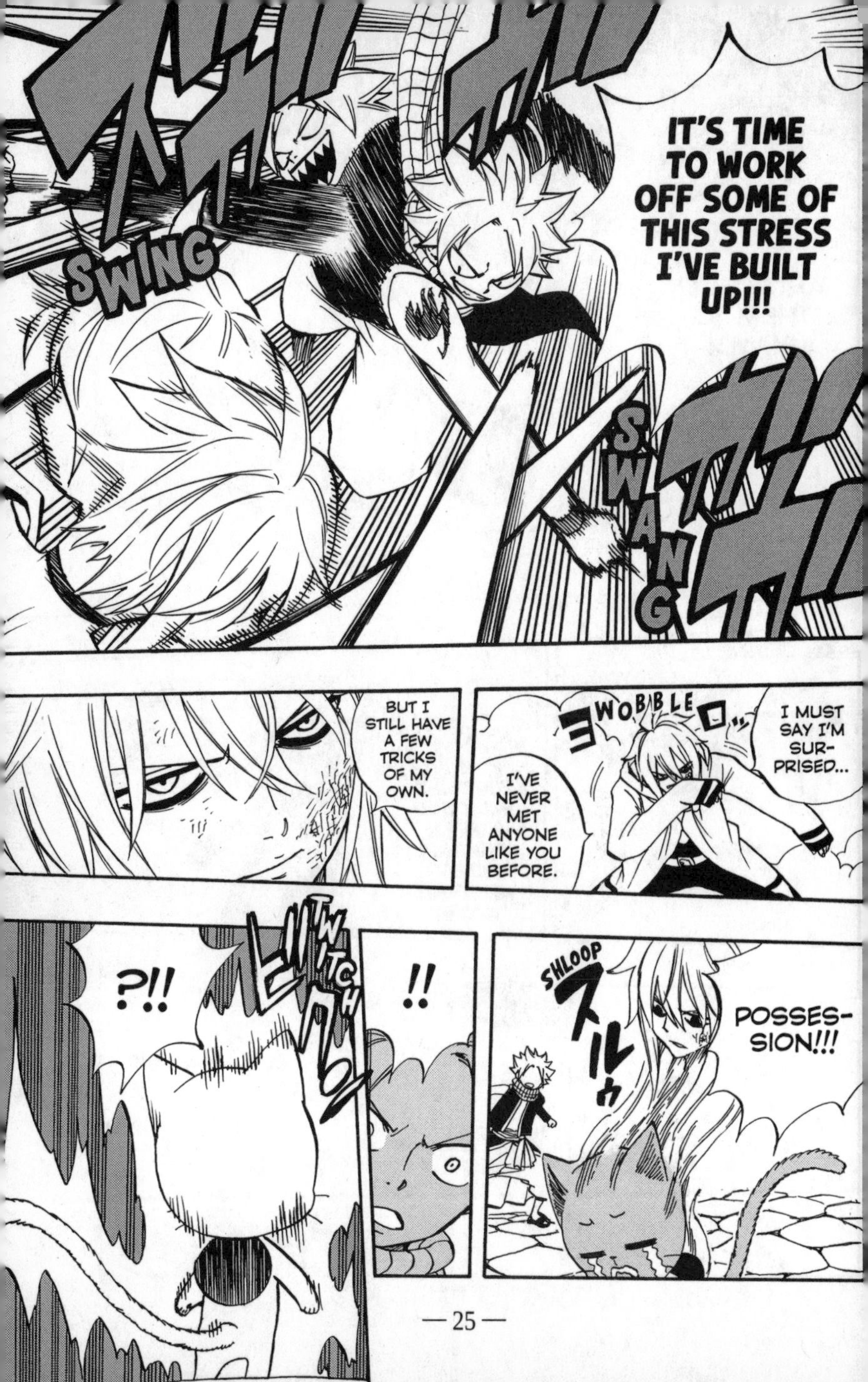
IT'S TIME TO WORK OFF SOME OF THIS STRESS I'VE BUILT UP!!!
SWANG
SWING
WOBBLE
I MUST SAY I'M SUR-PRISED...
I'VE NEVER MET ANYONE LIKE YOU BEFORE.
BUT I STILL HAVE A FEW TRICKS OF MY OWN.
SHLOOP
POSSES-SION!!!
!!
TWITCH
?!!

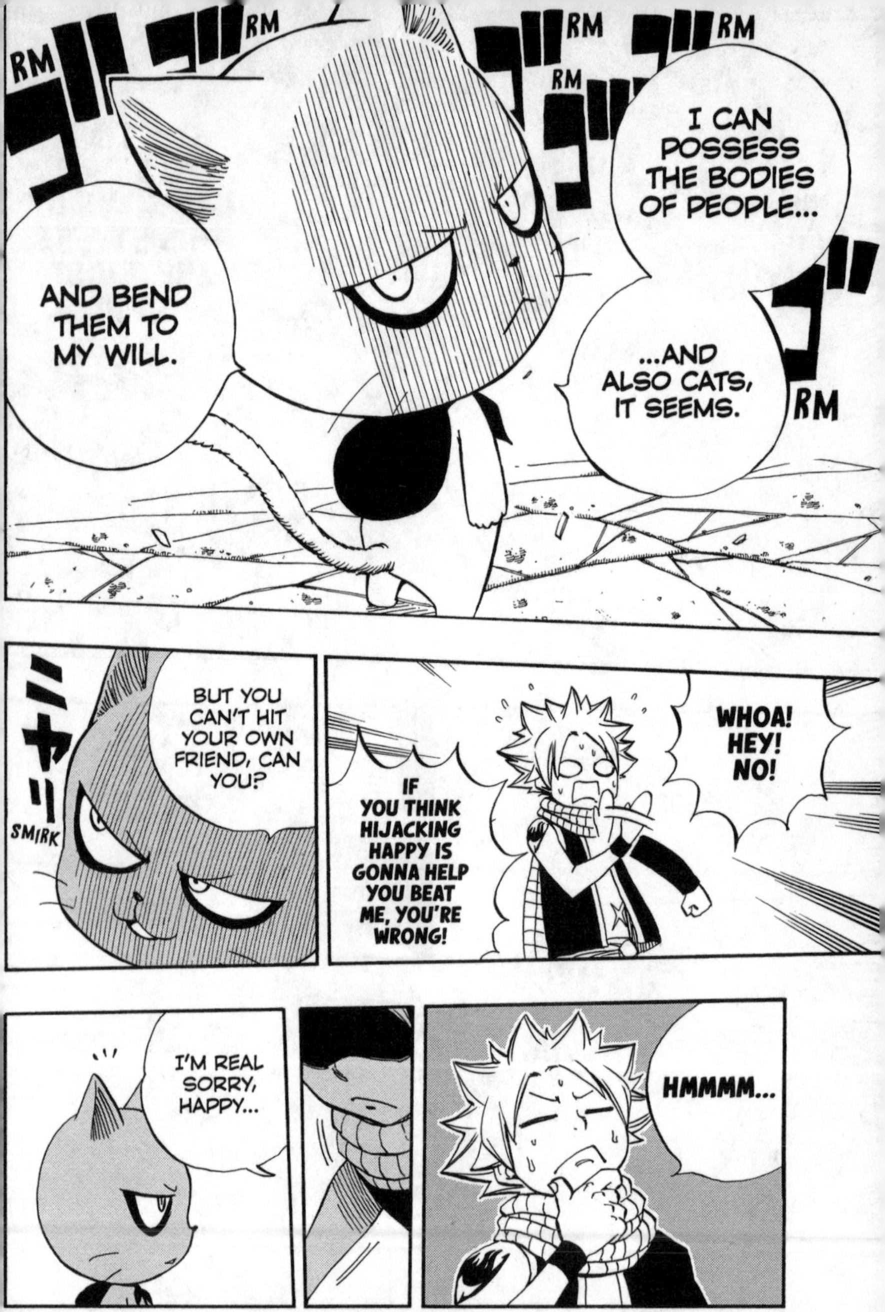
RM
RM
RM
RM
RM
I CAN POSSESS THE BODIES OF PEOPLE...
...AND ALSO CATS, IT SEEMS.
RM
AND BEND THEM TO MY WILL.
WHOA! HEY! NO!
IF YOU THINK HIJACKING HAPPY IS GONNA HELP YOU BEAT ME, YOU'RE WRONG!
BUT YOU CAN'T HIT YOUR OWN FRIEND, CAN YOU?
SMIRK
HMMMM...
I'M REAL SORRY, HAPPY...

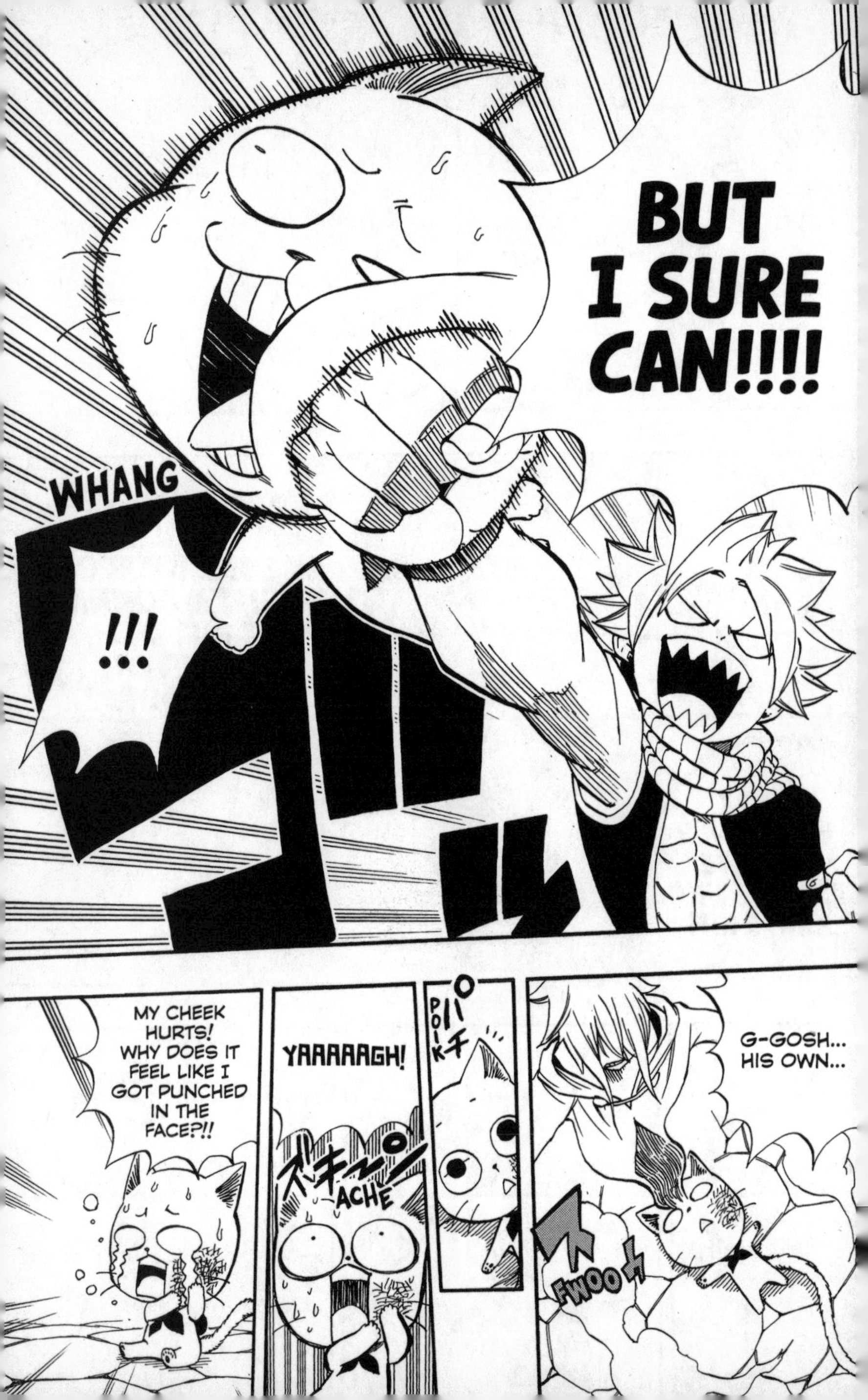
BUT I SURE CAN!!!!
WHANG
!!!
G-GOSH... HIS OWN...
FWOO
POIK
YAAAAAGH!
ACHE
MY CHEEK HURTS! WHY DOES IT FEEL LIKE I GOT PUNCHED IN THE FACE?!!

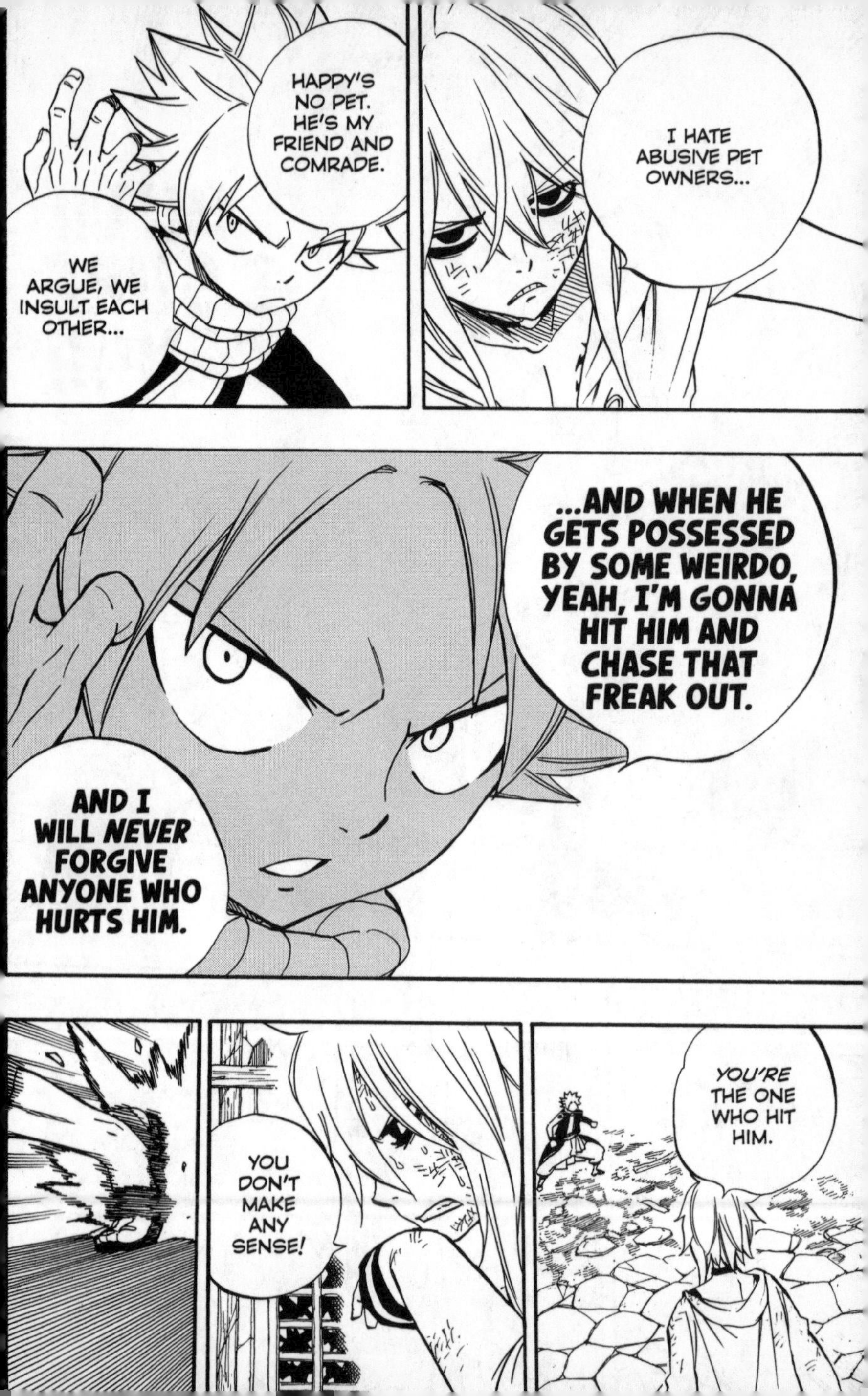
I HATE ABUSIVE PET OWNERS...
HAPPY'S NO PET. HE'S MY FRIEND AND COMRADE.
WE ARGUE, WE INSULT EACH OTHER...
...AND WHEN HE GETS POSSESSED BY SOME WEIRDO, YEAH, I'M GONNA HIT HIM AND CHASE THAT FREAK OUT.
AND I WILL *NEVER* FORGIVE ANYONE WHO HURTS HIM.
YOU'RE THE ONE WHO HIT HIM.
YOU DON'T MAKE ANY SENSE!

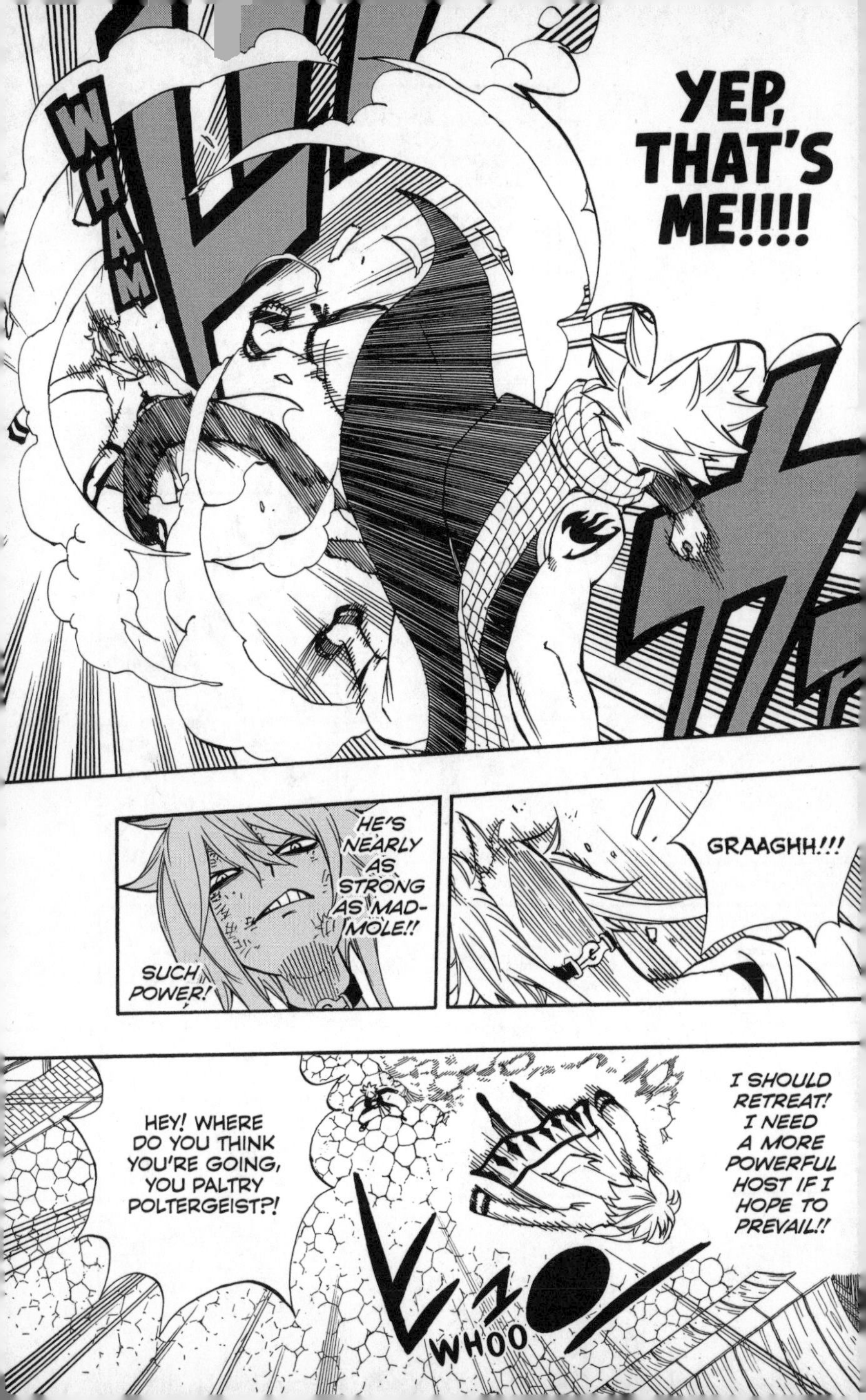
YEP, THAT'S ME!!!!
WHAM
GRAAGHH!!!
HE'S NEARLY AS STRONG AS MAD-MOLE!!
SUCH POWER!
I SHOULD RETREAT! I NEED A MORE POWERFUL HOST IF I HOPE TO PREVAIL!!
HEY! WHERE DO YOU THINK YOU'RE GOING, YOU PALTRY POLTERGEIST?!
WHOO

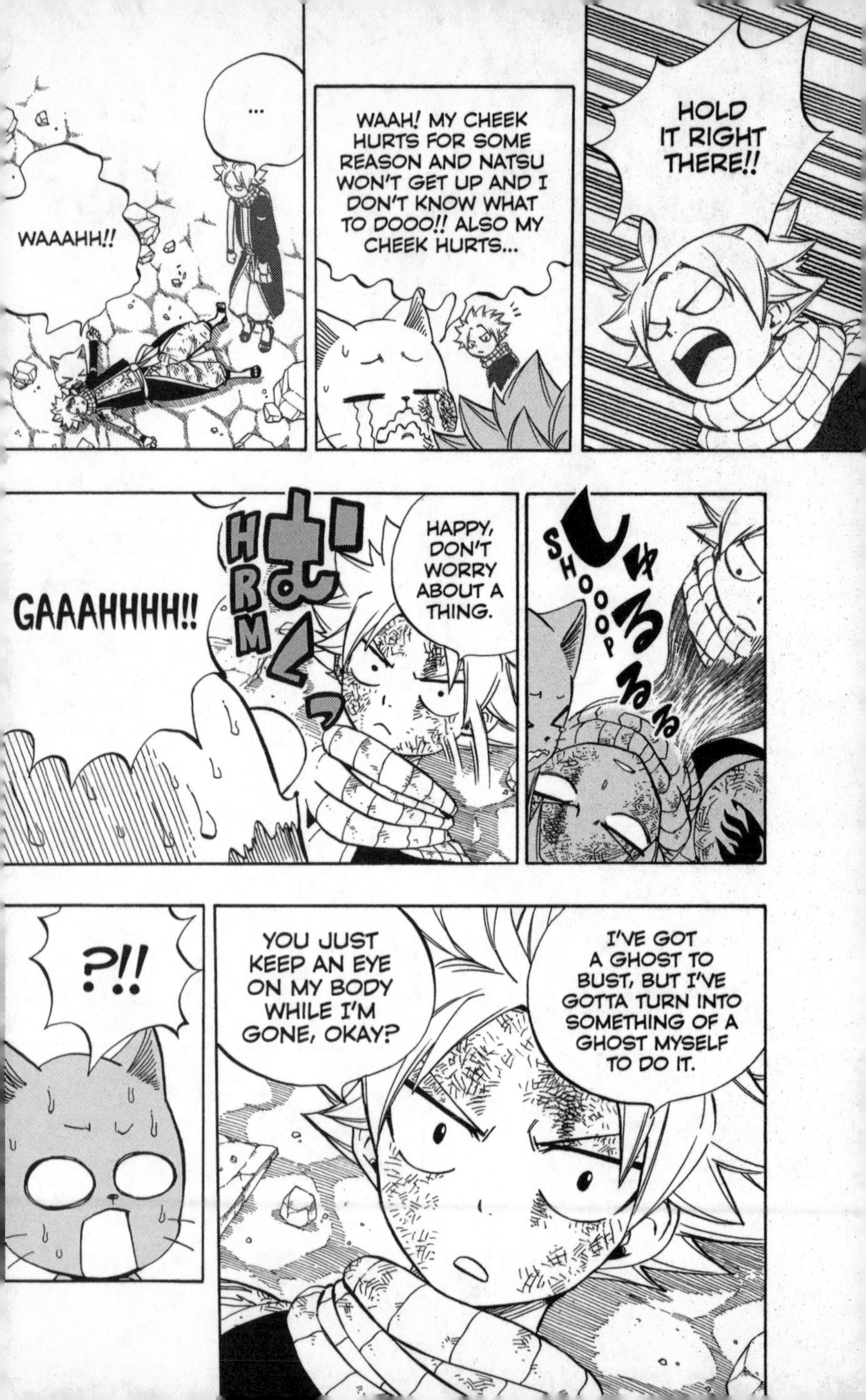
HOLD IT RIGHT THERE!!
WAAH! MY CHEEK HURTS FOR SOME REASON AND NATSU WON'T GET UP AND I DON'T KNOW WHAT TO DOOO!! ALSO MY CHEEK HURTS...
...
WAAAHH!!
SHOOOOP
HAPPY, DON'T WORRY ABOUT A THING.
HRM
GAAAHHHH!!
I'VE GOT A GHOST TO BUST, BUT I'VE GOTTA TURN INTO SOMETHING OF A GHOST MYSELF TO DO IT.
YOU JUST KEEP AN EYE ON MY BODY WHILE I'M GONE, OKAY?
?!!

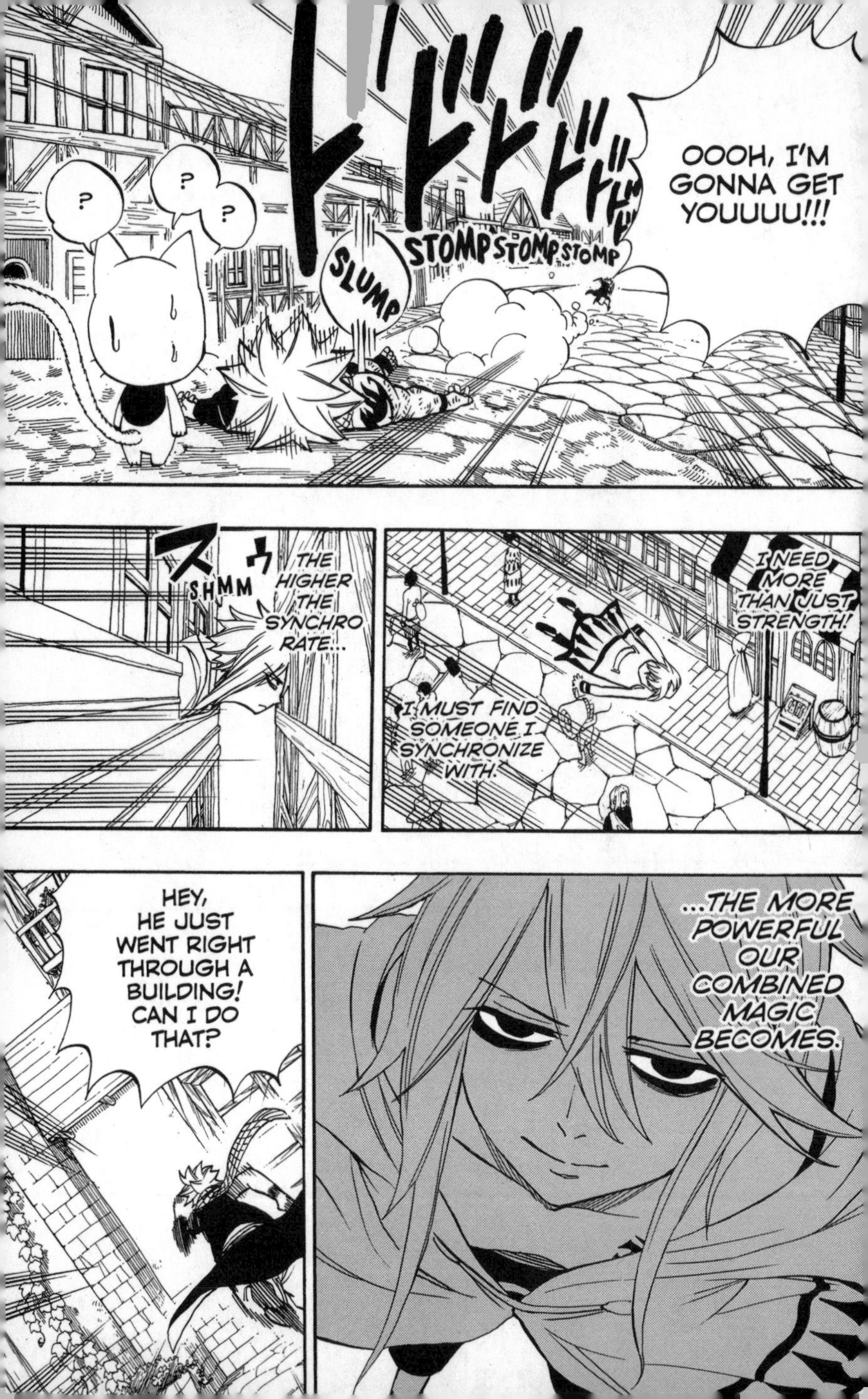
OOOH, I'M GONNA GET YOUUUU!!!
STOMP STOMP STOMP
SLUMP
?
?
?
I NEED MORE THAN JUST STRENGTH!
I MUST FIND SOMEONE I SYNCHRONIZE WITH.
SHMM
THE HIGHER THE SYNCHRO RATE...
...THE MORE POWERFUL OUR COMBINED MAGIC BECOMES.
HEY, HE JUST WENT RIGHT THROUGH A BUILDING! CAN I DO THAT?

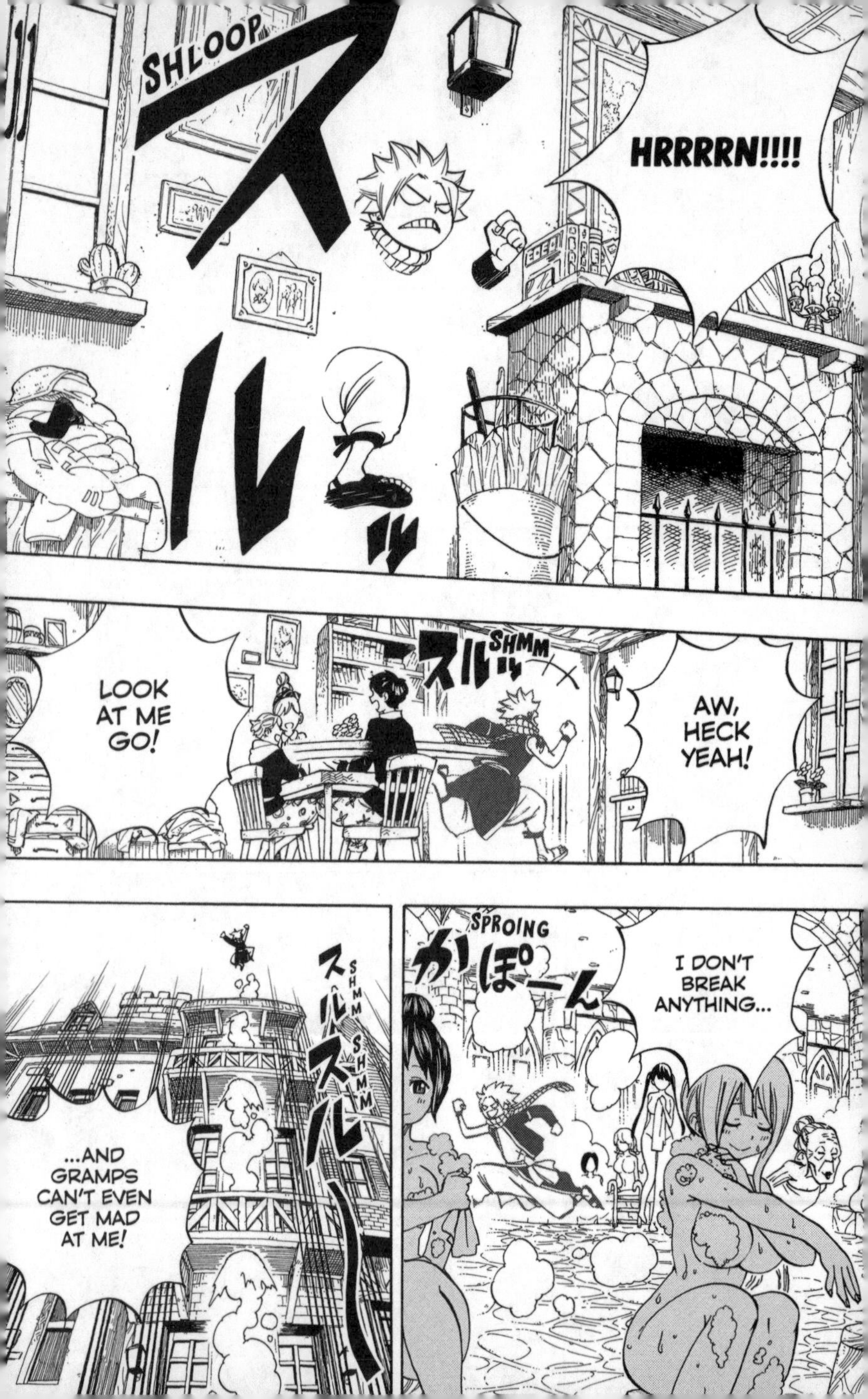
HRRRRN!!!!
SHLOOP
AW, HECK YEAH!
SHMM
LOOK AT ME GO!
SPROING
I DON'T BREAK ANYTHING...
SHMM SHMM
...AND GRAMPS CAN'T EVEN GET MAD AT ME!

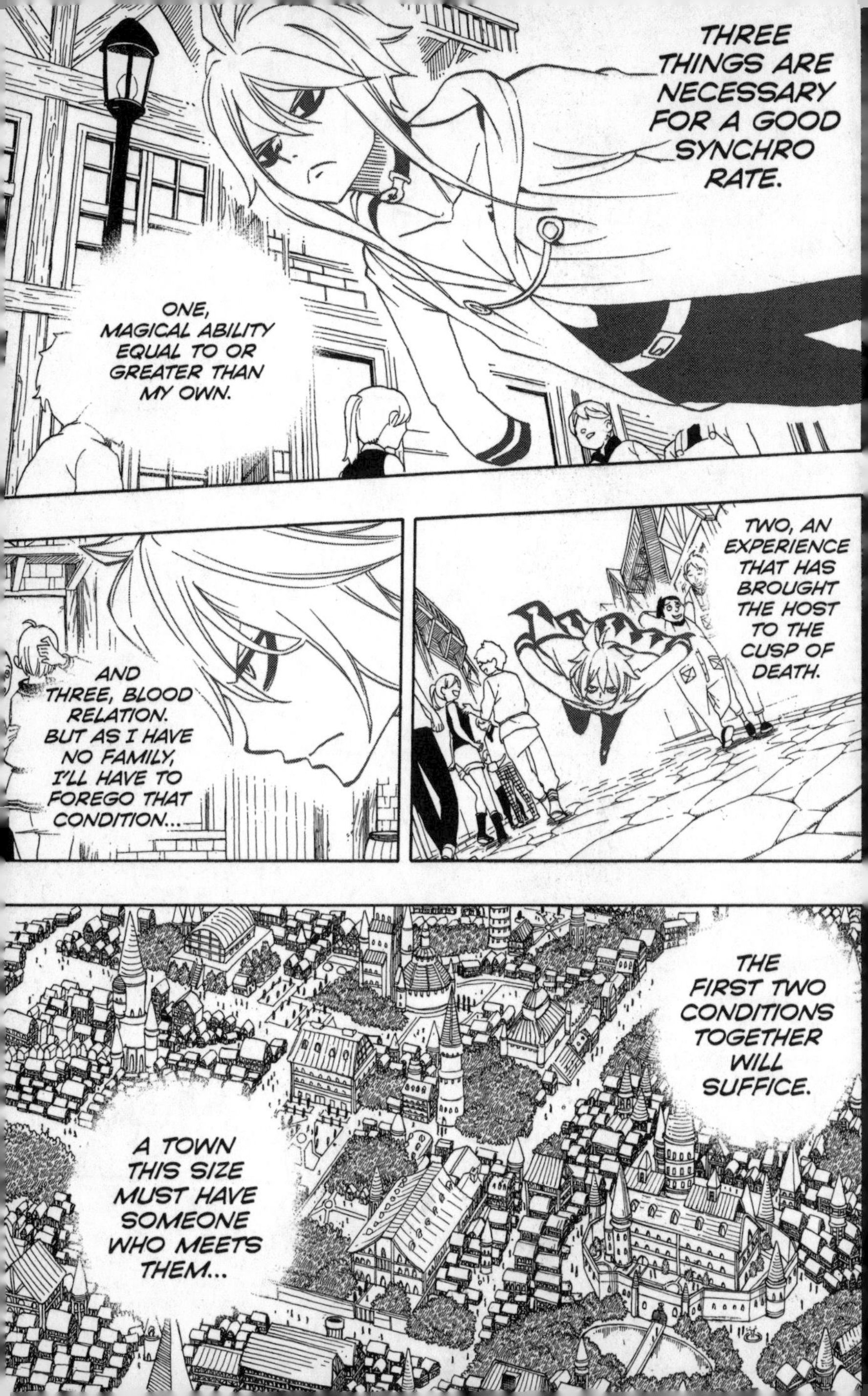
THREE THINGS ARE NECESSARY FOR A GOOD SYNCHRO RATE.
ONE, MAGICAL ABILITY EQUAL TO OR GREATER THAN MY OWN.
TWO, AN EXPERIENCE THAT HAS BROUGHT THE HOST TO THE CUSP OF DEATH.
AND THREE, BLOOD RELATION. BUT AS I HAVE NO FAMILY, I'LL HAVE TO FOREGO THAT CONDITION...
THE FIRST TWO CONDITIONS TOGETHER WILL SUFFICE.
A TOWN THIS SIZE MUST HAVE SOMEONE WHO MEETS THEM...

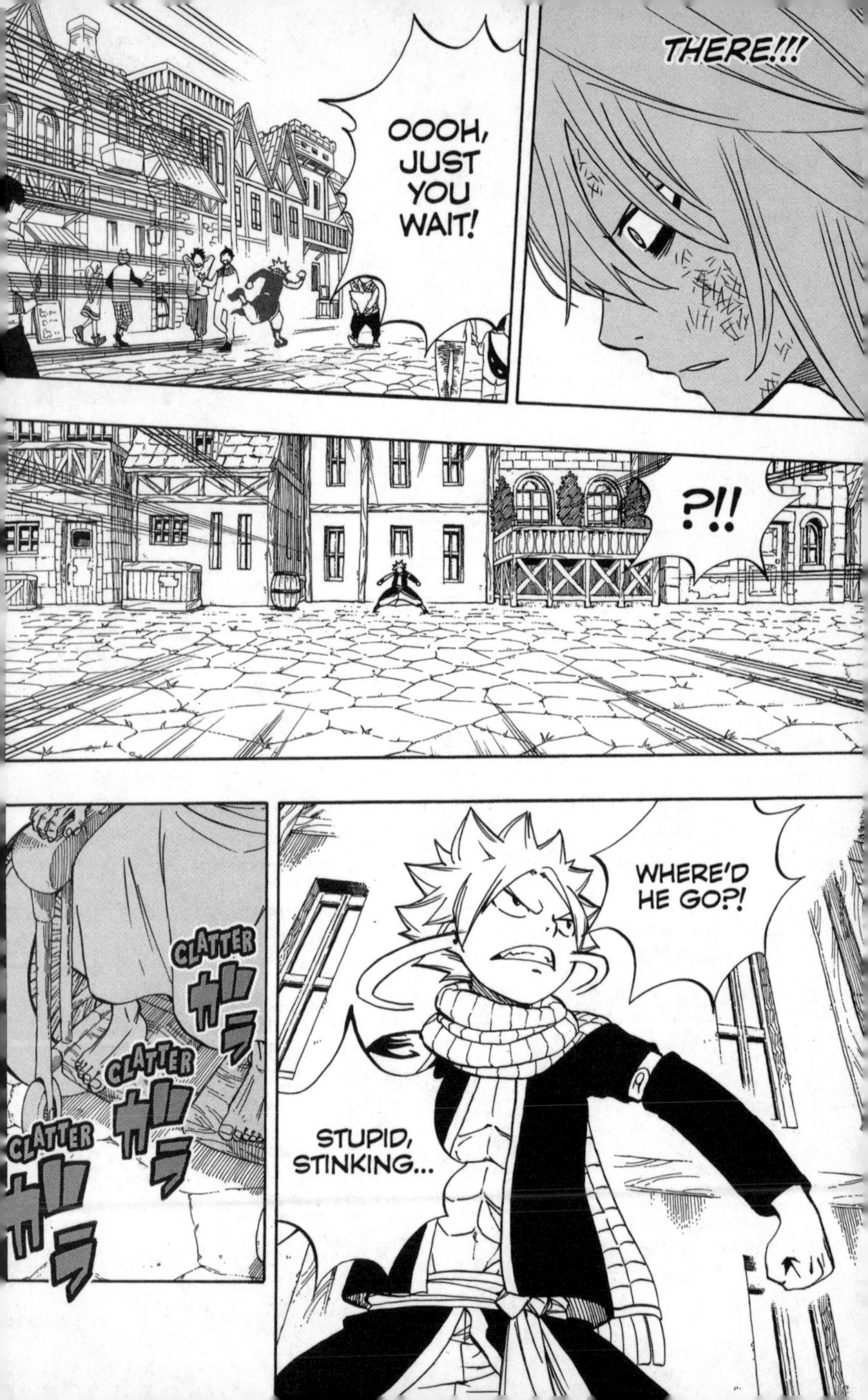
THERE!!!
OOOH, JUST YOU WAIT!
?!!
WHERE'D HE GO?!
STUPID, STINKING...
CLATTER
ガラ
CLATTER
ガラ
CLATTER
ガラ

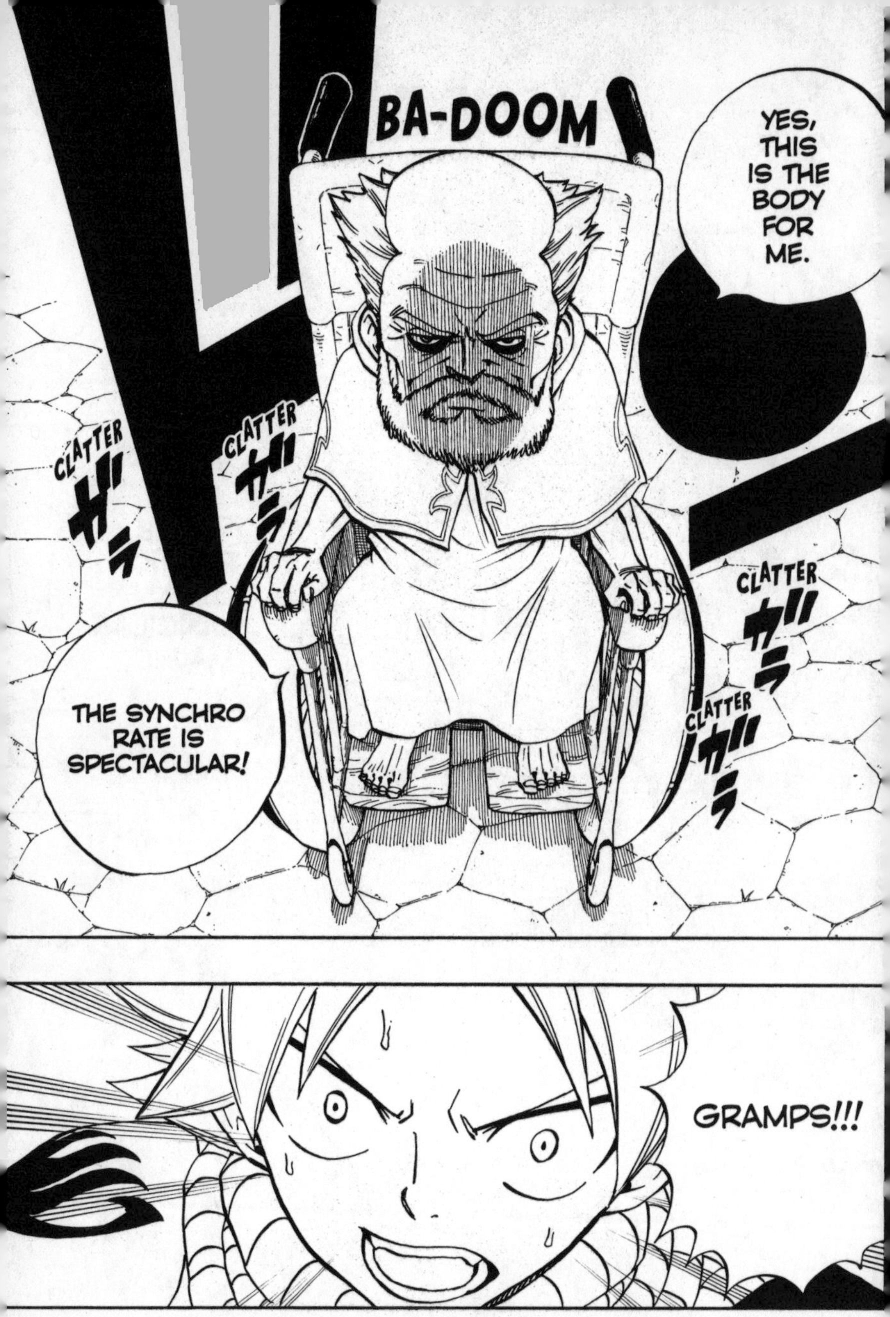
YES, THIS IS THE BODY FOR ME.
BA-DOOM
CLATTER
ガラ
CLATTER
ガラ
CLATTER
ガラ
CLATTER
ガラ
THE SYNCHRO RATE IS SPECTACULAR!
GRAMPS!!!

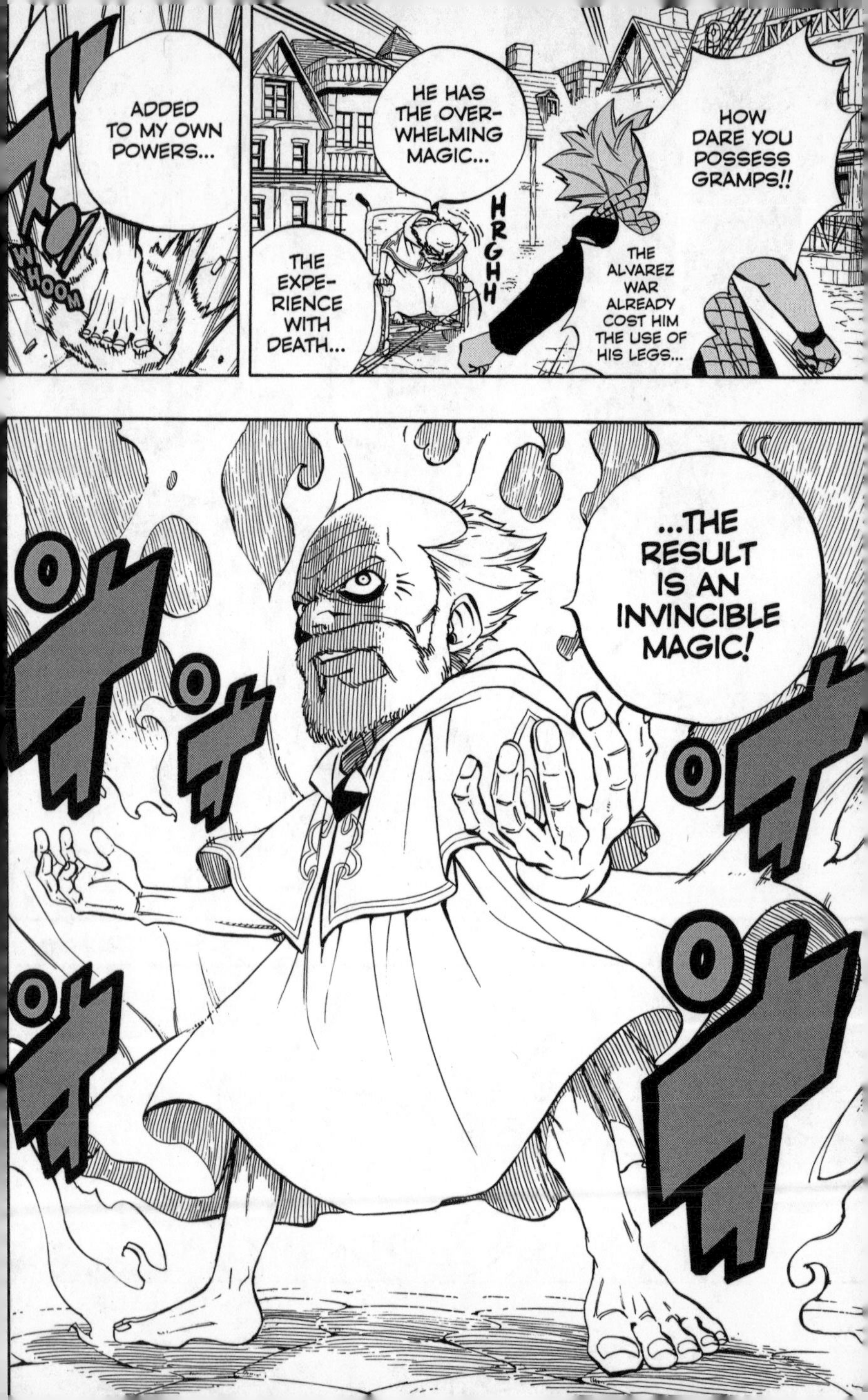
HOW DARE YOU POSSESS GRAMPS!!
THE ALVAREZ WAR ALREADY COST HIM THE USE OF HIS LEGS...
HE HAS THE OVER-WHELMING MAGIC...
HRGHH
THE EXPE-RIENCE WITH DEATH...
ADDED TO MY OWN POWERS...
WHOOM
...THE RESULT IS AN INVINCIBLE MAGIC!

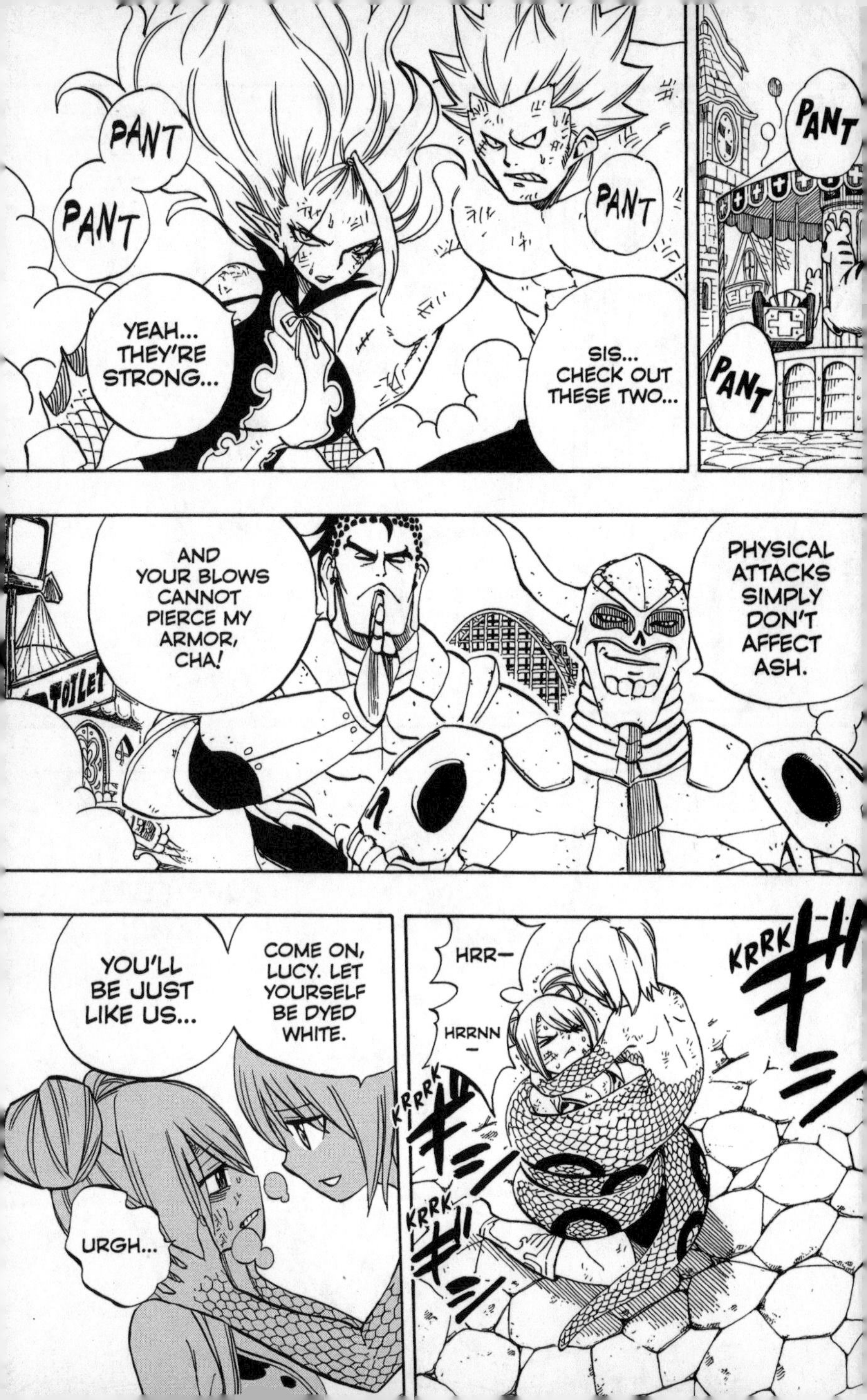
PANT
PANT
PANT
SIS... CHECK OUT THESE TWO...
PANT
PANT
YEAH... THEY'RE STRONG...
PHYSICAL ATTACKS SIMPLY DON'T AFFECT ASH.
AND YOUR BLOWS CANNOT PIERCE MY ARMOR, CHA!
TOILET
KRRK
HRR—
HRRNN—
KRRK
KRRK
COME ON, LUCY. LET YOURSELF BE DYED WHITE.
YOU'LL BE JUST LIKE US...
URGH...

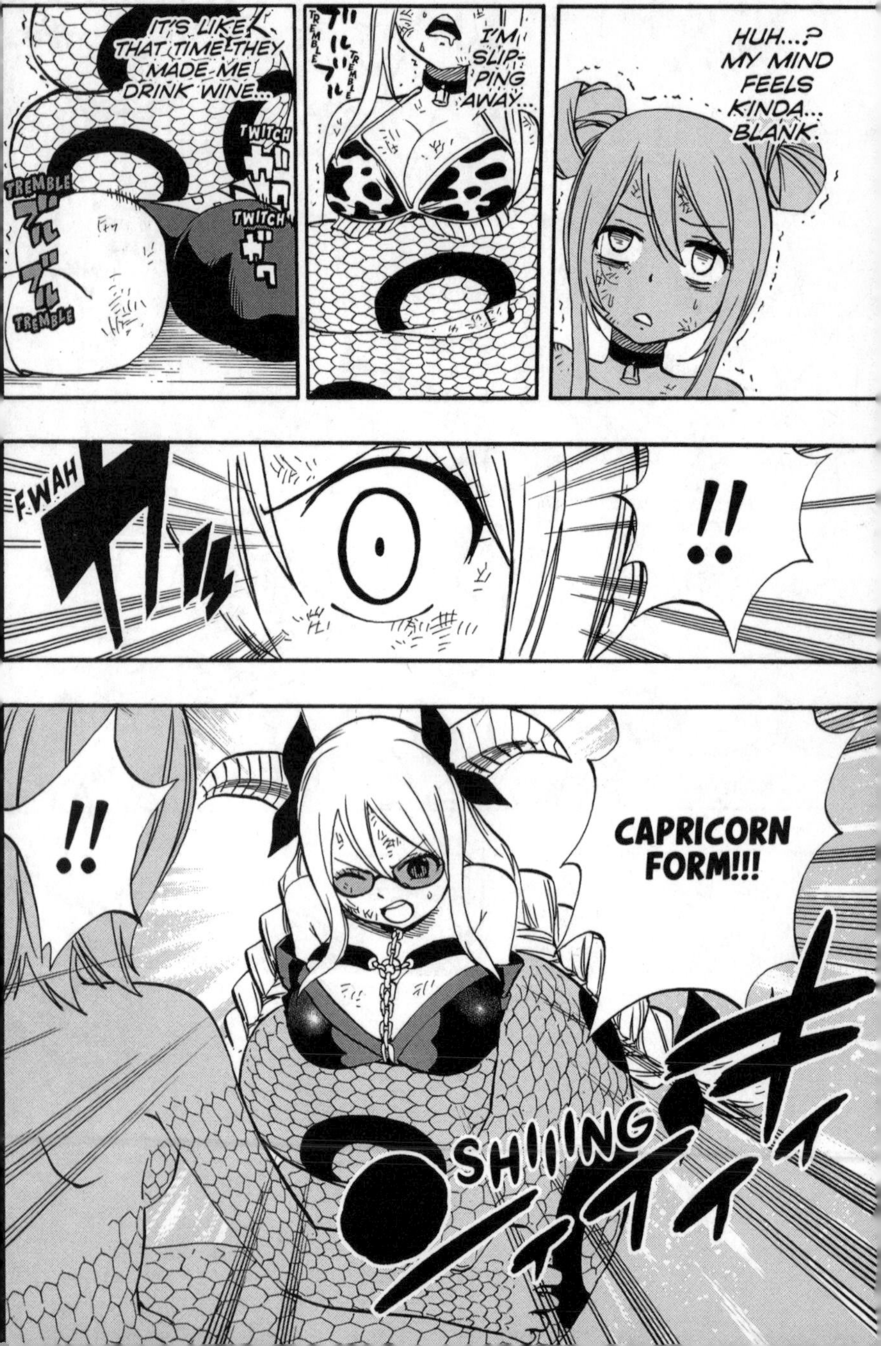
HUH...? MY MIND FEELS KINDA... BLANK.
I'M SLIP-PING AWAY...
TREMBLE
TREMBLE
IT'S LIKE THAT TIME THEY MADE ME DRINK WINE...
TWITCH
TWITCH
TREMBLE
TREMBLE
!!
FWAH
CAPRICORN FORM!!!
!!
SHIIING

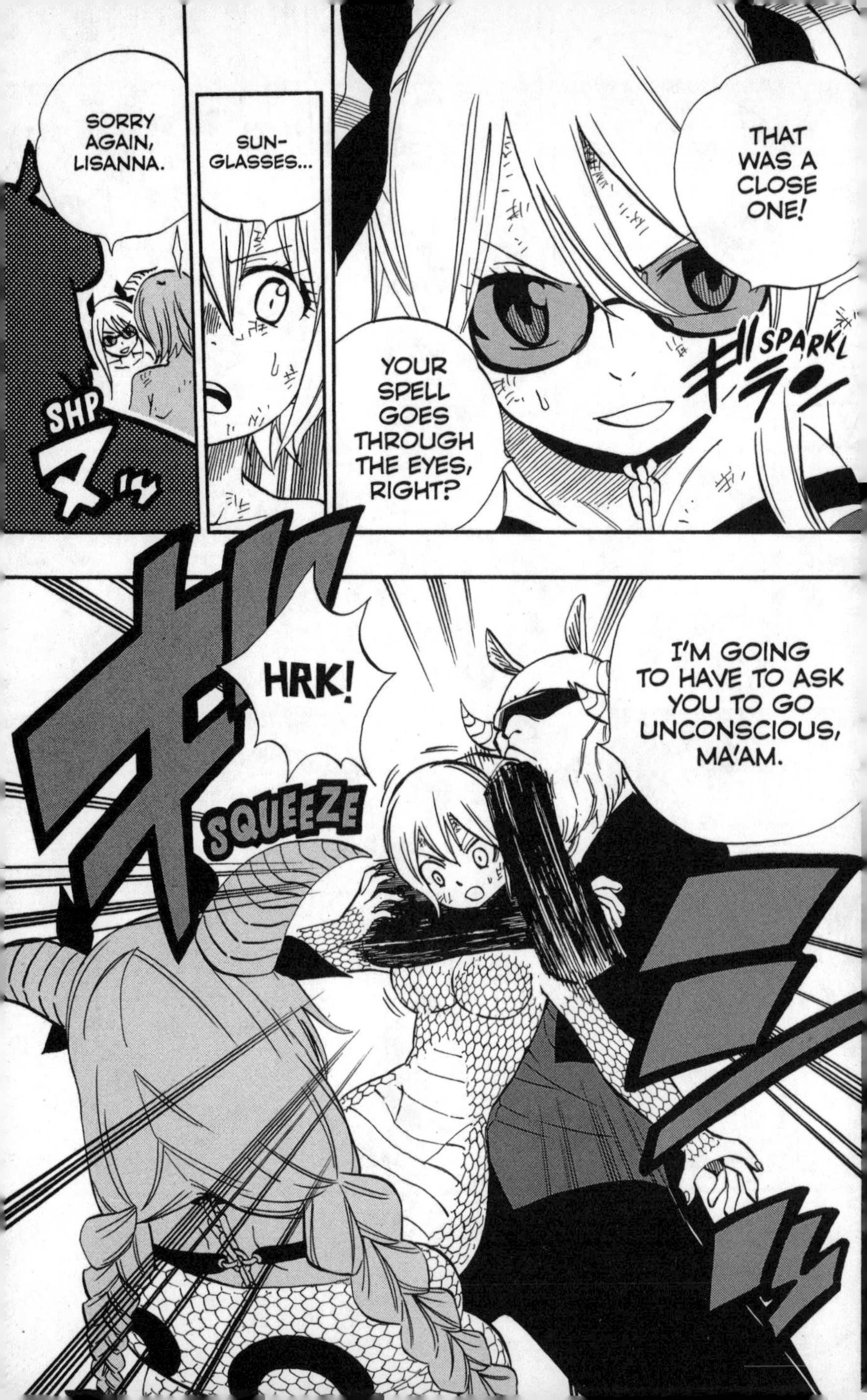
THAT WAS A CLOSE ONE!
SPARKL
YOUR SPELL GOES THROUGH THE EYES, RIGHT?
SUN-GLASSES...
SORRY AGAIN, LISANNA.
SHP
I'M GOING TO HAVE TO ASK YOU TO GO UNCONSCIOUS, MA'AM.
HRK!
SQUEEZE

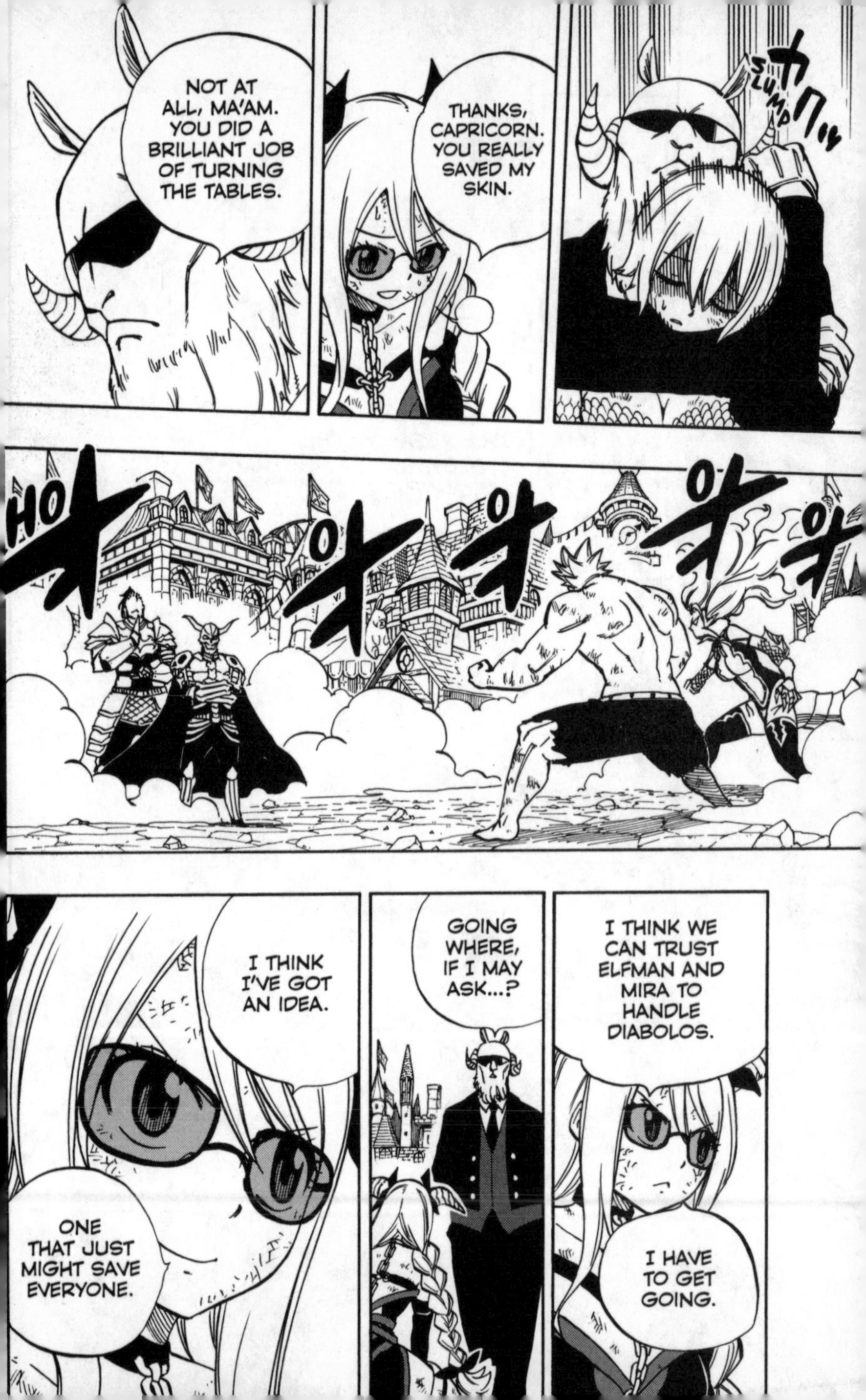
SLUMP
THANKS, CAPRICORN. YOU REALLY SAVED MY SKIN.
NOT AT ALL, MA'AM. YOU DID A BRILLIANT JOB OF TURNING THE TABLES.
HO
O
O
O
I THINK WE CAN TRUST ELFMAN AND MIRA TO HANDLE DIABOLOS.
I HAVE TO GET GOING.
GOING WHERE, IF I MAY ASK...?
I THINK I'VE GOT AN IDEA.
ONE THAT JUST MIGHT SAVE EVERYONE.

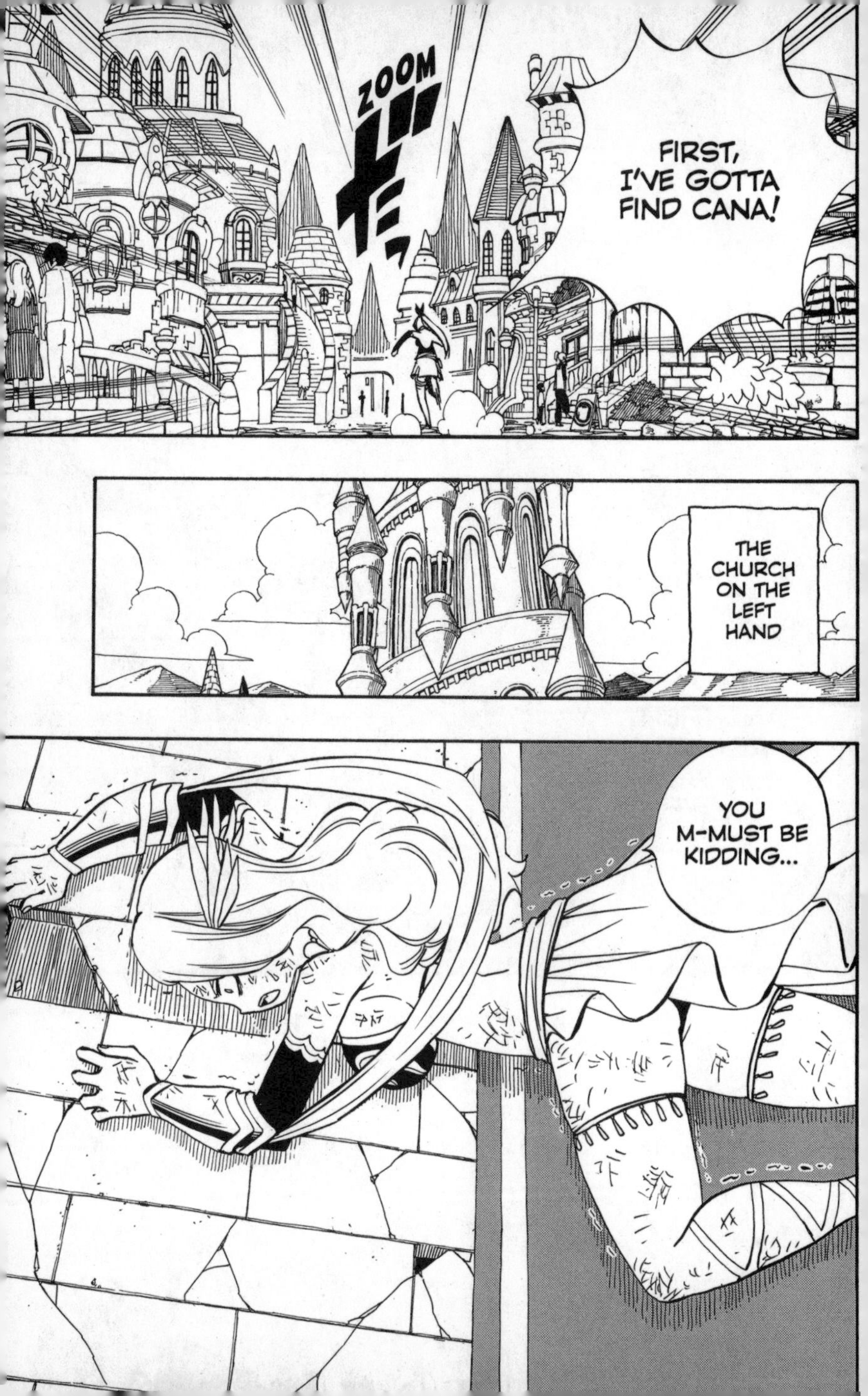
FIRST, I'VE GOTTA FIND CANA!
ZOOM
THE CHURCH ON THE LEFT HAND
YOU M-MUST BE KIDDING...

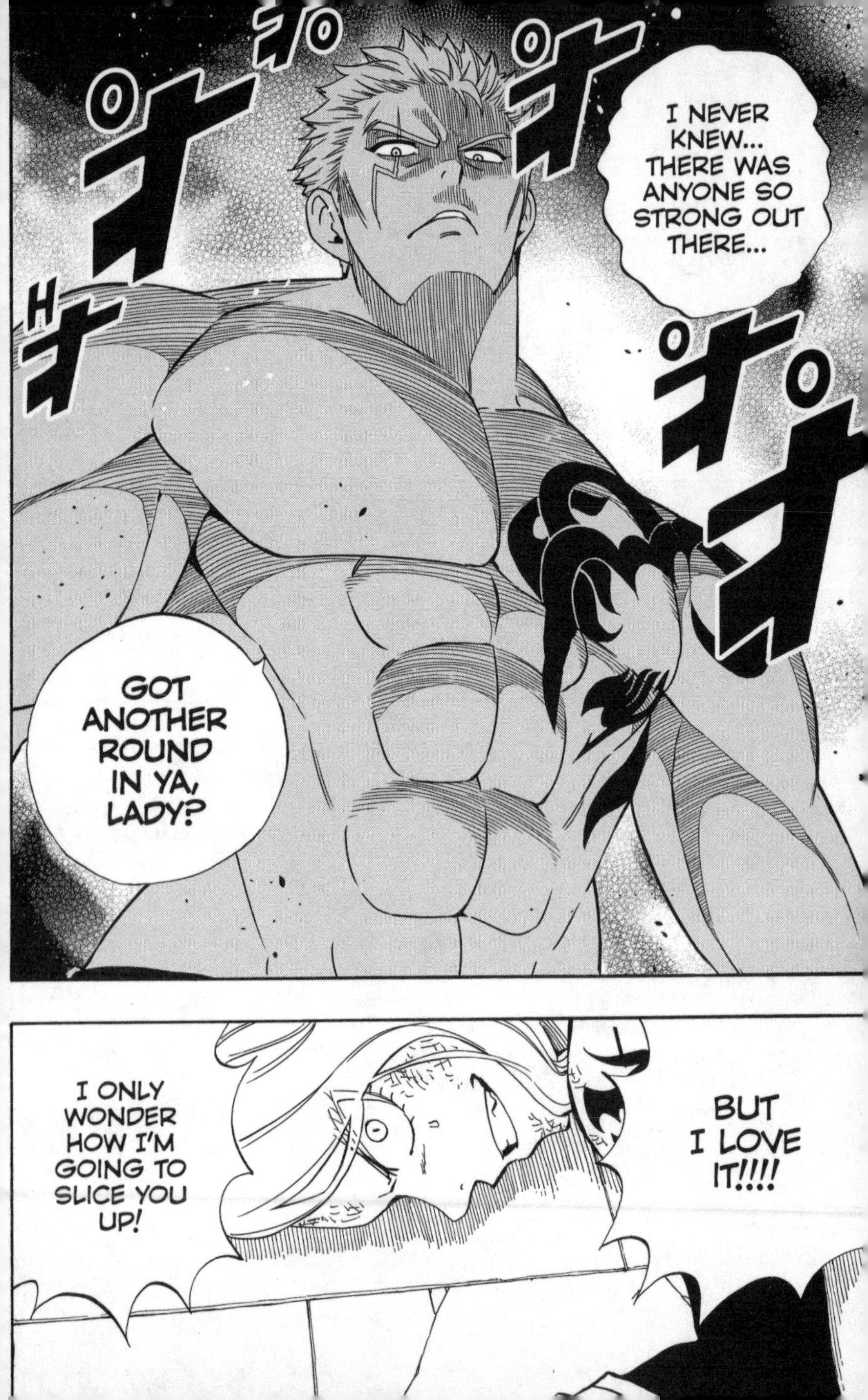
I NEVER KNEW... THERE WAS ANYONE SO STRONG OUT THERE...
GOT ANOTHER ROUND IN YA, LADY?
BUT I LOVE IT!!!!
I ONLY WONDER HOW I'M GOING TO SLICE YOU UP!

FAIRY TAIL 100 YEARS QUEST

Chapter 39: Coo-Coo, the Cocoon Dragon

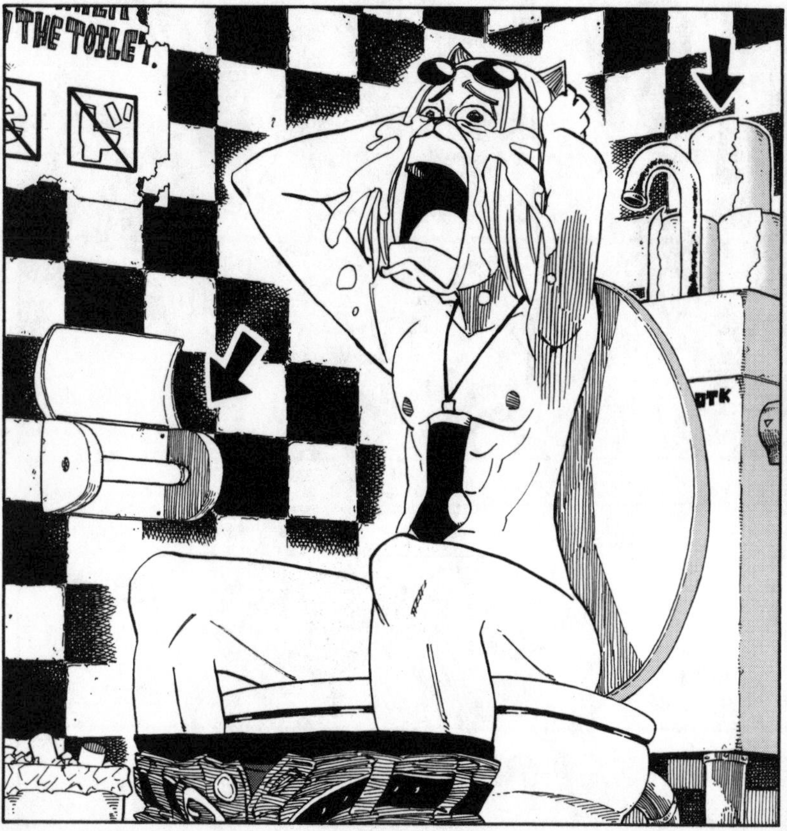
THE TOILET.
OTK

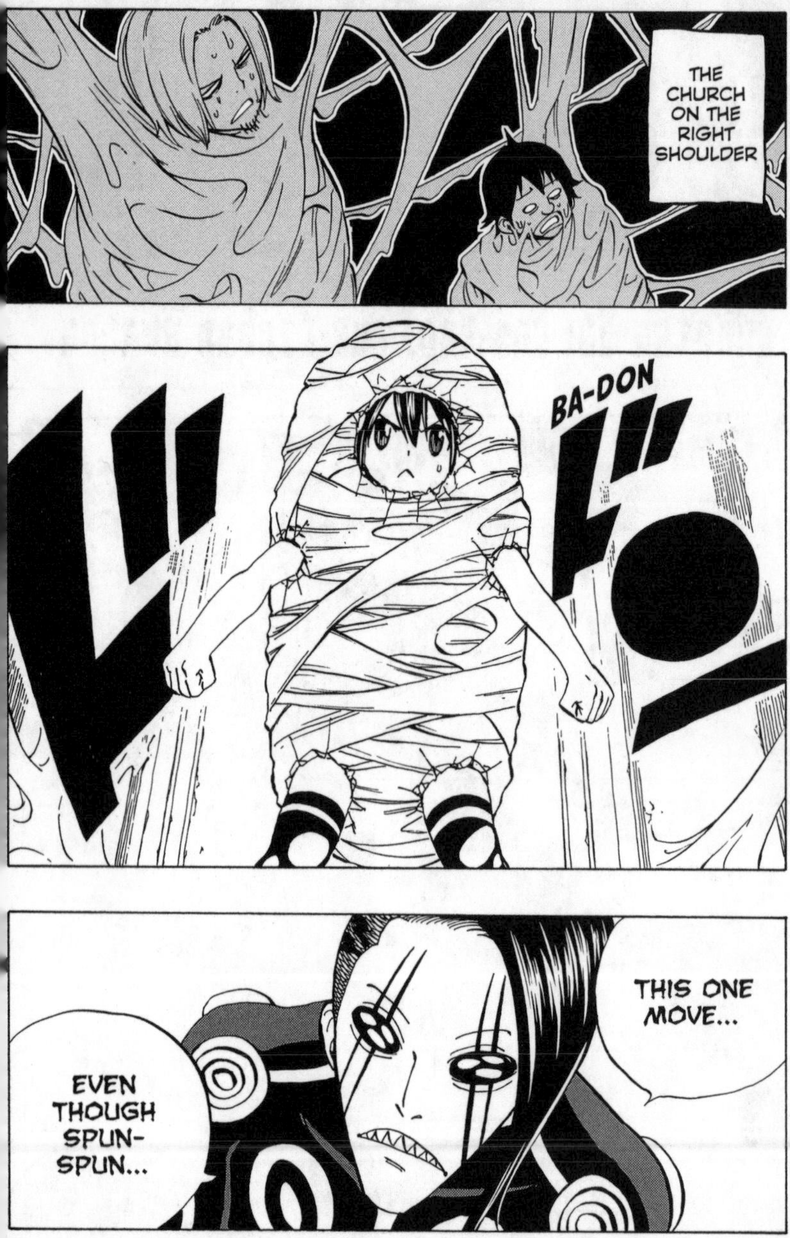
THE CHURCH ON THE RIGHT SHOULDER
BA-DON
THIS ONE MOVE...
EVEN THOUGH SPUN-SPUN...

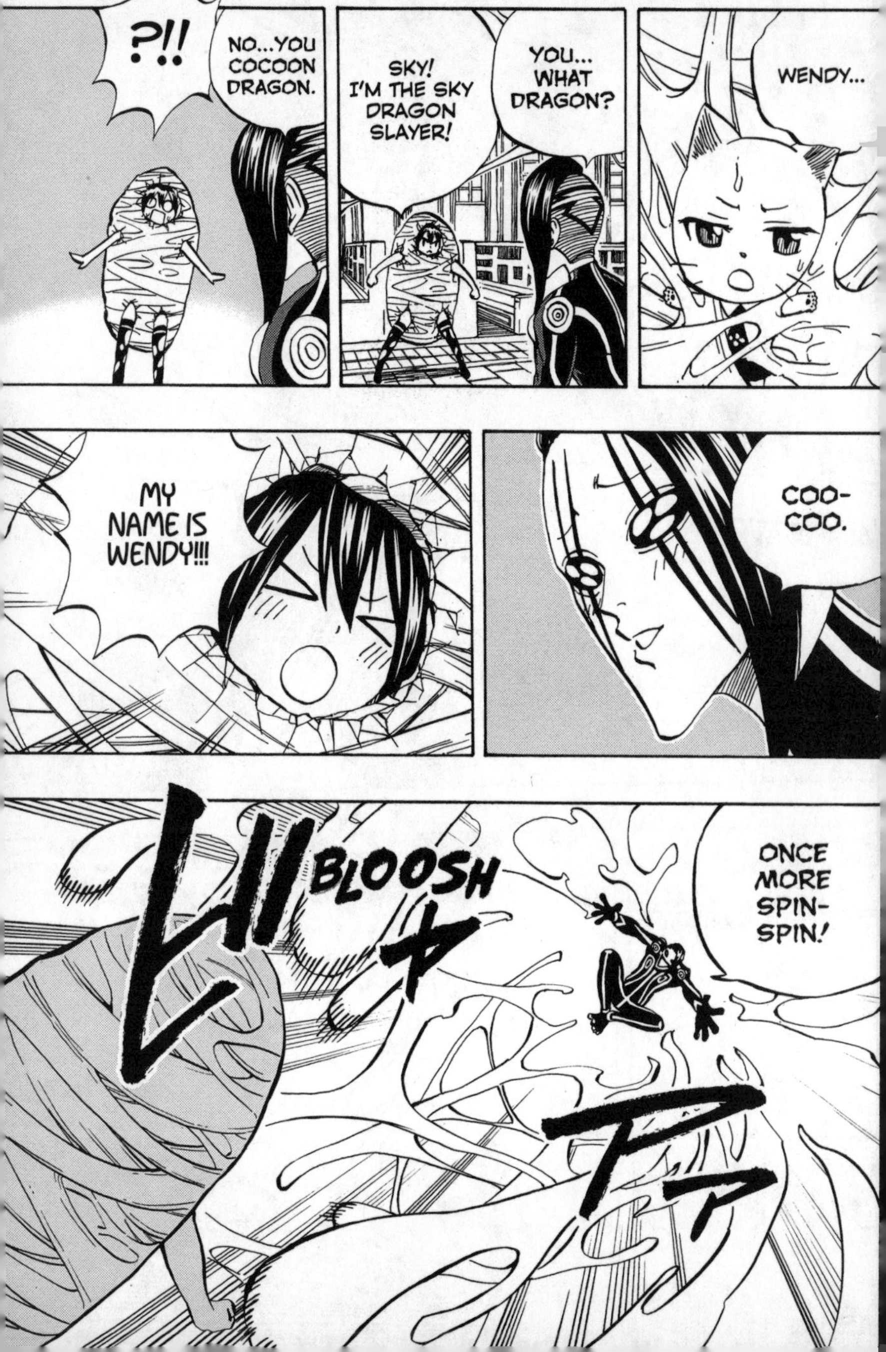
WENDY...
YOU... WHAT DRAGON?
SKY! I'M THE SKY DRAGON SLAYER!
NO...YOU COCOON DRAGON.
?!!
COO-COO.
MY NAME IS WENDY!!!
ONCE MORE SPIN-SPIN!
BLOOSH

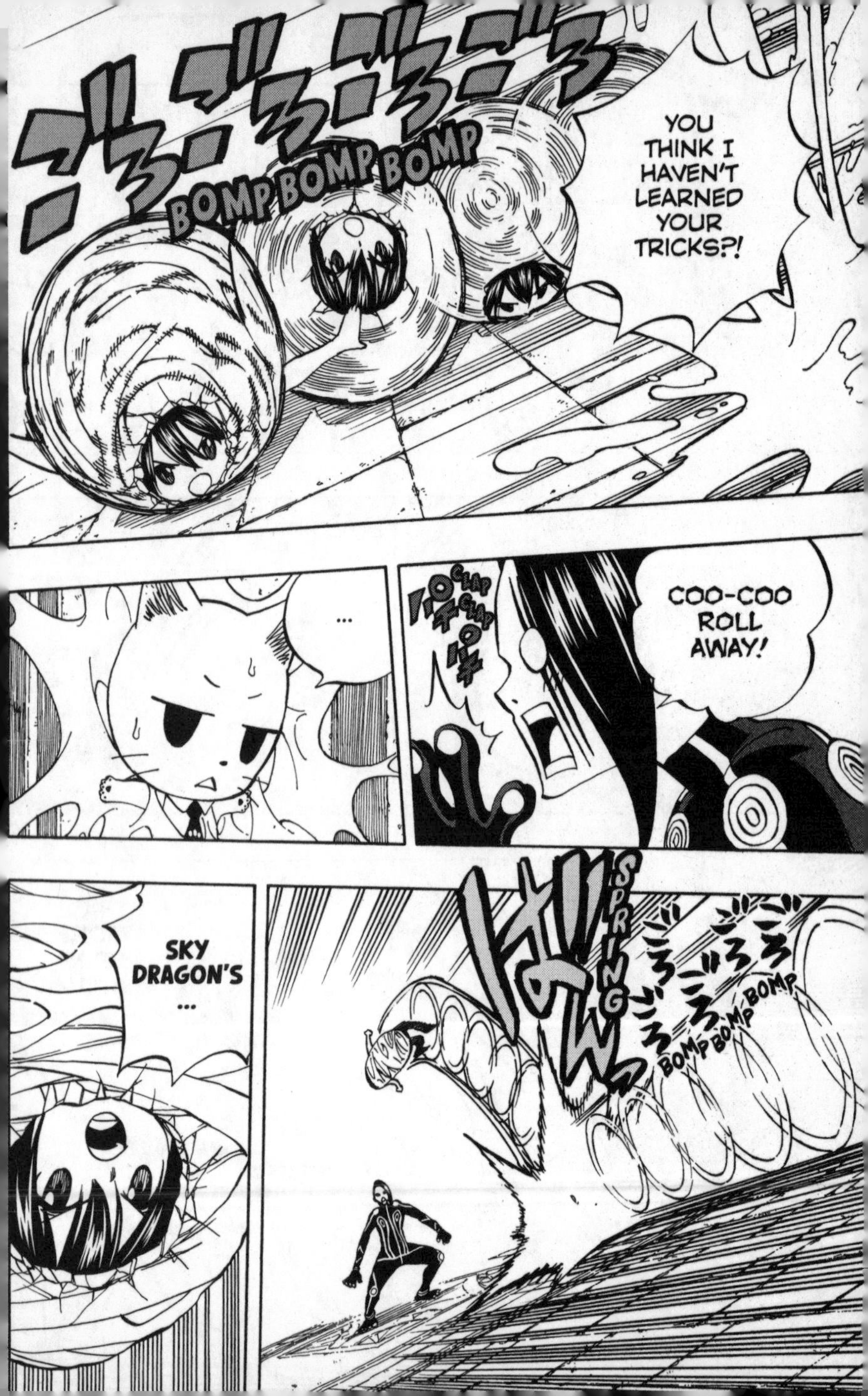
BOMP BOMP BOMP
YOU THINK I HAVEN'T LEARNED YOUR TRICKS?!
CLAP CLAP
COO-COO ROLL AWAY!
...
SPRING
BOMP BOMP BOMP
SKY DRAGON'S ...

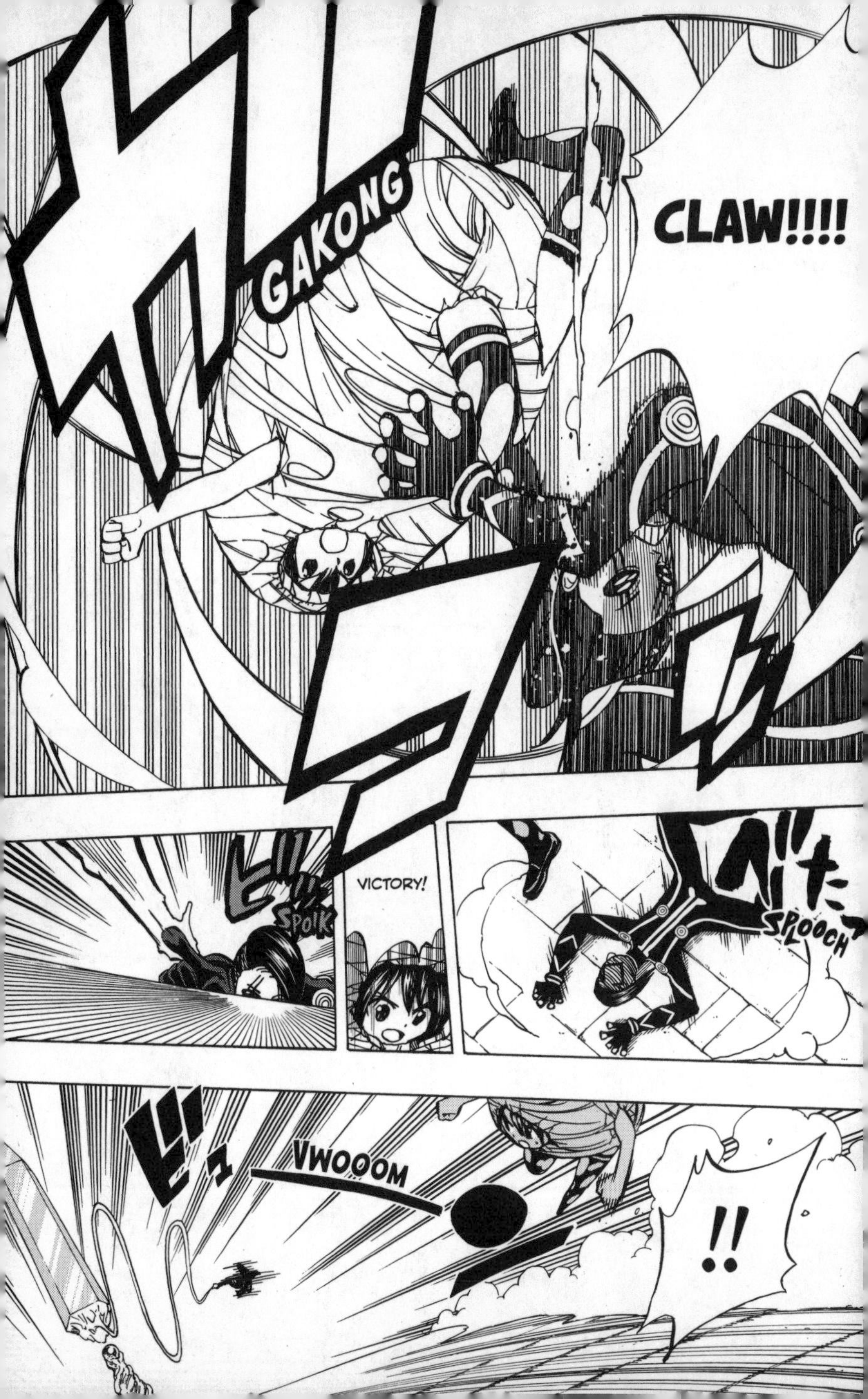
CLAW!!!!
GAKONG
SPLOOCH
VICTORY!
SPOIK
!!
VWOOOM

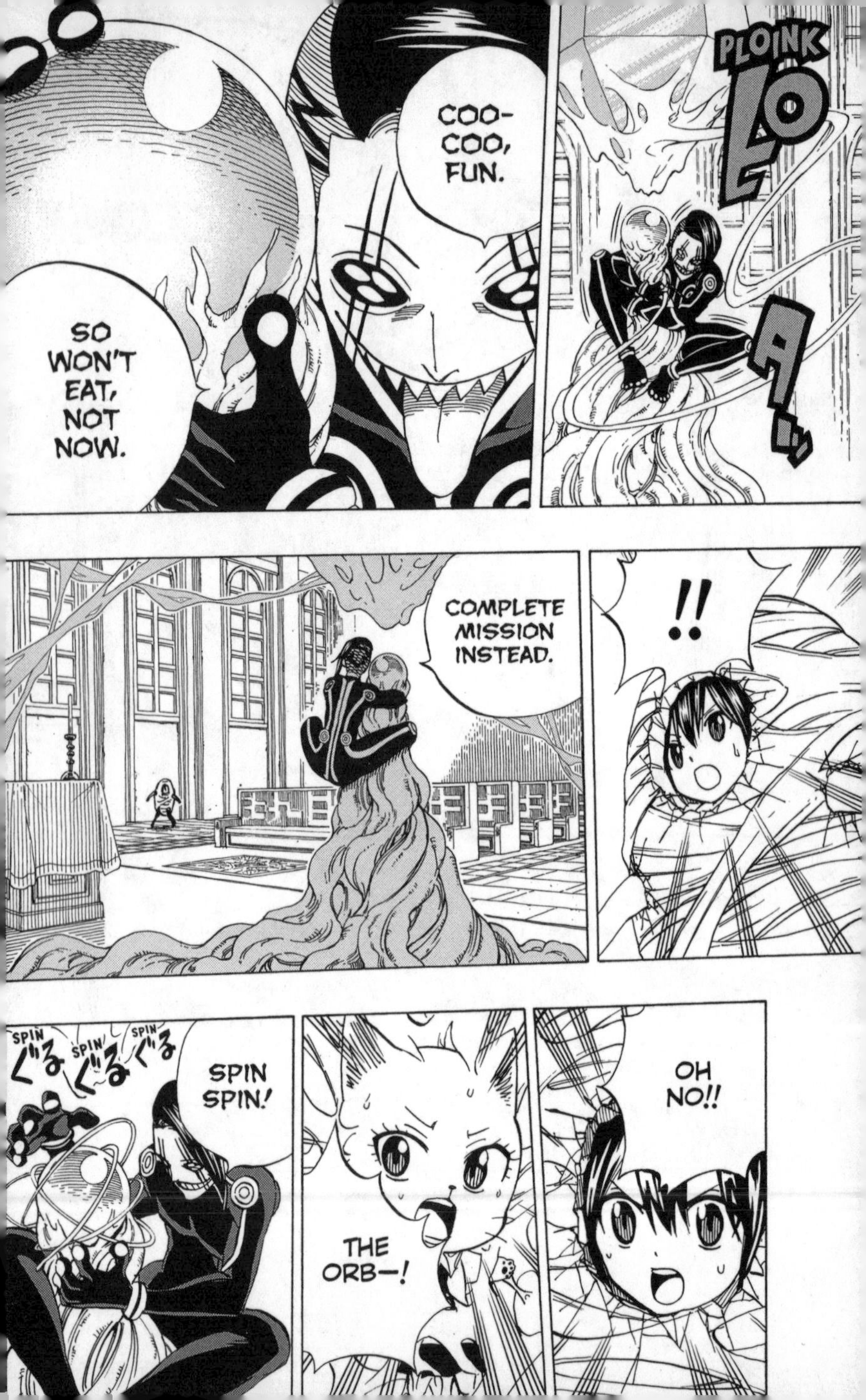
PLOINK
A..!
COO-COO, FUN.
SO WON'T EAT, NOT NOW.
!!
COMPLETE MISSION INSTEAD.
OH NO!!
THE ORB—!
SPIN ぐる SPIN ぐる SPIN ぐる
SPIN SPIN!

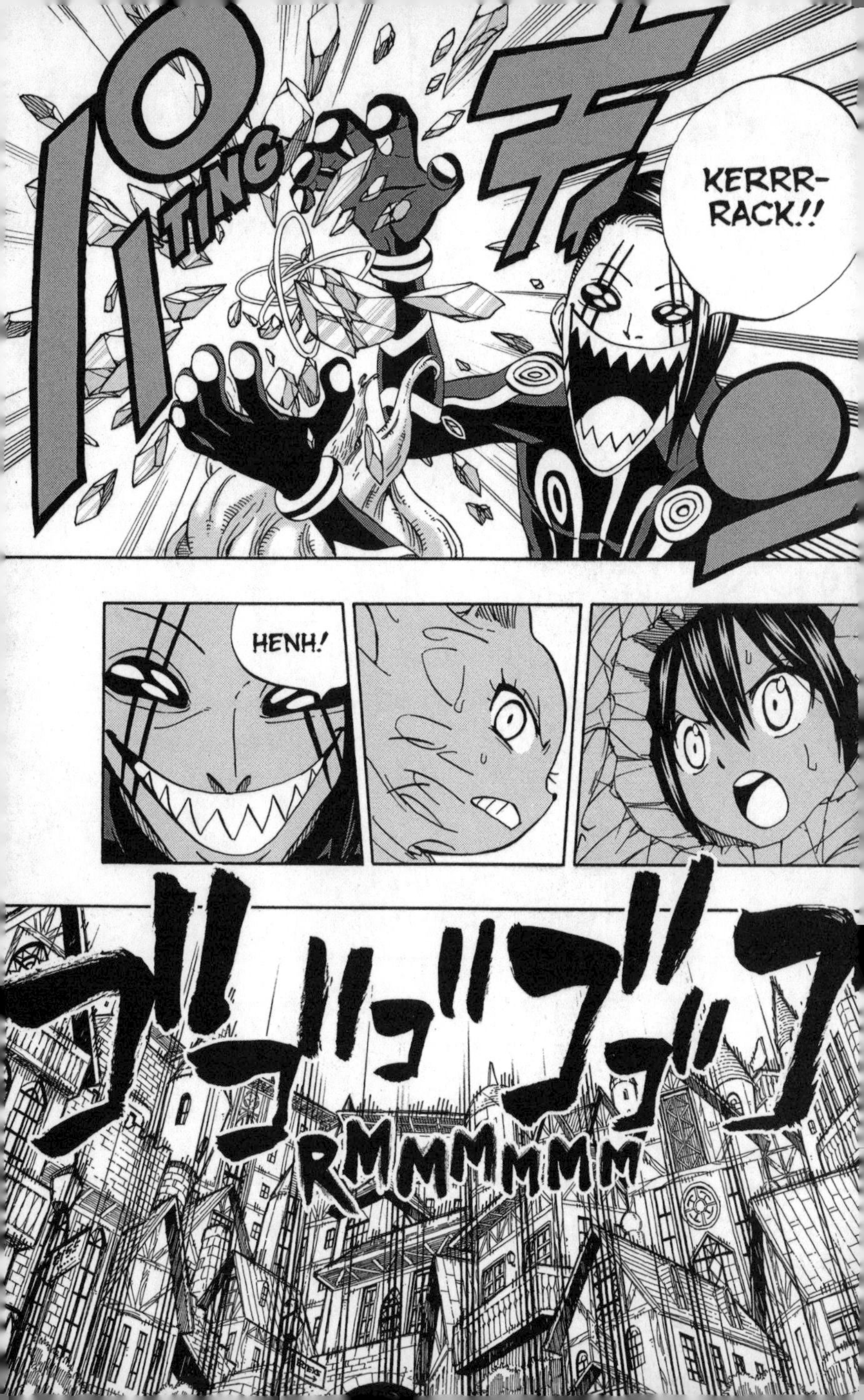
KERRR-
RACK!!
TING
HENH!
RMMMMMMM

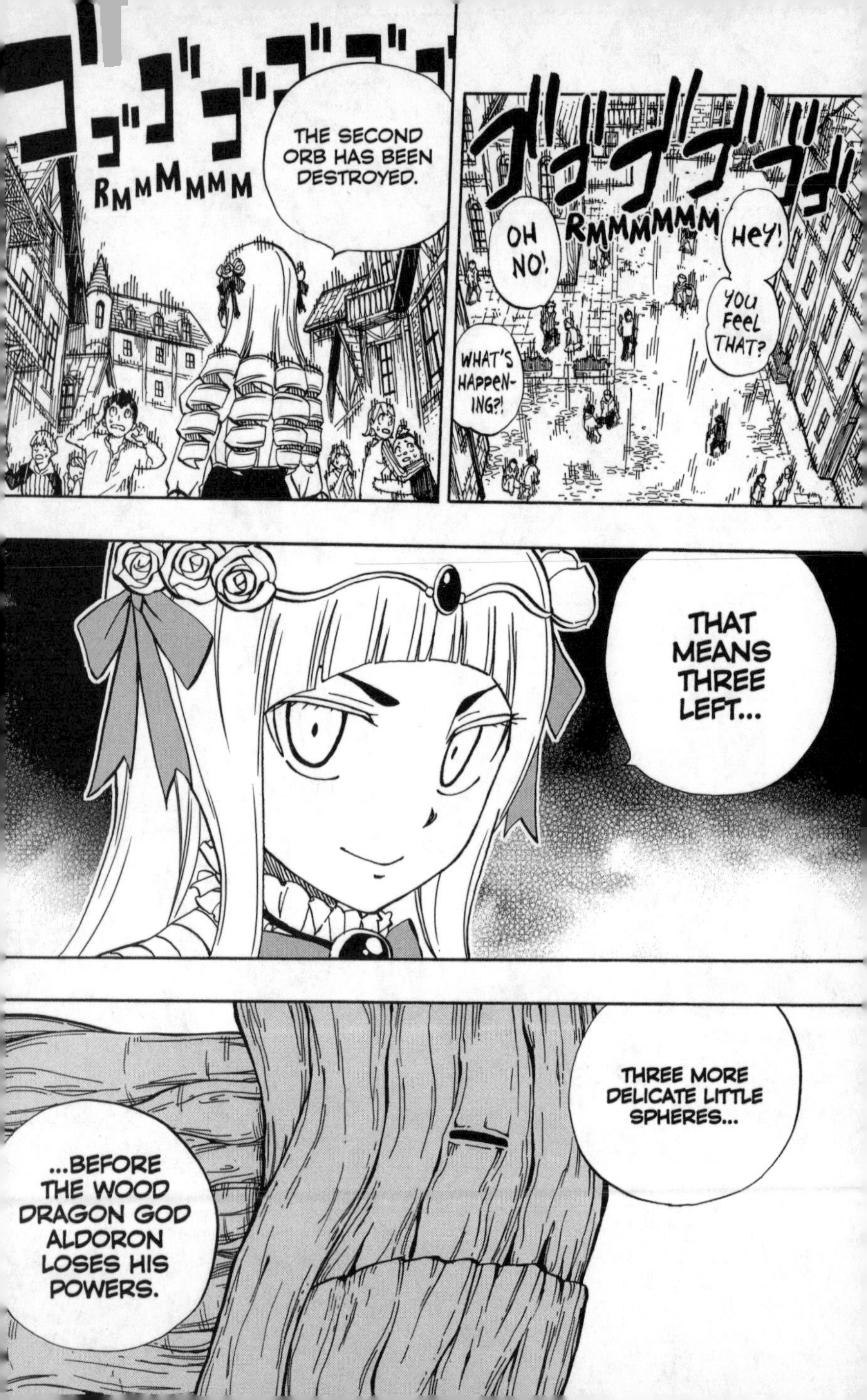
HEY!
YOU FEEL THAT?
RMMMMMM
OH NO!
WHAT'S HAPPENING?!
THE SECOND ORB HAS BEEN DESTROYED.
RMMMMMMM
THAT MEANS THREE LEFT...
THREE MORE DELICATE LITTLE SPHERES...
...BEFORE THE WOOD DRAGON GOD ALDORON LOSES HIS POWERS.

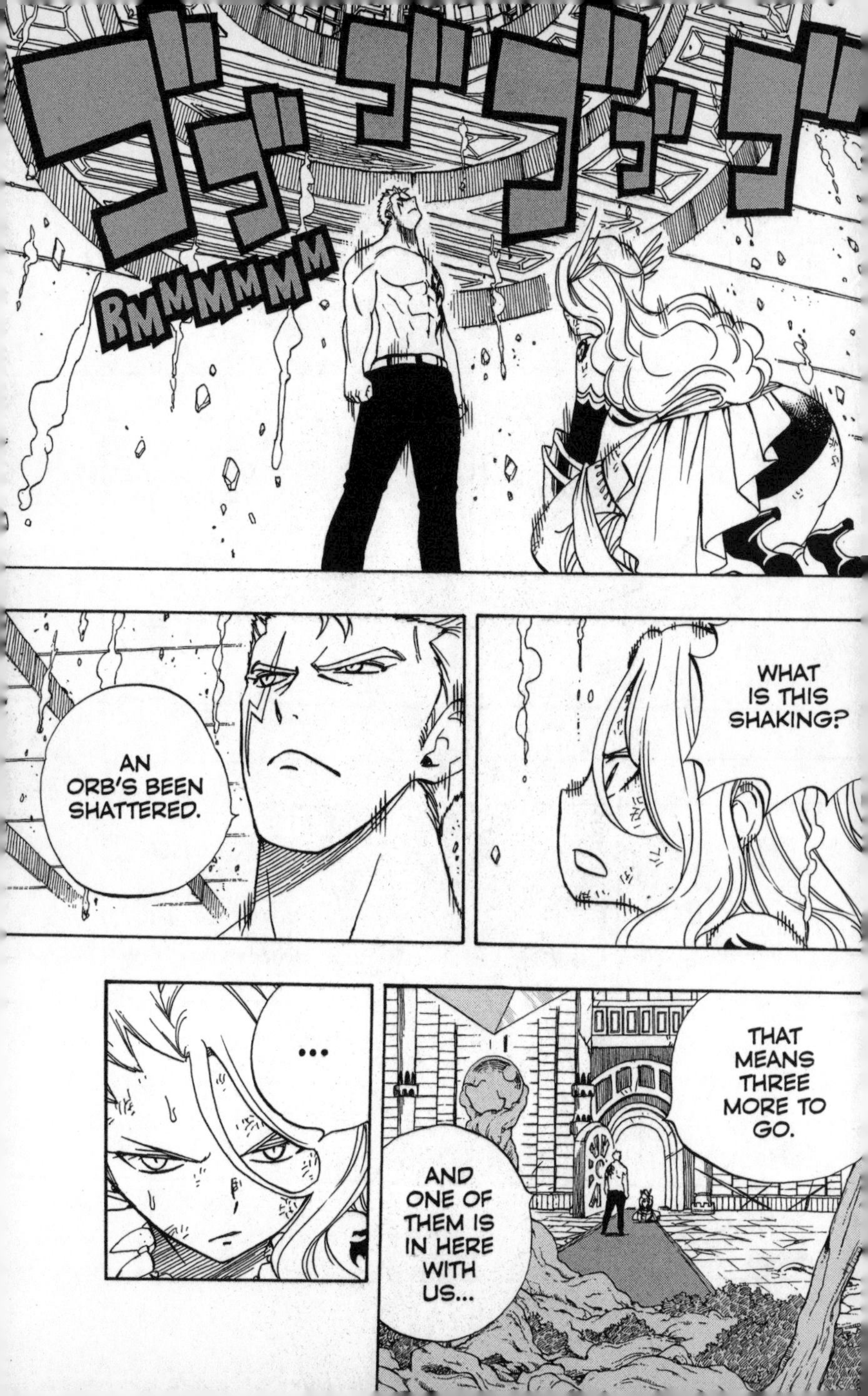
RMMMMMM
WHAT IS THIS SHAKING?
AN ORB'S BEEN SHATTERED.
THAT MEANS THREE MORE TO GO.
AND ONE OF THEM IS IN HERE WITH US...
...

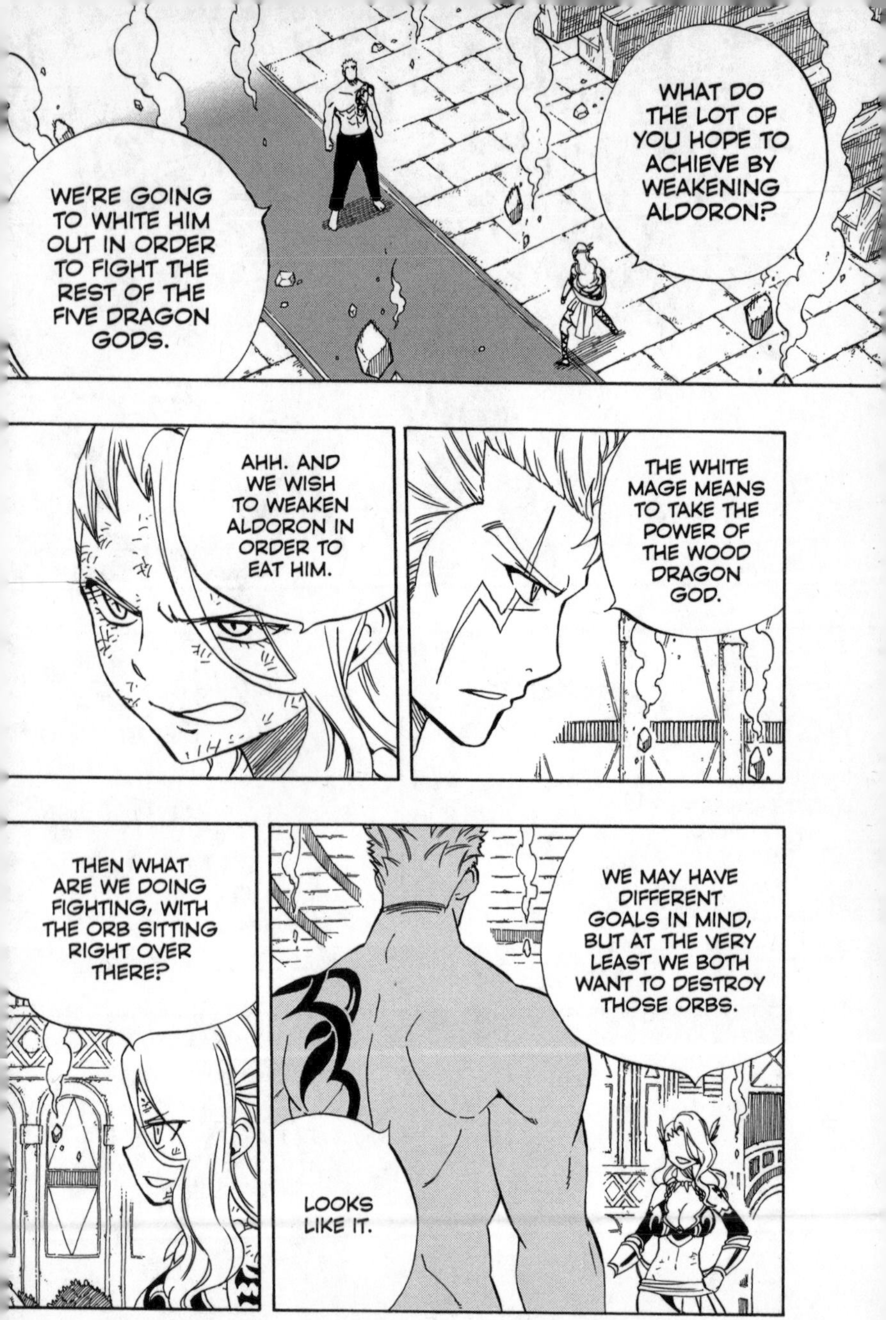
WHAT DO THE LOT OF YOU HOPE TO ACHIEVE BY WEAKENING ALDORON?
WE'RE GOING TO WHITE HIM OUT IN ORDER TO FIGHT THE REST OF THE FIVE DRAGON GODS.
THE WHITE MAGE MEANS TO TAKE THE POWER OF THE WOOD DRAGON GOD.
AHH. AND WE WISH TO WEAKEN ALDORON IN ORDER TO EAT HIM.
WE MAY HAVE DIFFERENT GOALS IN MIND, BUT AT THE VERY LEAST WE BOTH WANT TO DESTROY THOSE ORBS.
LOOKS LIKE IT.
THEN WHAT ARE WE DOING FIGHTING, WITH THE ORB SITTING RIGHT OVER THERE?

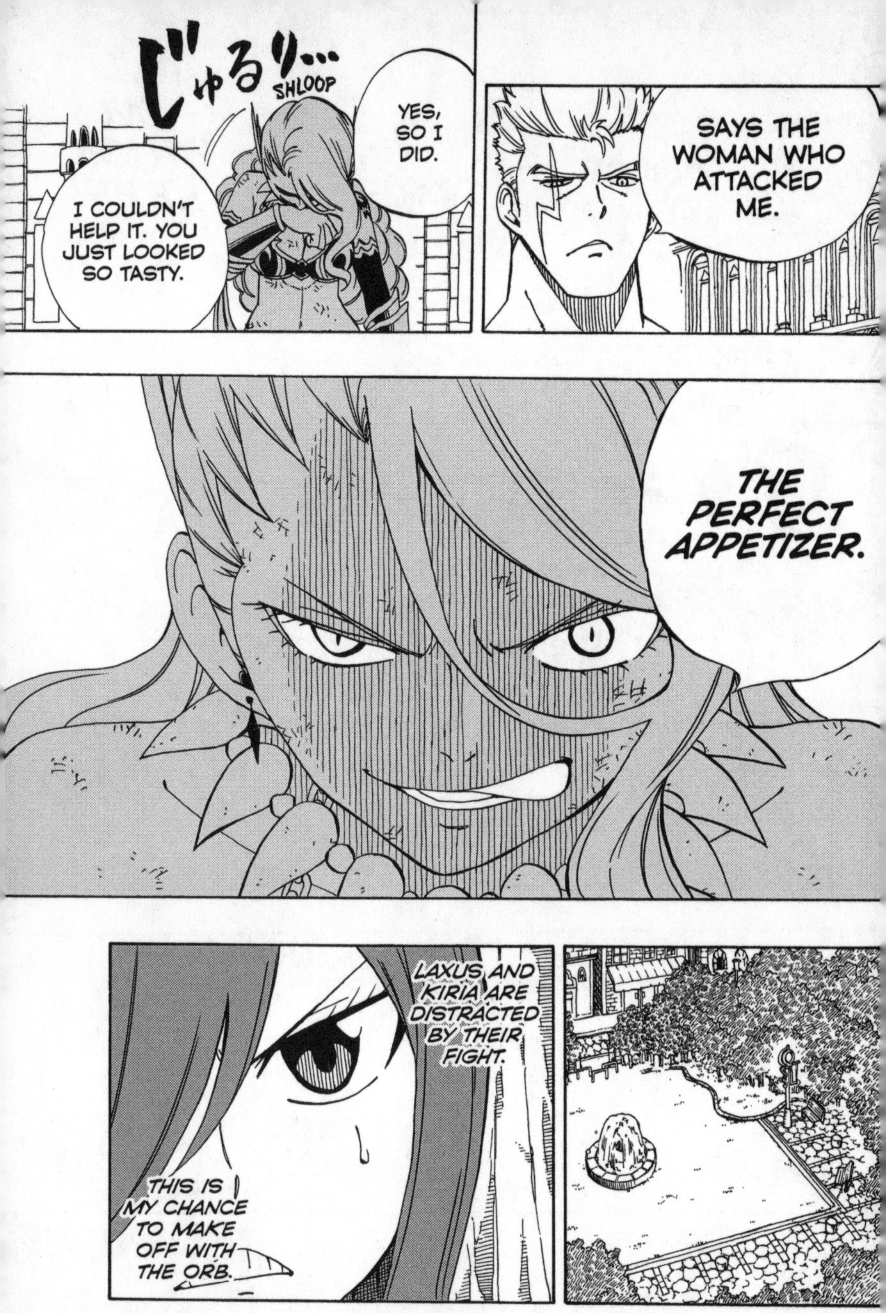
SAYS THE WOMAN WHO ATTACKED ME.
YES, SO I DID.
じゅるり…
SHLOOP
I COULDN'T HELP IT. YOU JUST LOOKED SO TASTY.
THE PERFECT APPETIZER.
LAXUS AND KIRIA ARE DISTRACTED BY THEIR FIGHT.
THIS IS MY CHANCE TO MAKE OFF WITH THE ORB.

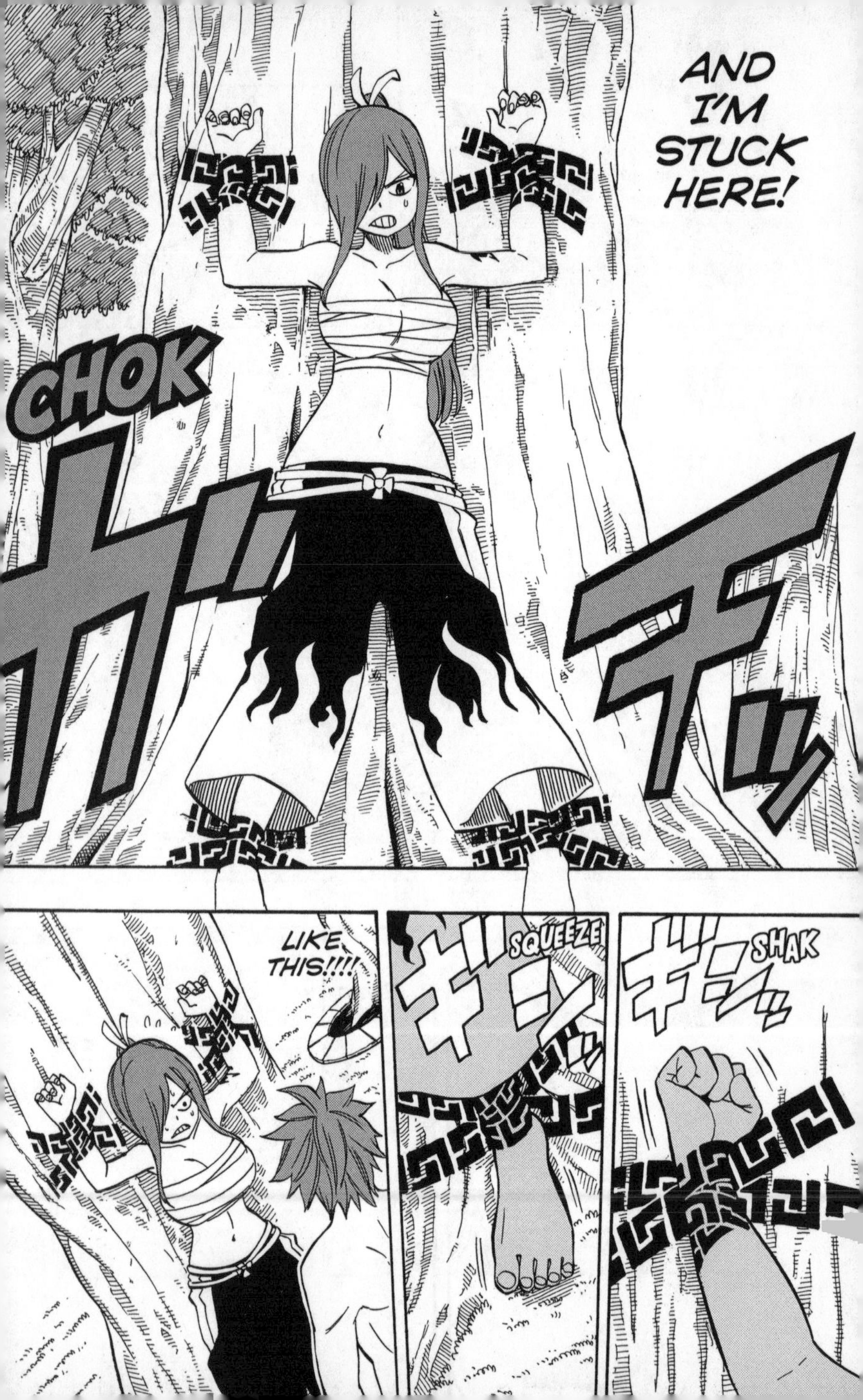
AND I'M STUCK HERE!
CHOK
SHAK
SQUEEZE
LIKE THIS!!!!

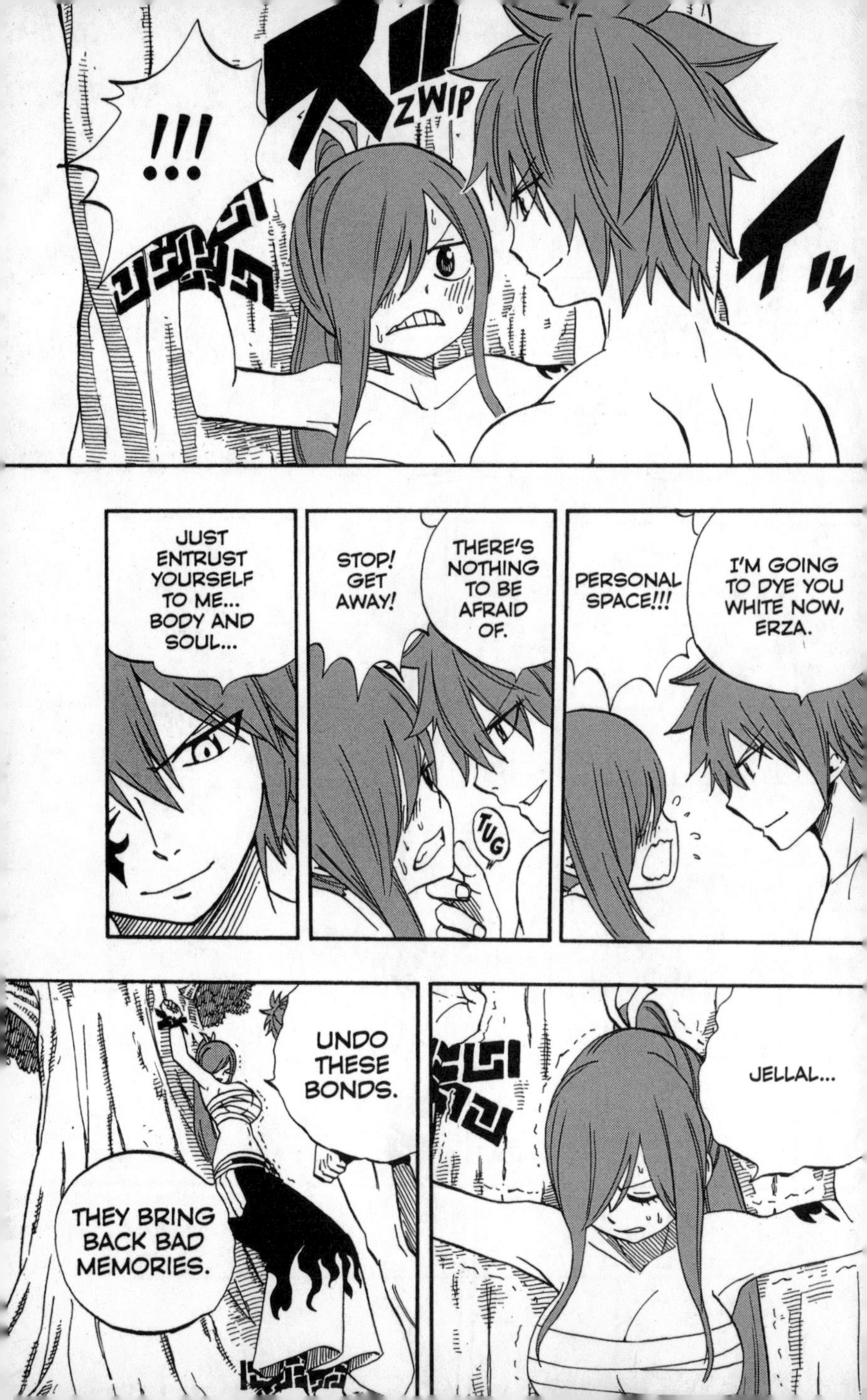
ZWIP
!!!
I'M GOING TO DYE YOU WHITE NOW, ERZA.
PERSONAL SPACE!!!
THERE'S NOTHING TO BE AFRAID OF.
STOP! GET AWAY!
TUG
JUST ENTRUST YOURSELF TO ME... BODY AND SOUL...
JELLAL...
UNDO THESE BONDS.
THEY BRING BACK BAD MEMORIES.

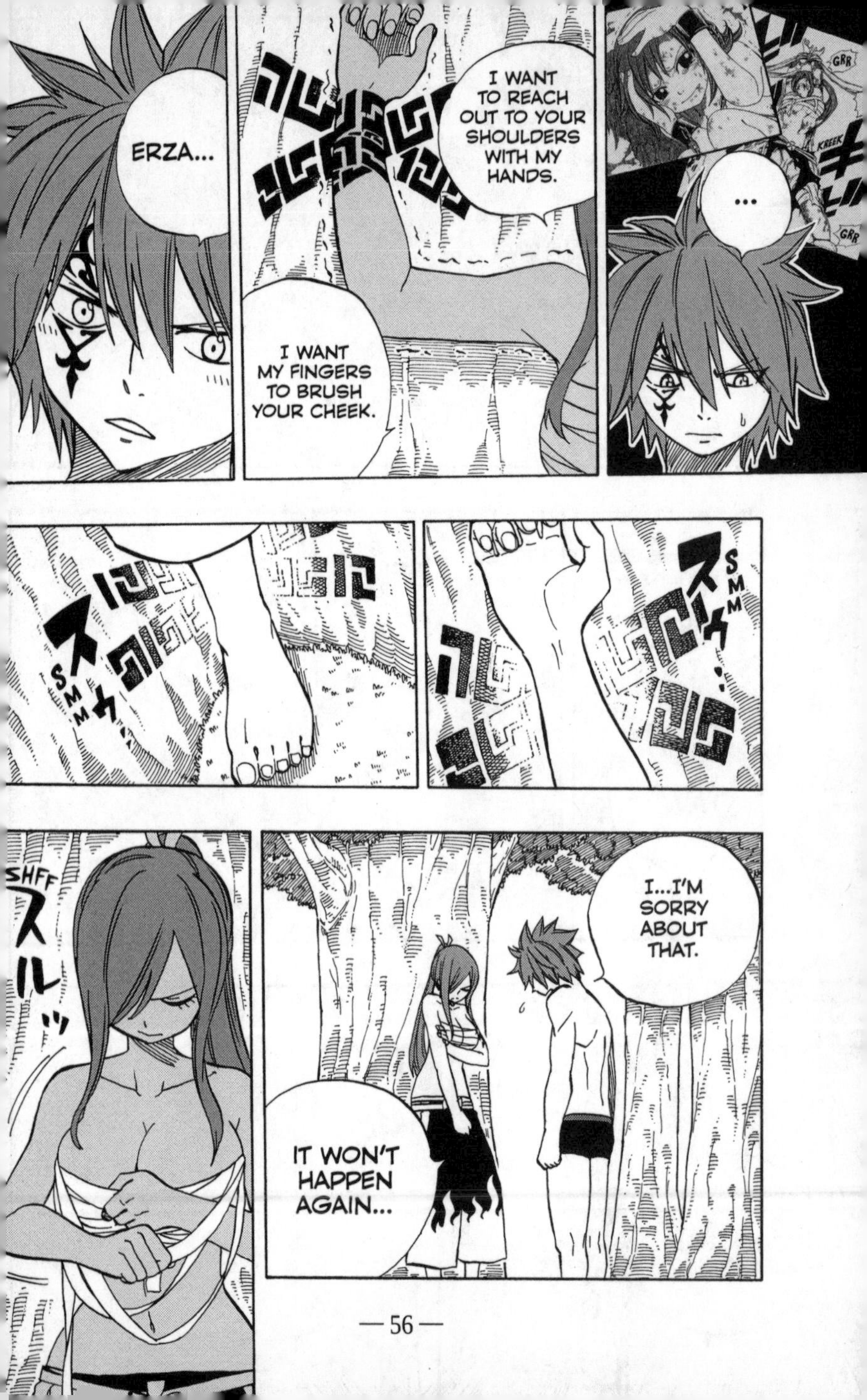
GRR
KREEK
GRR
...
I WANT TO REACH OUT TO YOUR SHOULDERS WITH MY HANDS.
I WANT MY FINGERS TO BRUSH YOUR CHEEK.
ERZA...
SMM
SMM
I...I'M SORRY ABOUT THAT.
IT WON'T HAPPEN AGAIN...
SHFF

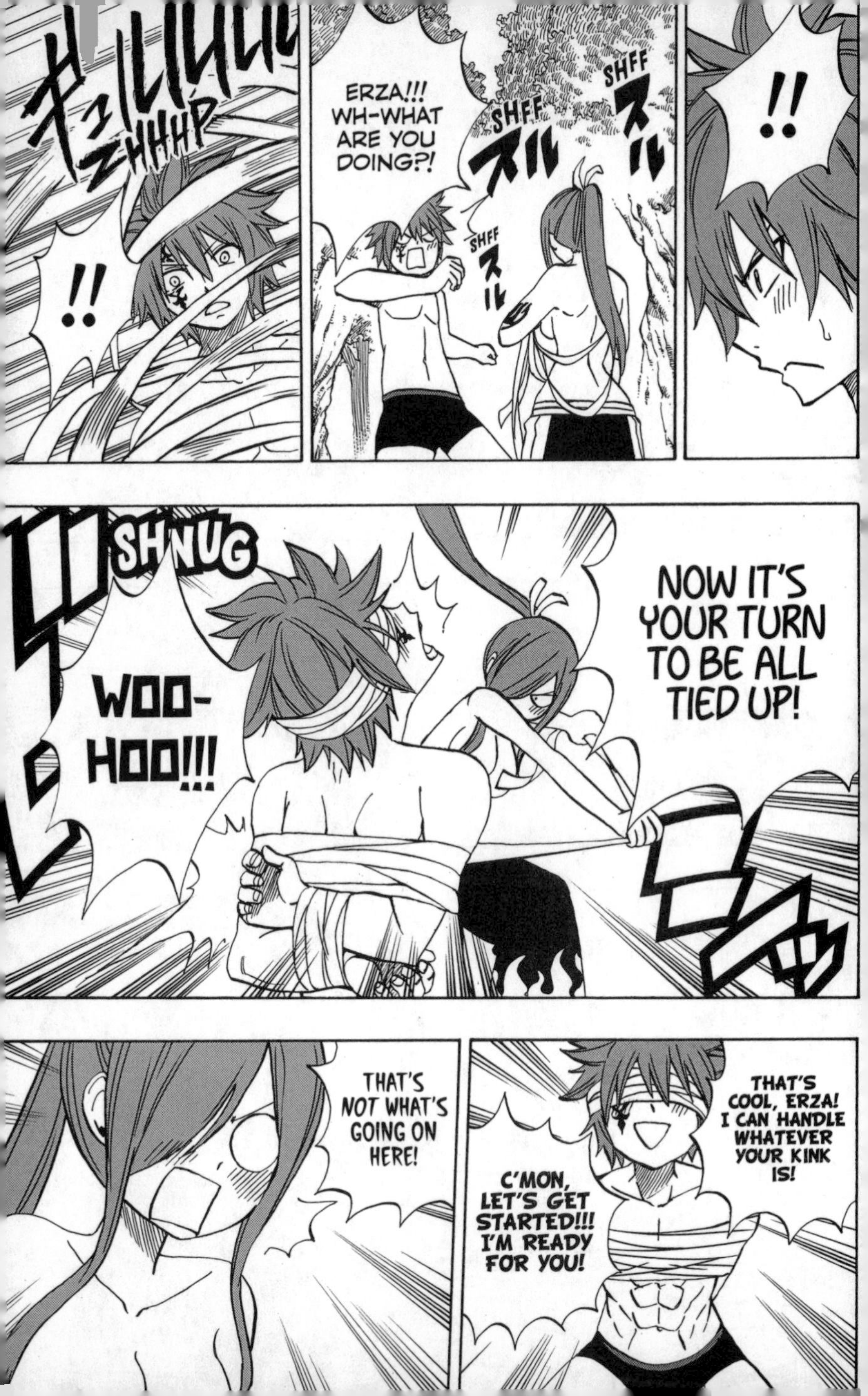
!!
ERZA!!! WH-WHAT ARE YOU DOING?!
SHFF
SHFF
SHFF
ZHHHP
!!
NOW IT'S YOUR TURN TO BE ALL TIED UP!
SHNUG
WOO-HOO!!!
THAT'S COOL, ERZA! I CAN HANDLE WHATEVER YOUR KINK IS!
C'MON, LET'S GET STARTED!!! I'M READY FOR YOU!
THAT'S NOT WHAT'S GOING ON HERE!

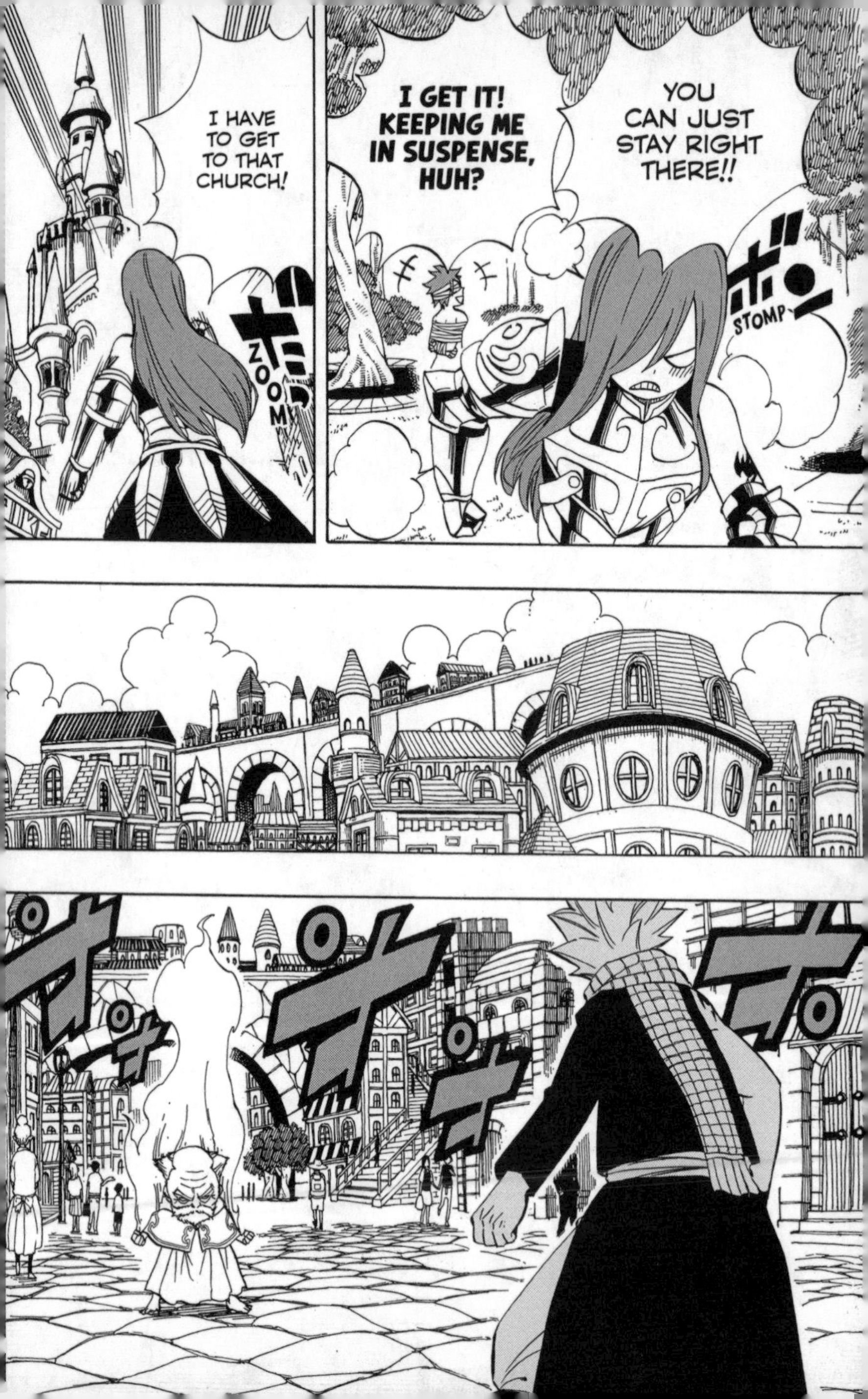
YOU CAN JUST STAY RIGHT THERE!!
I GET IT! KEEPING ME IN SUSPENSE, HUH?
STOMP
I HAVE TO GET TO THAT CHURCH!
ZOOM

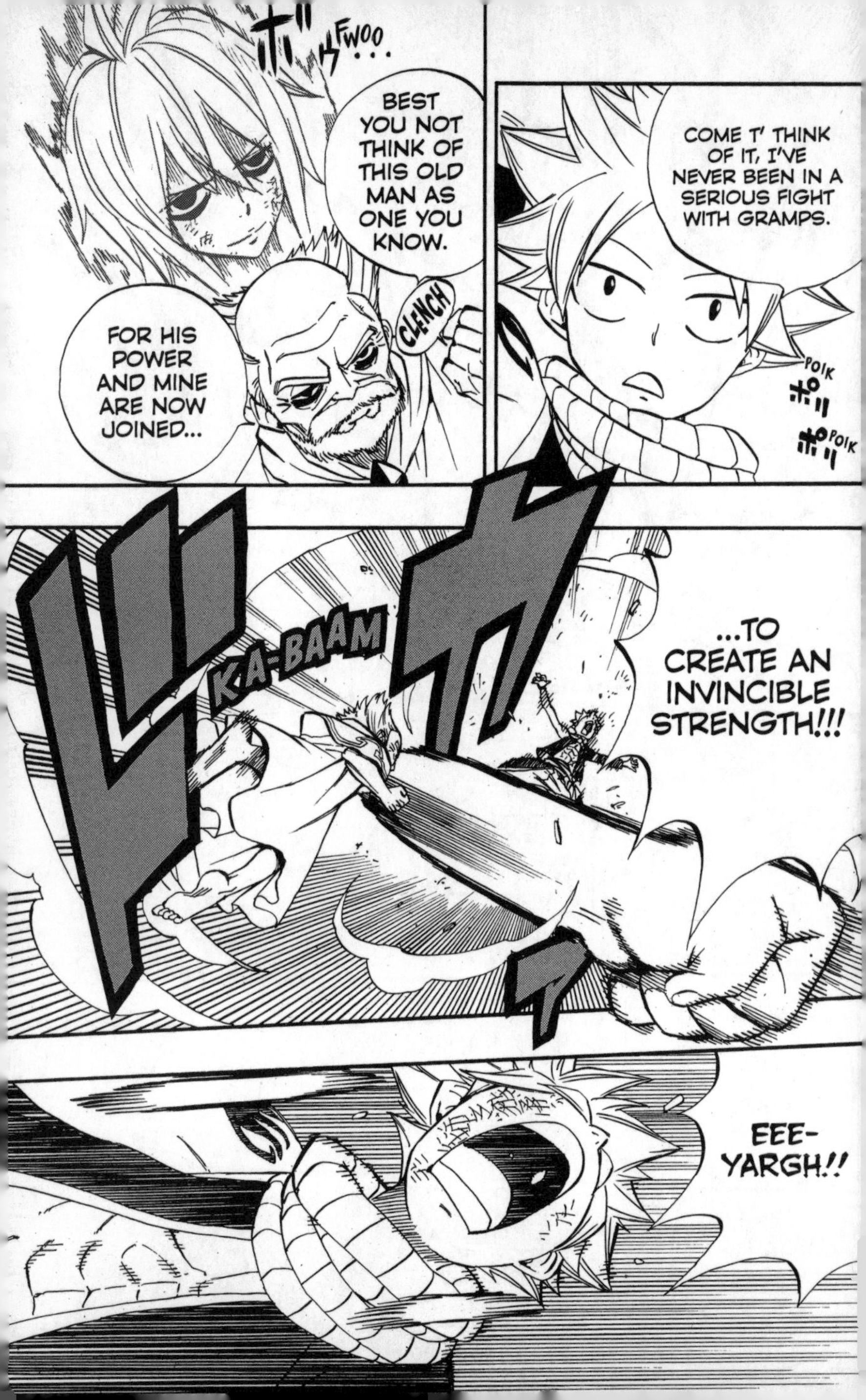
COME T' THINK OF IT, I'VE NEVER BEEN IN A SERIOUS FIGHT WITH GRAMPS.
POIK
POIK
FWOO...
BEST YOU NOT THINK OF THIS OLD MAN AS ONE YOU KNOW.
CLENCH
FOR HIS POWER AND MINE ARE NOW JOINED...
KA-BAAM
...TO CREATE AN INVINCIBLE STRENGTH!!!
EEE-YARGH!!

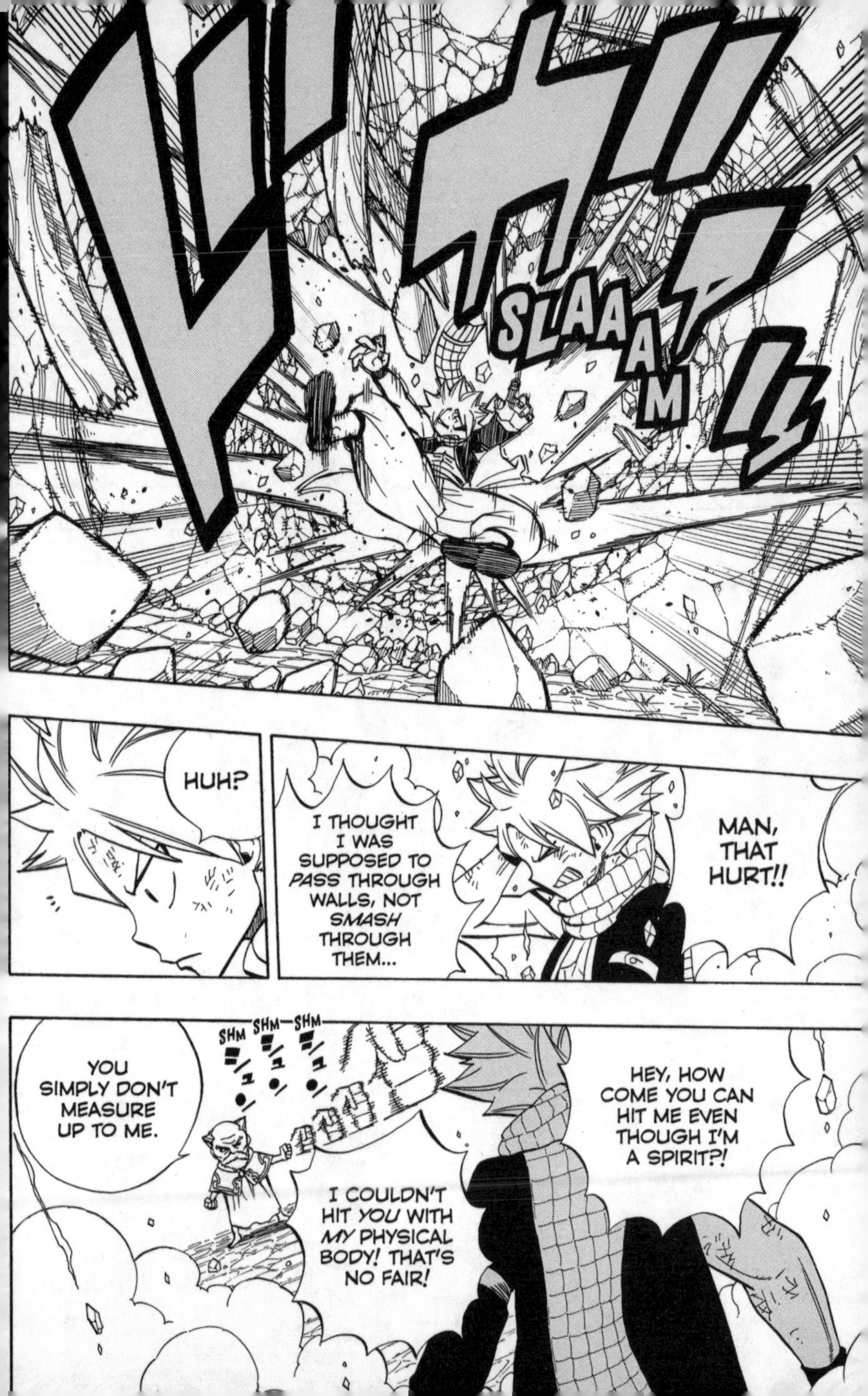
SLAAAAM
MAN, THAT HURT!!
I THOUGHT I WAS SUPPOSED TO *PASS* THROUGH WALLS, NOT *SMASH* THROUGH THEM...
HUH?
HEY, HOW COME YOU CAN HIT ME EVEN THOUGH I'M A SPIRIT?!
I COULDN'T HIT *YOU* WITH *MY* PHYSICAL BODY! THAT'S NO FAIR!
SHM SHM SHM
YOU SIMPLY DON'T MEASURE UP TO ME.

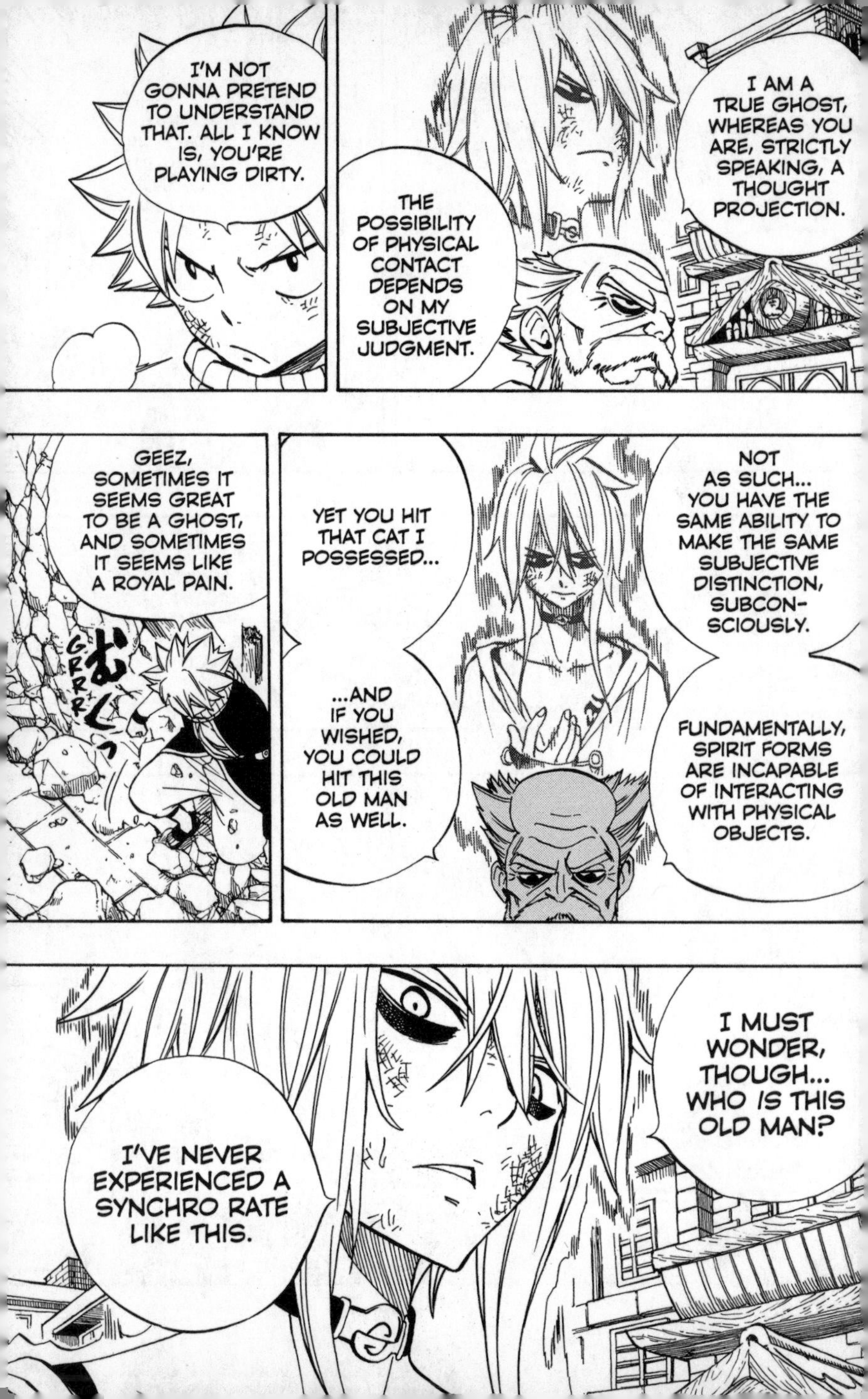
I AM A TRUE GHOST, WHEREAS YOU ARE, STRICTLY SPEAKING, A THOUGHT PROJECTION.
THE POSSIBILITY OF PHYSICAL CONTACT DEPENDS ON MY SUBJECTIVE JUDGMENT.
I'M NOT GONNA PRETEND TO UNDERSTAND THAT. ALL I KNOW IS, YOU'RE PLAYING DIRTY.
NOT AS SUCH... YOU HAVE THE SAME ABILITY TO MAKE THE SAME SUBJECTIVE DISTINCTION, SUBCON-SCIOUSLY.
YET YOU HIT THAT CAT I POSSESSED...
FUNDAMENTALLY, SPIRIT FORMS ARE INCAPABLE OF INTERACTING WITH PHYSICAL OBJECTS.
...AND IF YOU WISHED, YOU COULD HIT THIS OLD MAN AS WELL.
GEEZ, SOMETIMES IT SEEMS GREAT TO BE A GHOST, AND SOMETIMES IT SEEMS LIKE A ROYAL PAIN.
GRRR
I MUST WONDER, THOUGH... WHO *IS* THIS OLD MAN?
I'VE NEVER EXPERIENCED A SYNCHRO RATE LIKE THIS.

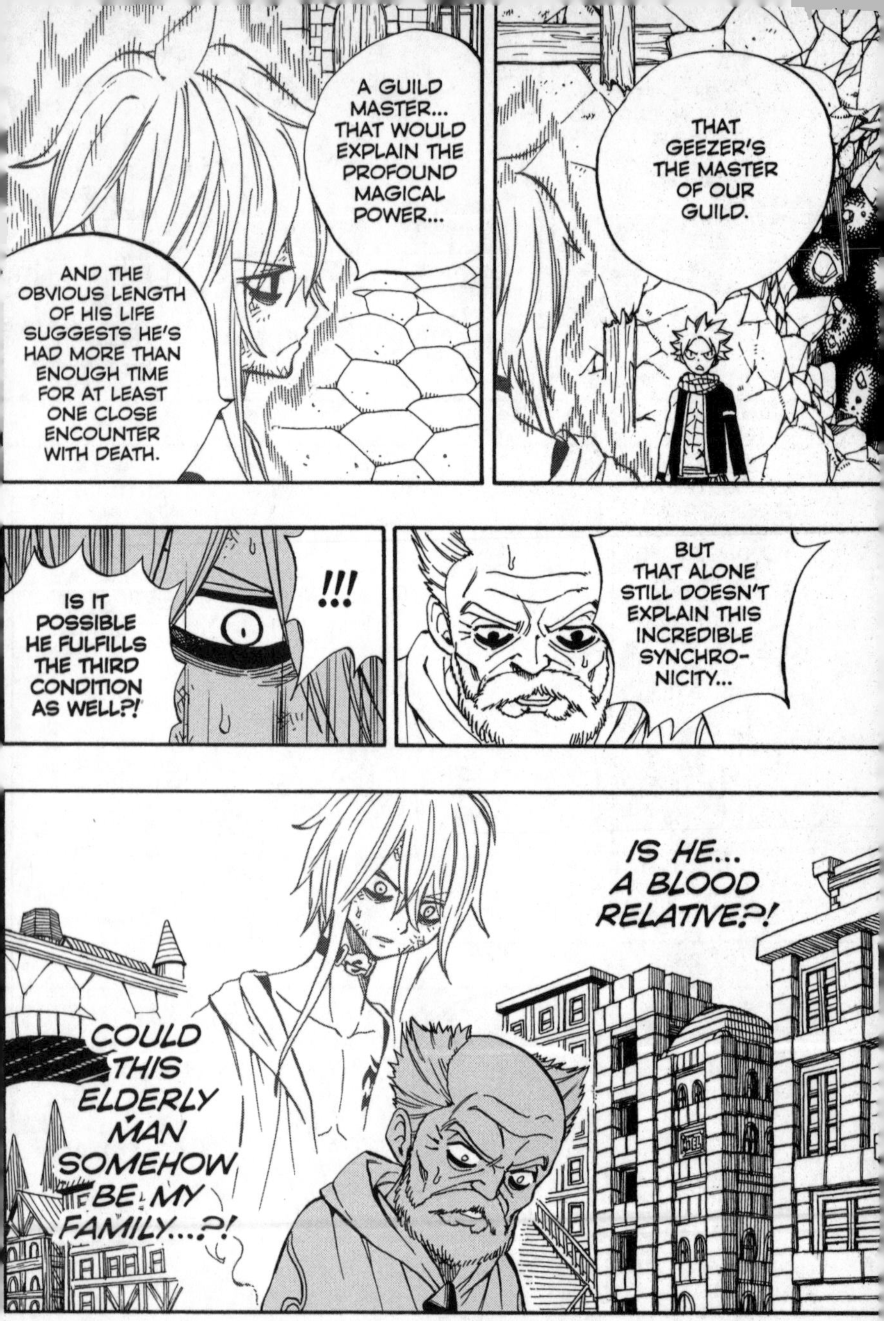
THAT GEEZER'S THE MASTER OF OUR GUILD.
A GUILD MASTER... THAT WOULD EXPLAIN THE PROFOUND MAGICAL POWER...
AND THE OBVIOUS LENGTH OF HIS LIFE SUGGESTS HE'S HAD MORE THAN ENOUGH TIME FOR AT LEAST ONE CLOSE ENCOUNTER WITH DEATH.
BUT THAT ALONE STILL DOESN'T EXPLAIN THIS INCREDIBLE SYNCHRO-NICITY...
!!!
IS IT POSSIBLE HE FULFILLS THE THIRD CONDITION AS WELL?!
IS HE... A BLOOD RELATIVE?!
COULD THIS ELDERLY MAN SOMEHOW BE MY FAMILY...?!

FAIRY TAIL 100 YEARS QUEST

Chapter 48: Thicker Than Blood

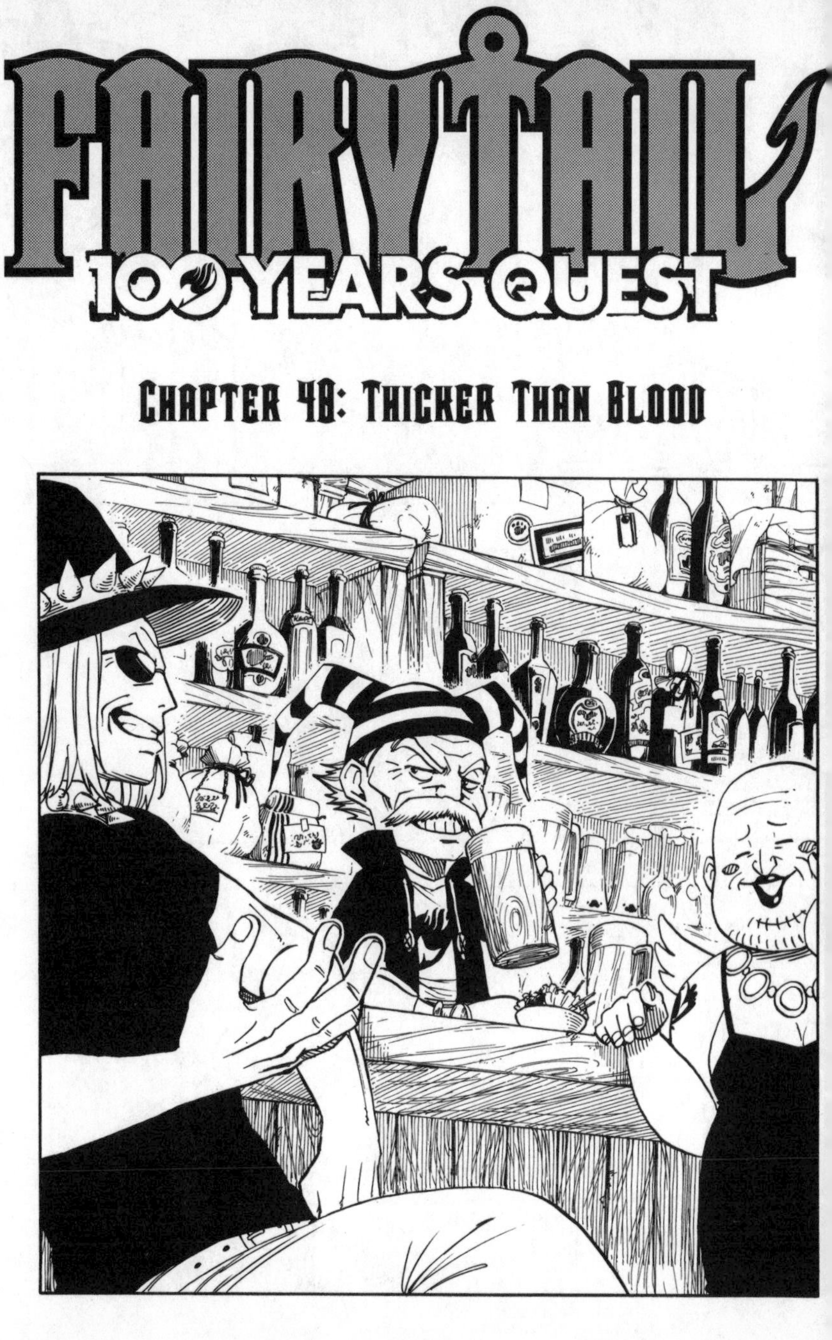

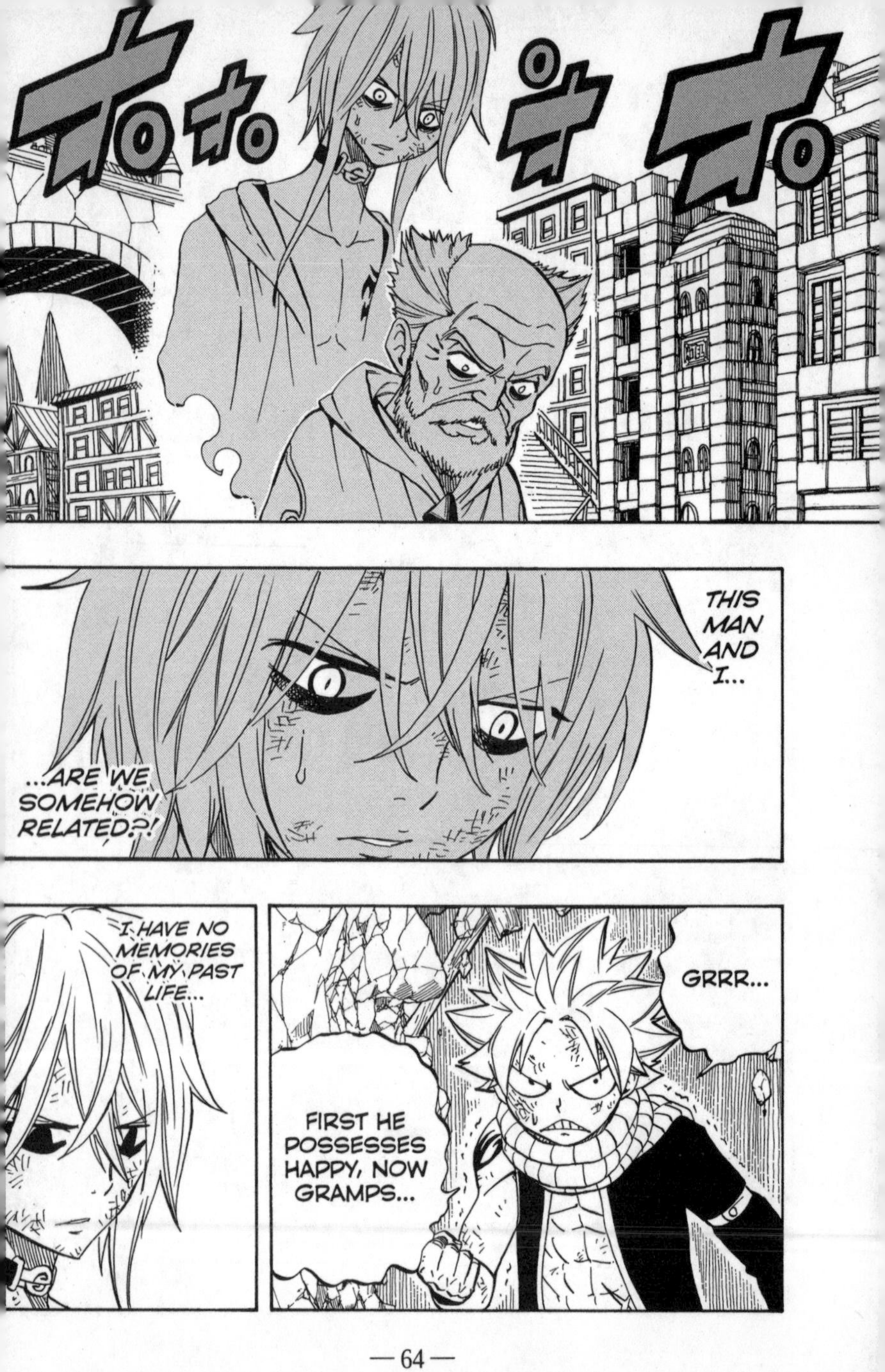
THIS MAN AND I...
...ARE WE SOMEHOW RELATED?!
GRRR...
FIRST HE POSSESSES HAPPY, NOW GRAMPS...
I HAVE NO MEMORIES OF MY PAST LIFE...

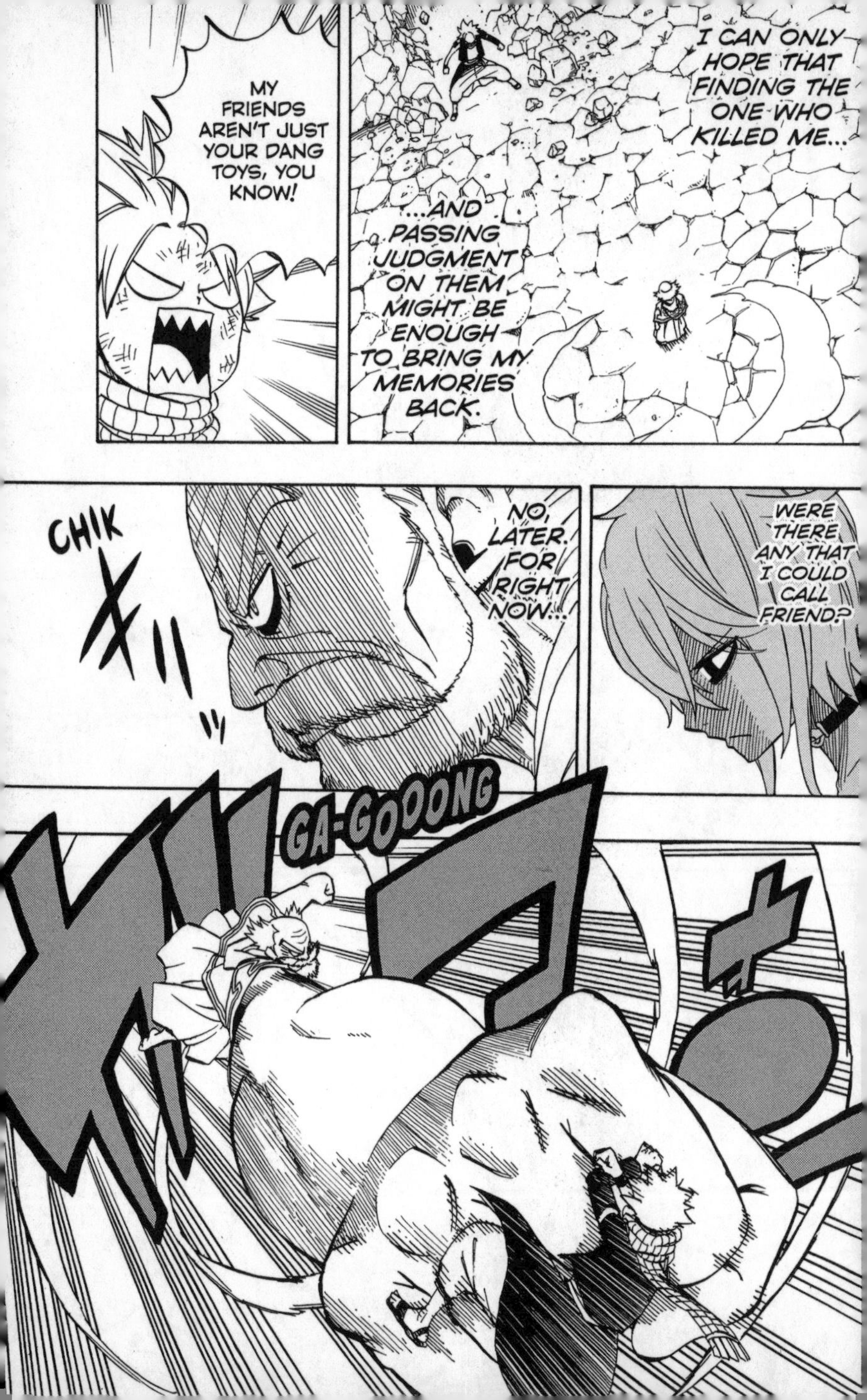
I CAN ONLY HOPE THAT FINDING THE ONE WHO KILLED ME...
...AND PASSING JUDGMENT ON THEM MIGHT BE ENOUGH TO BRING MY MEMORIES BACK.
MY FRIENDS AREN'T JUST YOUR DANG TOYS, YOU KNOW!
WERE THERE ANY THAT I COULD CALL FRIEND?
NO, LATER. FOR RIGHT NOW...
CHIK
GA-GOOONG

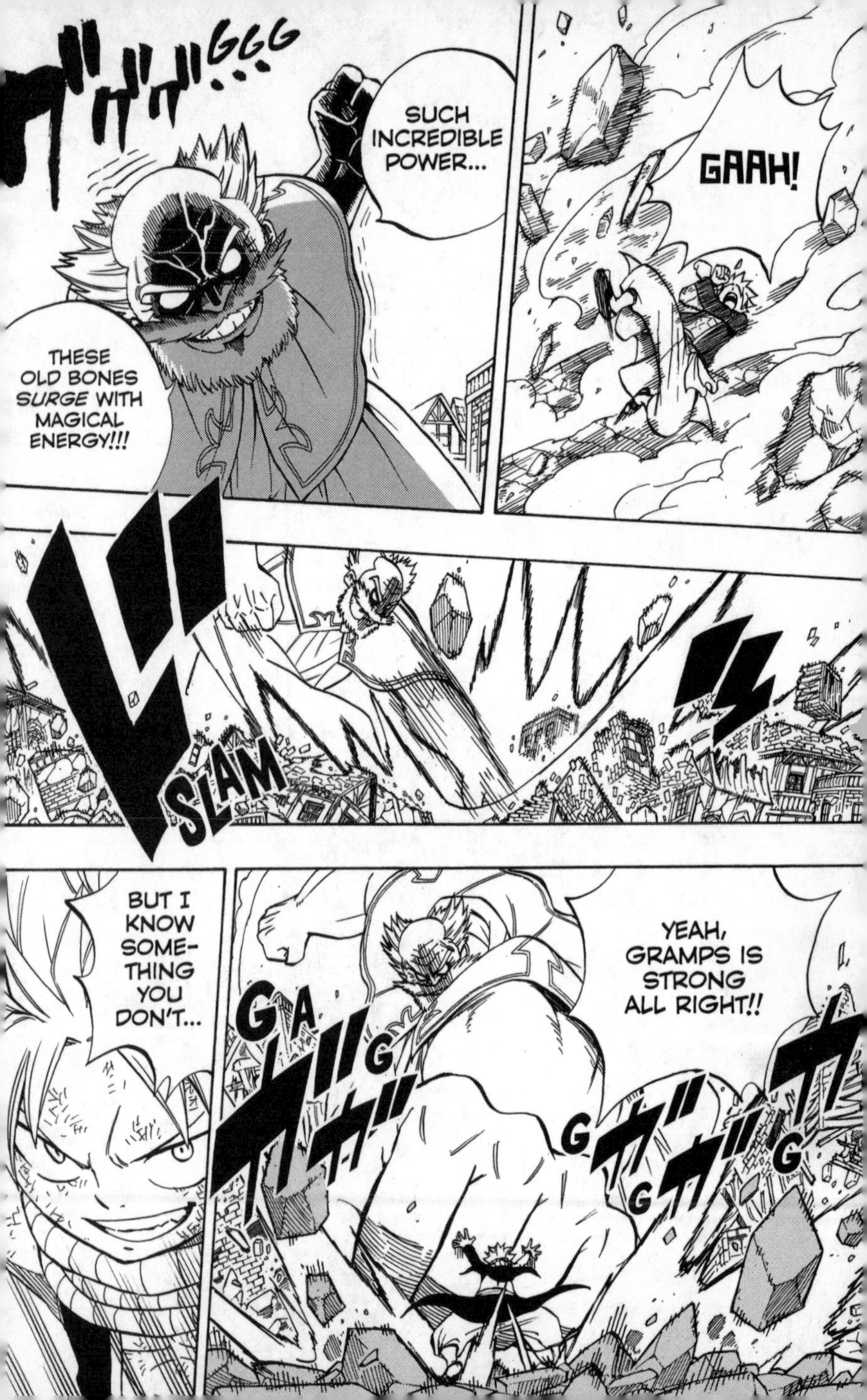
GAAH!
GGG
SUCH INCREDIBLE POWER...
THESE OLD BONES *SURGE* WITH MAGICAL ENERGY!!!
SLAM
YEAH, GRAMPS IS STRONG ALL RIGHT!!
GA
G
G
G
G
BUT I KNOW SOME-THING YOU DON'T...

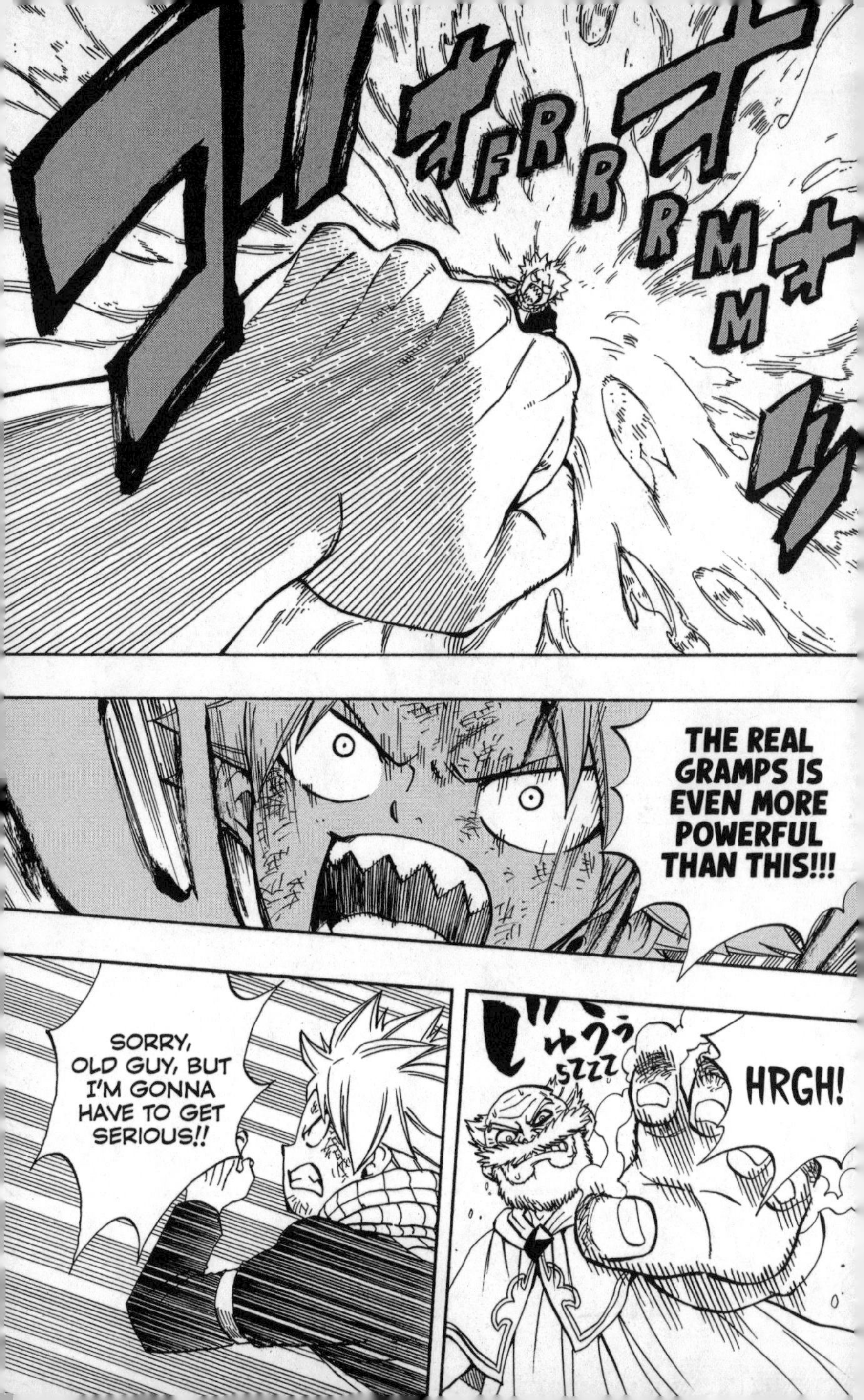
FRRRMM
THE REAL GRAMPS IS EVEN MORE POWERFUL THAN THIS!!!
SZZZ
HRGH!
SORRY, OLD GUY, BUT I'M GONNA HAVE TO GET SERIOUS!!

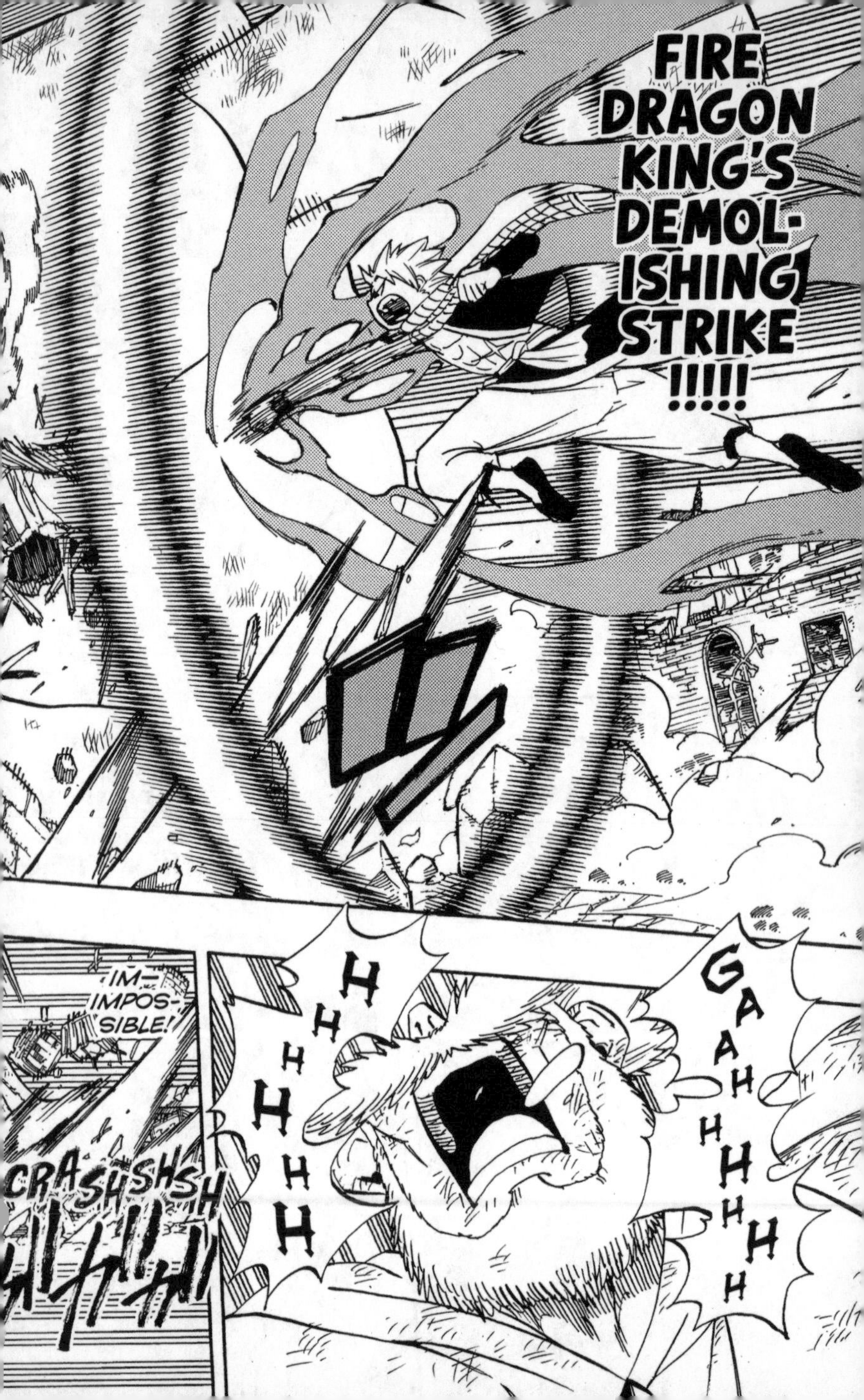
FIRE DRAGON KING'S DEMOL-ISHING STRIKE!!!!!
GAAHHHHHHH
HHHHHHHHH
IM-IMPOS-SIBLE!
CRASHSHSH

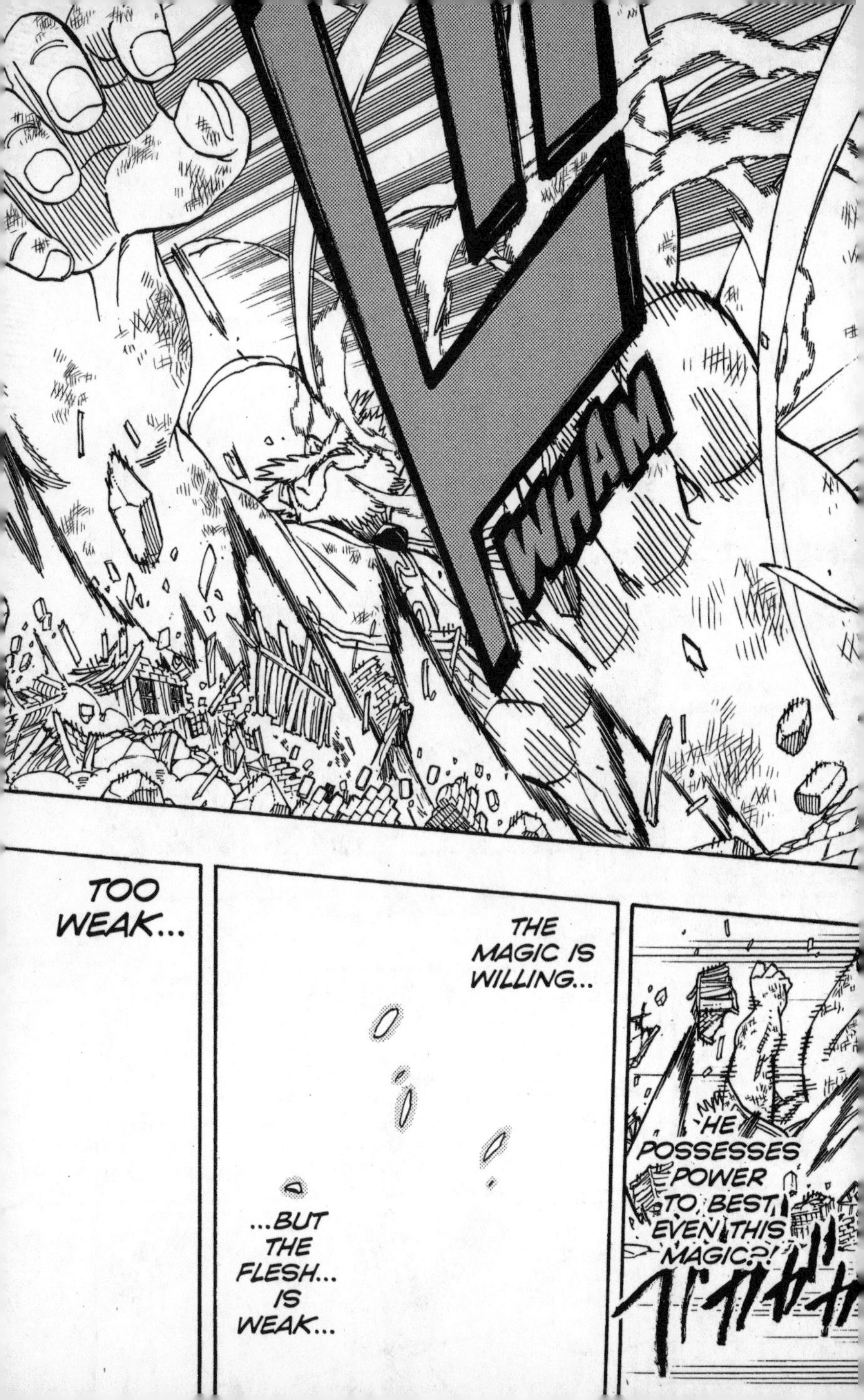
WHAM
HE POSSESSES POWER TO BEST EVEN THIS MAGIC?!
THE MAGIC IS WILLING...
...BUT THE FLESH... IS WEAK...
TOO WEAK...

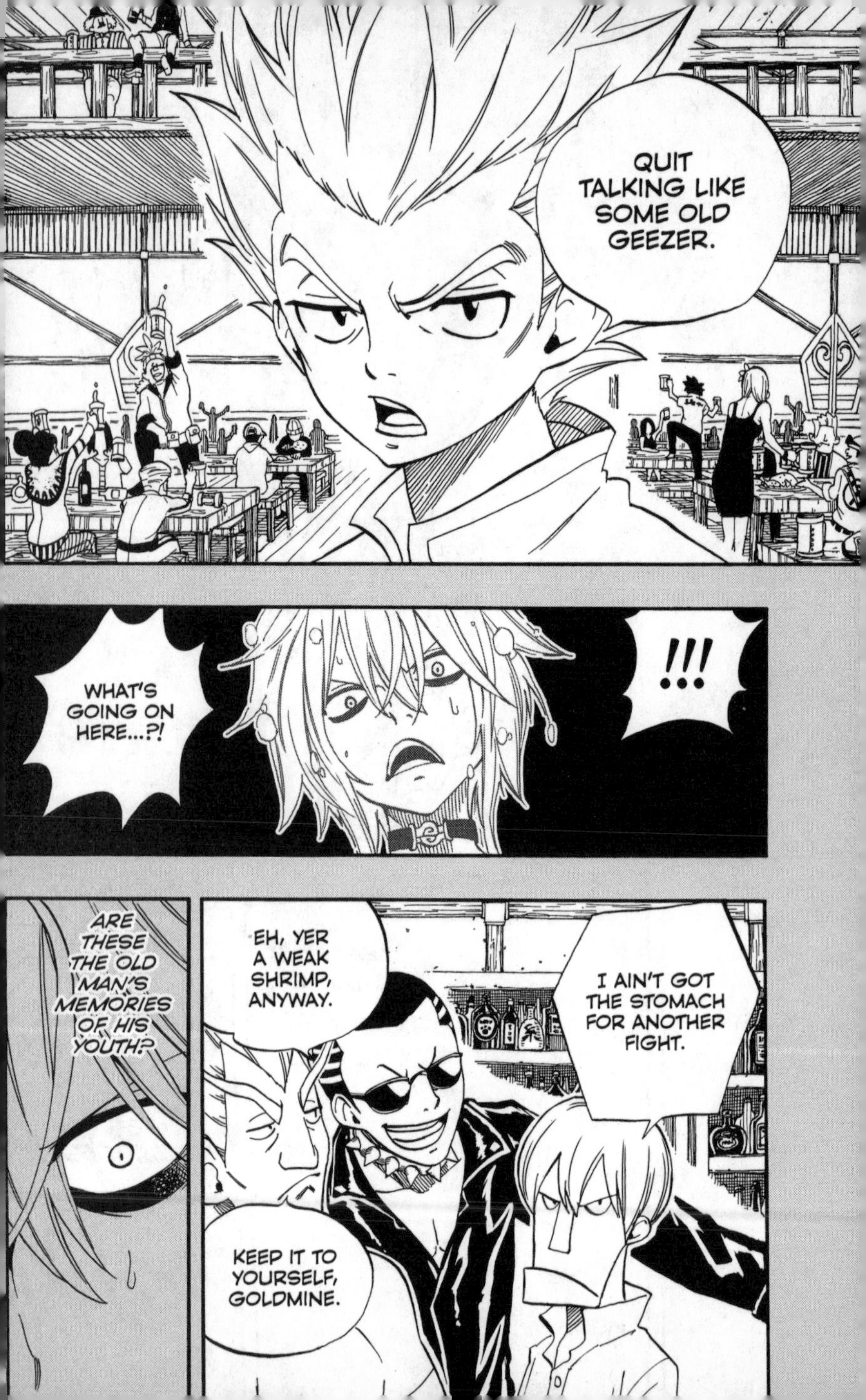
QUIT TALKING LIKE SOME OLD GEEZER.
!!!
WHAT'S GOING ON HERE...?!
I AIN'T GOT THE STOMACH FOR ANOTHER FIGHT.
EH, YER A WEAK SHRIMP, ANYWAY.
KEEP IT TO YOURSELF, GOLDMINE.
ARE THESE THE OLD MAN'S MEMORIES OF HIS YOUTH?

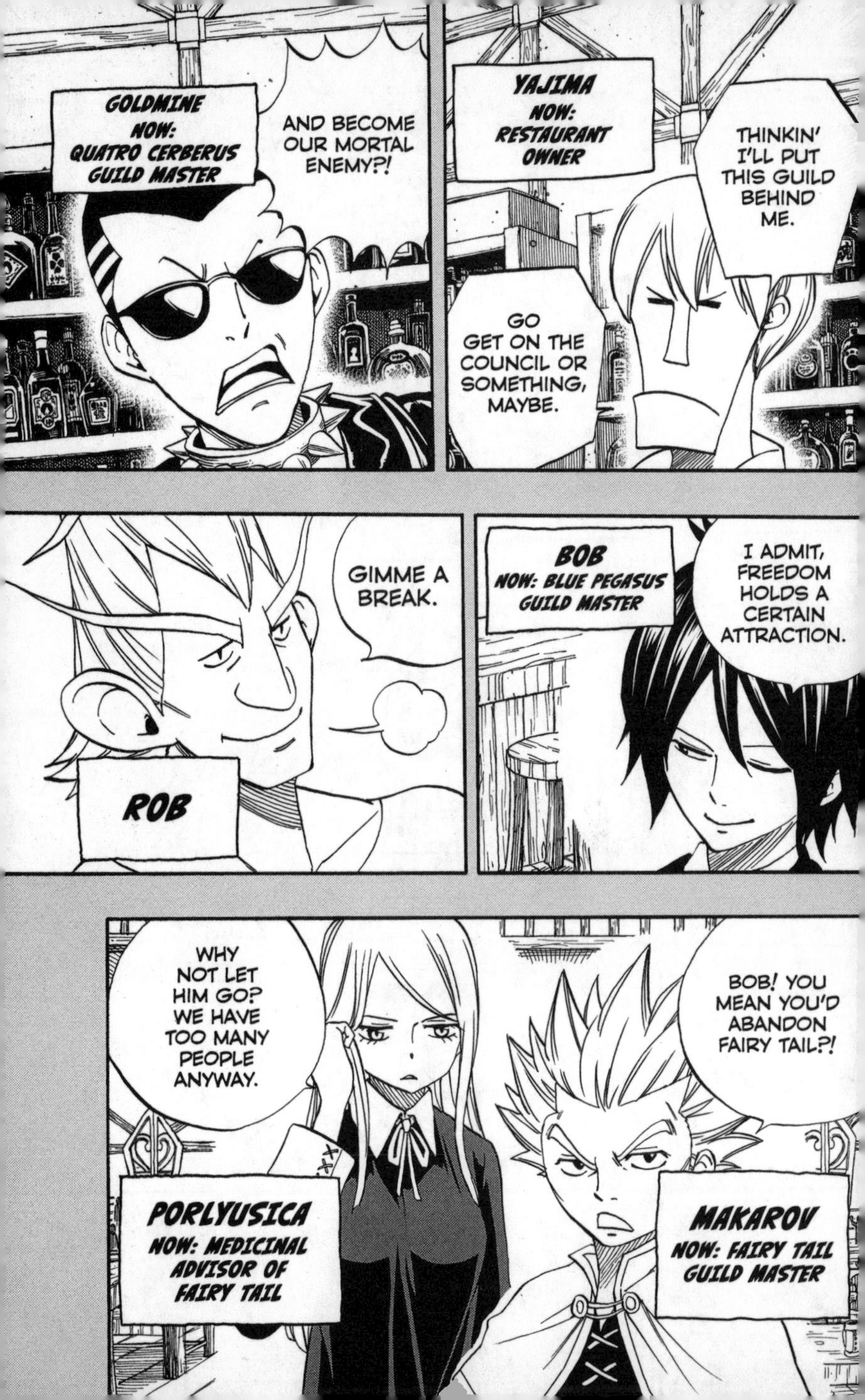

THINKIN' I'LL PUT THIS GUILD BEHIND ME.
YAJIMA NOW: RESTAURANT OWNER
GO GET ON THE COUNCIL OR SOMETHING, MAYBE.
AND BECOME OUR MORTAL ENEMY?!
GOLDMINE NOW: QUATRO CERBERUS GUILD MASTER
I ADMIT, FREEDOM HOLDS A CERTAIN ATTRACTION.
BOB NOW: BLUE PEGASUS GUILD MASTER
GIMME A BREAK.
ROB
BOB! YOU MEAN YOU'D ABANDON FAIRY TAIL?!
WHY NOT LET HIM GO? WE HAVE TOO MANY PEOPLE ANYWAY.
MAKAROV NOW: FAIRY TAIL GUILD MASTER
PORLYUSICA NOW: MEDICINAL ADVISOR OF FAIRY TAIL

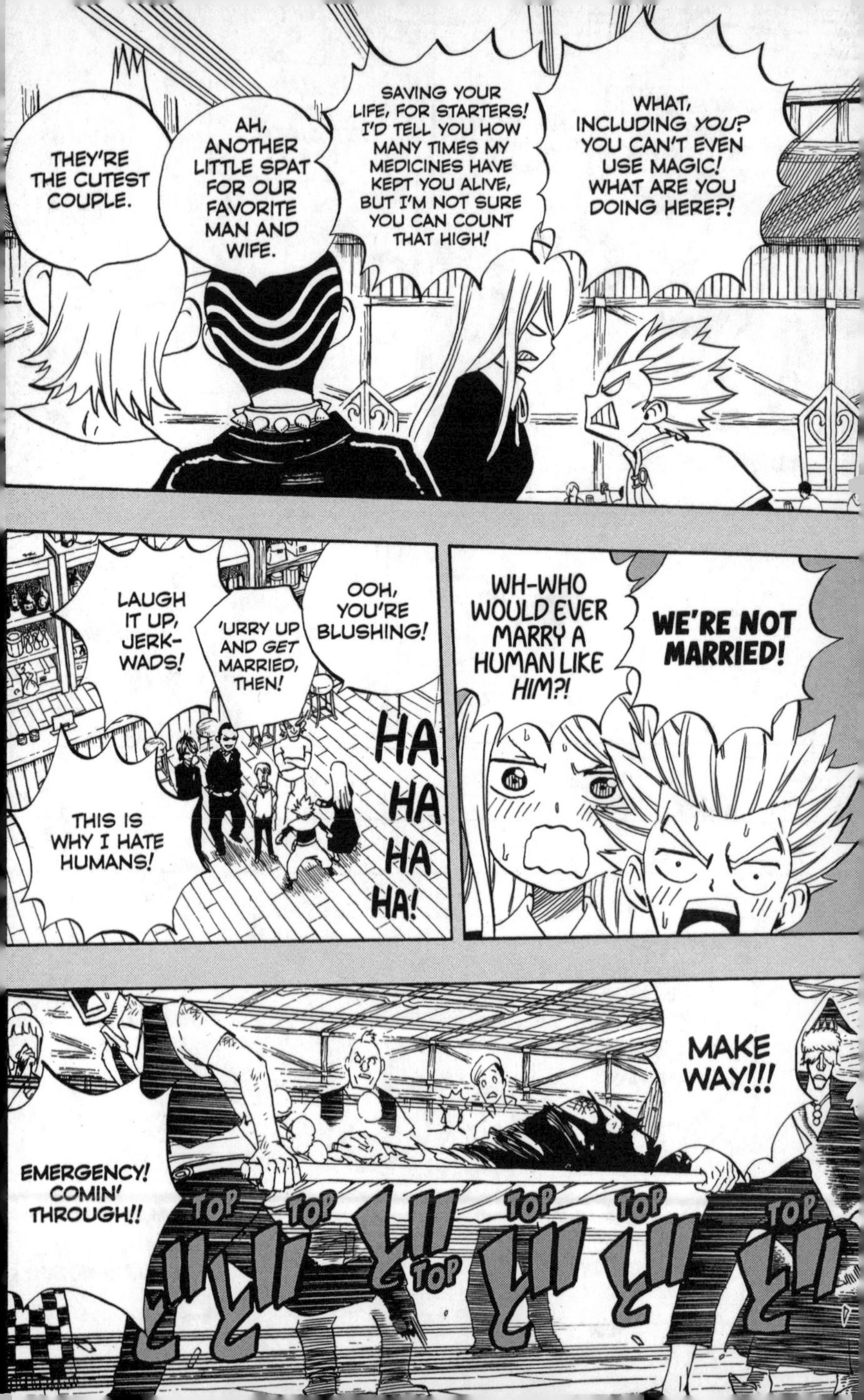
WHAT, INCLUDING *YOU*? YOU CAN'T EVEN USE MAGIC! WHAT ARE YOU DOING HERE?!
SAVING YOUR LIFE, FOR STARTERS! I'D TELL YOU HOW MANY TIMES MY MEDICINES HAVE KEPT YOU ALIVE, BUT I'M NOT SURE YOU CAN COUNT THAT HIGH!
AH, ANOTHER LITTLE SPAT FOR OUR FAVORITE MAN AND WIFE.
THEY'RE THE CUTEST COUPLE.
WE'RE NOT MARRIED!
WH-WHO WOULD EVER MARRY A HUMAN LIKE *HIM*?!
HA HA HA HA!
OOH, YOU'RE BLUSHING!
'URRY UP AND *GET* MARRIED, THEN!
LAUGH IT UP, JERK-WADS!
THIS IS WHY I HATE HUMANS!
MAKE WAY!!!
EMERGENCY! COMIN' THROUGH!!
TOP TOP TOP TOP TOP TOP

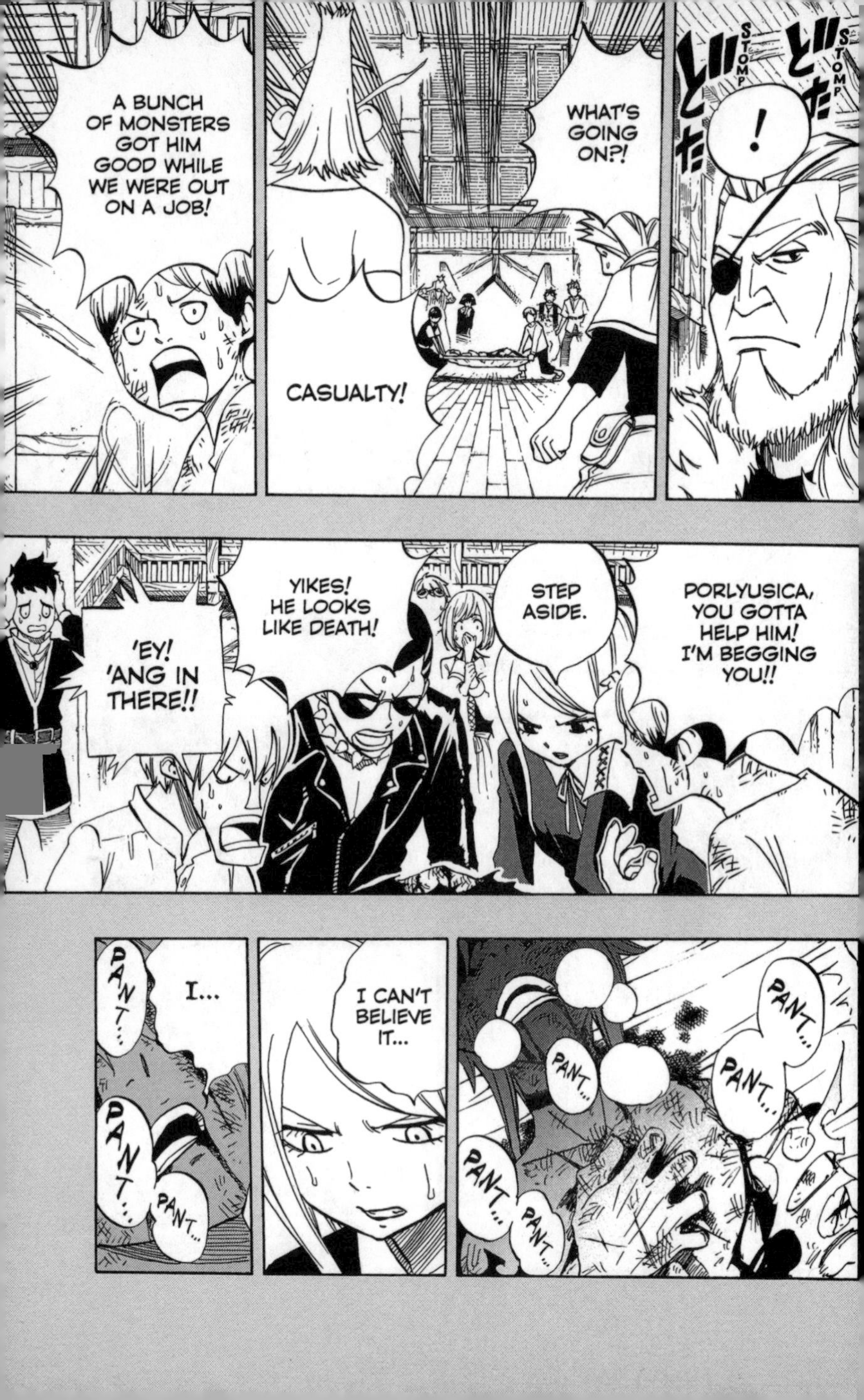
STOMP
STOMP
!
WHAT'S GOING ON?!
CASUALTY!
A BUNCH OF MONSTERS GOT HIM GOOD WHILE WE WERE OUT ON A JOB!
PORLYUSICA, YOU GOTTA HELP HIM! I'M BEGGING YOU!!
STEP ASIDE.
YIKES! HE LOOKS LIKE DEATH!
'EY! 'ANG IN THERE!!
PANT...
PANT...
PANT...
PANT...
PANT...
I CAN'T BELIEVE IT...
I...
PANT...
PANT...
PANT...

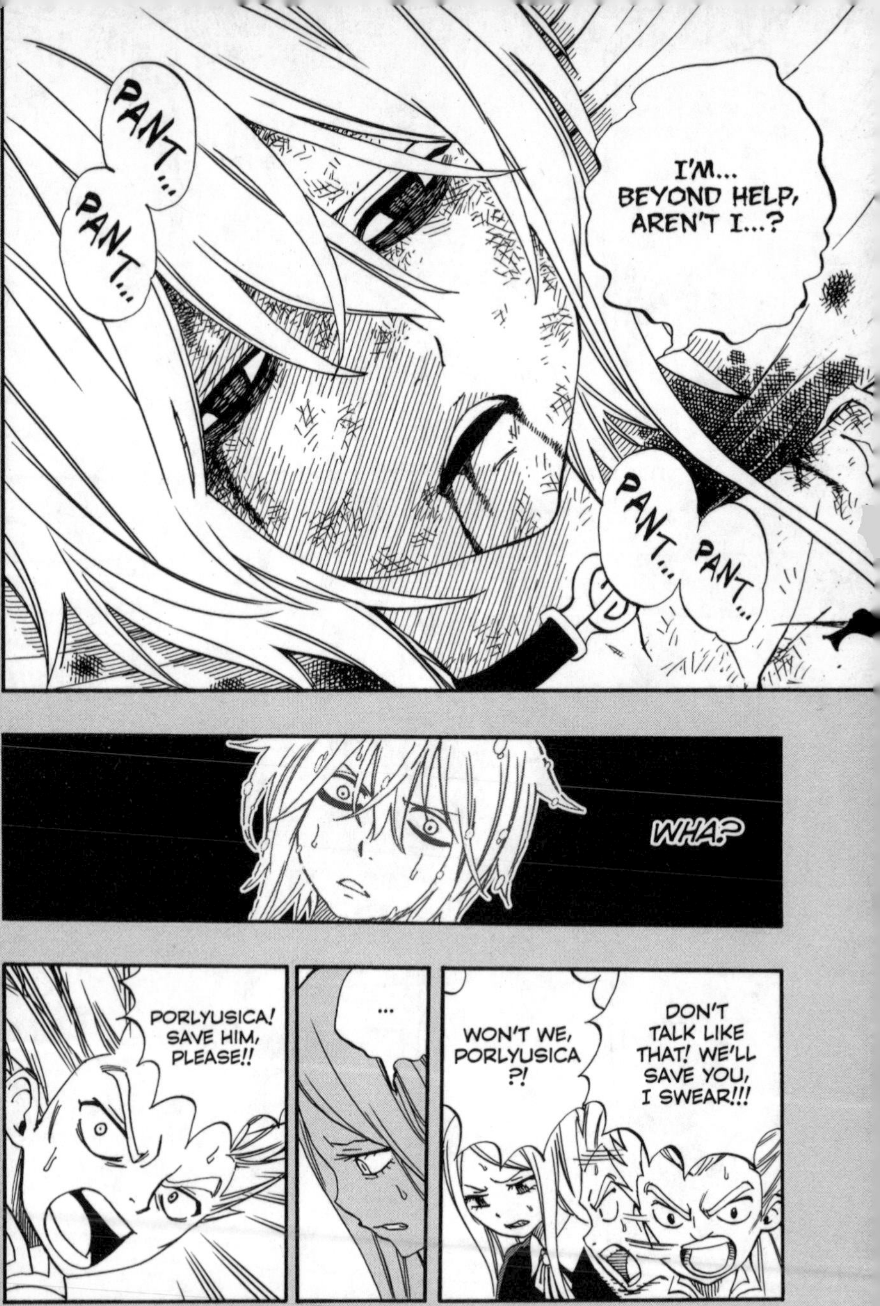
I'M... BEYOND HELP, AREN'T I...?
PANT... PANT...
PANT... PANT...
WHA?
DON'T TALK LIKE THAT! WE'LL SAVE YOU, I SWEAR!!!
WON'T WE, PORLYUSICA?!
...
PORLYUSICA! SAVE HIM, PLEASE!!

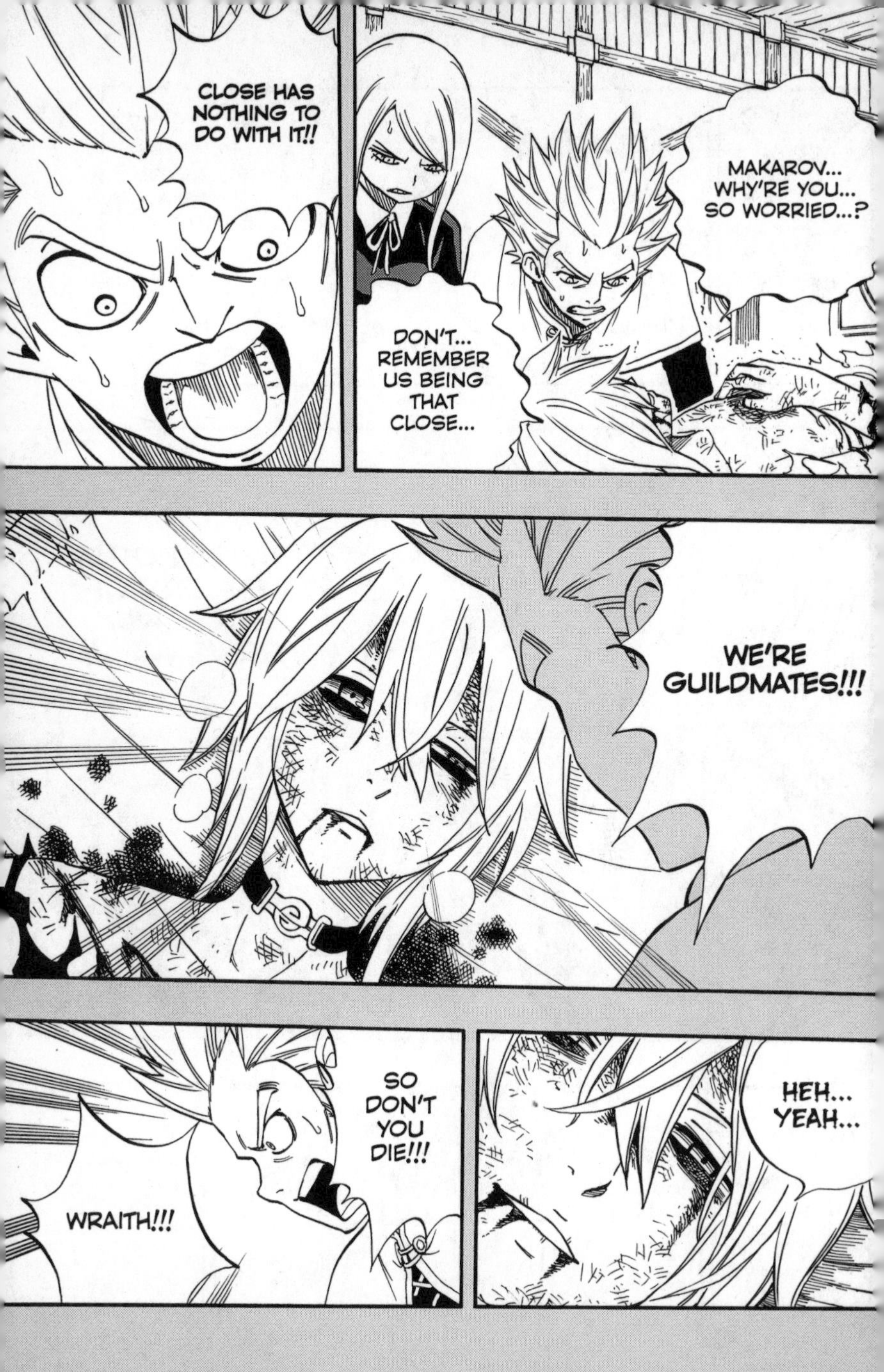
MAKAROV... WHY'RE YOU... SO WORRIED...?
DON'T... REMEMBER US BEING THAT CLOSE...
CLOSE HAS NOTHING TO DO WITH IT!!
WE'RE GUILDMATES!!!
HEH... YEAH...
SO DON'T YOU DIE!!!
WRAITH!!!

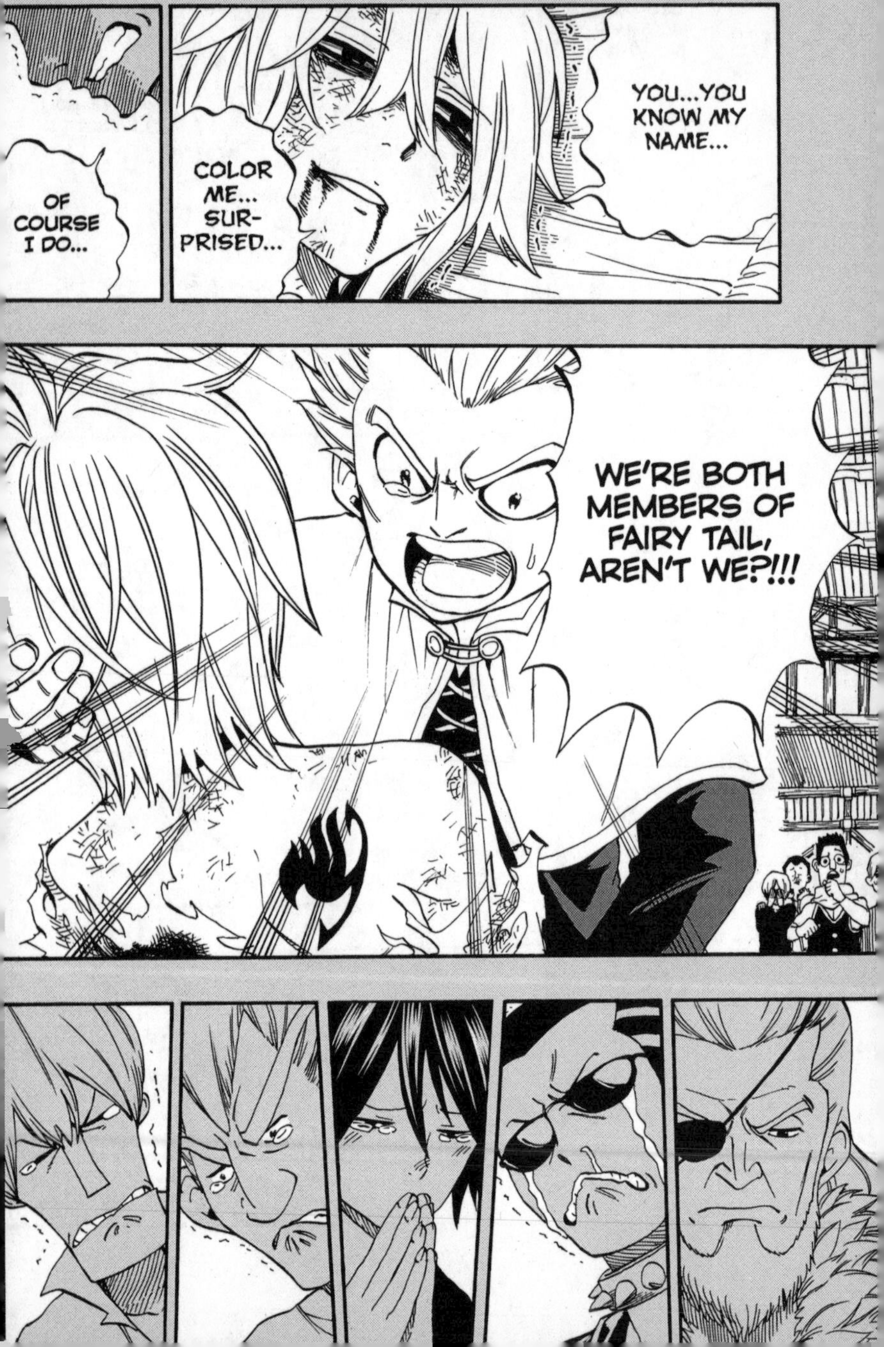
YOU...YOU KNOW MY NAME...
COLOR ME... SUR-PRISED...
OF COURSE I DO...
WE'RE BOTH MEMBERS OF FAIRY TAIL, AREN'T WE?!!!

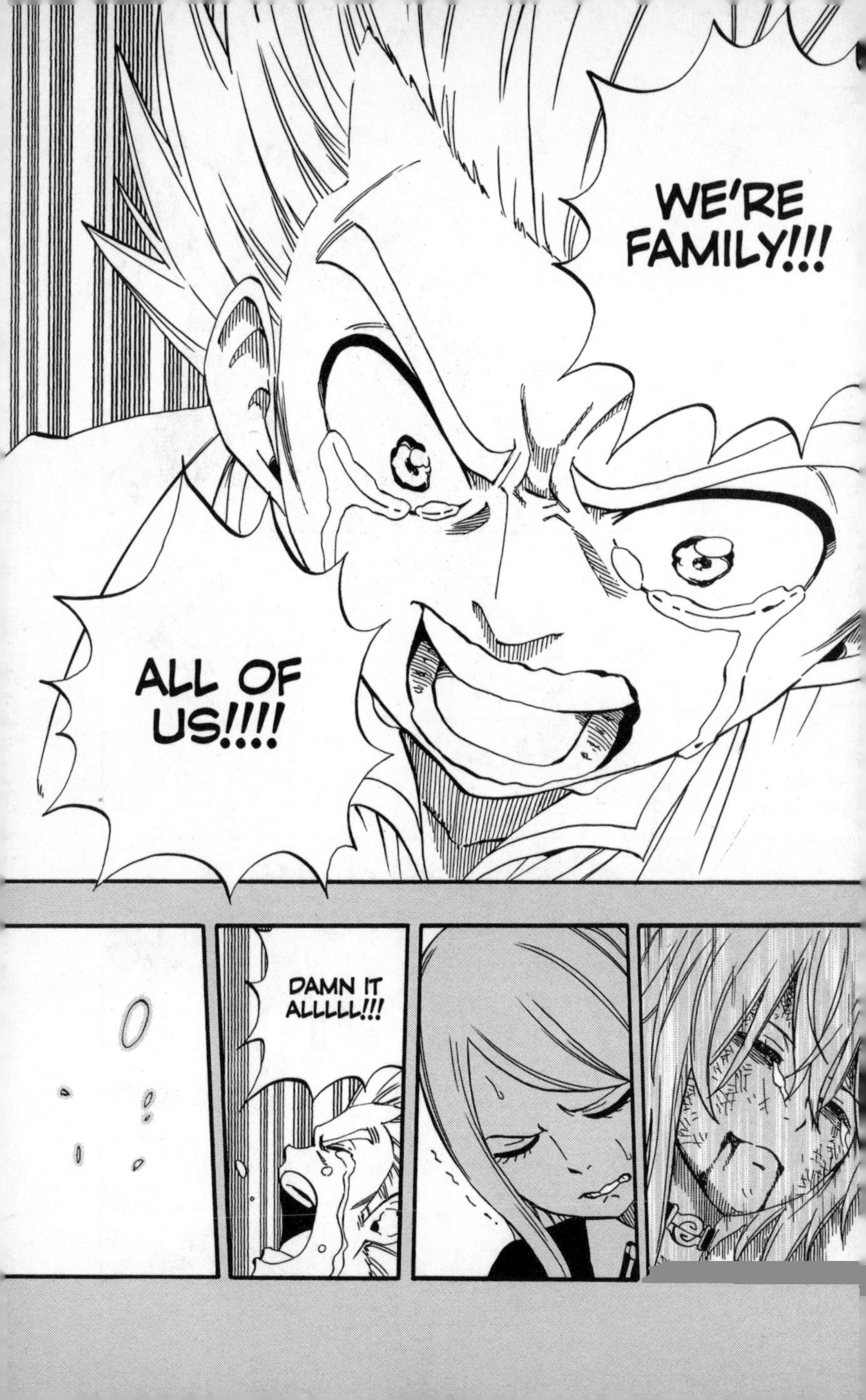
WE'RE FAMILY!!!
ALL OF US!!!!
DAMN IT ALLLLL!!!

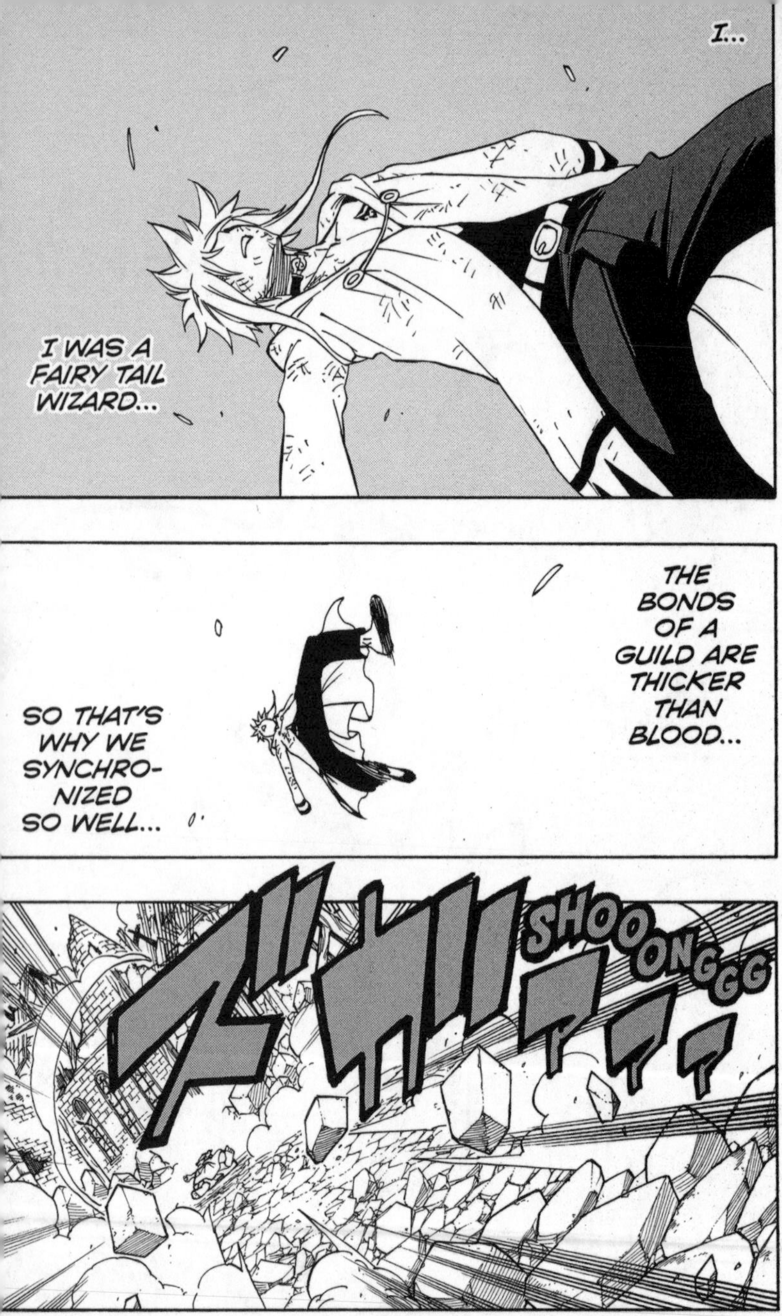
I...
I WAS A FAIRY TAIL WIZARD...
THE BONDS OF A GUILD ARE THICKER THAN BLOOD...
SO THAT'S WHY WE SYNCHRO-NIZED SO WELL...
SHOOOONGGG

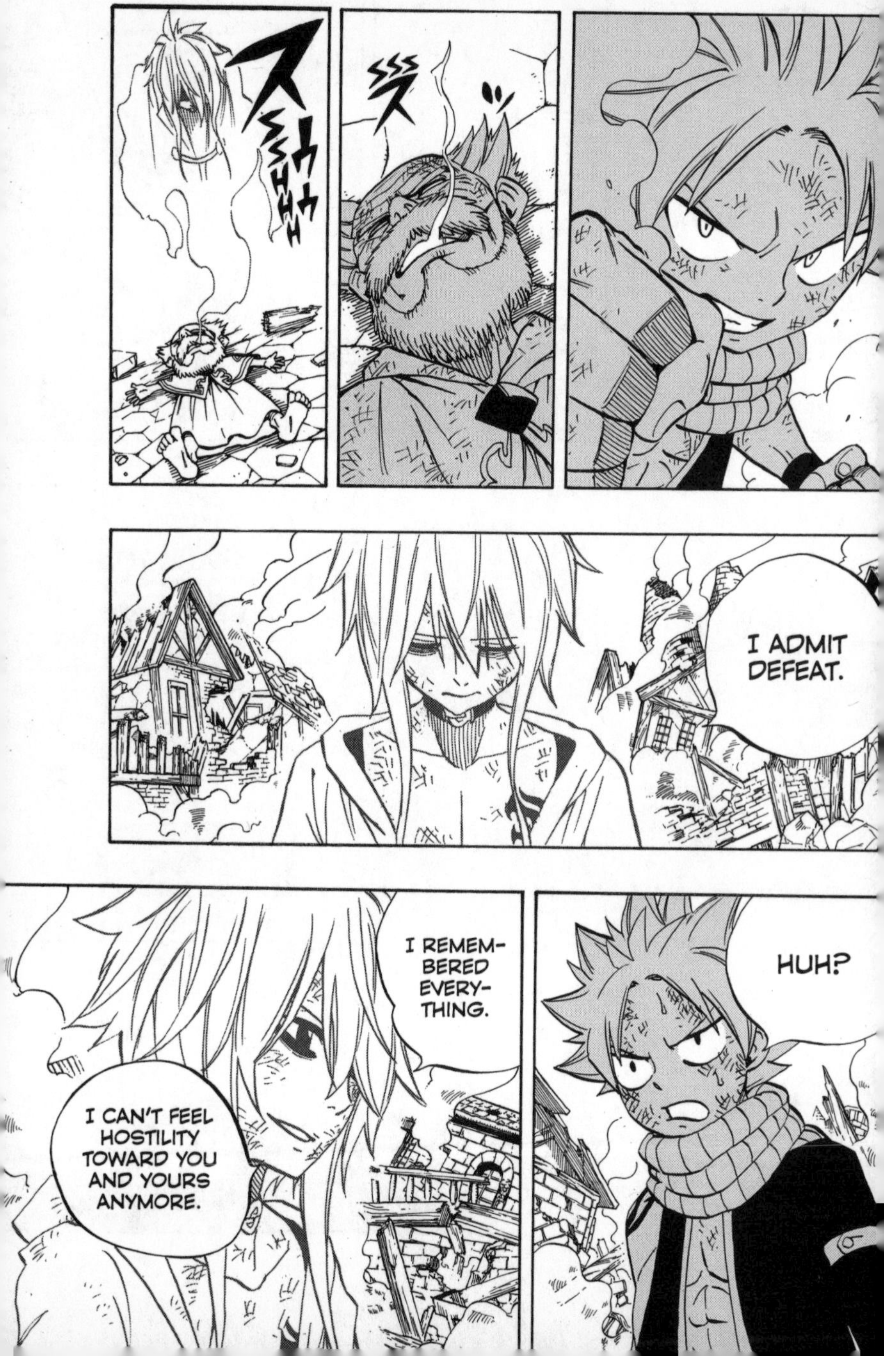
SSHHHH
I ADMIT DEFEAT.
HUH?
I REMEM-BERED EVERY-THING.
I CAN'T FEEL HOSTILITY TOWARD YOU AND YOURS ANYMORE.

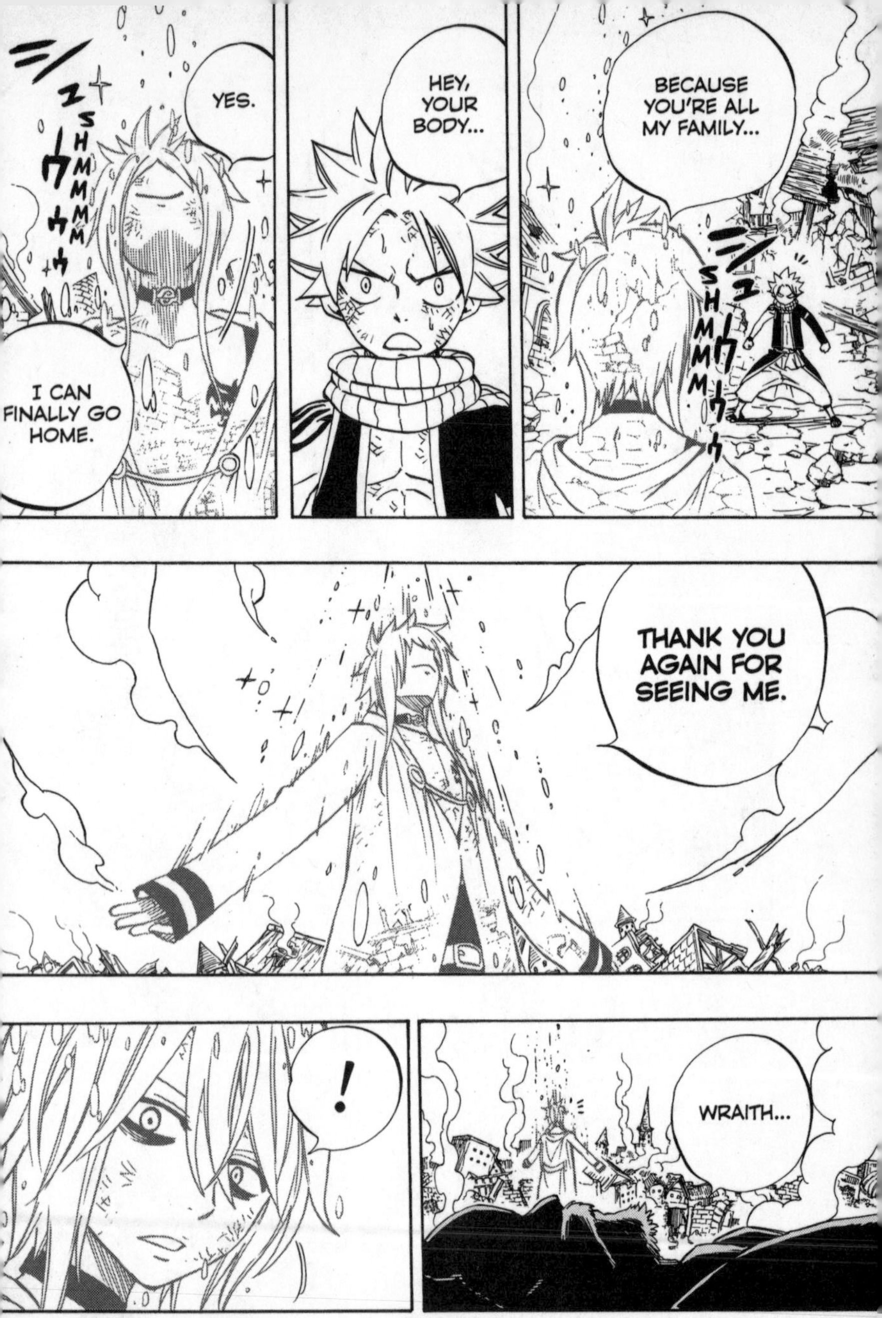
BECAUSE YOU'RE ALL MY FAMILY...
SHMMMM
HEY, YOUR BODY...
YES.
SHMMMM
I CAN FINALLY GO HOME.
THANK YOU AGAIN FOR SEEING ME.
WRAITH...
!

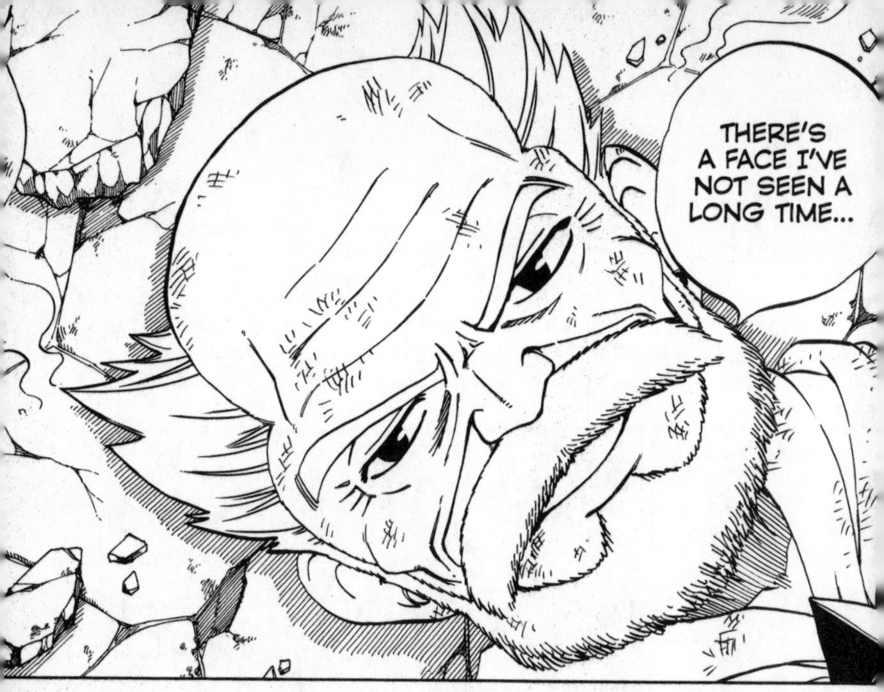
THERE'S A FACE I'VE NOT SEEN A LONG TIME...
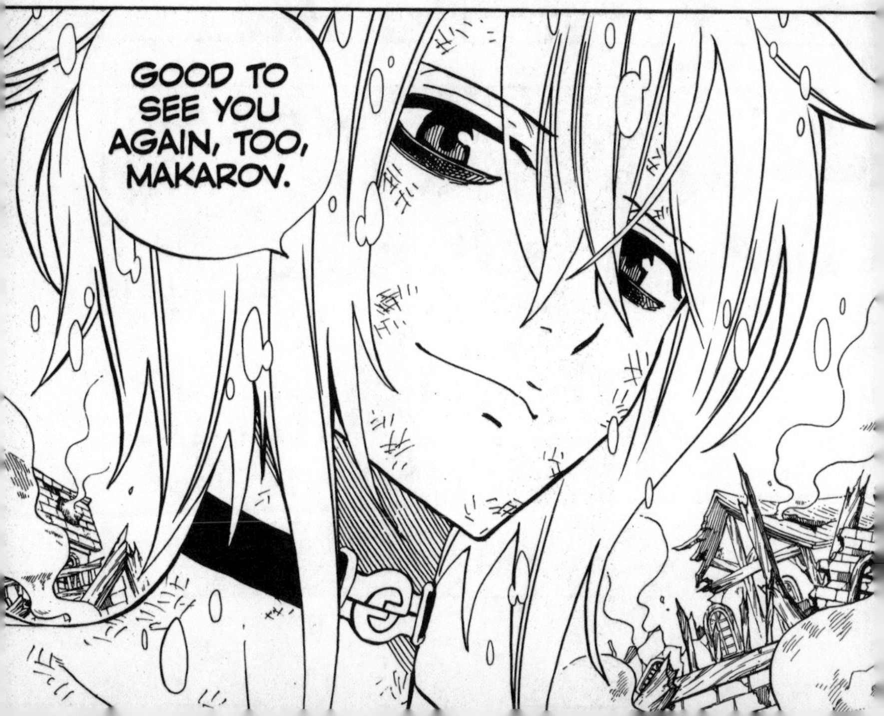
GOOD TO SEE YOU AGAIN, TOO, MAKAROV.

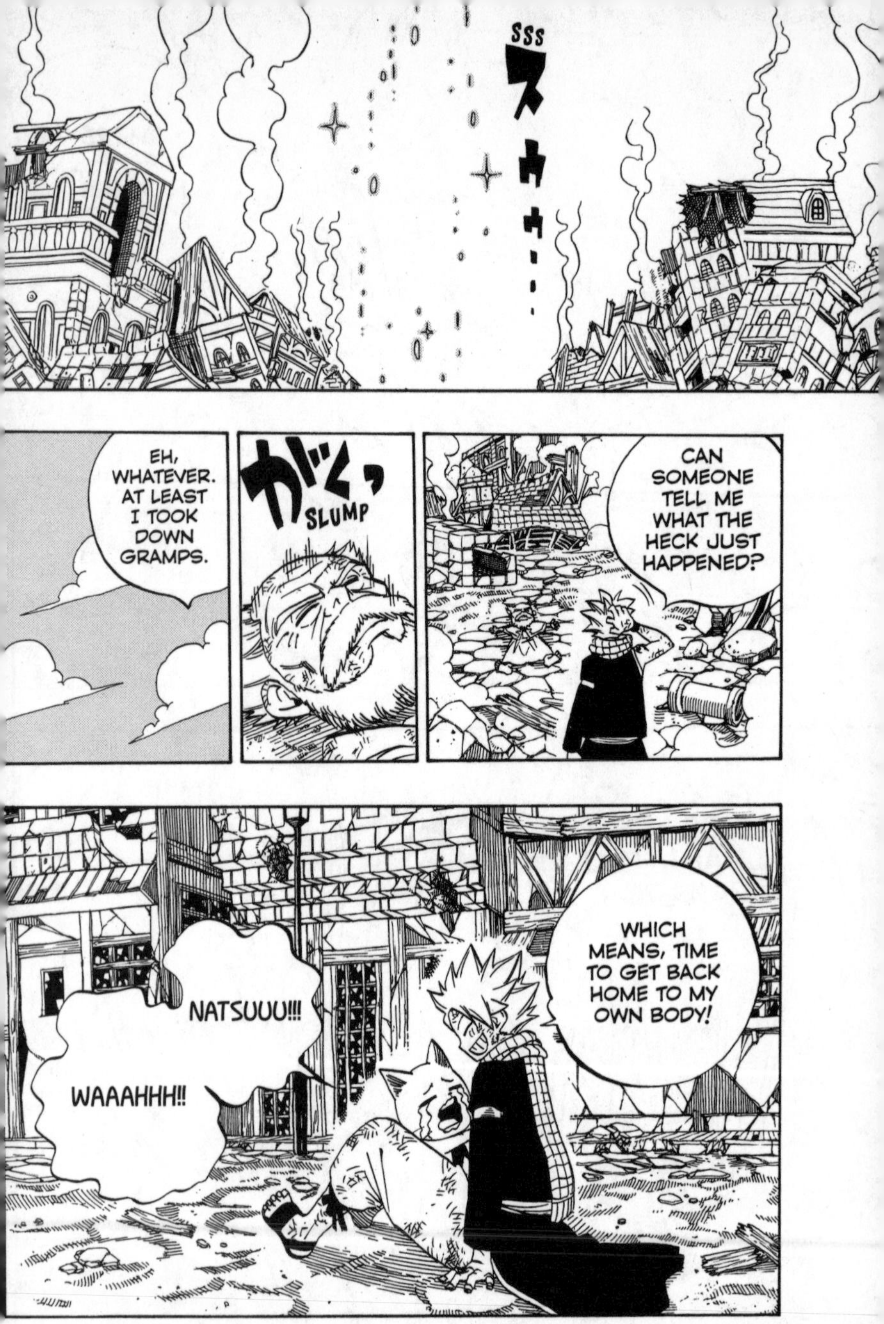
SSS
スゥゥ…
CAN SOMEONE TELL ME WHAT THE HECK JUST HAPPENED?
がくっ
SLUMP
EH, WHATEVER. AT LEAST I TOOK DOWN GRAMPS.
WHICH MEANS, TIME TO GET BACK HOME TO MY OWN BODY!
NATSUUU!!!
WAAAHHH!!

FAIRY TAIL 100 YEARS QUEST

Chapter 41: A Card in the Hand

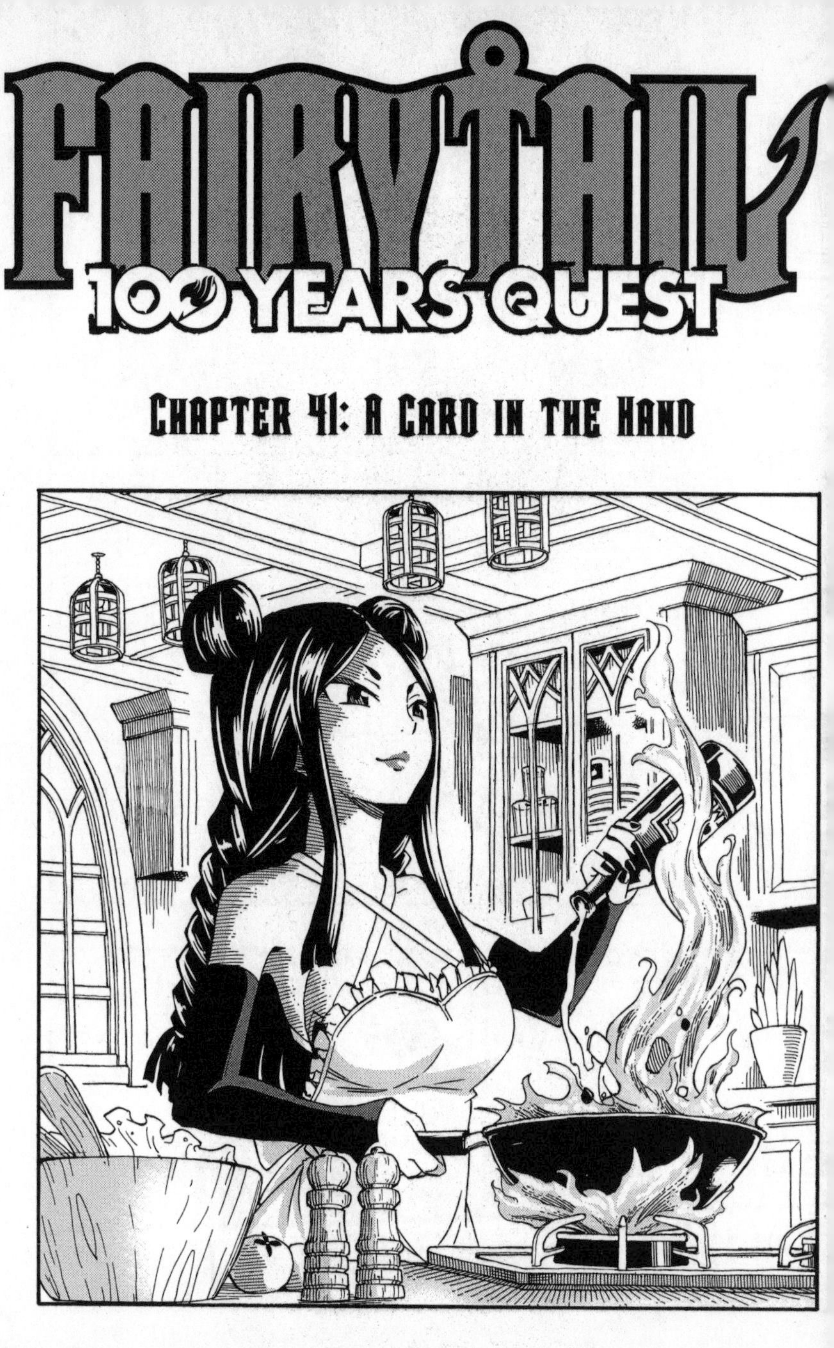

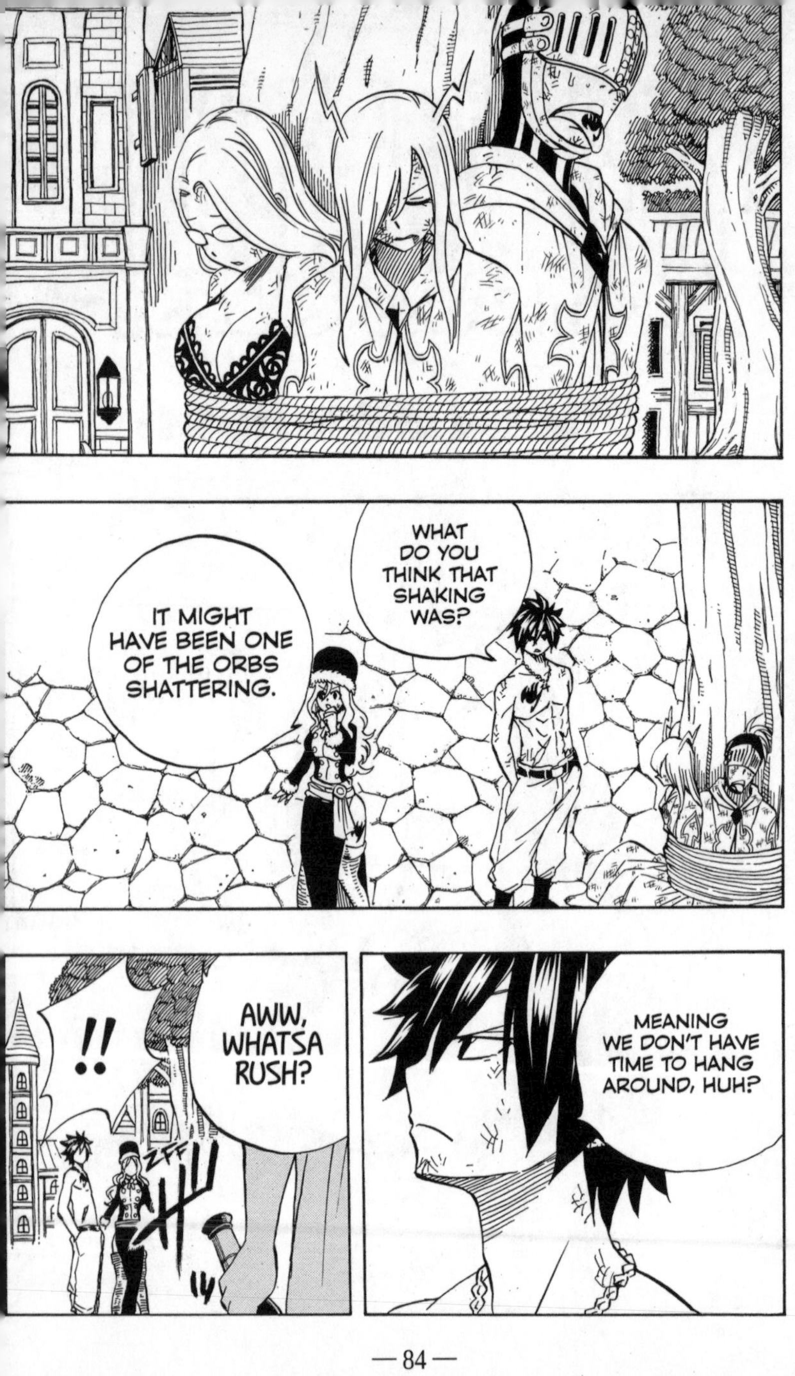
WHAT DO YOU THINK THAT SHAKING WAS?
IT MIGHT HAVE BEEN ONE OF THE ORBS SHATTERING.
MEANING WE DON'T HAVE TIME TO HANG AROUND, HUH?
AWW, WHATSA RUSH?
!!
ZFF

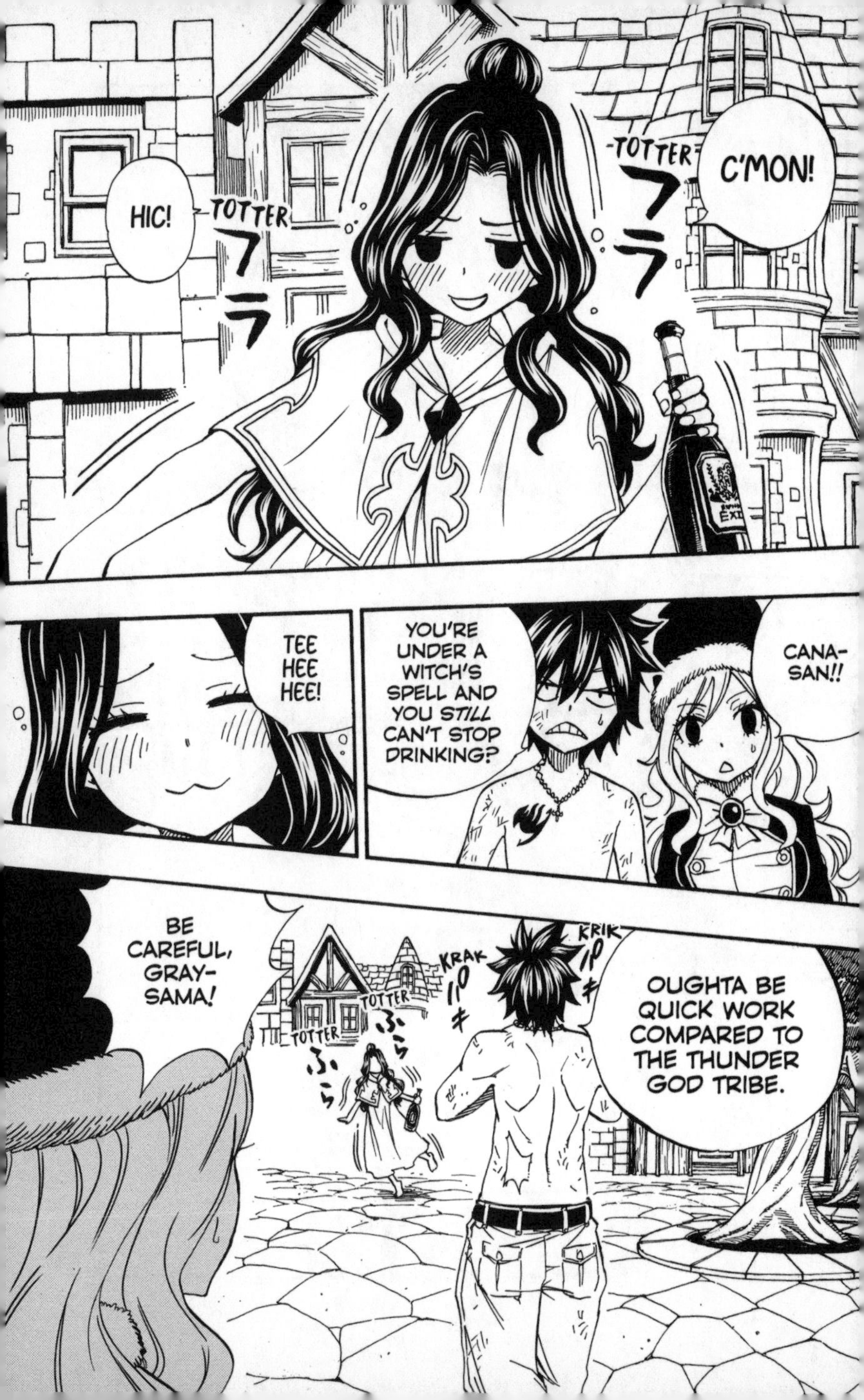
C'MON!
-TOTTER-
フラ
TOTTER
フラ
HIC!
CANA-SAN!!
YOU'RE UNDER A WITCH'S SPELL AND YOU *STILL* CAN'T STOP DRINKING?
TEE HEE HEE!
OUGHTA BE QUICK WORK COMPARED TO THE THUNDER GOD TRIBE.
KRIK
パキ
KRAK
パキ
TOTTER
ふら
TOTTER
ふら
BE CAREFUL, GRAY-SAMA!

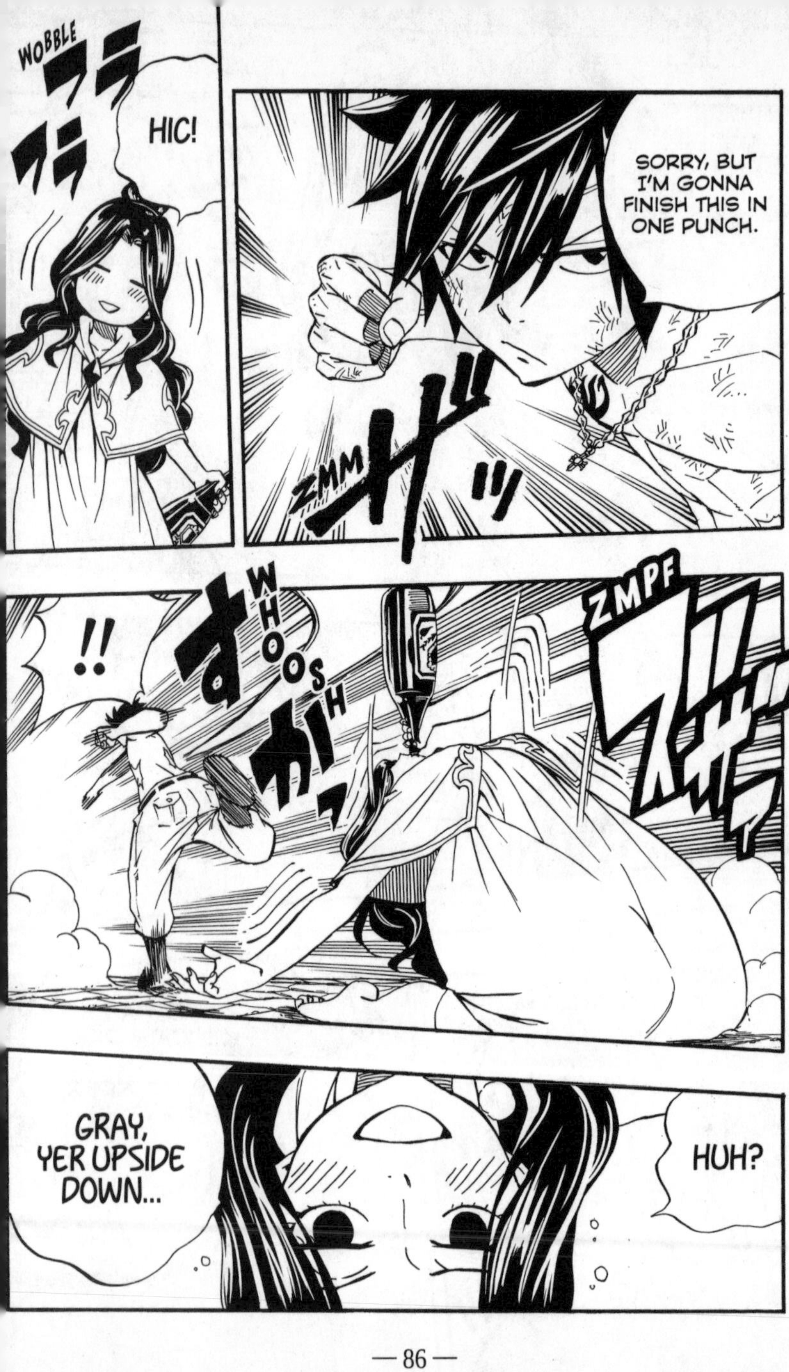
SORRY, BUT I'M GONNA FINISH THIS IN ONE PUNCH.
ZMM
WOBBLE
HIC!
ZMPF
WHOOSH
!!
HUH?
GRAY, YER UPSIDE DOWN...

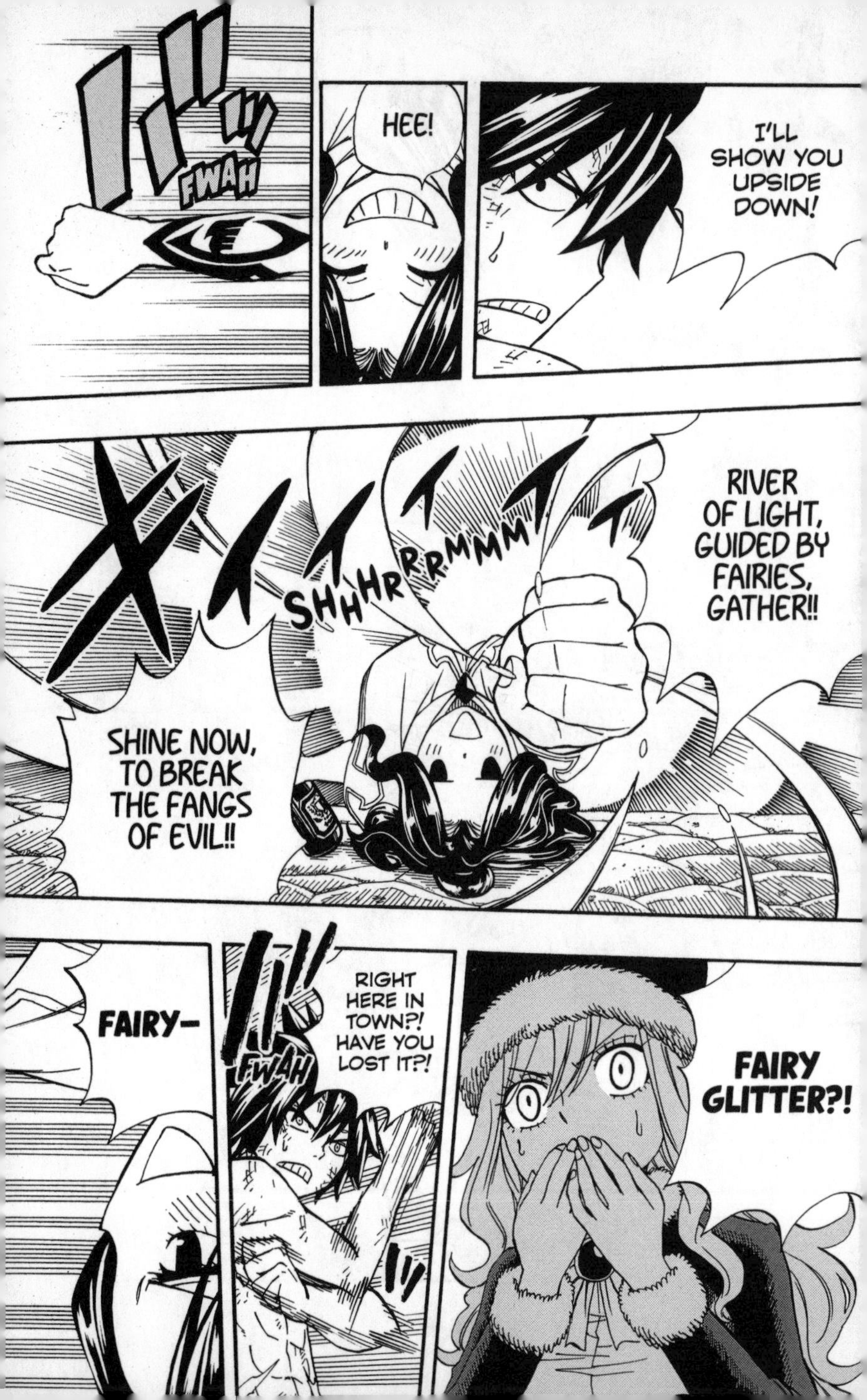
I'LL SHOW YOU UPSIDE DOWN!
HEE!
FWAH
RIVER OF LIGHT, GUIDED BY FAIRIES, GATHER!!
SHHHRRRMMMM
SHINE NOW, TO BREAK THE FANGS OF EVIL!!
FAIRY GLITTER?!
RIGHT HERE IN TOWN?! HAVE YOU LOST IT?!
FWAH
FAIRY–

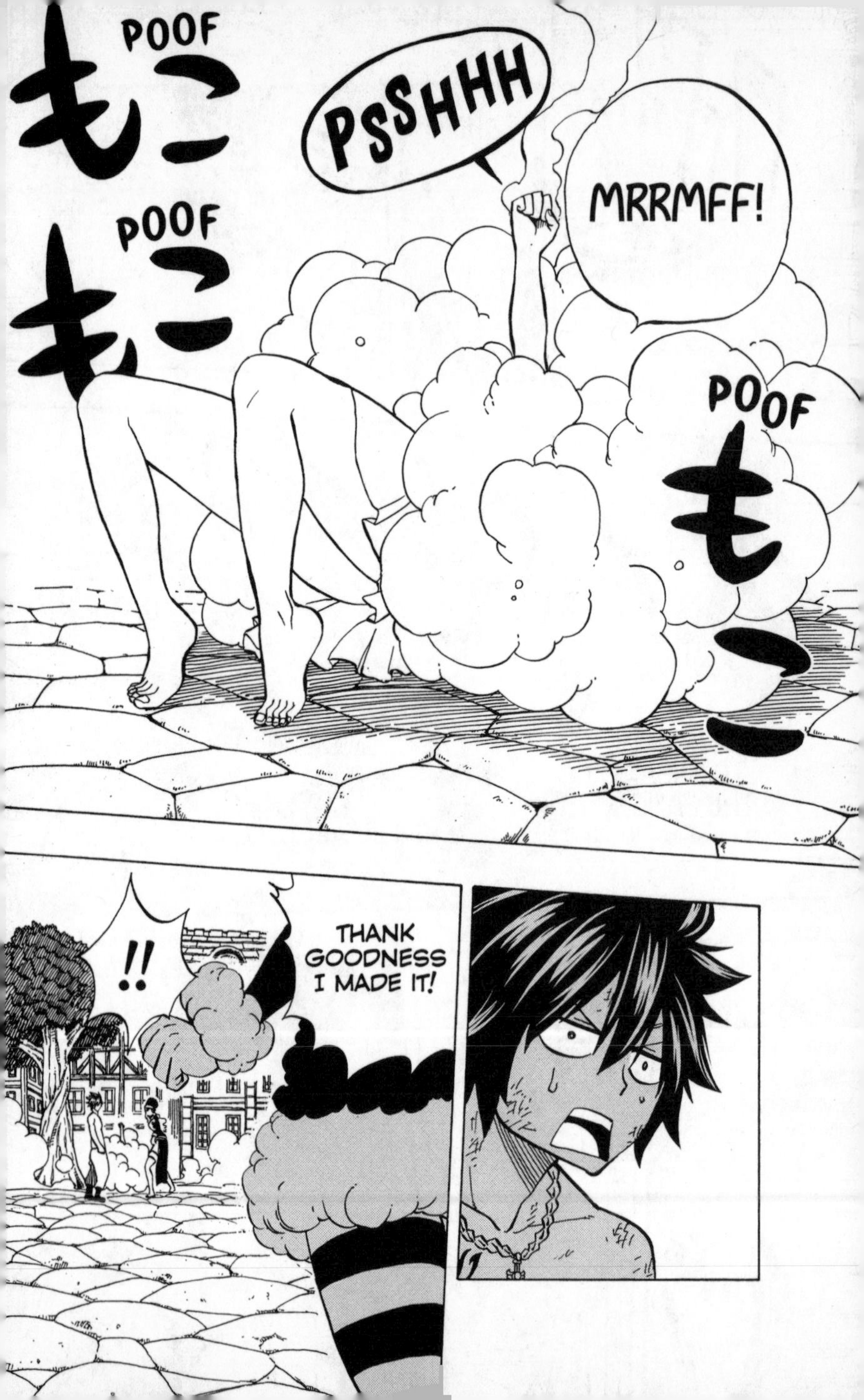

MRRMFF!
PSSHHH
POOF
もこ
POOF
もこ
POOF
もこ
THANK GOODNESS I MADE IT!
!!

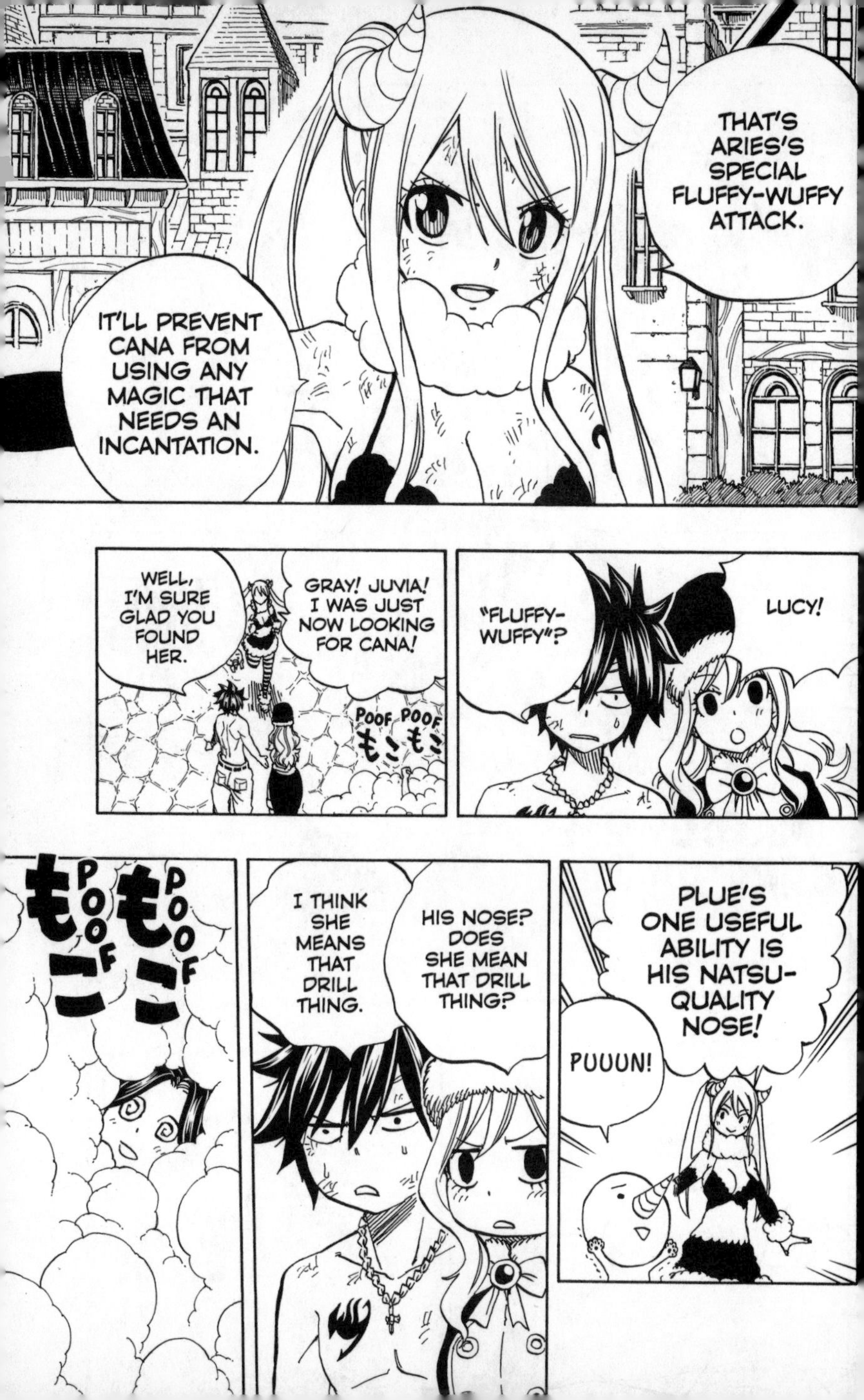
THAT'S ARIES'S SPECIAL FLUFFY-WUFFY ATTACK.
IT'LL PREVENT CANA FROM USING ANY MAGIC THAT NEEDS AN INCANTATION.
LUCY!
"FLUFFY-WUFFY"?
GRAY! JUVIA! I WAS JUST NOW LOOKING FOR CANA!
WELL, I'M SURE GLAD YOU FOUND HER.
POOF POOF
もこもこ
PLUE'S ONE USEFUL ABILITY IS HIS NATSU-QUALITY NOSE!
PUUUN!
HIS NOSE? DOES SHE MEAN THAT DRILL THING?
I THINK SHE MEANS THAT DRILL THING.
もこ POOF
もこ POOF

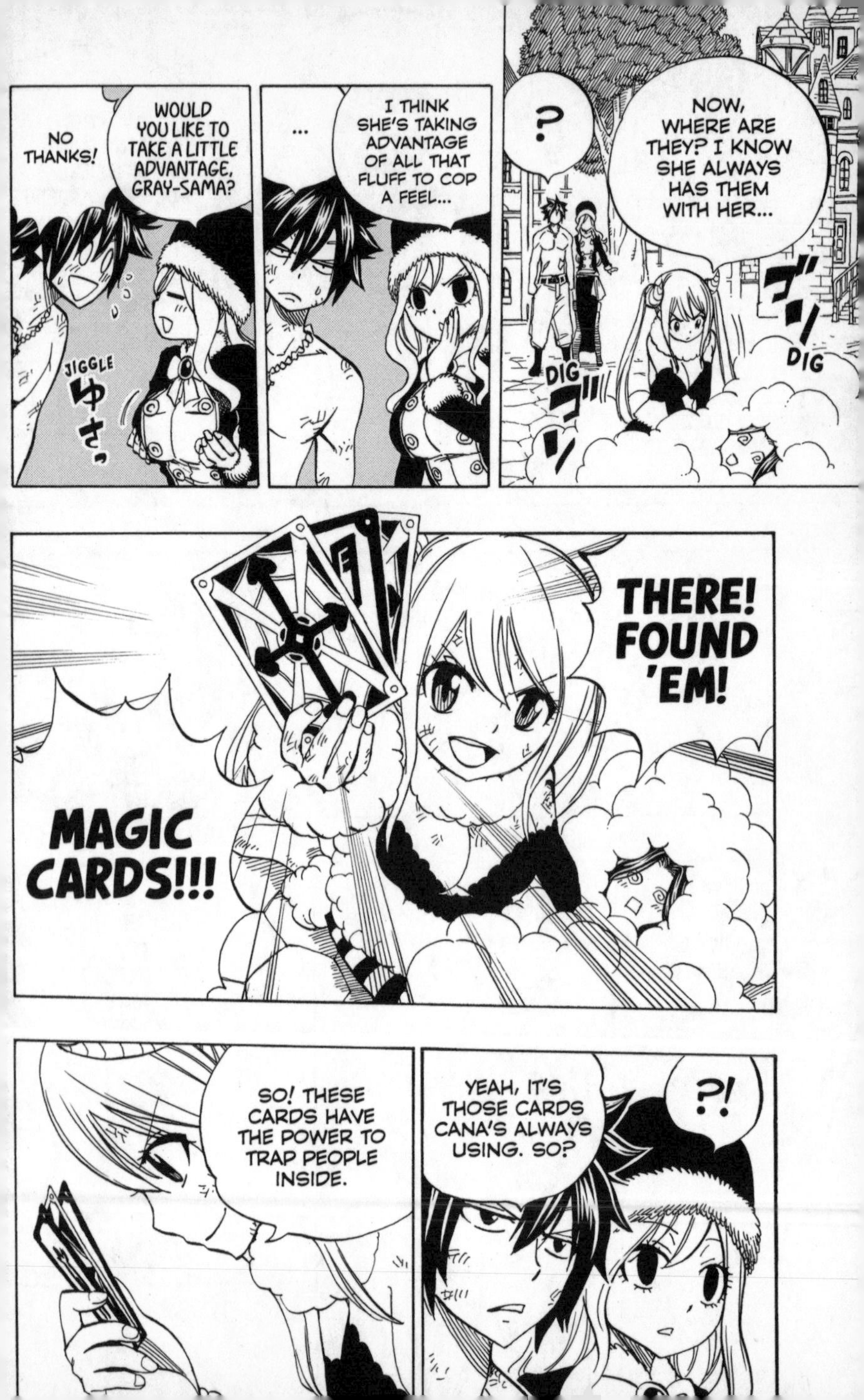
?
NOW, WHERE ARE THEY? I KNOW SHE ALWAYS HAS THEM WITH HER...
DIG
DIG
I THINK SHE'S TAKING ADVANTAGE OF ALL THAT FLUFF TO COP A FEEL...
...
WOULD YOU LIKE TO TAKE A LITTLE ADVANTAGE, GRAY-SAMA?
NO THANKS!
JIGGLE
ゆさ
THERE! FOUND 'EM!
MAGIC CARDS!!!
?!
YEAH, IT'S THOSE CARDS CANA'S ALWAYS USING. SO?
SO! THESE CARDS HAVE THE POWER TO TRAP PEOPLE INSIDE.

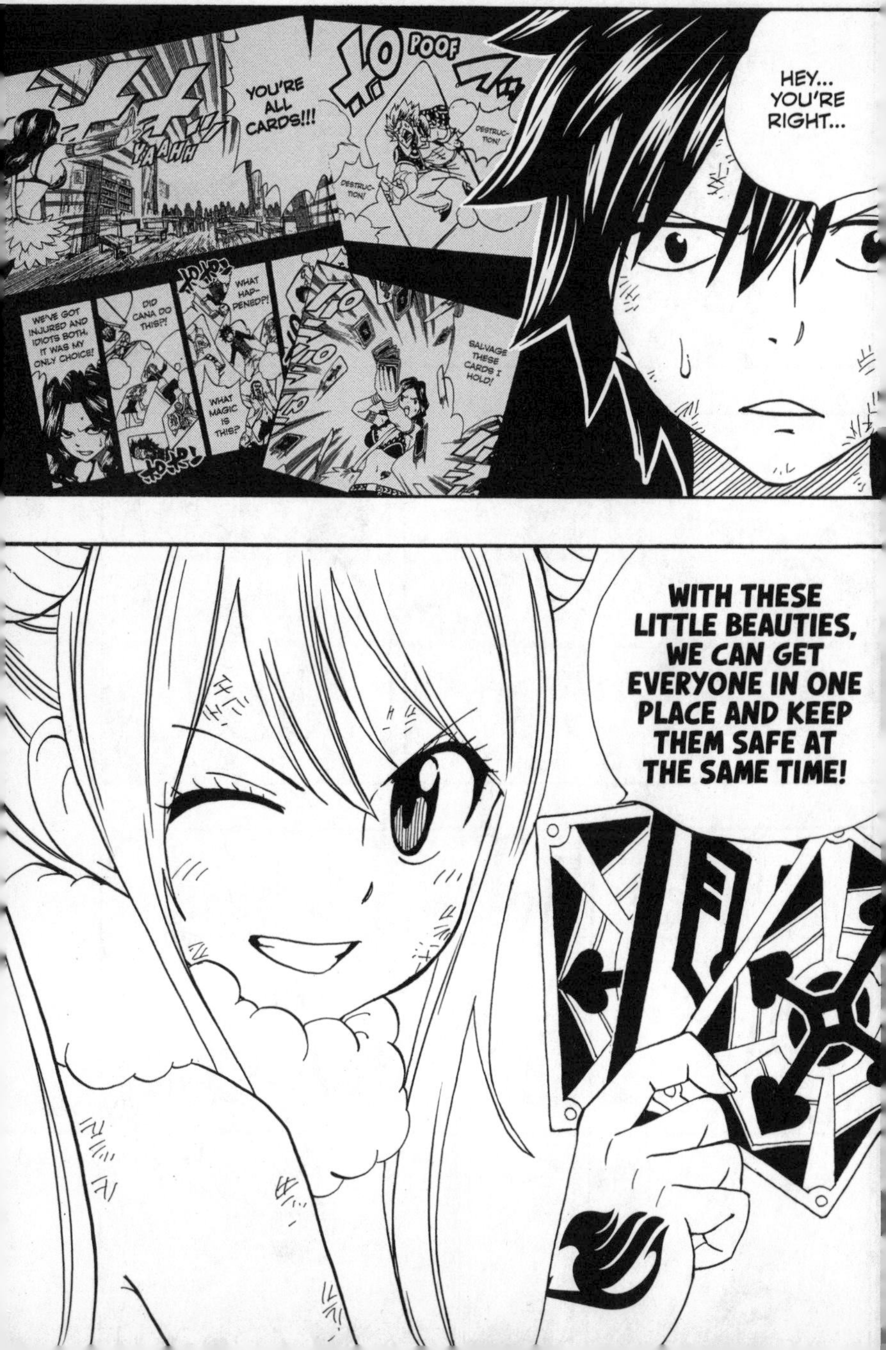
HEY... YOU'RE RIGHT...
POOF
DESTRUCTION!
DESTRUCTION!
YOU'RE ALL CARDS!!!
YAAHH
SALVAGE THESE CARDS I HOLD!
WHAT HAPPENED?!
WHAT MAGIC IS THIS?
DID CANA DO THIS?!
WE'VE GOT INJURED AND IDIOTS BOTH, IT WAS MY ONLY CHOICE!
WITH THESE LITTLE BEAUTIES, WE CAN GET EVERYONE IN ONE PLACE AND KEEP THEM SAFE AT THE SAME TIME!

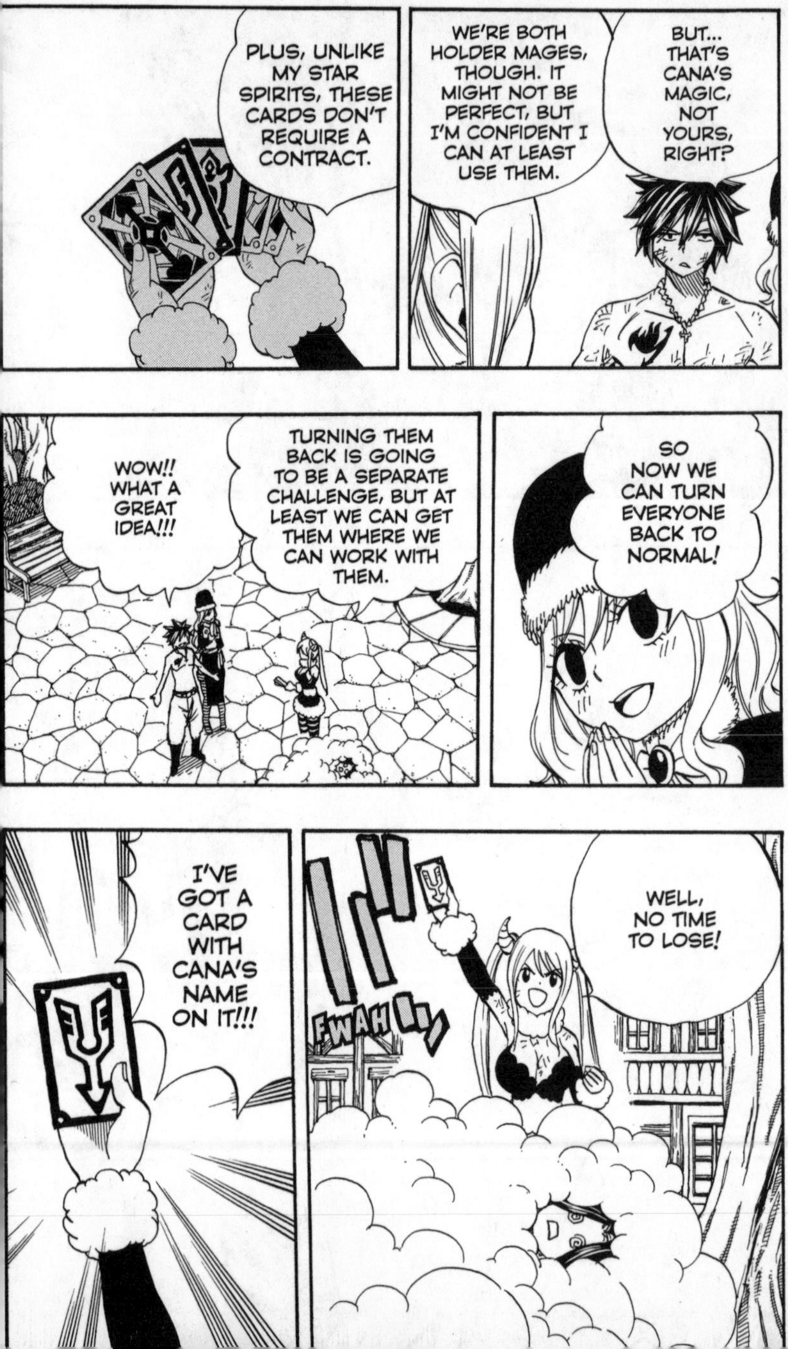
BUT... THAT'S CANA'S MAGIC, NOT YOURS, RIGHT?
WE'RE BOTH HOLDER MAGES, THOUGH. IT MIGHT NOT BE PERFECT, BUT I'M CONFIDENT I CAN AT LEAST USE THEM.
PLUS, UNLIKE MY STAR SPIRITS, THESE CARDS DON'T REQUIRE A CONTRACT.
SO NOW WE CAN TURN EVERYONE BACK TO NORMAL!
TURNING THEM BACK IS GOING TO BE A SEPARATE CHALLENGE, BUT AT LEAST WE CAN GET THEM WHERE WE CAN WORK WITH THEM.
WOW!! WHAT A GREAT IDEA!!!
WELL, NO TIME TO LOSE!
FWAH
I'VE GOT A CARD WITH CANA'S NAME ON IT!!!

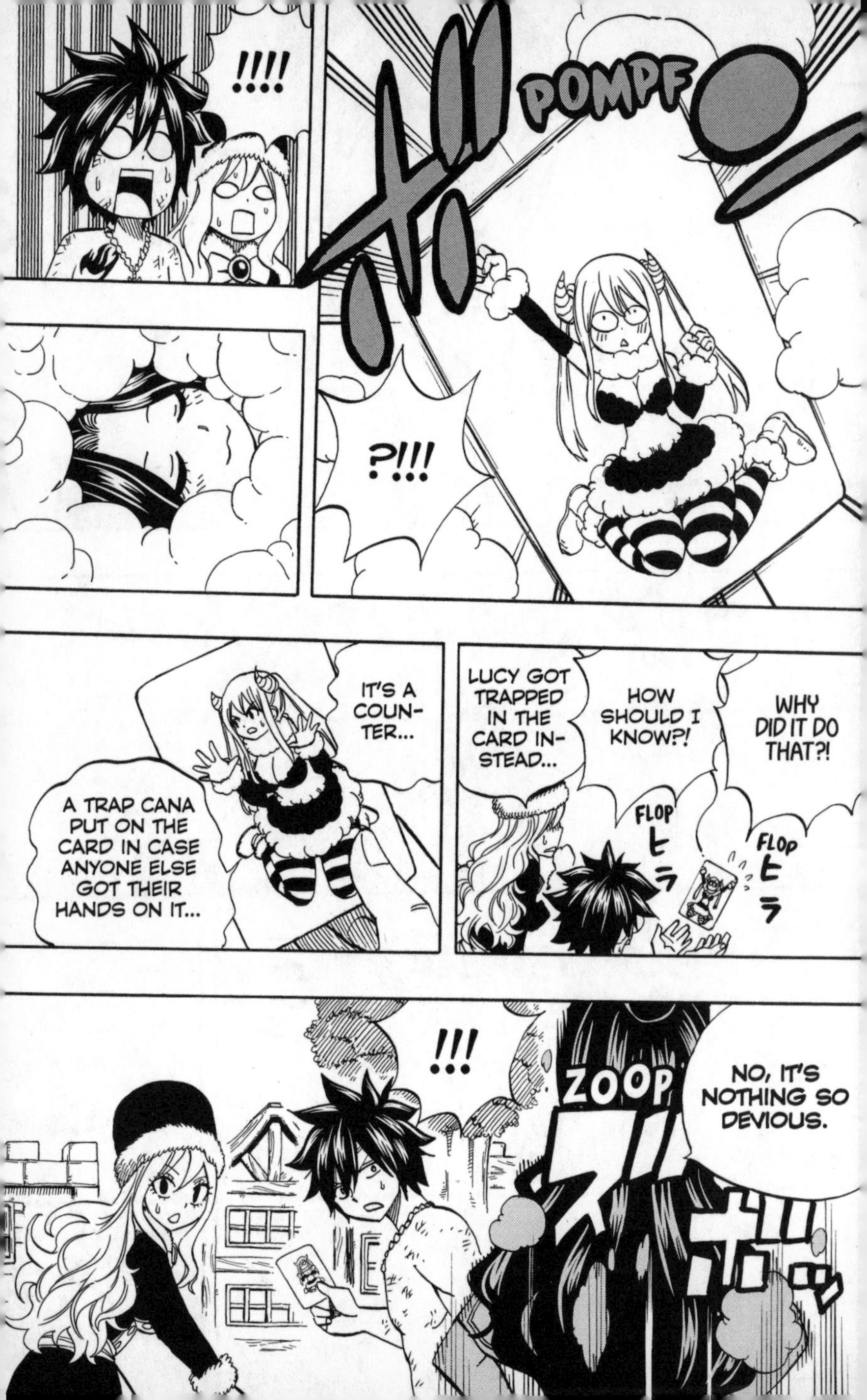
POMPF
?!!!
!!!!
WHY DID IT DO THAT?!
HOW SHOULD I KNOW?!
LUCY GOT TRAPPED IN THE CARD IN-STEAD...
FLOP
FLOP
IT'S A COUN-TER...
A TRAP CANA PUT ON THE CARD IN CASE ANYONE ELSE GOT THEIR HANDS ON IT...
NO, IT'S NOTHING SO DEVIOUS.
ZOOP
!!!

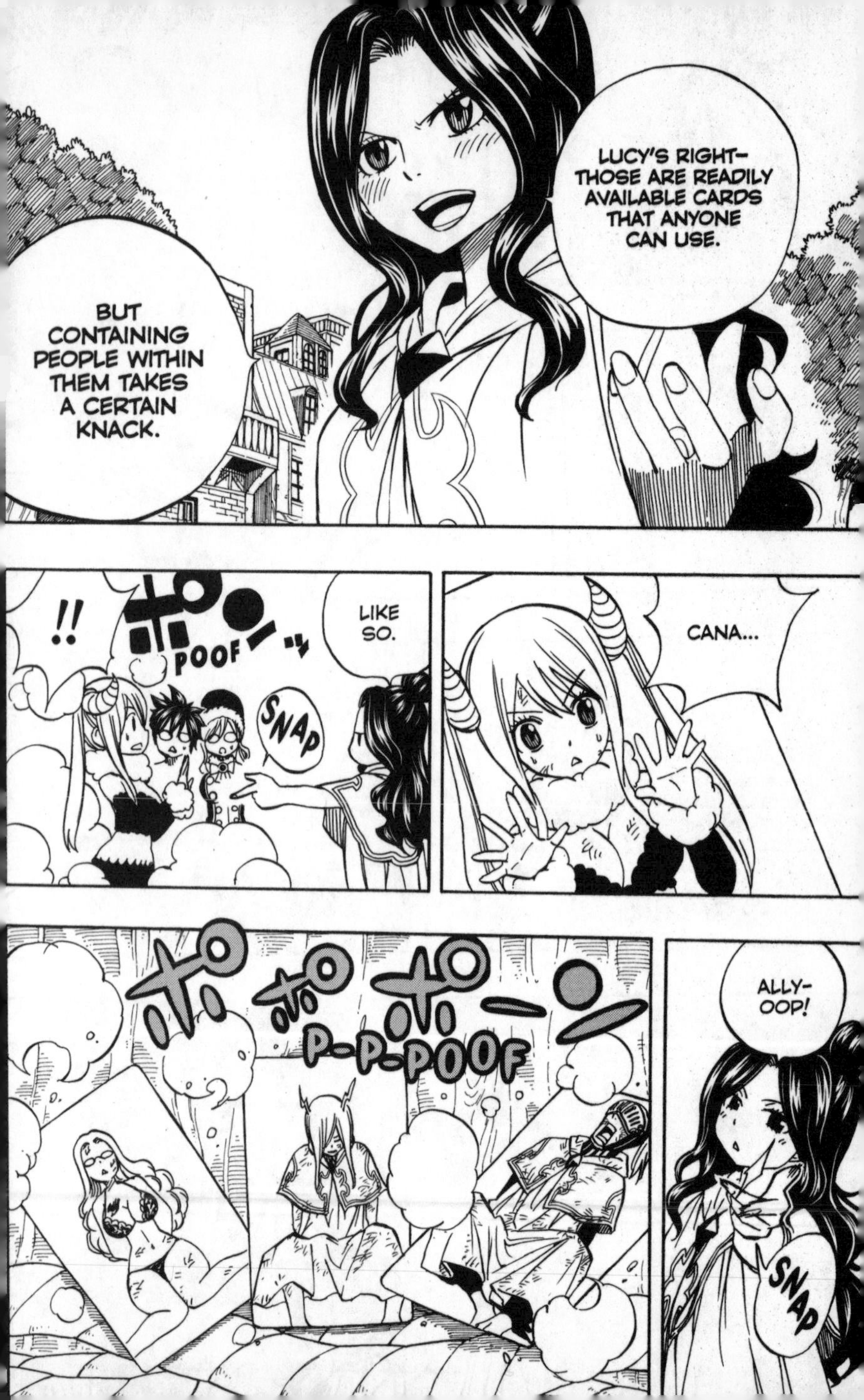
LUCY'S RIGHT— THOSE ARE READILY AVAILABLE CARDS THAT ANYONE CAN USE.
BUT CONTAINING PEOPLE WITHIN THEM TAKES A CERTAIN KNACK.
CANA...
LIKE SO.
POOF
!!
SNAP
ALLY-OOP!
SNAP
P-P-POOF

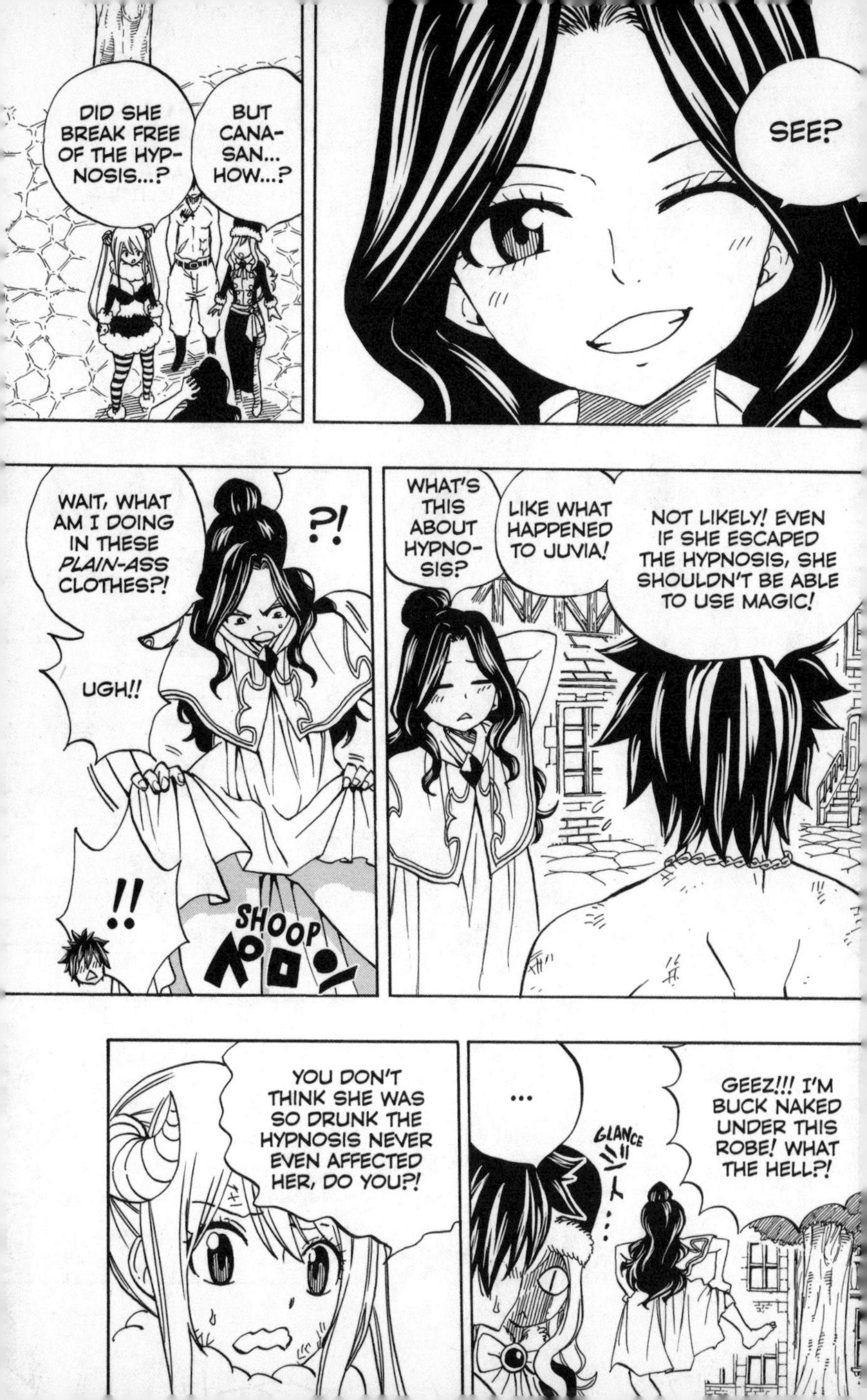
SEE?
BUT CANA-SAN... HOW...?
DID SHE BREAK FREE OF THE HYPNOSIS...?
NOT LIKELY! EVEN IF SHE ESCAPED THE HYPNOSIS, SHE SHOULDN'T BE ABLE TO USE MAGIC!
LIKE WHAT HAPPENED TO JUVIA!
WHAT'S THIS ABOUT HYPNOSIS?
?!
WAIT, WHAT AM I DOING IN THESE *PLAIN*-ASS CLOTHES?!
UGH!!
!!
SHOOP
GEEZ!!! I'M BUCK NAKED UNDER THIS ROBE! WHAT THE HELL?!
...
GLANCE
YOU DON'T THINK SHE WAS SO DRUNK THE HYPNOSIS NEVER EVEN AFFECTED HER, DO YOU?!

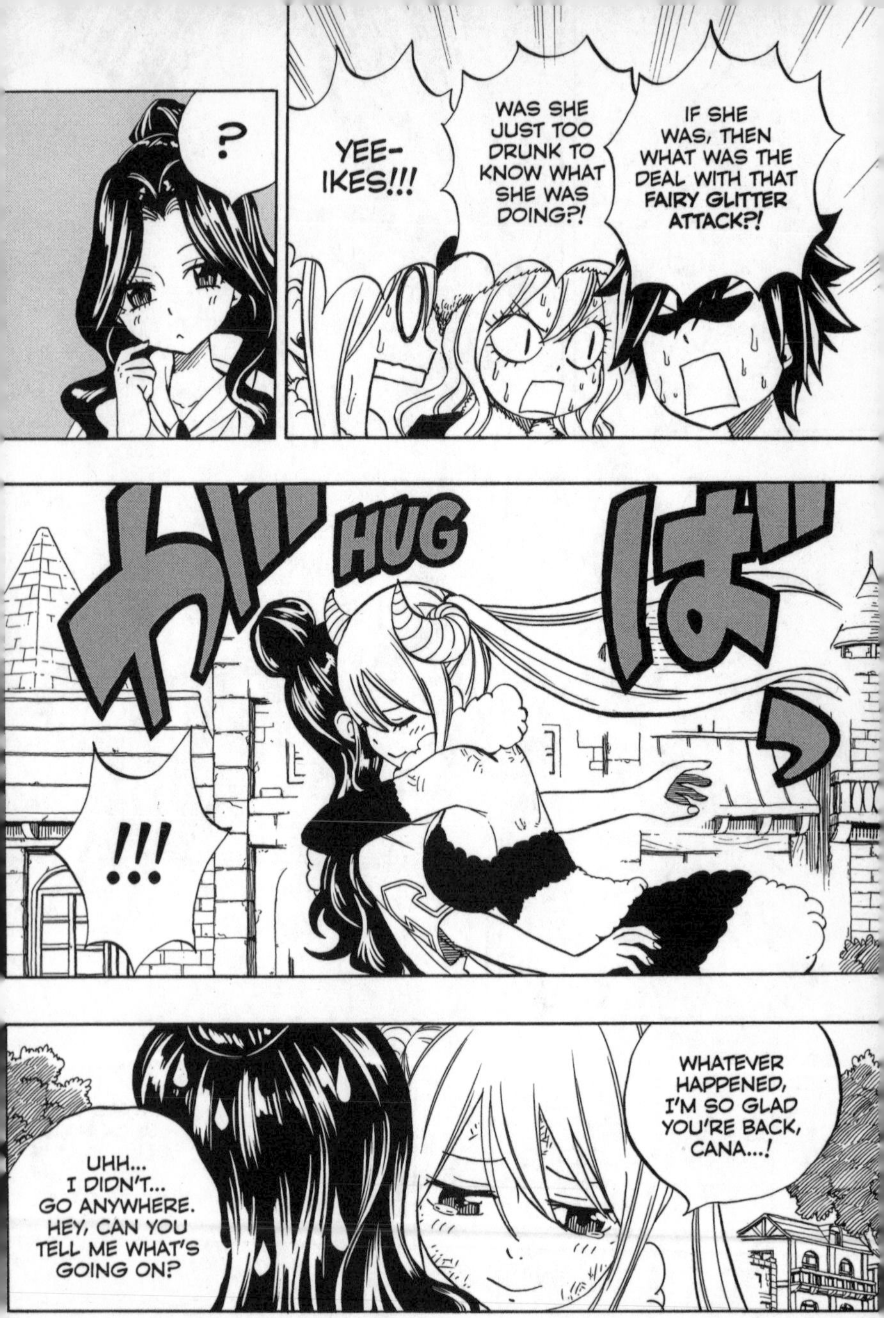
IF SHE WAS, THEN WHAT WAS THE DEAL WITH THAT FAIRY GLITTER ATTACK?!
WAS SHE JUST TOO DRUNK TO KNOW WHAT SHE WAS DOING?!
YEE-IKES!!!
?
HUG
!!!
WHATEVER HAPPENED, I'M SO GLAD YOU'RE BACK, CANA...!
UHH... I DIDN'T... GO ANYWHERE. HEY, CAN YOU TELL ME WHAT'S GOING ON?

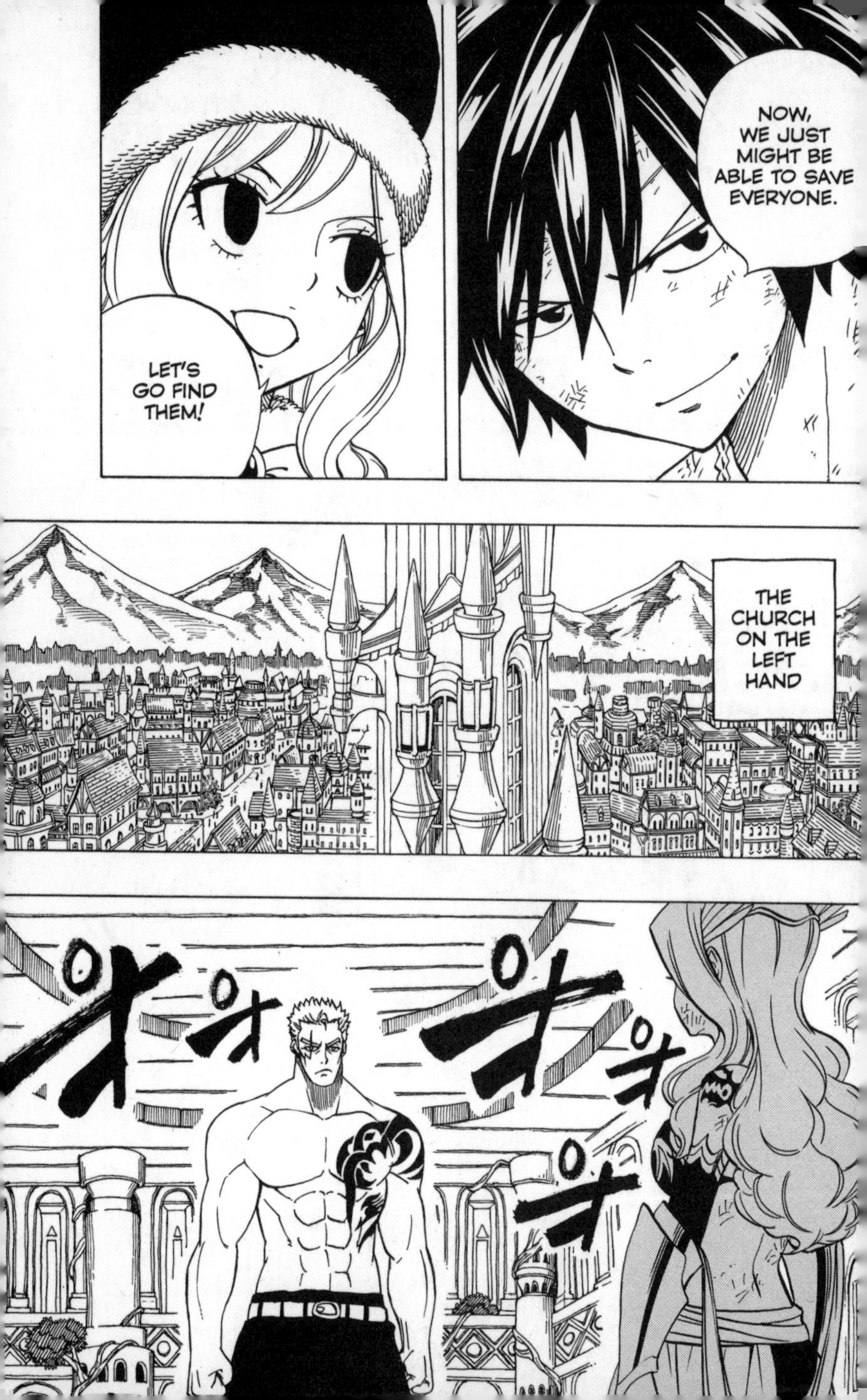
NOW, WE JUST MIGHT BE ABLE TO SAVE EVERYONE.
LET'S GO FIND THEM!
THE CHURCH ON THE LEFT HAND

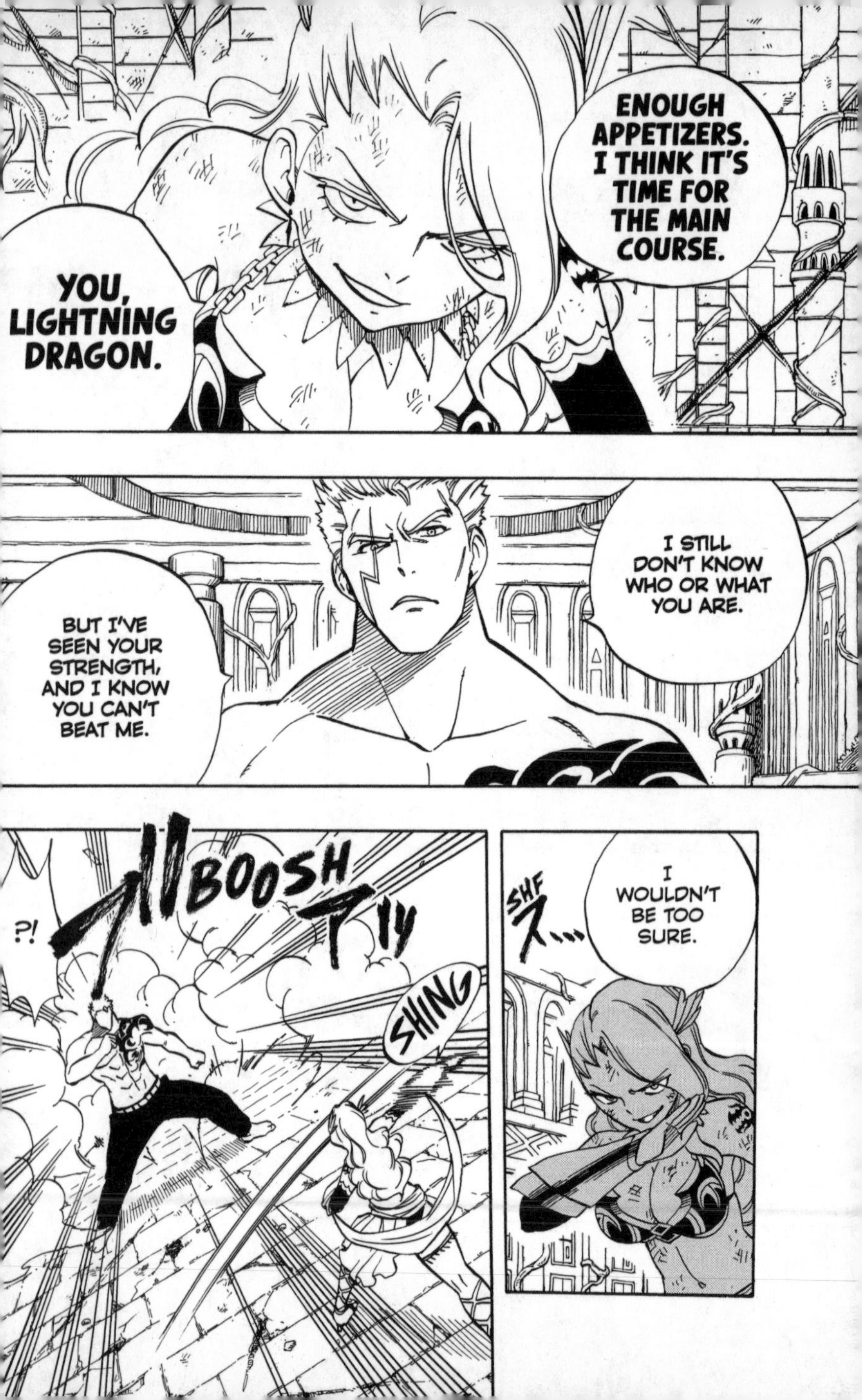
ENOUGH APPETIZERS. I THINK IT'S TIME FOR THE MAIN COURSE.
YOU, LIGHTNING DRAGON.
I STILL DON'T KNOW WHO OR WHAT YOU ARE.
BUT I'VE SEEN YOUR STRENGTH, AND I KNOW YOU CAN'T BEAT ME.
SHF
I WOULDN'T BE TOO SURE.
BOOSH
SHING
?!

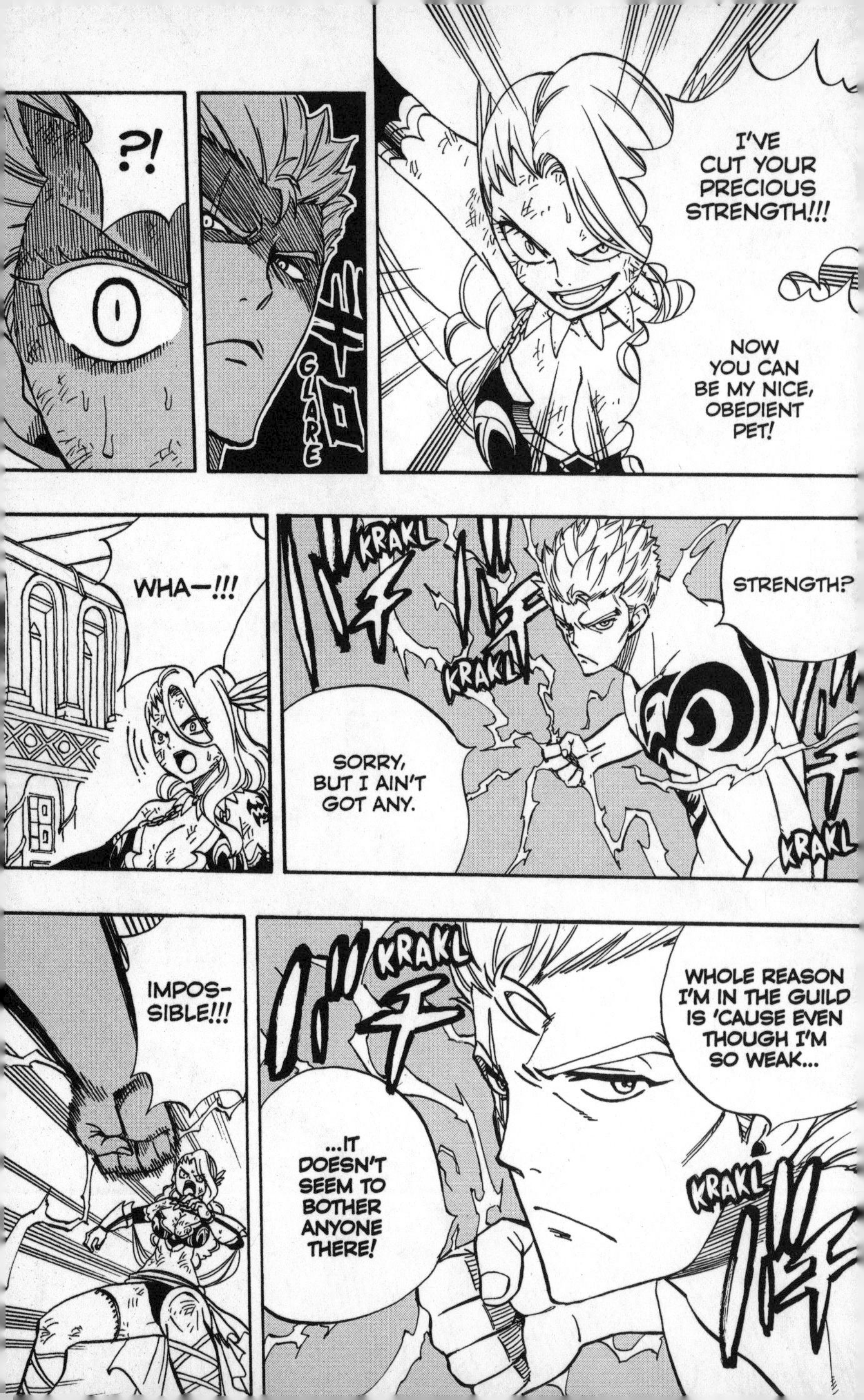
I'VE CUT YOUR PRECIOUS STRENGTH!!!
NOW YOU CAN BE MY NICE, OBEDIENT PET!
GLARE
?!
STRENGTH?
KRAKL
KRAKL
SORRY, BUT I AIN'T GOT ANY.
KRAKL
WHA-!!!
WHOLE REASON I'M IN THE GUILD IS 'CAUSE EVEN THOUGH I'M SO WEAK...
KRAKL
KRAKL
...IT DOESN'T SEEM TO BOTHER ANYONE THERE!
IMPOS-SIBLE!!!

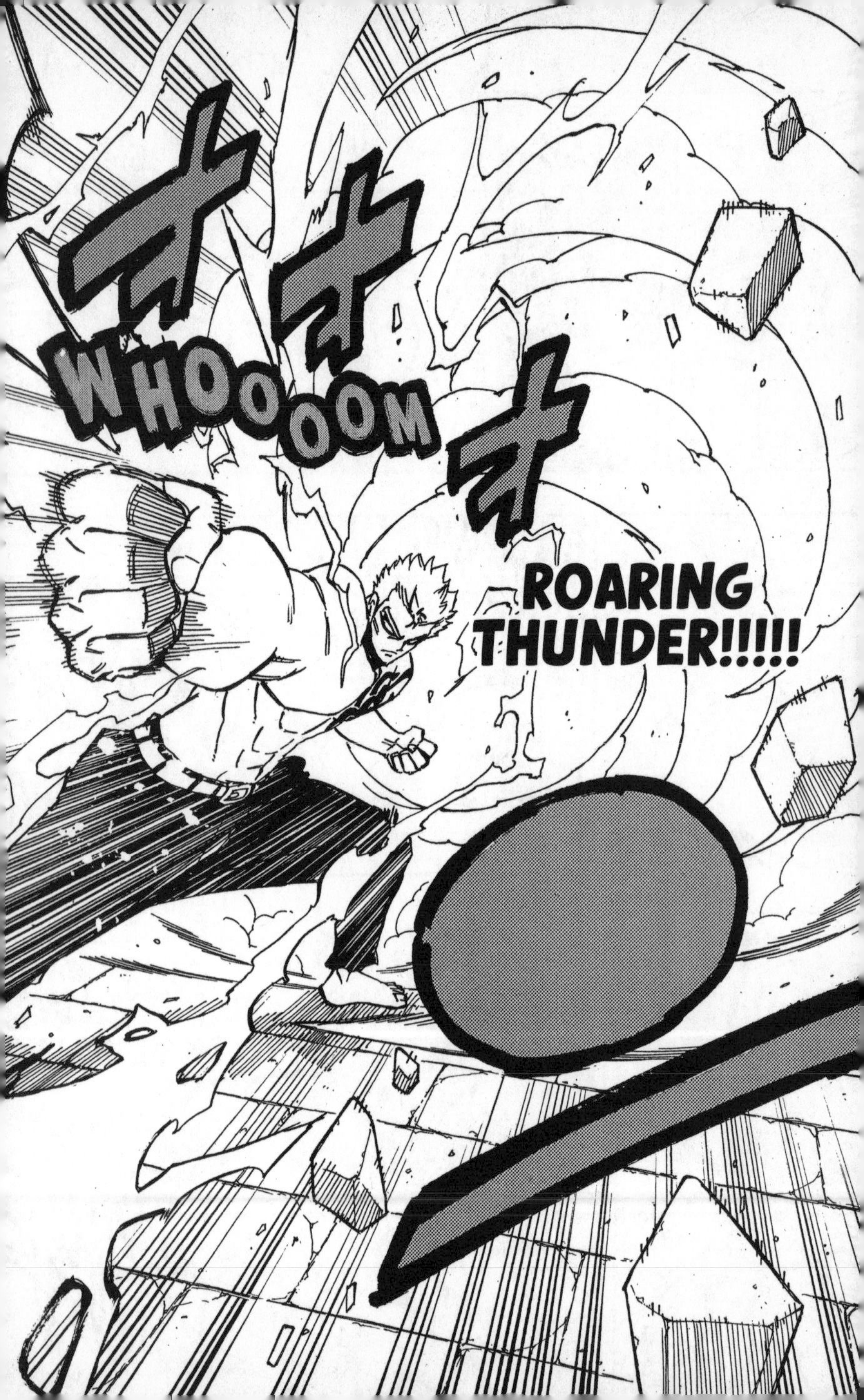
WHOOOOM
ROARING THUNDER!!!!!

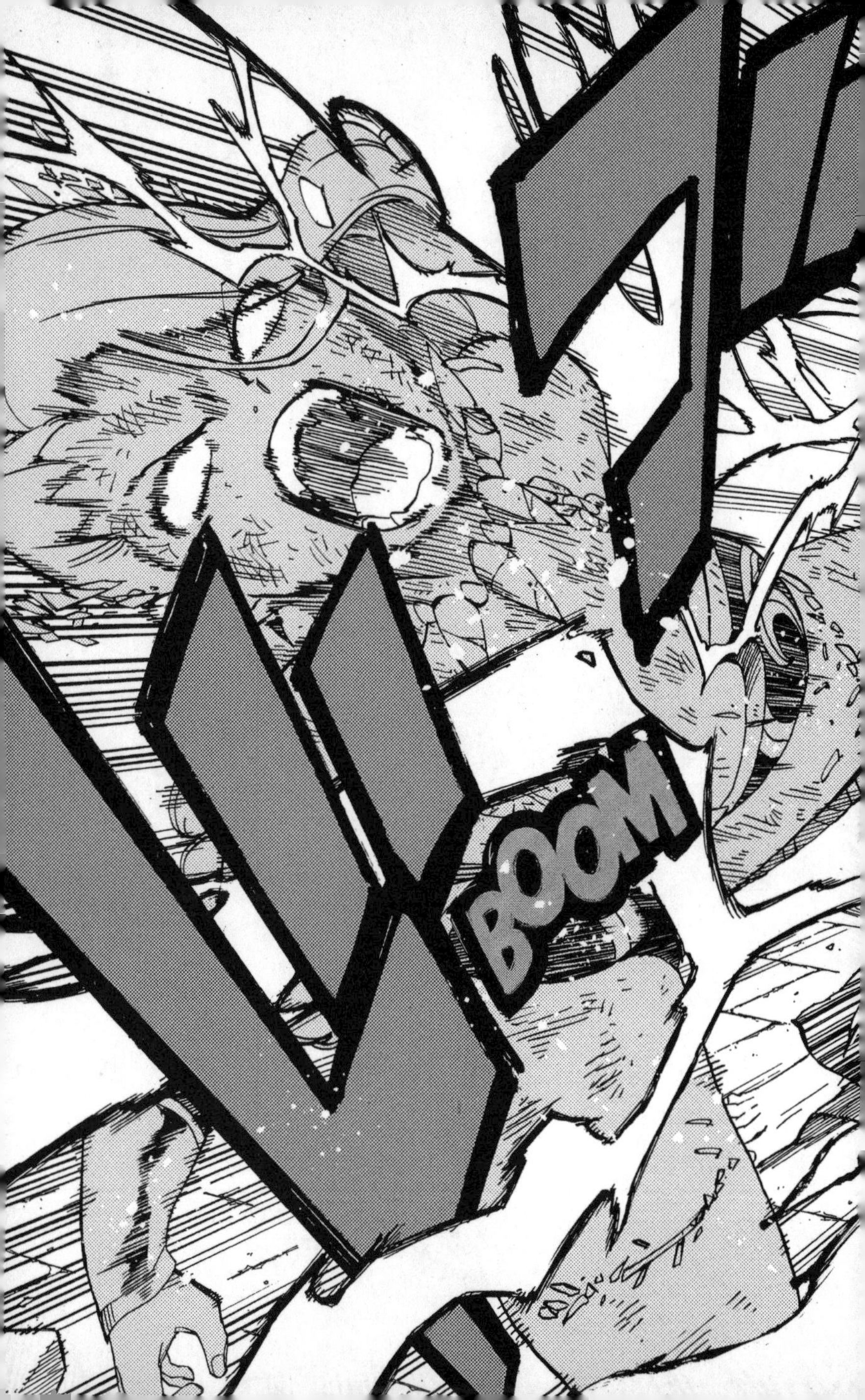
BOOM

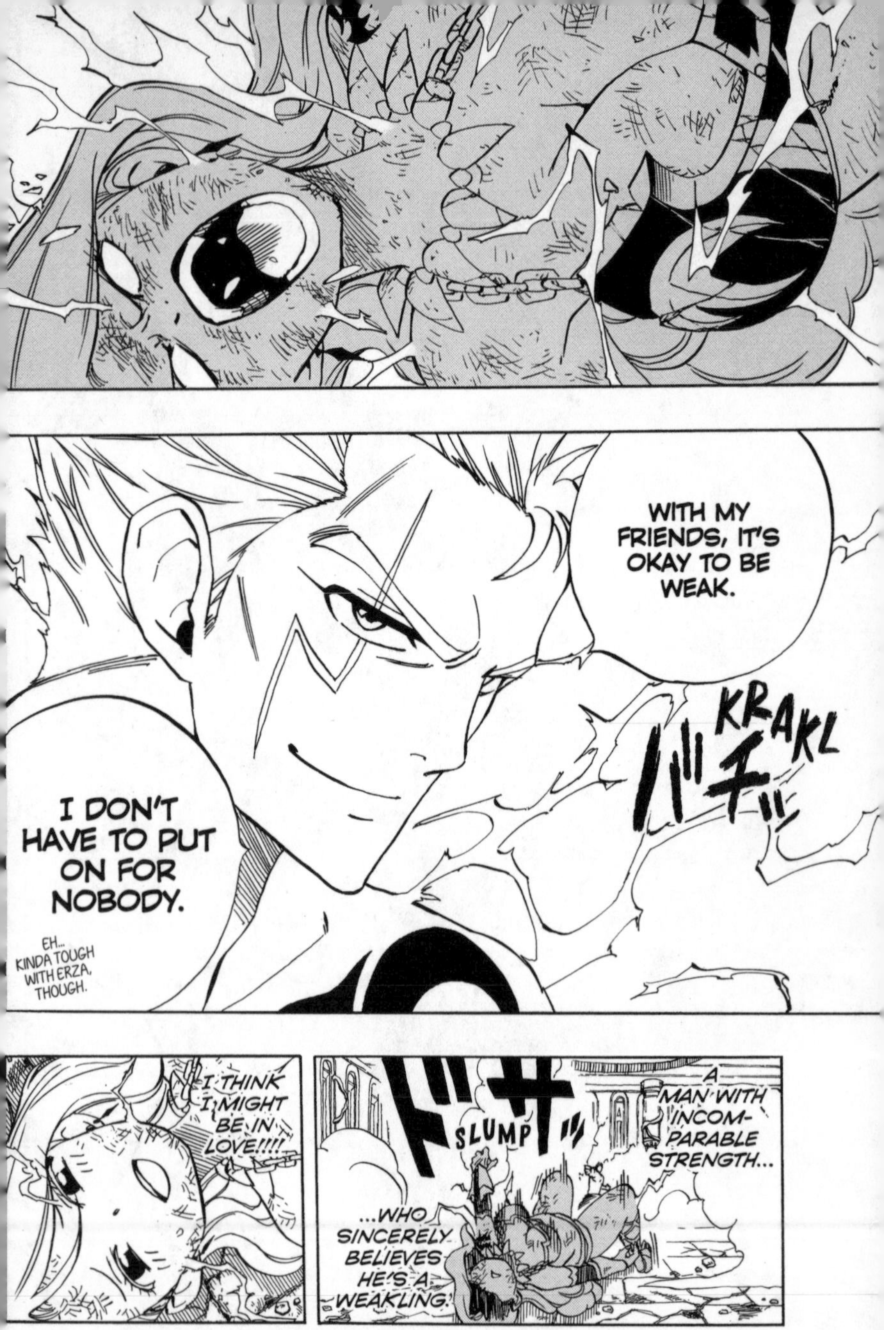
WITH MY FRIENDS, IT'S OKAY TO BE WEAK.
KRAKL
I DON'T HAVE TO PUT ON FOR NOBODY.
EH... KINDA TOUGH WITH ERZA, THOUGH.
A MAN WITH INCOM-PARABLE STRENGTH...
SLUMP
...WHO SINCERELY BELIEVES HE'S A WEAKLING.
I THINK I MIGHT BE IN LOVE!!!!

FAIRY TAIL 100 YEARS QUEST

Chapter 42: For the Guild, I Would

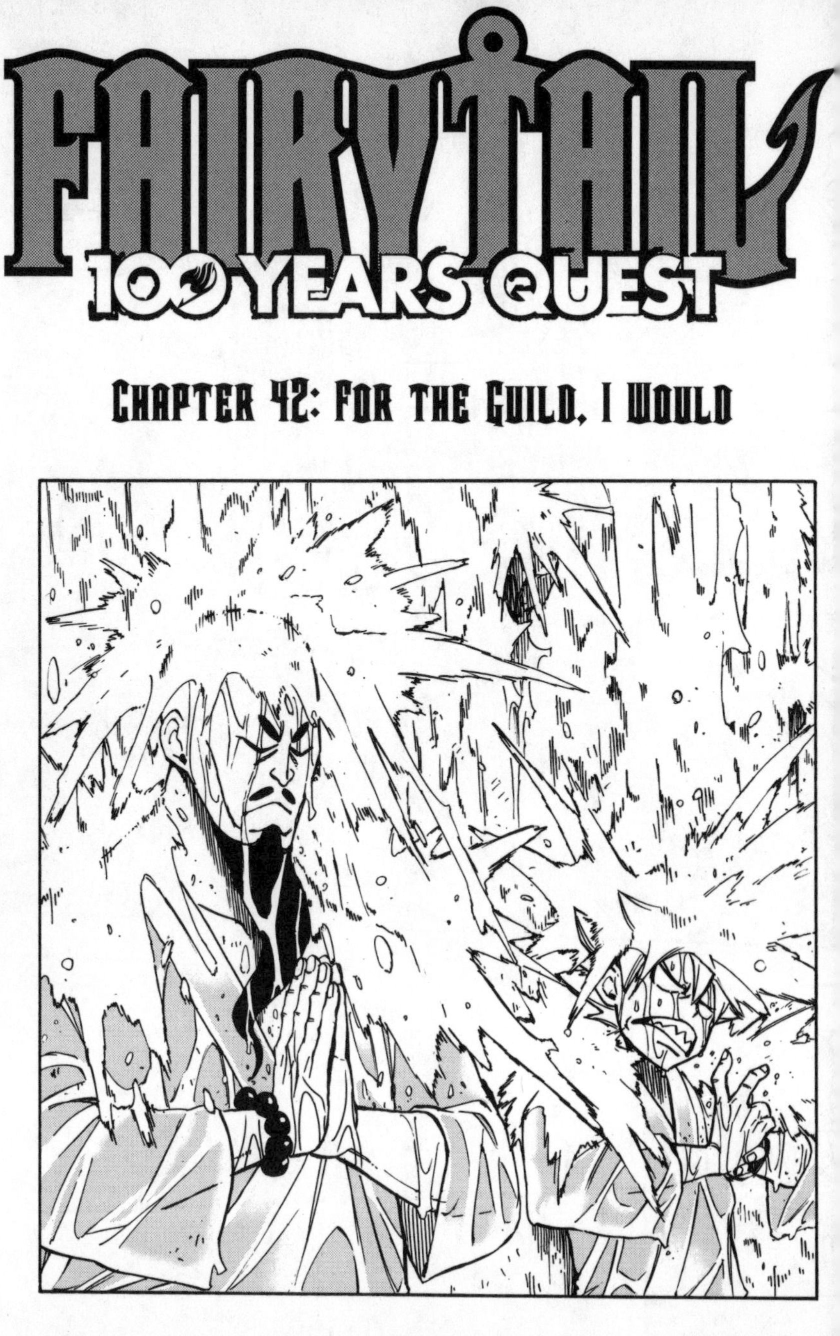

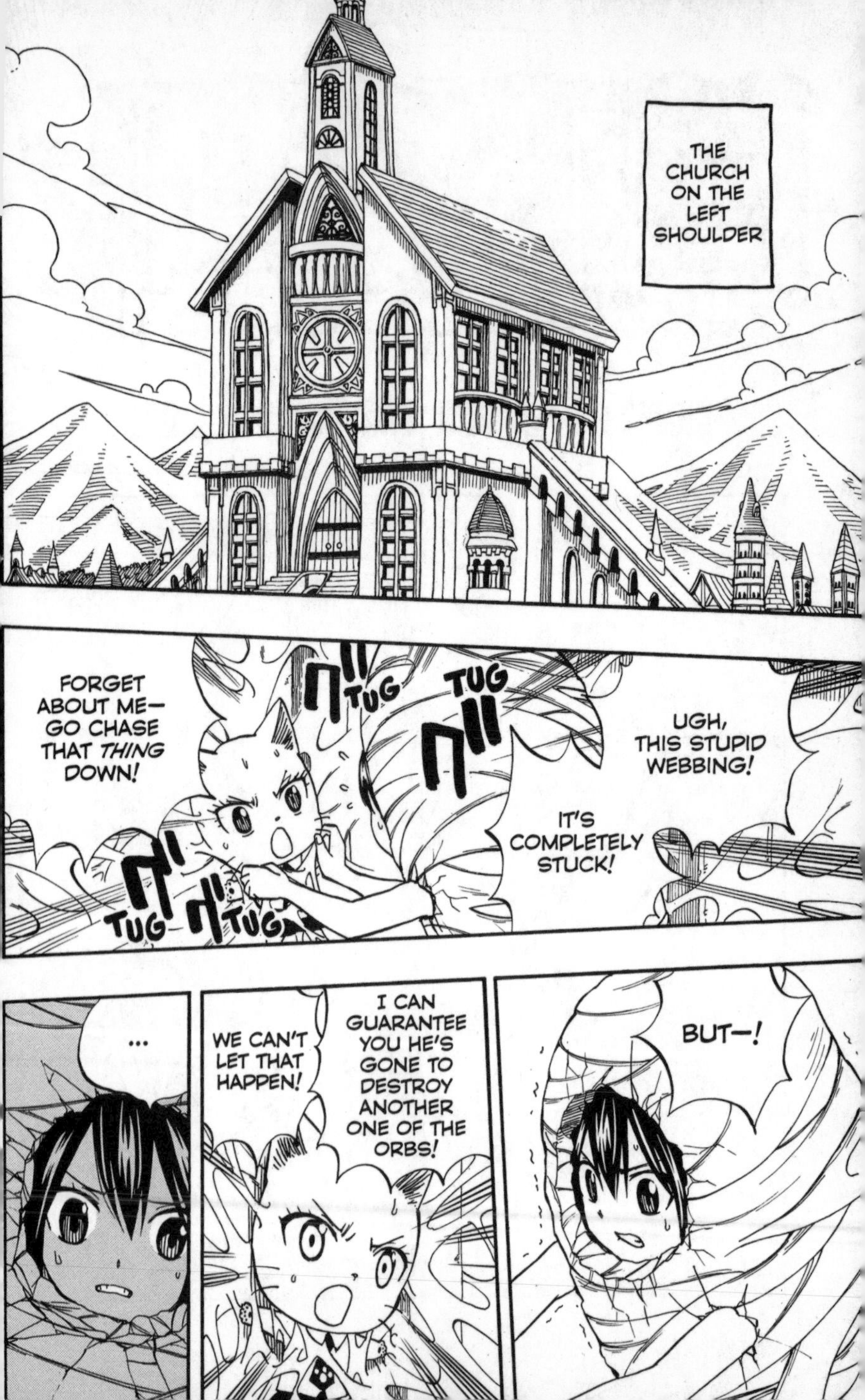
THE CHURCH ON THE LEFT SHOULDER
UGH, THIS STUPID WEBBING!
IT'S COMPLETELY STUCK!
TUG
TUG
FORGET ABOUT ME— GO CHASE THAT *THING* DOWN!
TUG
TUG
BUT—!
I CAN GUARANTEE YOU HE'S GONE TO DESTROY ANOTHER ONE OF THE ORBS!
WE CAN'T LET THAT HAPPEN!
...

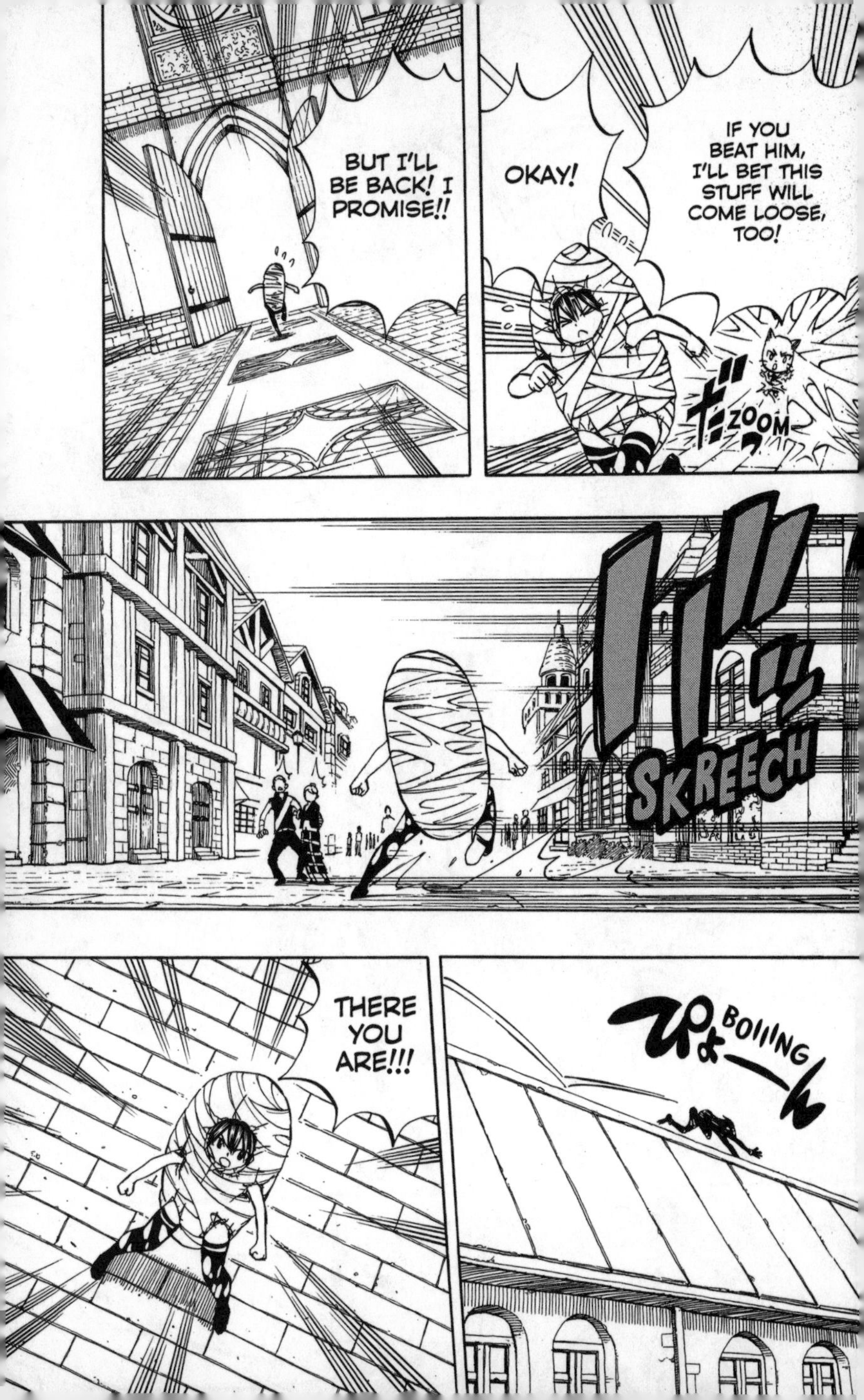
IF YOU BEAT HIM, I'LL BET THIS STUFF WILL COME LOOSE, TOO!
OKAY!
ZOOM
BUT I'LL BE BACK! I PROMISE!!
SKREECH
BOIIING
THERE YOU ARE!!!

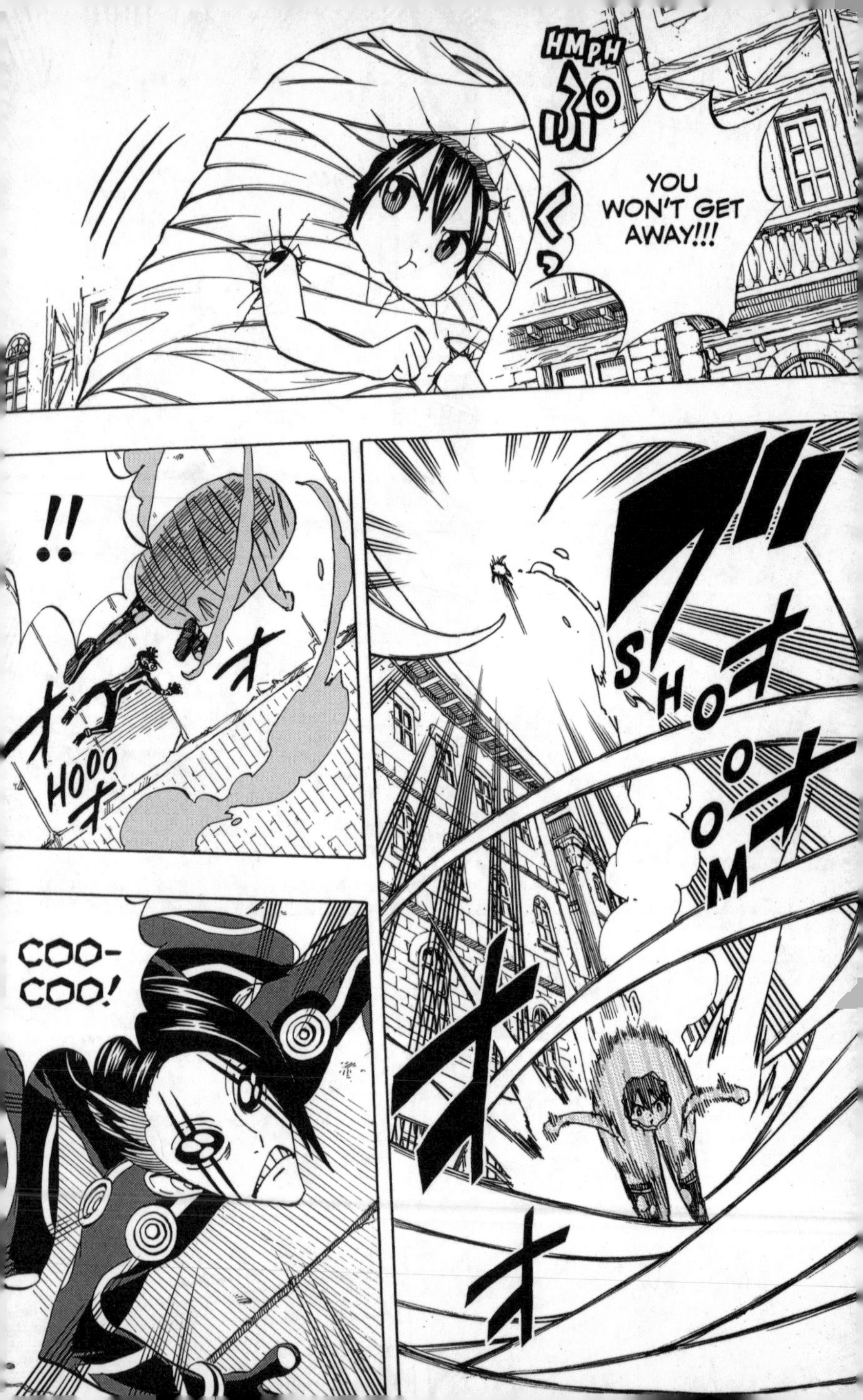
HMPH
YOU WON'T GET AWAY!!!
SHOOOOM
!!
HOOO
COO-COO!

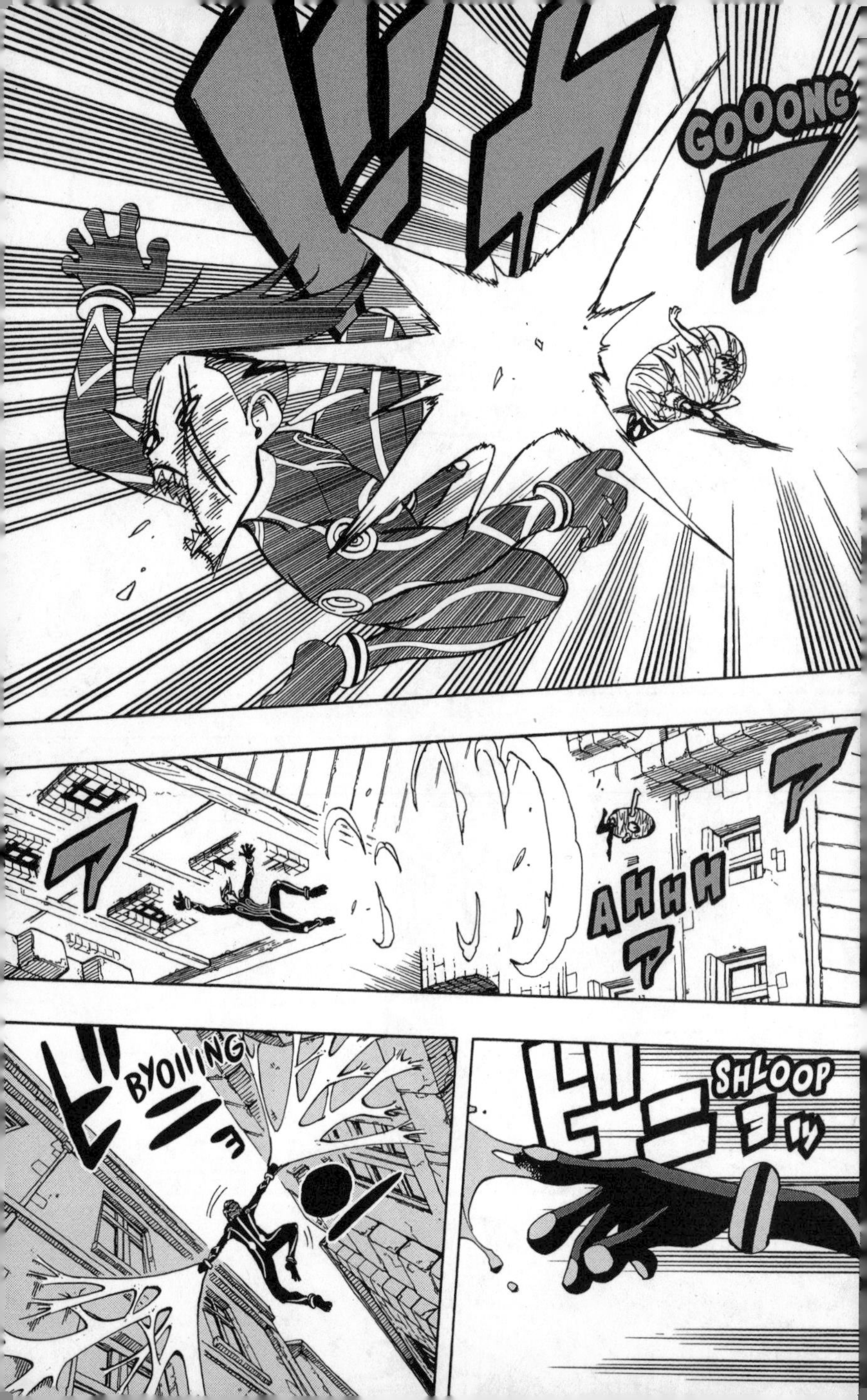
GOOONG
AHHH
SHLOOP
BYOIIIING

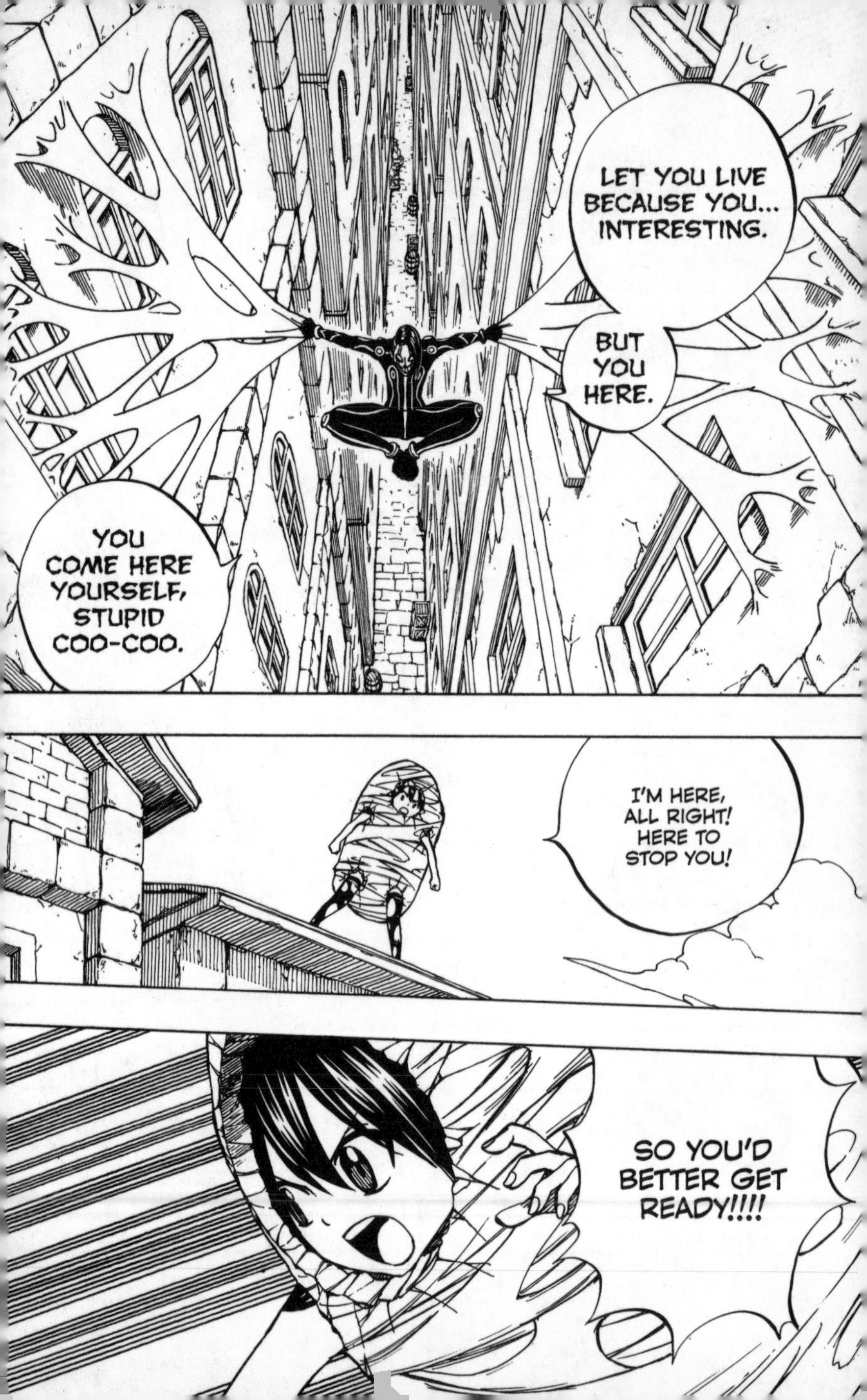
LET YOU LIVE BECAUSE YOU... INTERESTING.
BUT YOU HERE.
YOU COME HERE YOURSELF, STUPID COO-COO.
I'M HERE, ALL RIGHT! HERE TO STOP YOU!
SO YOU'D BETTER GET READY!!!!

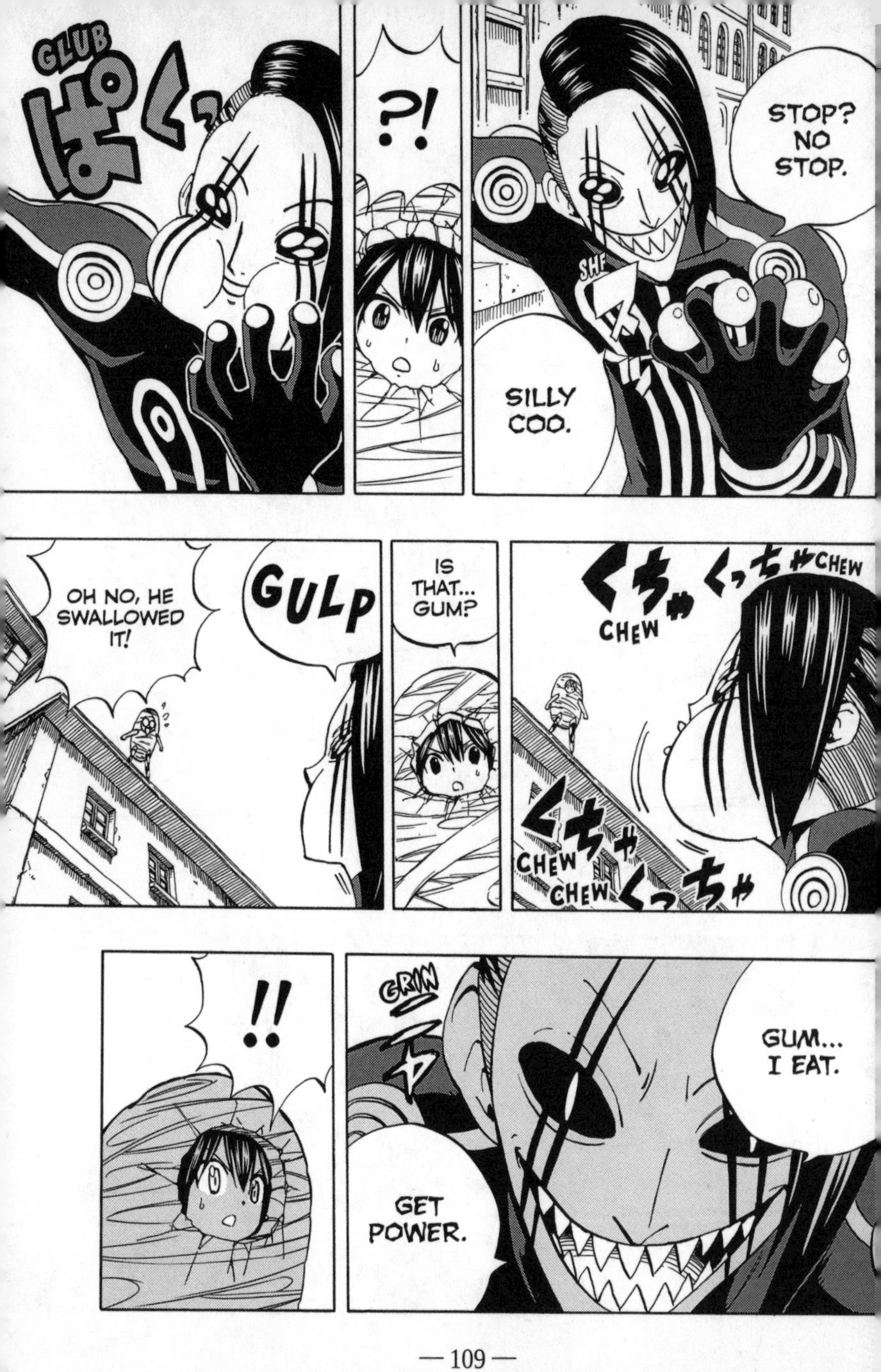
STOP? NO STOP.
SHF
SILLY COO.
?!
GLUB
ぱくっ
くちゃ
くっちゃ
CHEW
CHEW
くちゃ
くっちゃ
CHEW
CHEW
IS THAT... GUM?
GULP
OH NO, HE SWALLOWED IT!
GRIN
GUM... I EAT.
GET POWER.
!!

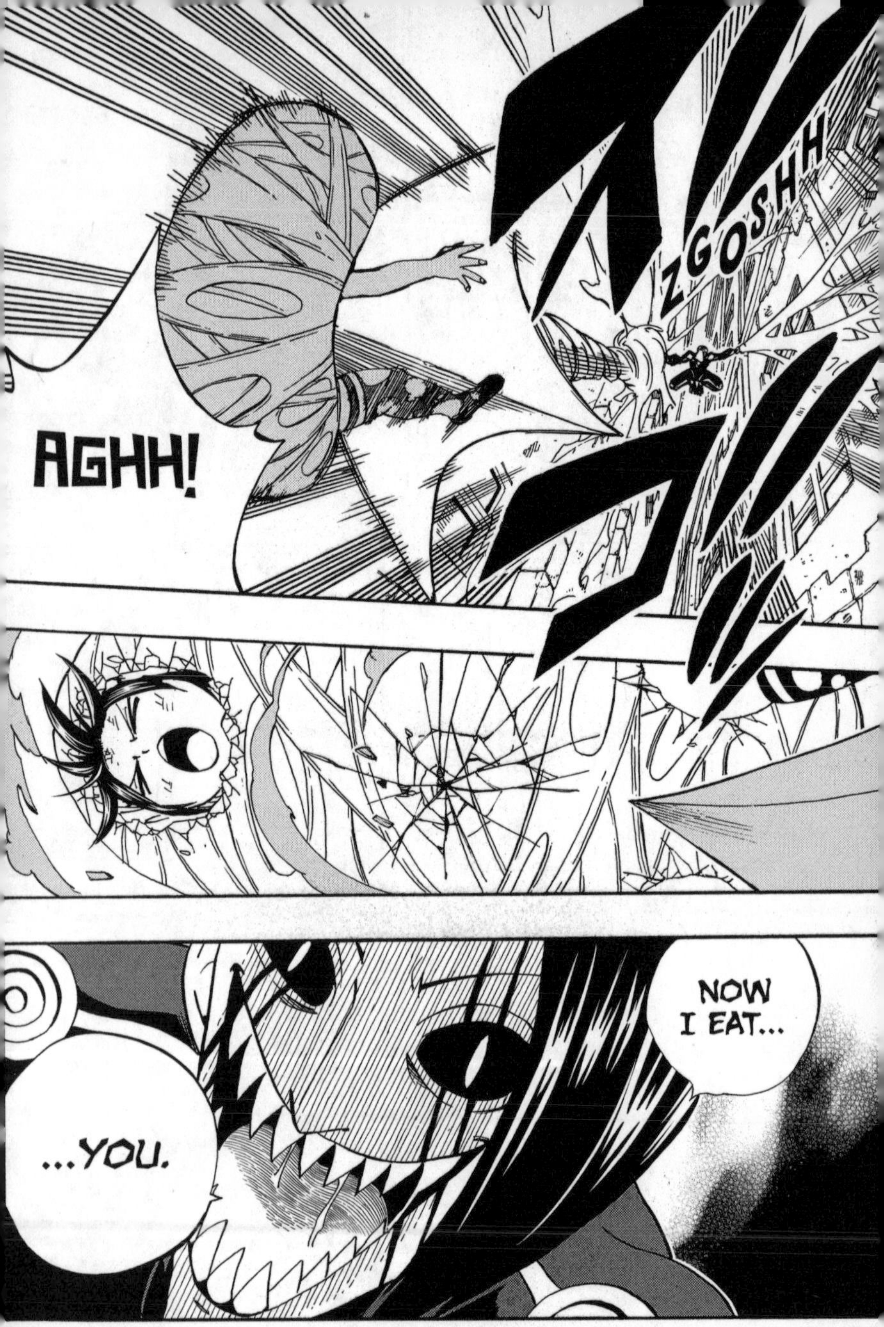
ZGOSHH
AGHH!
NOW I EAT...
...YOU.

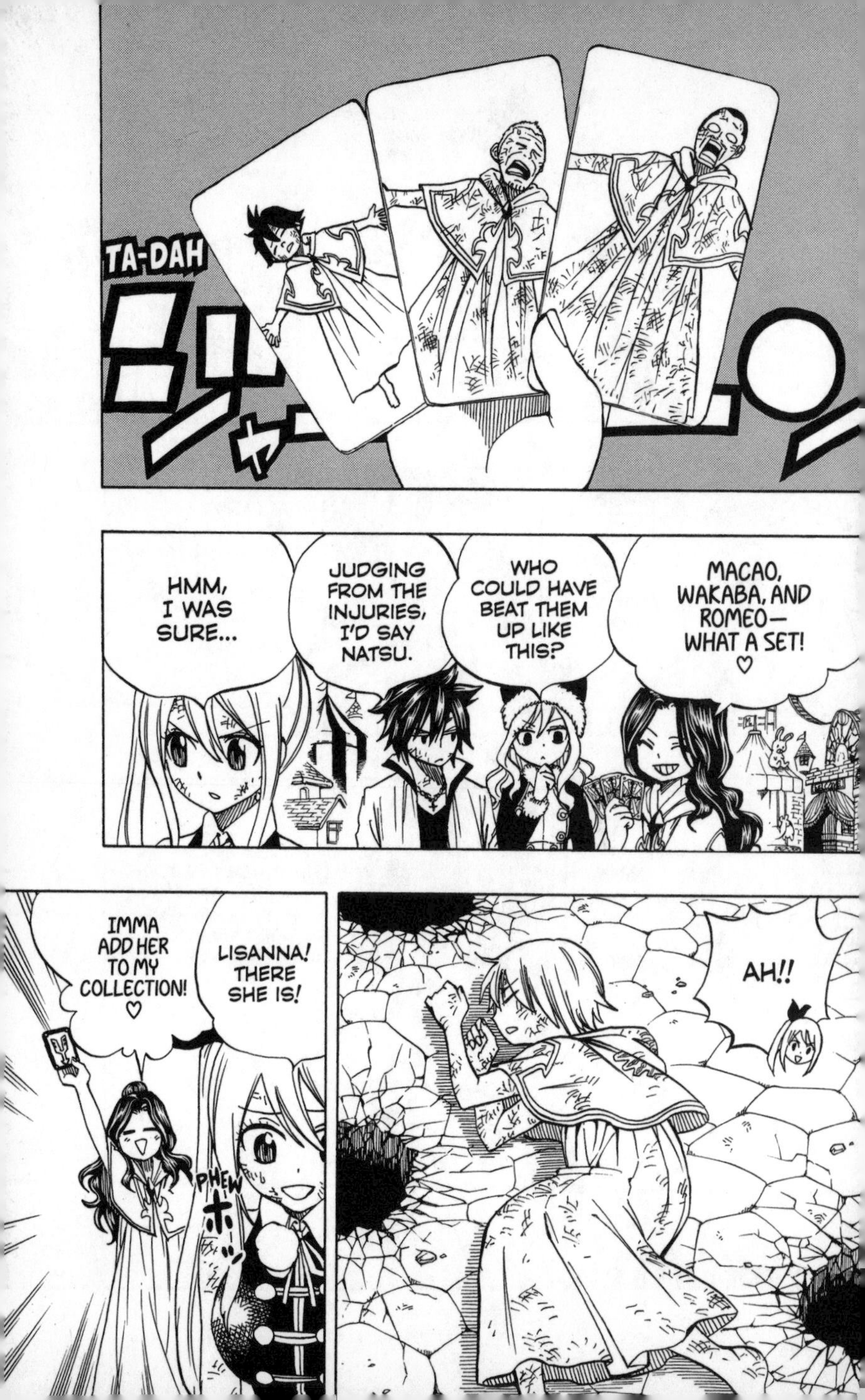
TA-DAH
MACAO, WAKABA, AND ROMEO— WHAT A SET! ♡
WHO COULD HAVE BEAT THEM UP LIKE THIS?
JUDGING FROM THE INJURIES, I'D SAY NATSU.
HMM, I WAS SURE...
AH!!
LISANNA! THERE SHE IS!
IMMA ADD HER TO MY COLLECTION! ♡
PHEW

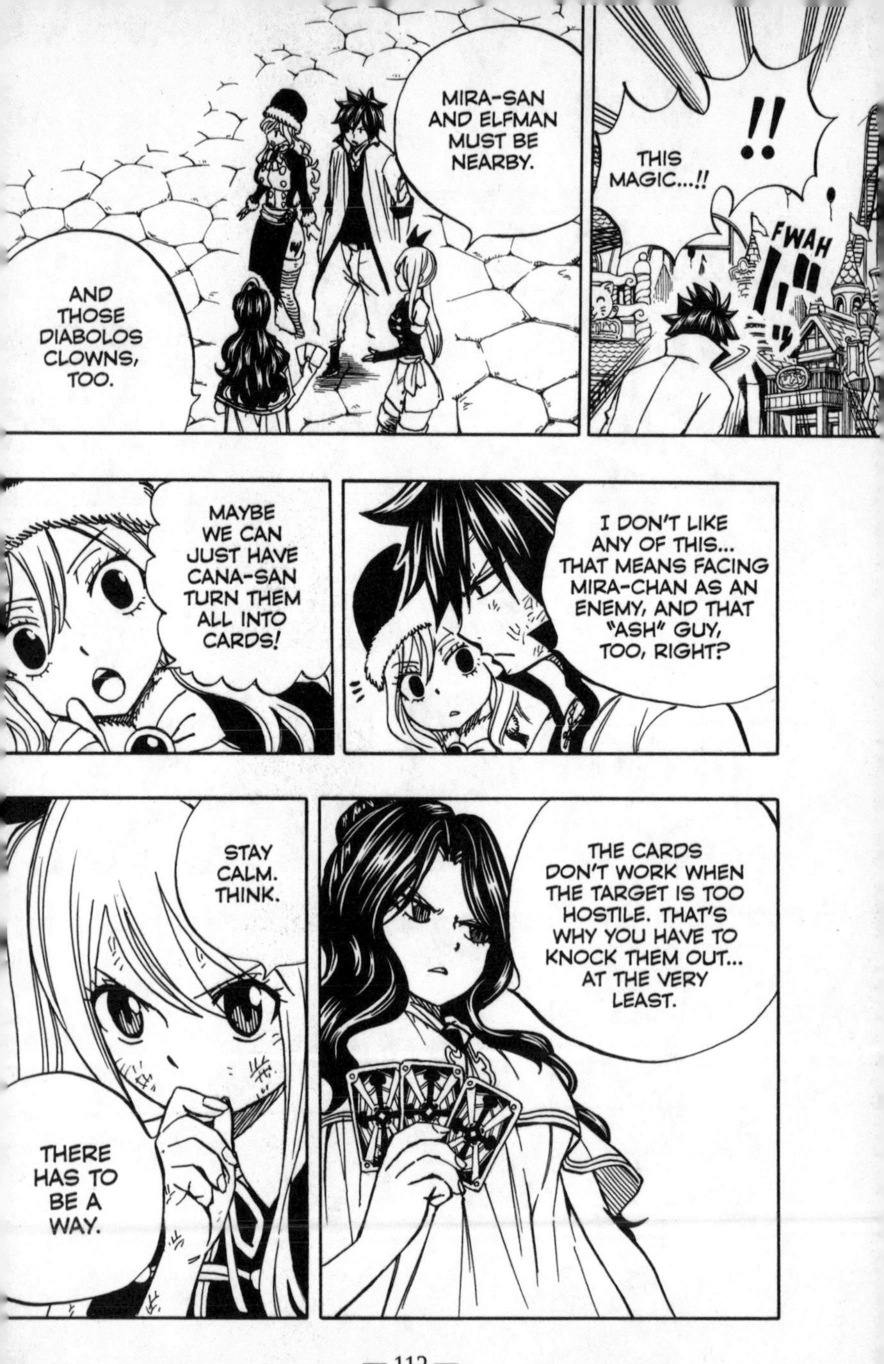
!!
THIS MAGIC...!!
FWAH
MIRA-SAN AND ELFMAN MUST BE NEARBY.
AND THOSE DIABOLOS CLOWNS, TOO.
I DON'T LIKE ANY OF THIS... THAT MEANS FACING MIRA-CHAN AS AN ENEMY, AND THAT "ASH" GUY, TOO, RIGHT?
MAYBE WE CAN JUST HAVE CANA-SAN TURN THEM ALL INTO CARDS!
THE CARDS DON'T WORK WHEN THE TARGET IS TOO HOSTILE. THAT'S WHY YOU HAVE TO KNOCK THEM OUT... AT THE VERY LEAST.
STAY CALM. THINK.
THERE HAS TO BE A WAY.

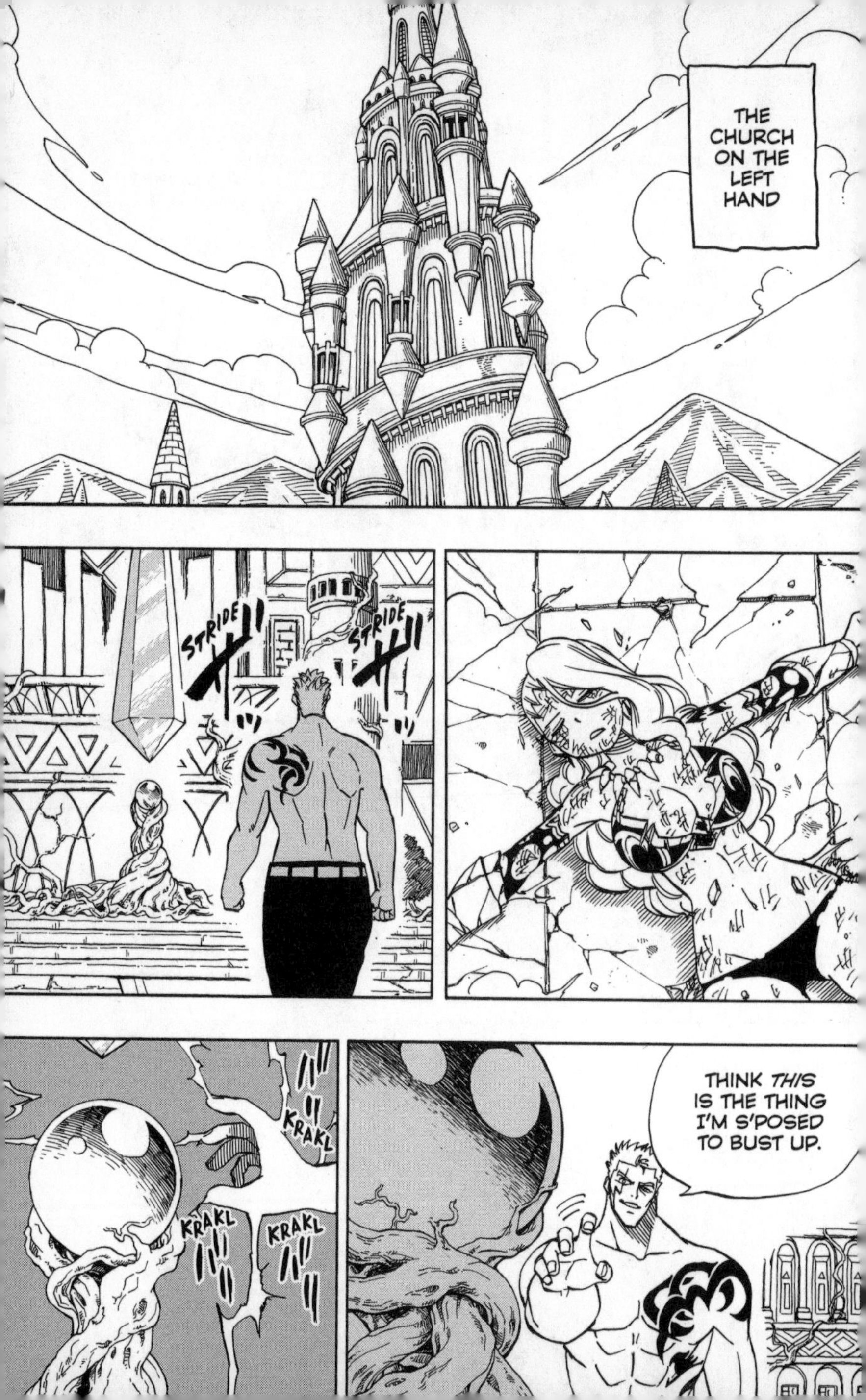
THE CHURCH ON THE LEFT HAND
STRIDE
STRIDE
THINK *THIS* IS THE THING I'M S'POSED TO BUST UP.
KRAKL
KRAKL
KRAKL

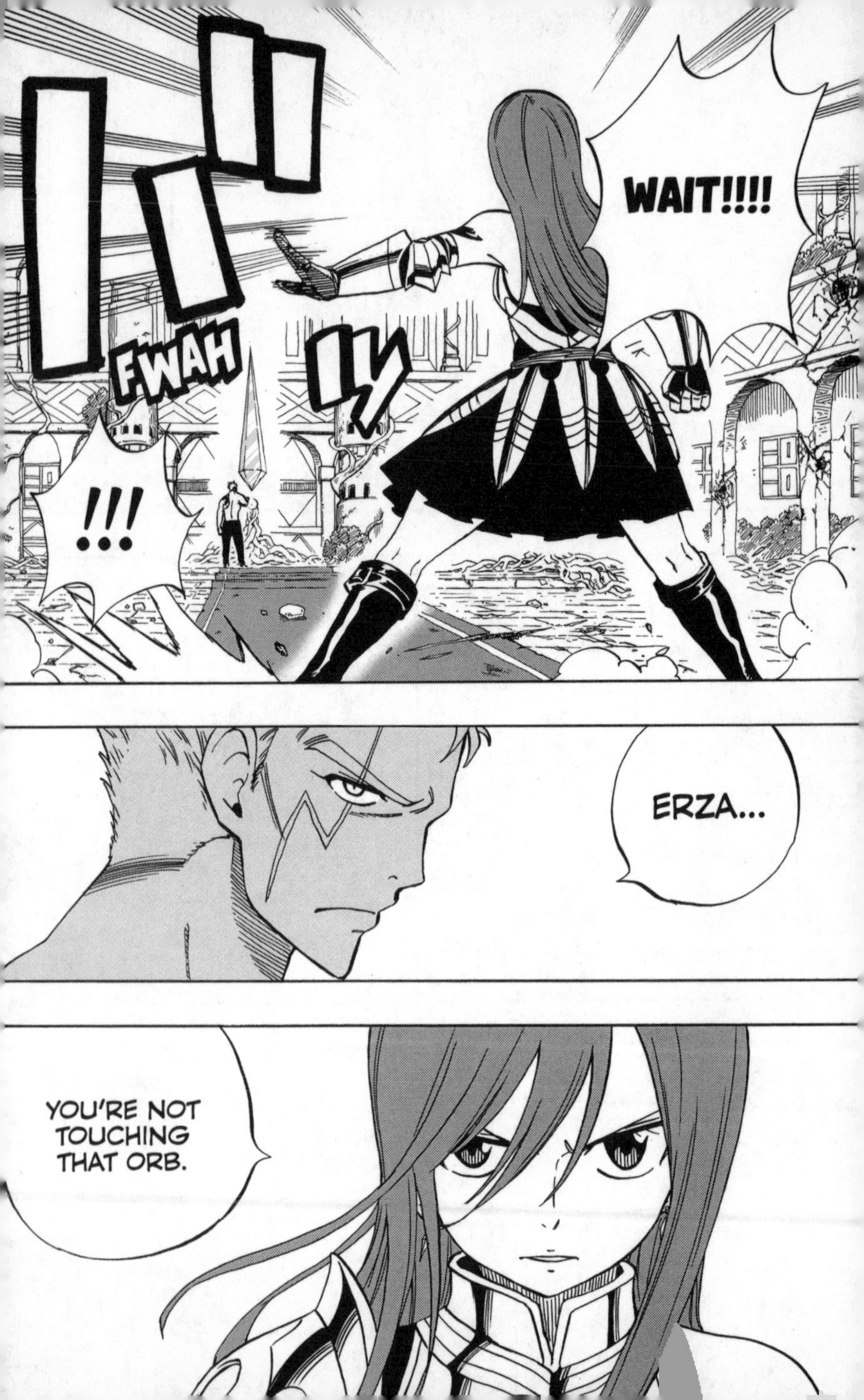
WAIT!!!!
FWAH
!!!
ERZA...
YOU'RE NOT TOUCHING THAT ORB.

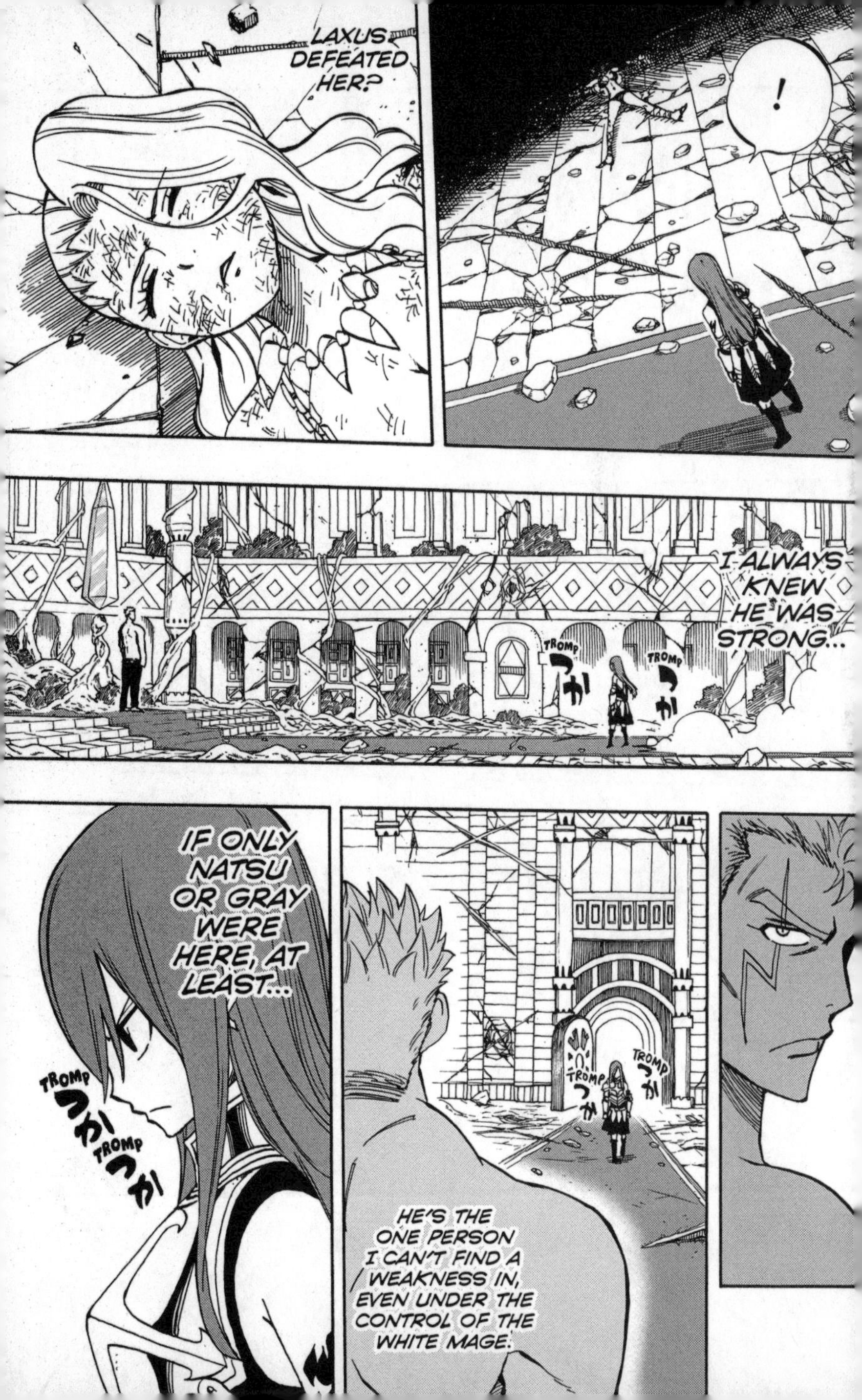
!
LAXUS DEFEATED HER?
I ALWAYS KNEW HE WAS STRONG...
TROMP つか
TROMP つか
TROMP つか
TROMP つか
HE'S THE ONE PERSON I CAN'T FIND A WEAKNESS IN, EVEN UNDER THE CONTROL OF THE WHITE MAGE.
IF ONLY NATSU OR GRAY WERE HERE, AT LEAST...
TROMP つか
TROMP つか

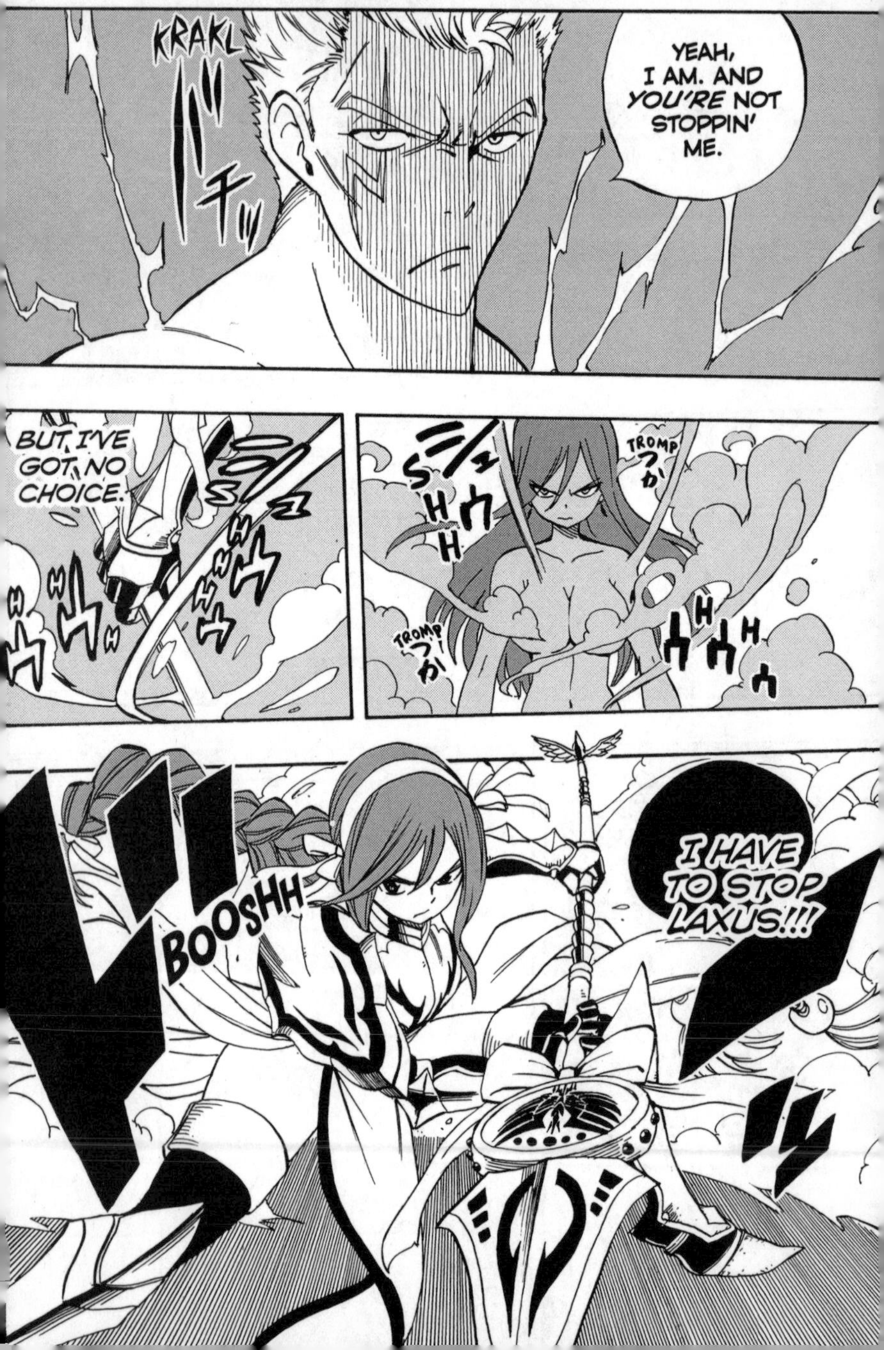
YEAH, I AM. AND YOU'RE NOT STOPPIN' ME.
KRAKL
TROMP
BUT I'VE GOT NO CHOICE.
I HAVE TO STOP LAXUS!!!
BOOSHH

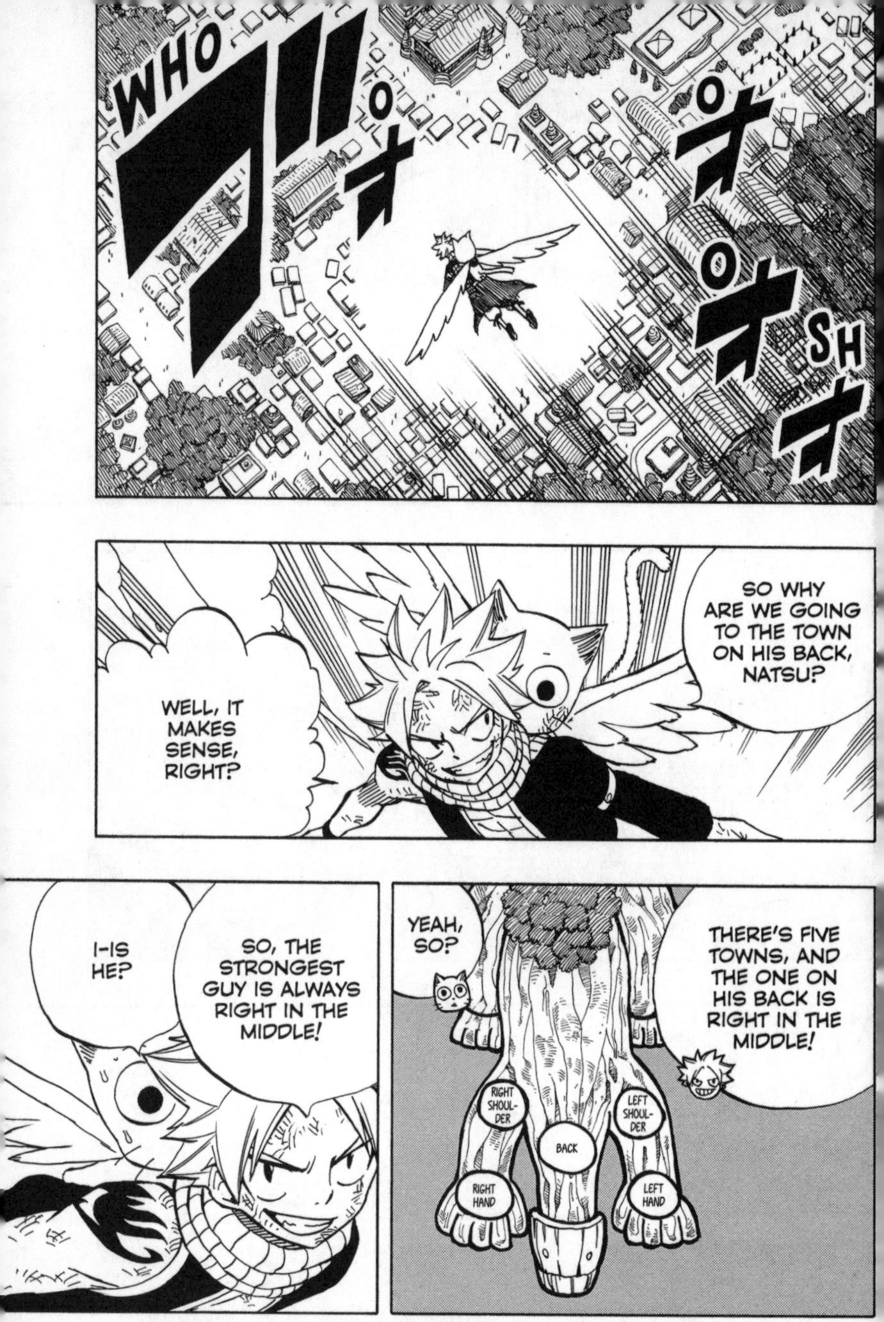
WHO
O
O
O
SH
SO WHY ARE WE GOING TO THE TOWN ON HIS BACK, NATSU?
WELL, IT MAKES SENSE, RIGHT?
THERE'S FIVE TOWNS, AND THE ONE ON HIS BACK IS RIGHT IN THE MIDDLE!
YEAH, SO?
LEFT SHOUL-DER
RIGHT SHOUL-DER
BACK
LEFT HAND
RIGHT HAND
SO, THE STRONGEST GUY IS ALWAYS RIGHT IN THE MIDDLE!
I-IS HE?

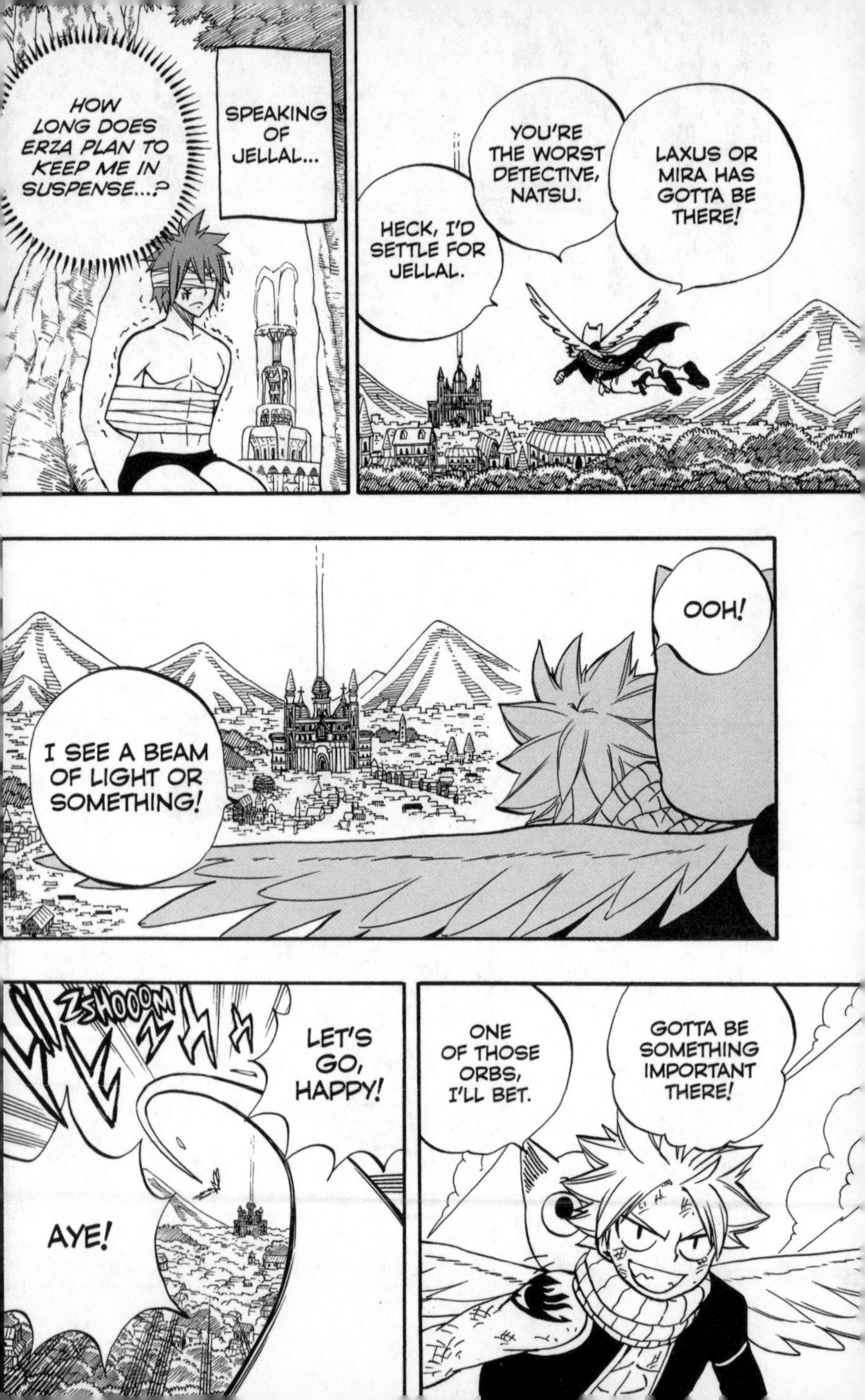
LAXUS OR MIRA HAS GOTTA BE THERE!
YOU'RE THE WORST DETECTIVE, NATSU.
HECK, I'D SETTLE FOR JELLAL.
SPEAKING OF JELLAL...
HOW LONG DOES ERZA PLAN TO KEEP ME IN SUSPENSE...?
OOH!
I SEE A BEAM OF LIGHT OR SOMETHING!
GOTTA BE SOMETHING IMPORTANT THERE!
ONE OF THOSE ORBS, I'LL BET.
ZSHOOOM
LET'S GO, HAPPY!
AYE!

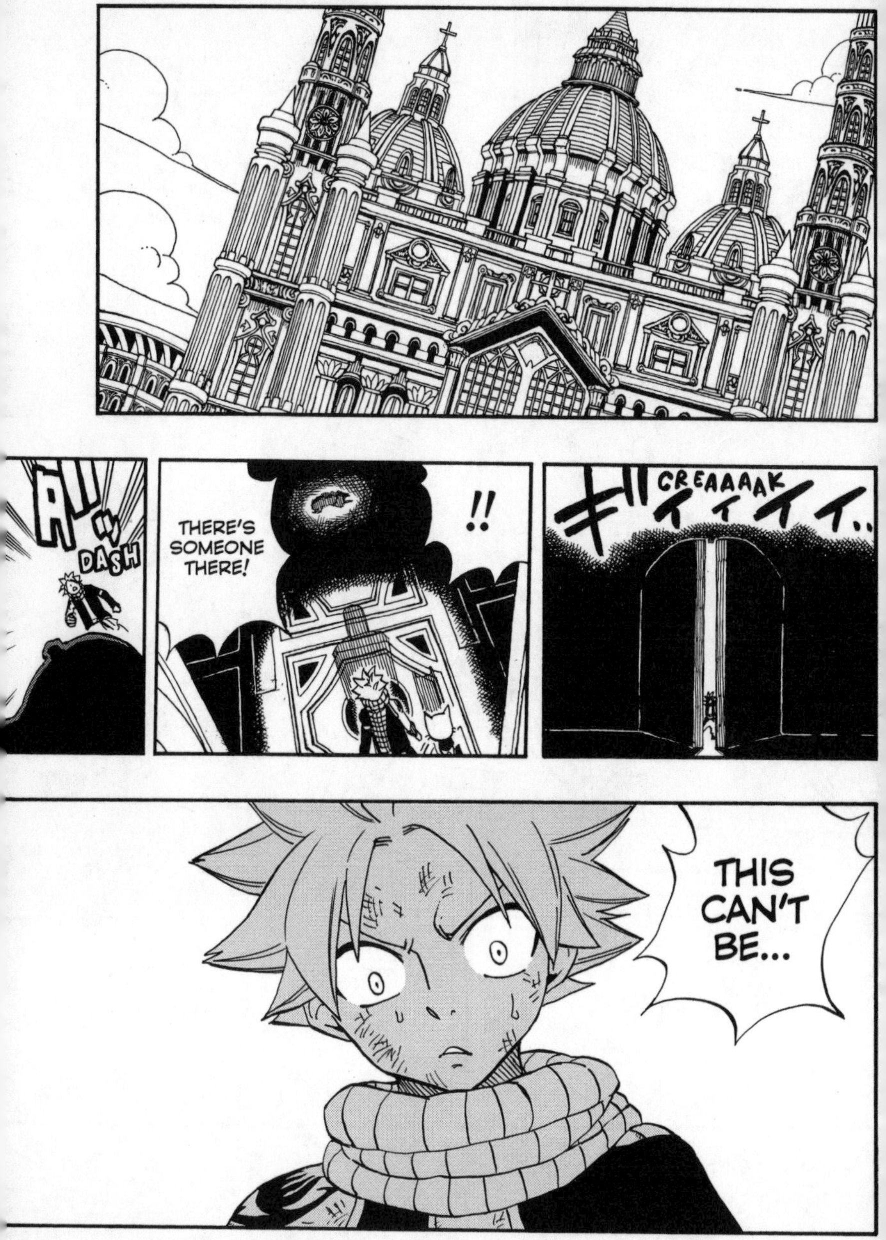
CREAAAK
!!
THERE'S SOMEONE THERE!
DASH
THIS CAN'T BE...

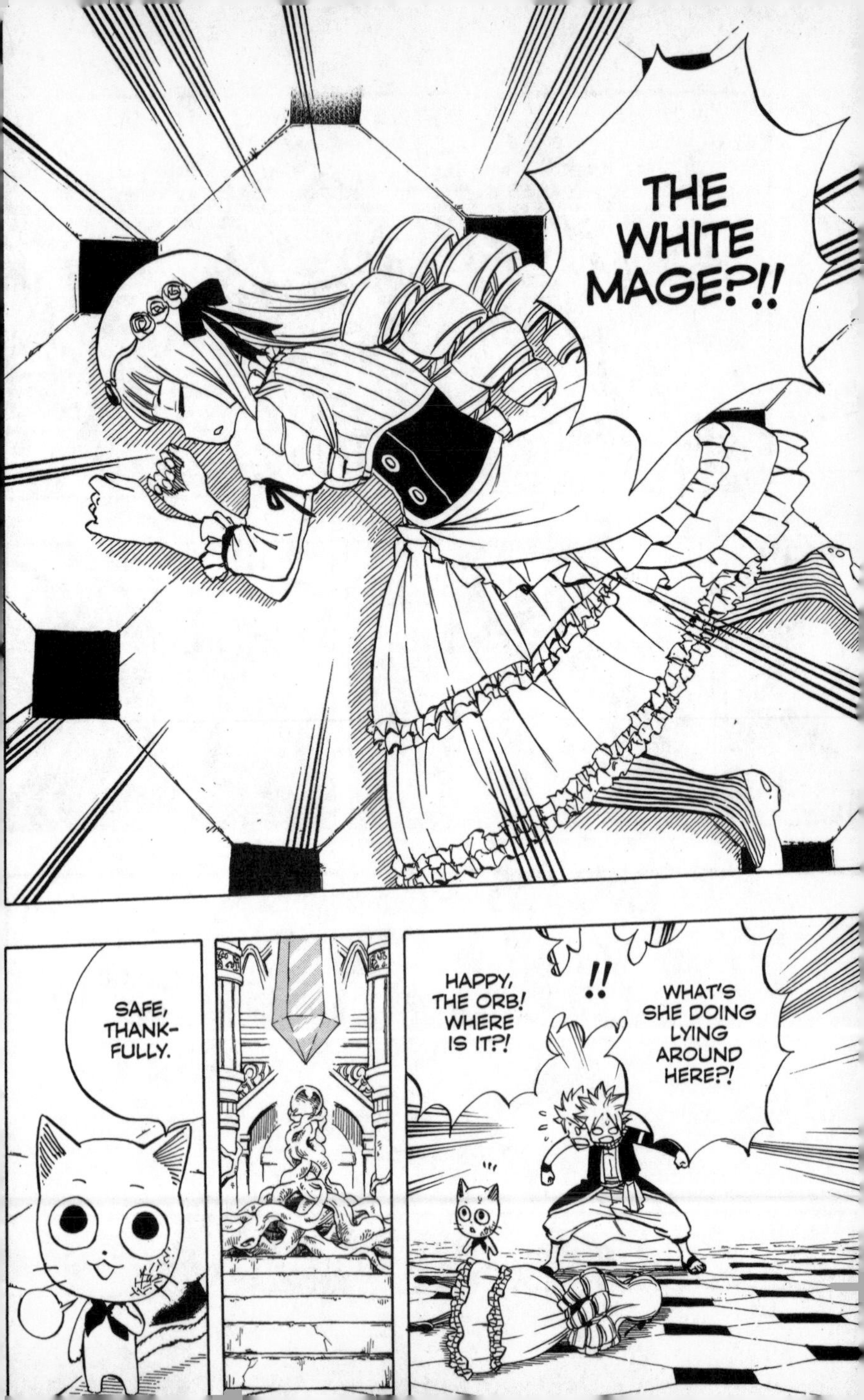
THE WHITE MAGE?!!
WHAT'S SHE DOING LYING AROUND HERE?!
!!
HAPPY, THE ORB! WHERE IS IT?!
SAFE, THANK-FULLY.

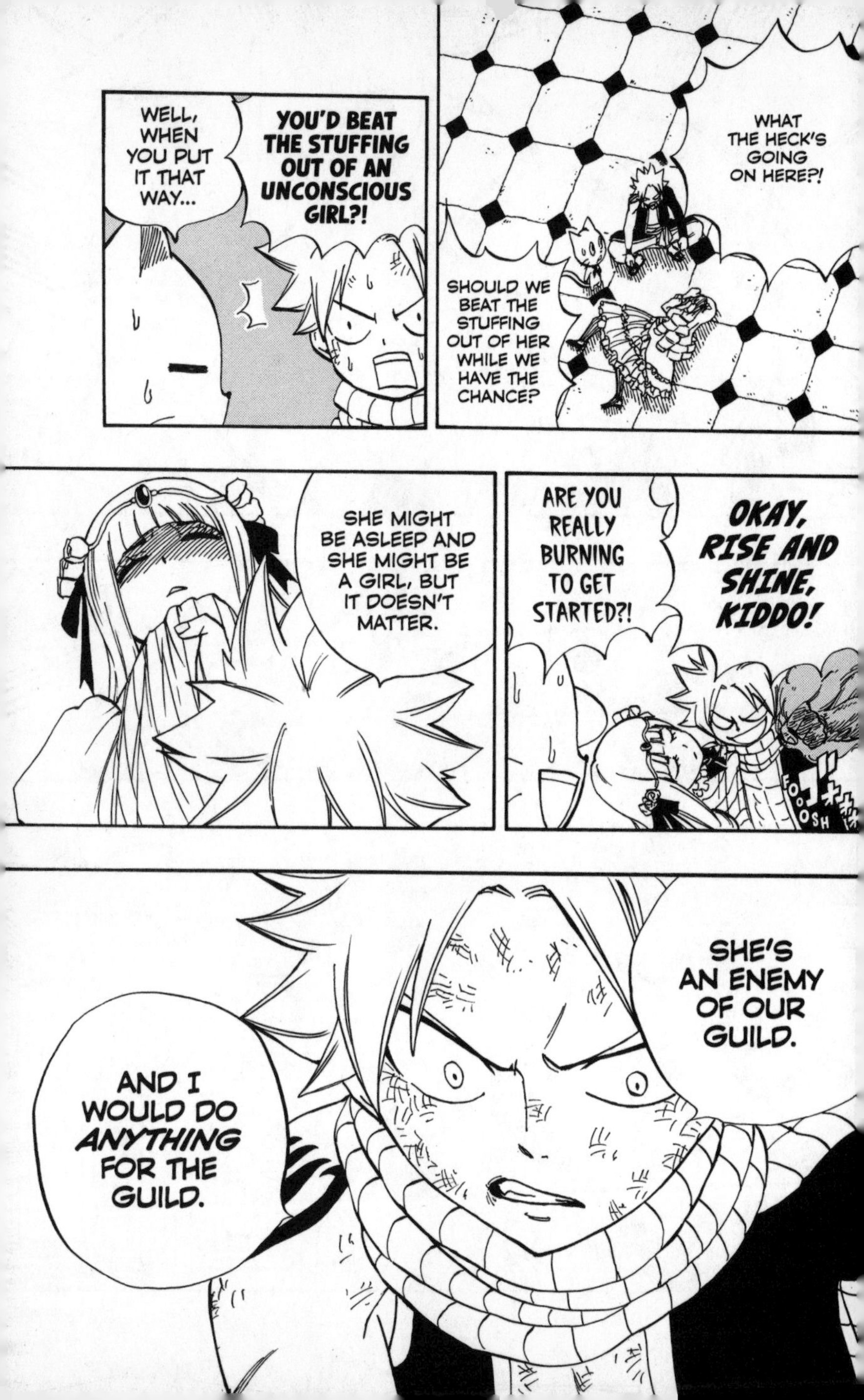
WHAT THE HECK'S GOING ON HERE?!
SHOULD WE BEAT THE STUFFING OUT OF HER WHILE WE HAVE THE CHANCE?
YOU'D BEAT THE STUFFING OUT OF AN UNCONSCIOUS GIRL?!
WELL, WHEN YOU PUT IT THAT WAY...
OKAY, RISE AND SHINE, KIDDO!
ARE YOU REALLY BURNING TO GET STARTED?!
FOOOSH
SHE MIGHT BE ASLEEP AND SHE MIGHT BE A GIRL, BUT IT DOESN'T MATTER.
SHE'S AN ENEMY OF OUR GUILD.
AND I WOULD DO *ANYTHING* FOR THE GUILD.

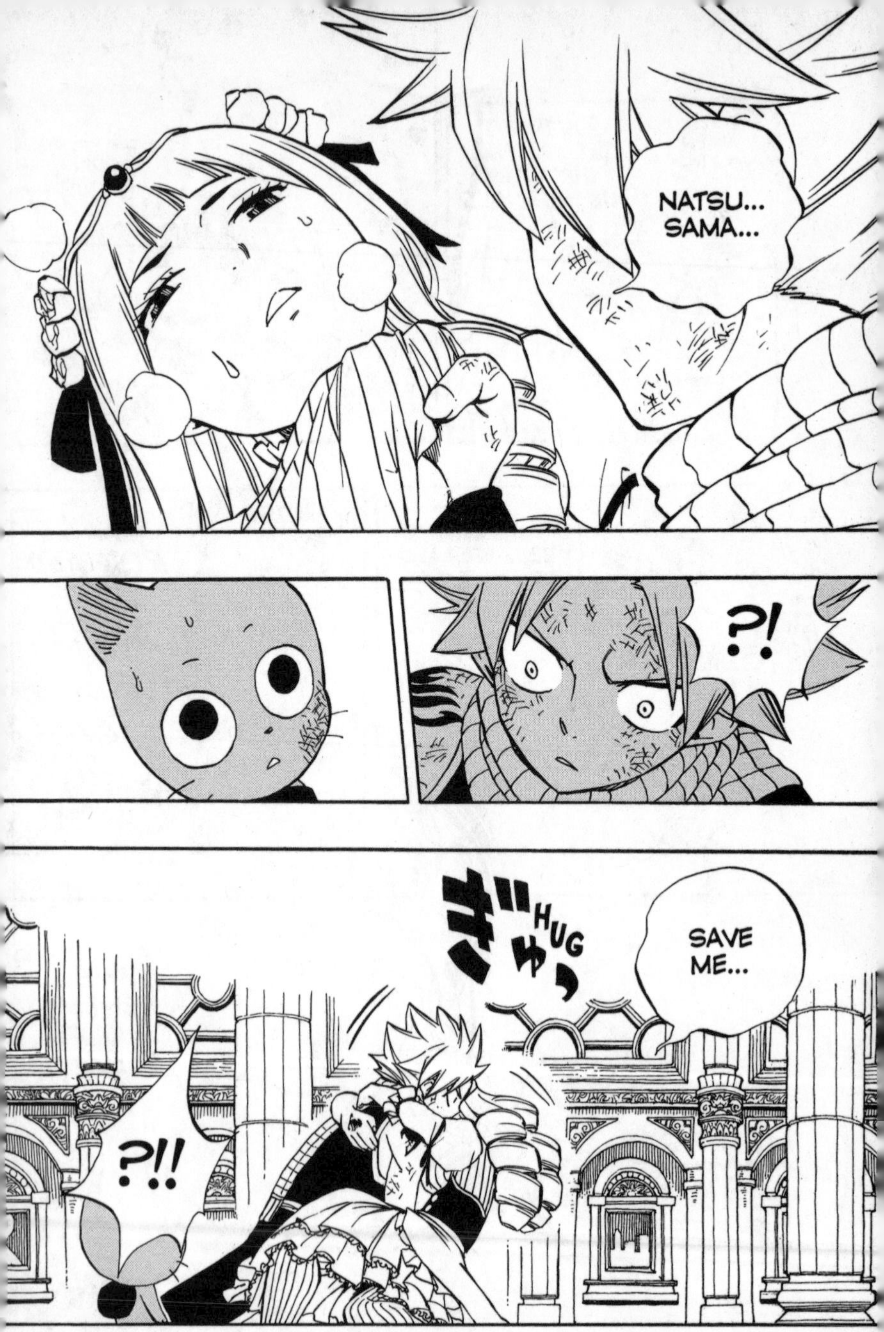
NATSU... SAMA...
?!
SAVE ME...
ぎゅっ
HUG
?!!

FAIRY TAIL 100 YEARS QUEST

Chapter 43: Mistakes & Misapprehensions

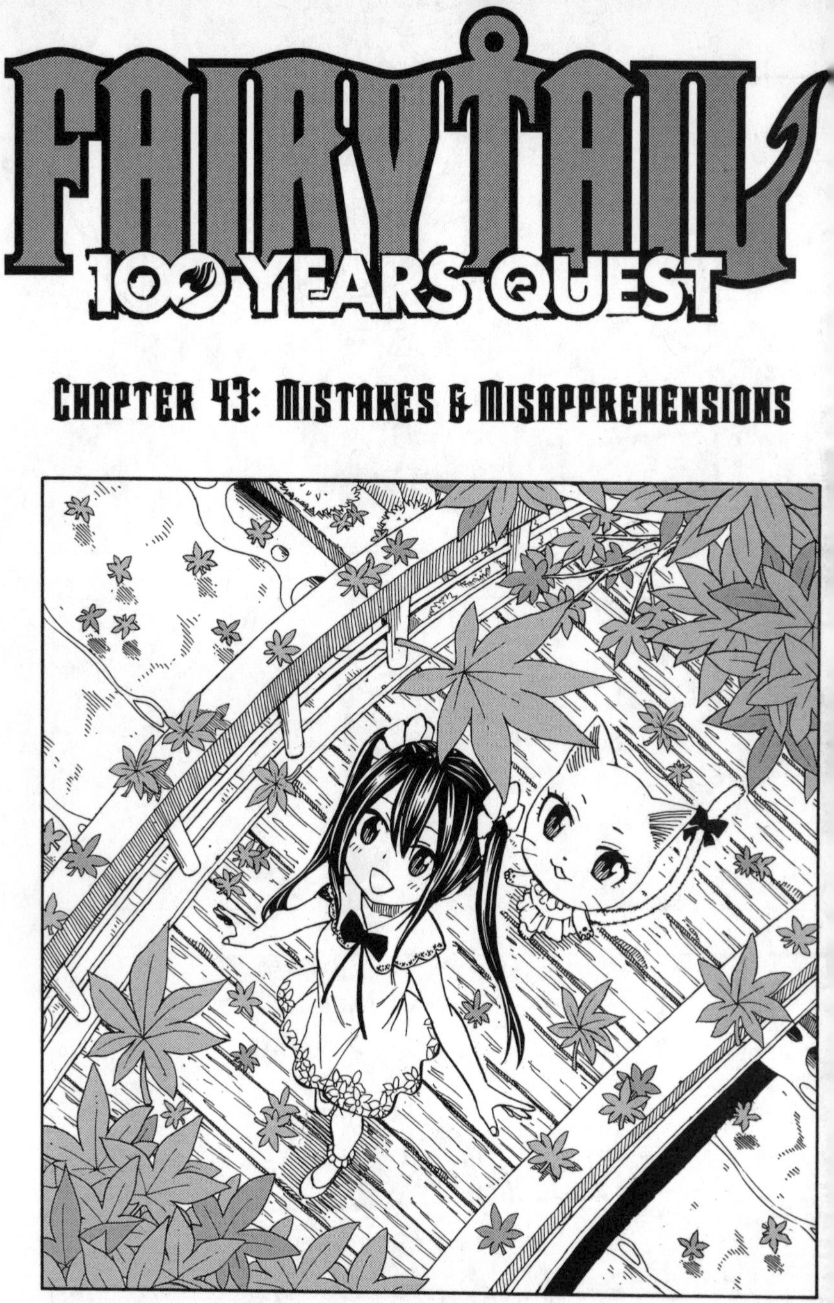

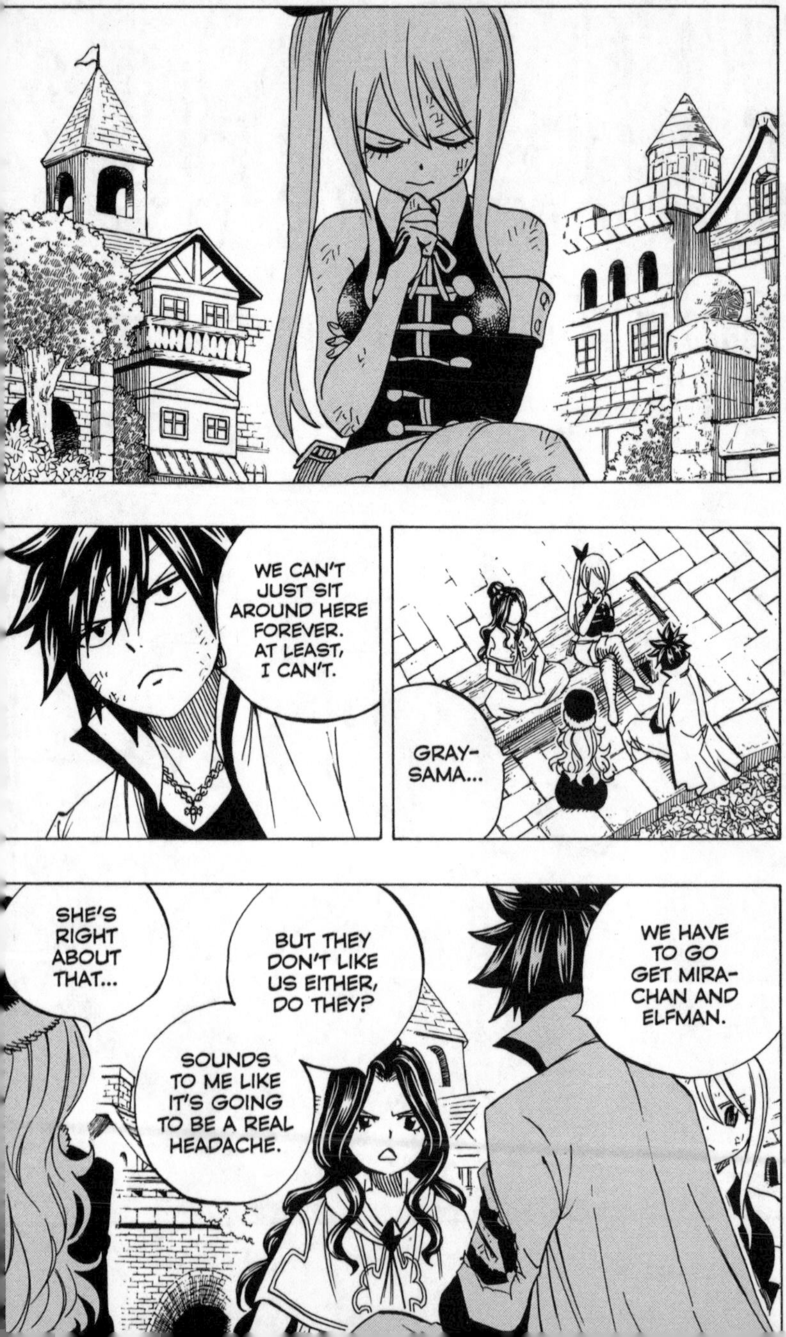
GRAY-SAMA...
WE CAN'T JUST SIT AROUND HERE FOREVER. AT LEAST, I CAN'T.
WE HAVE TO GO GET MIRA-CHAN AND ELFMAN.
SHE'S RIGHT ABOUT THAT...
BUT THEY DON'T LIKE US EITHER, DO THEY?
SOUNDS TO ME LIKE IT'S GOING TO BE A REAL HEADACHE.

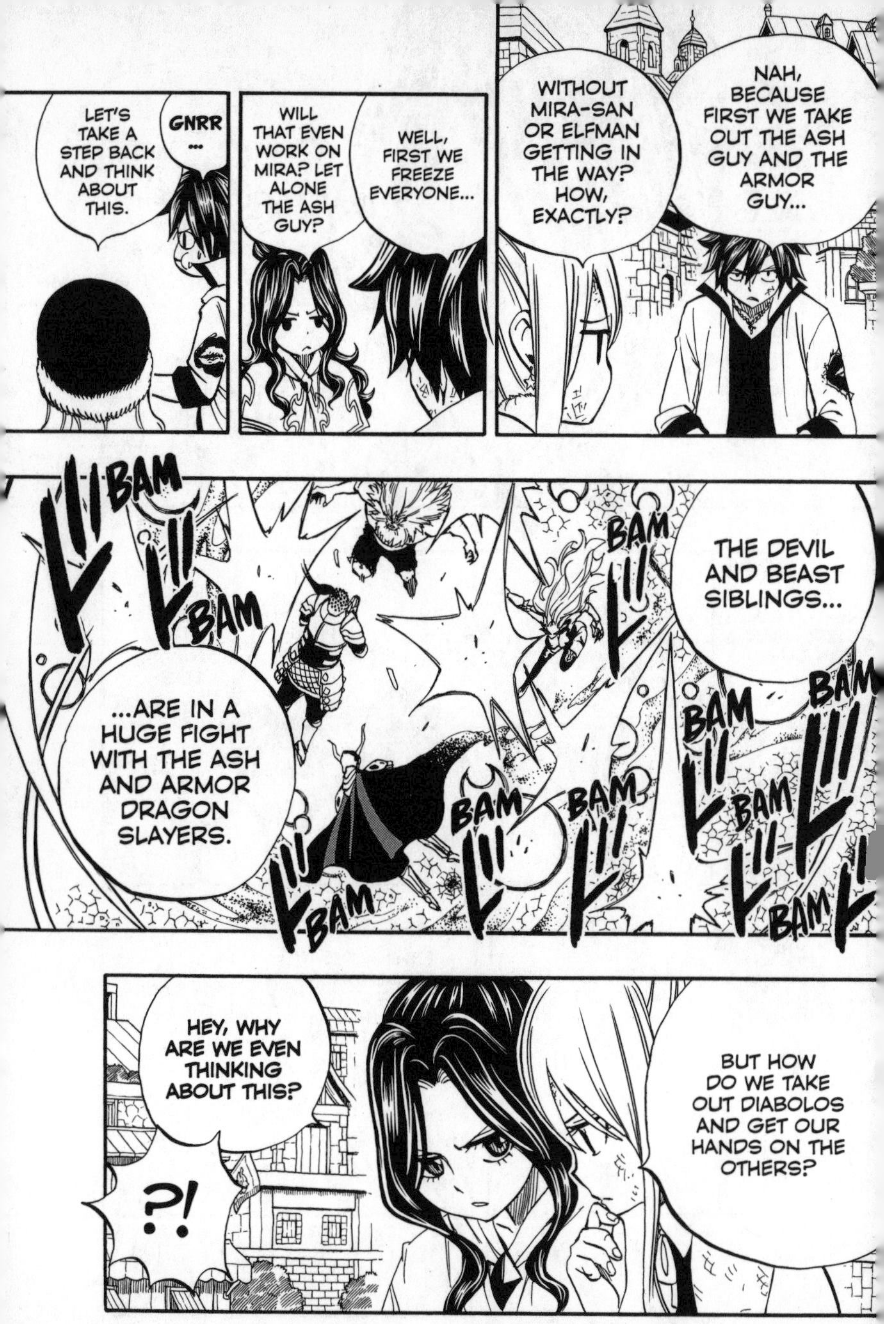
NAH, BECAUSE FIRST WE TAKE OUT THE ASH GUY AND THE ARMOR GUY...
WITHOUT MIRA-SAN OR ELFMAN GETTING IN THE WAY? HOW, EXACTLY?
WELL, FIRST WE FREEZE EVERYONE...
WILL THAT EVEN WORK ON MIRA? LET ALONE THE ASH GUY?
GNRR...
LET'S TAKE A STEP BACK AND THINK ABOUT THIS.
THE DEVIL AND BEAST SIBLINGS...
BAM
BAM
BAM
BAM
BAM
BAM
BAM
BAM
BAM
BAM
...ARE IN A HUGE FIGHT WITH THE ASH AND ARMOR DRAGON SLAYERS.
BUT HOW DO WE TAKE OUT DIABOLOS AND GET OUR HANDS ON THE OTHERS?
HEY, WHY ARE WE EVEN THINKING ABOUT THIS?
?!

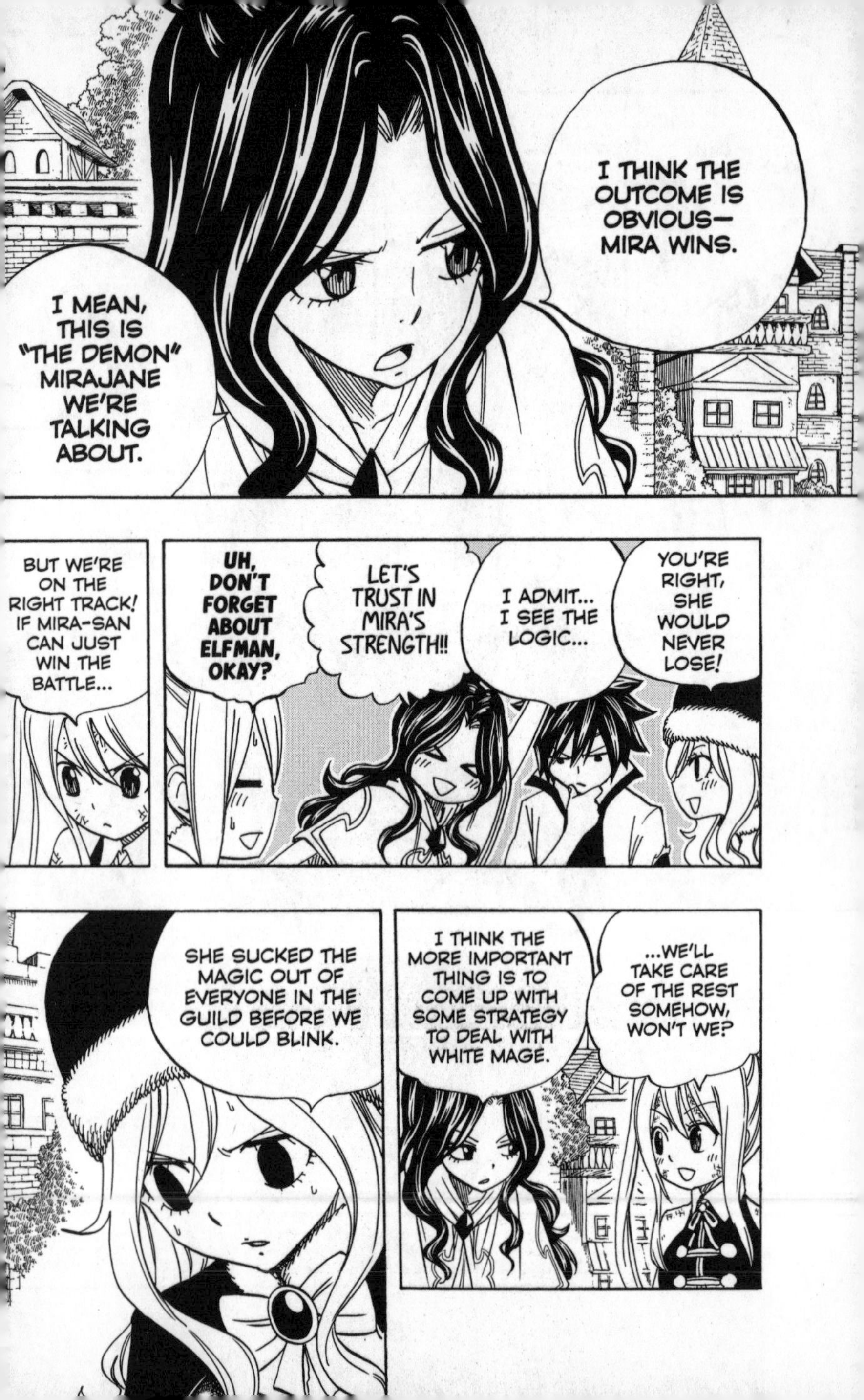
I THINK THE OUTCOME IS OBVIOUS— MIRA WINS.
I MEAN, THIS IS "THE DEMON" MIRAJANE WE'RE TALKING ABOUT.
YOU'RE RIGHT, SHE WOULD NEVER LOSE!
I ADMIT... I SEE THE LOGIC...
LET'S TRUST IN MIRA'S STRENGTH!!
UH, DON'T FORGET ABOUT ELFMAN, OKAY?
BUT WE'RE ON THE RIGHT TRACK! IF MIRA-SAN CAN JUST WIN THE BATTLE...
...WE'LL TAKE CARE OF THE REST SOMEHOW, WON'T WE?
I THINK THE MORE IMPORTANT THING IS TO COME UP WITH SOME STRATEGY TO DEAL WITH WHITE MAGE.
SHE SUCKED THE MAGIC OUT OF EVERYONE IN THE GUILD BEFORE WE COULD BLINK.

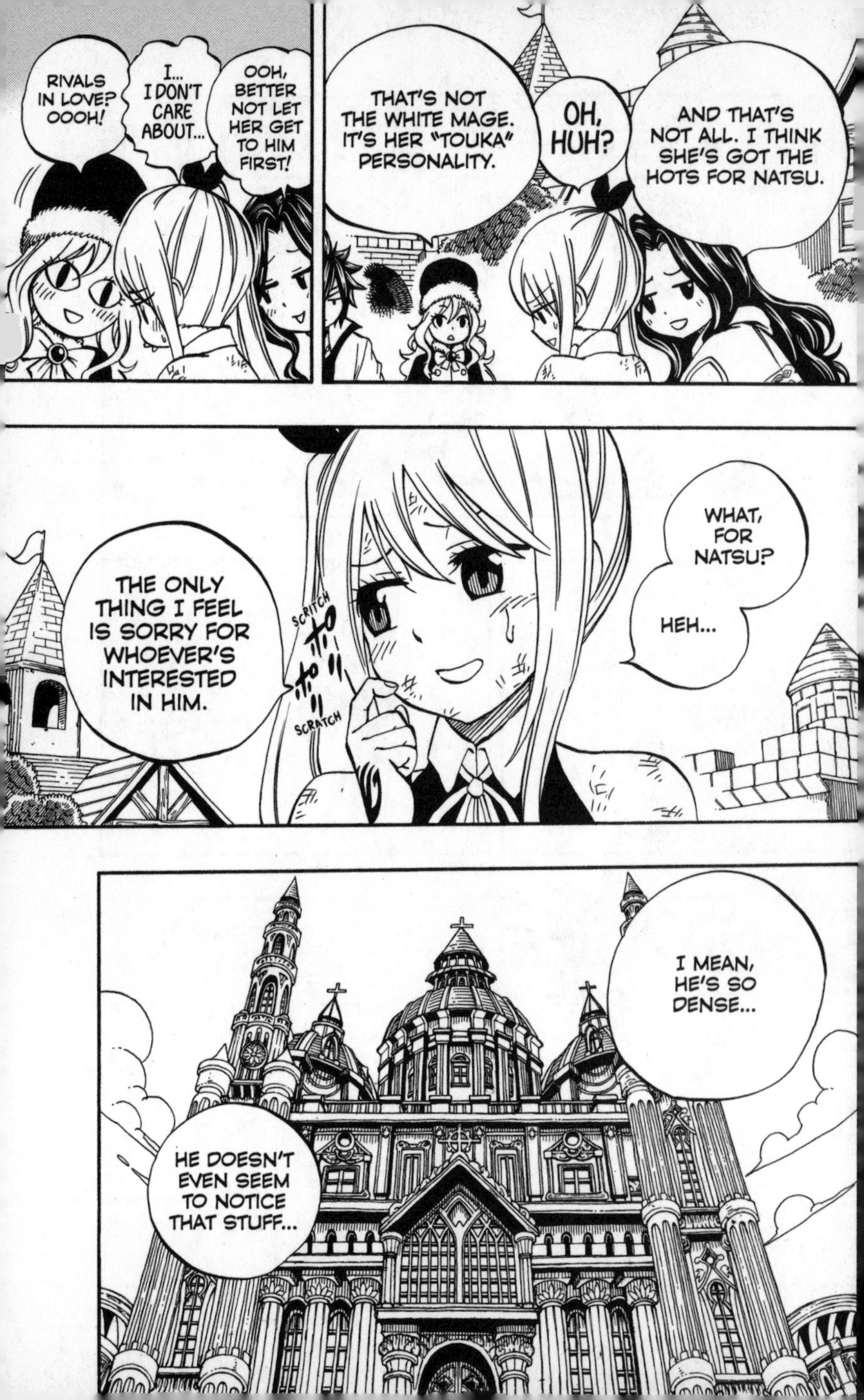
THAT'S NOT THE WHITE MAGE. IT'S HER "TOUKA" PERSONALITY.
OH, HUH?
AND THAT'S NOT ALL. I THINK SHE'S GOT THE HOTS FOR NATSU.
OOH, BETTER NOT LET HER GET TO HIM FIRST!
I... I DON'T CARE ABOUT...
RIVALS IN LOVE? OOOH!
WHAT, FOR NATSU?
HEH...
SCRITCH
SCRATCH
THE ONLY THING I FEEL IS SORRY FOR WHOEVER'S INTERESTED IN HIM.
I MEAN, HE'S SO DENSE...
HE DOESN'T EVEN SEEM TO NOTICE THAT STUFF...

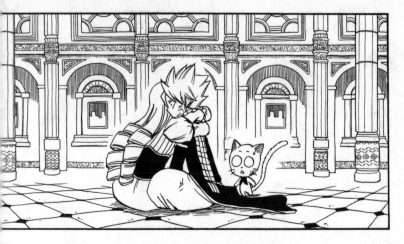

SHOVE

O-OH!
I'M SORRY...

I...

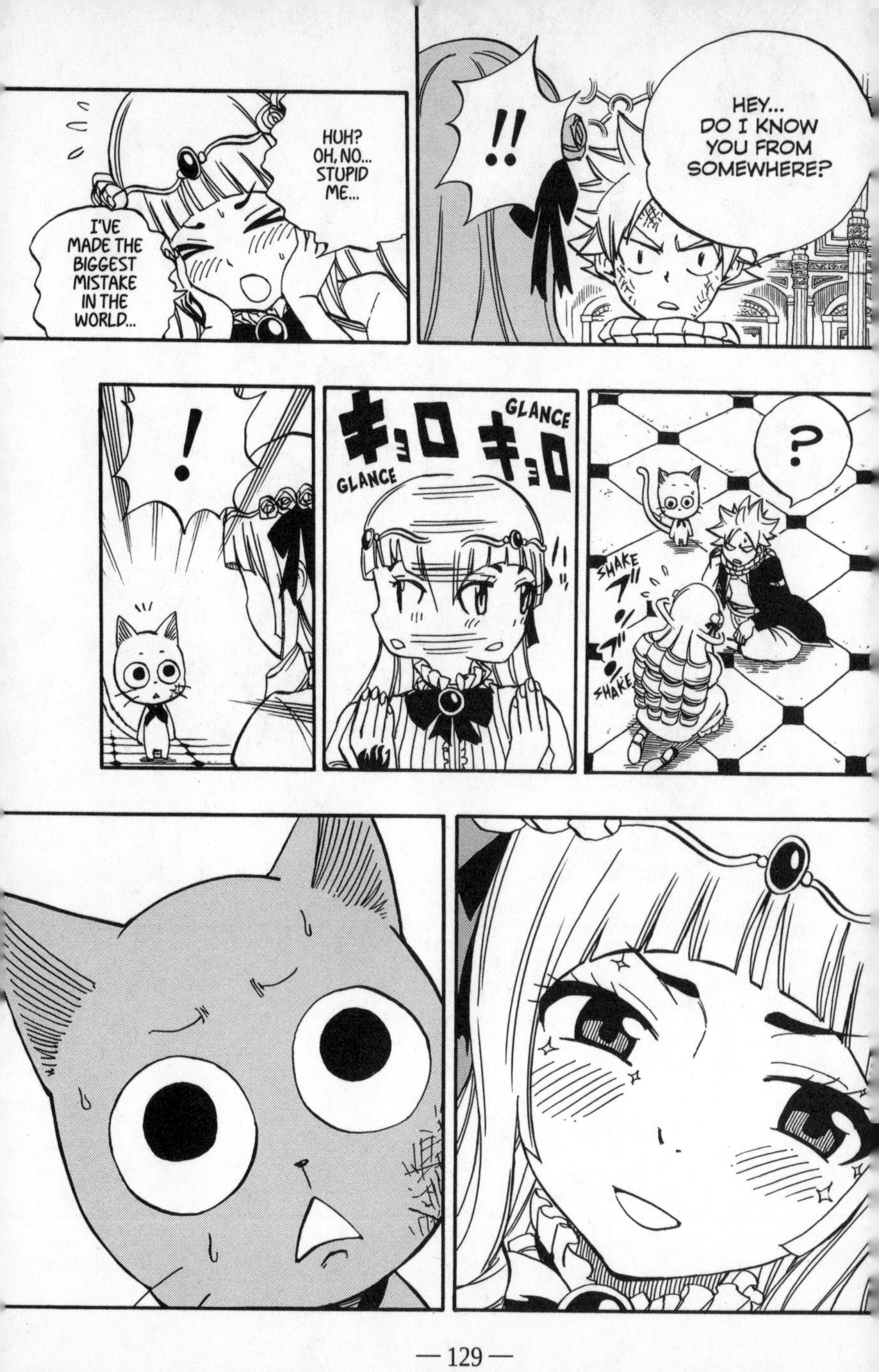
!!
HEY... DO I KNOW YOU FROM SOMEWHERE?
HUH? OH, NO... STUPID ME...
I'VE MADE THE BIGGEST MISTAKE IN THE WORLD...
?
SHAKE
SHAKE
キョロ
GLANCE
キョロ
GLANCE
!

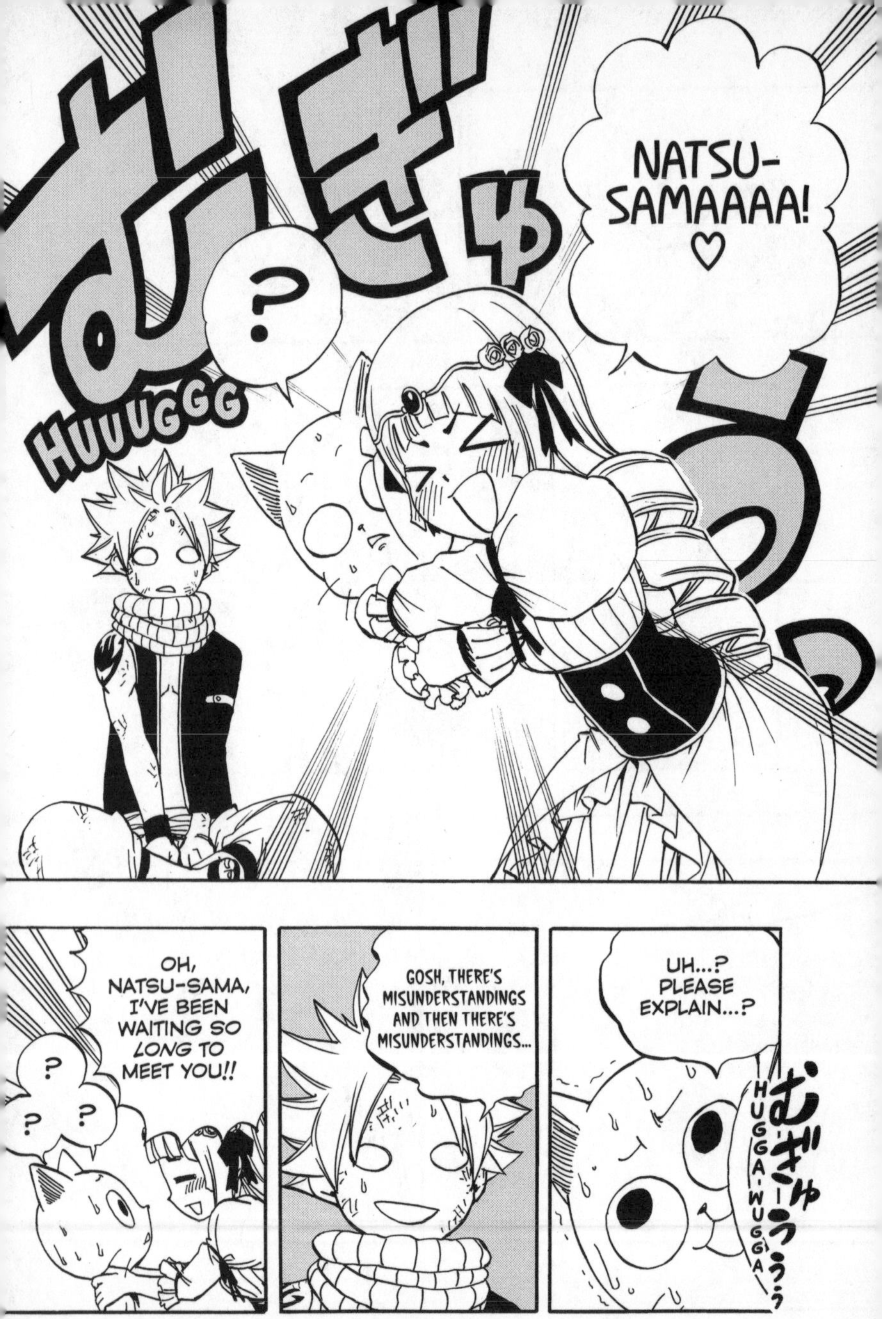
NATSU-SAMAAAA! ♥
?
むぎゅ
HUUUGGG
UH...? PLEASE EXPLAIN...?
むぎゅううう
HUGGA-WUGGA
GOSH, THERE'S MISUNDERSTANDINGS AND THEN THERE'S MISUNDERSTANDINGS...
OH, NATSU-SAMA, I'VE BEEN WAITING SO *LONG* TO MEET YOU!!
? ? ?

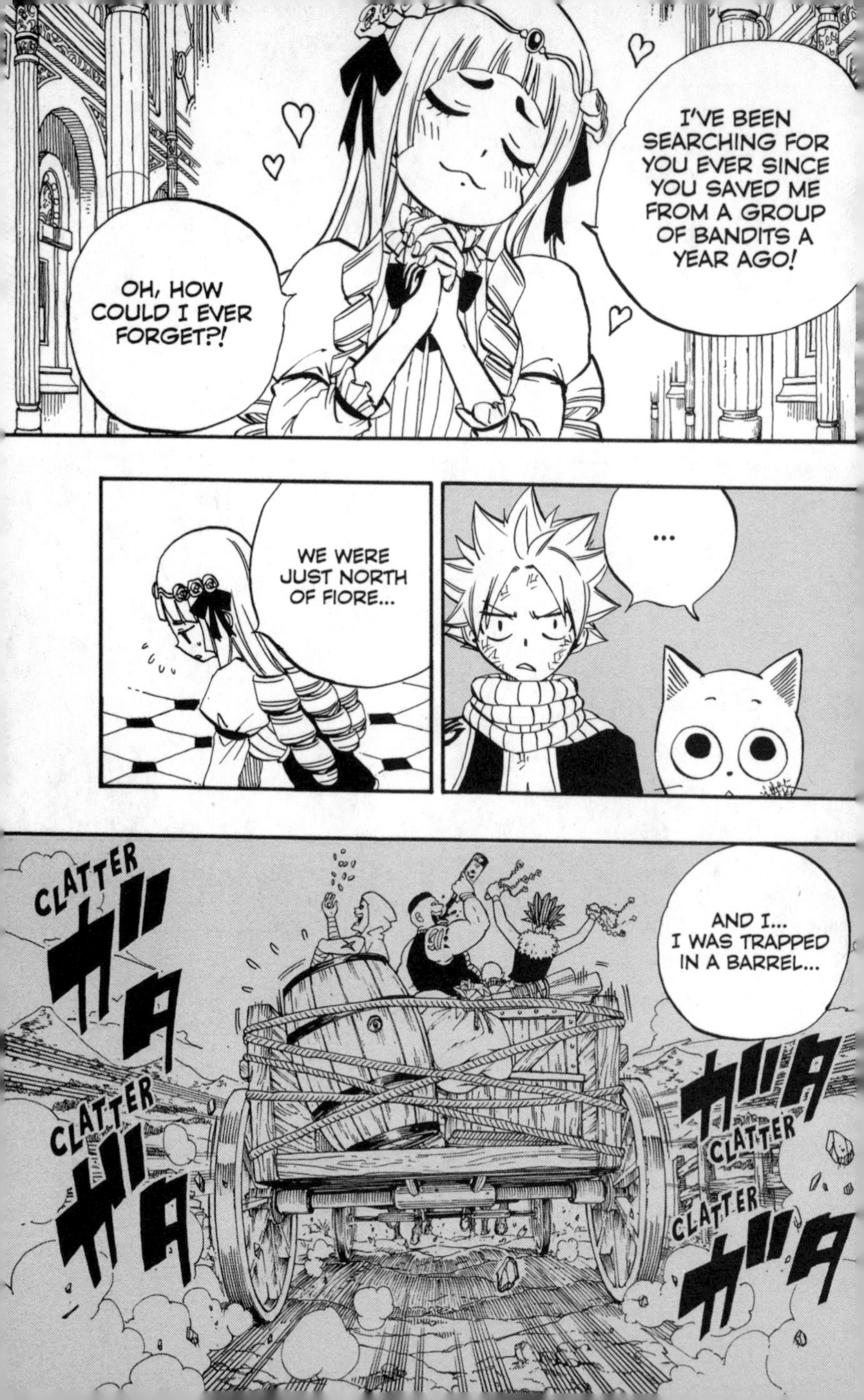
I'VE BEEN SEARCHING FOR YOU EVER SINCE YOU SAVED ME FROM A GROUP OF BANDITS A YEAR AGO!
OH, HOW COULD I EVER FORGET?!
...
WE WERE JUST NORTH OF FIORE...
AND I... I WAS TRAPPED IN A BARREL...
CLATTER
CLATTER
CLATTER
CLATTER

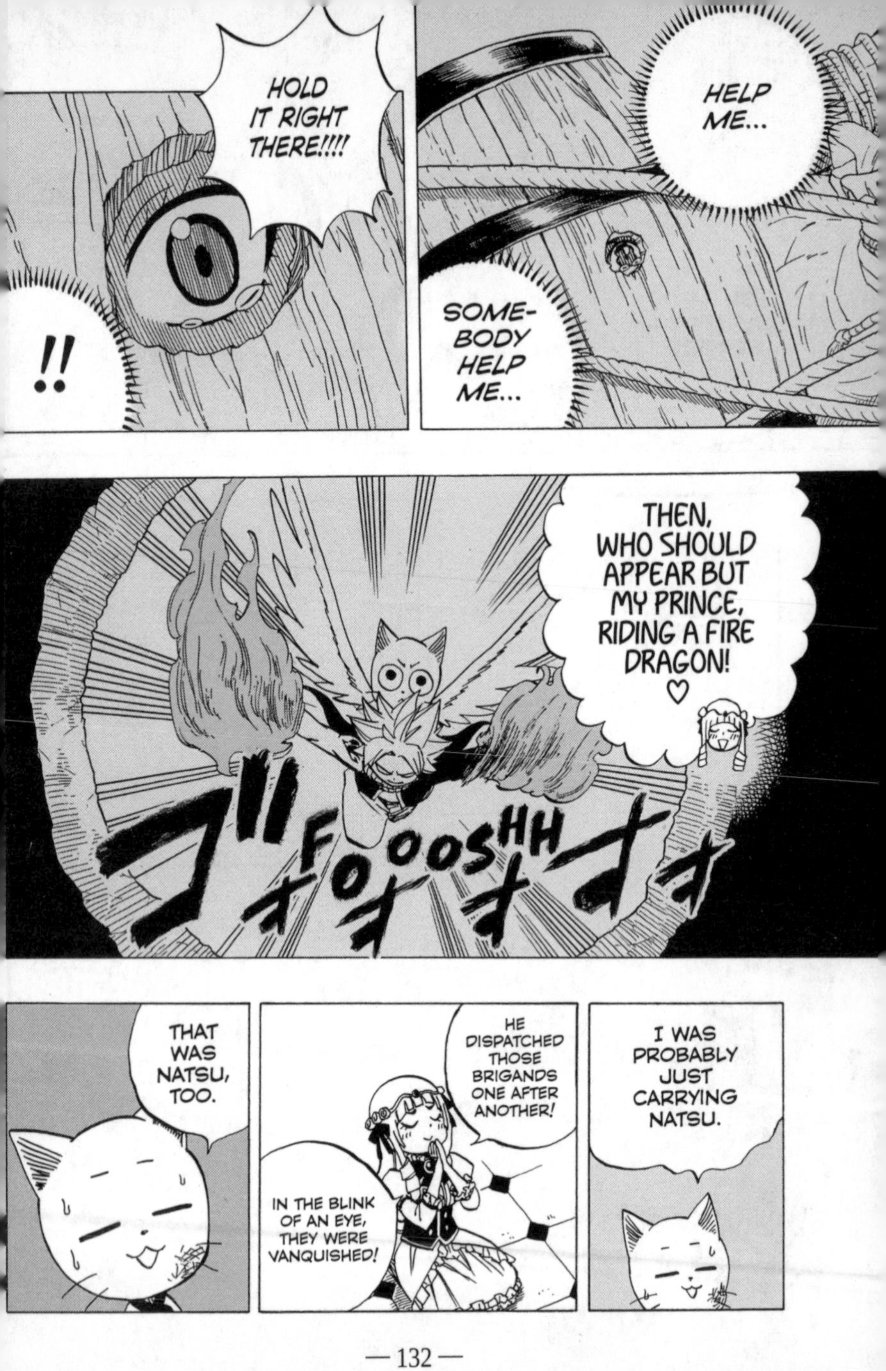
HELP ME...
SOMEBODY HELP ME...
HOLD IT RIGHT THERE!!!!
!!
THEN, WHO SHOULD APPEAR BUT MY PRINCE, RIDING A FIRE DRAGON! ♡
FOOOSHH
I WAS PROBABLY JUST CARRYING NATSU.
HE DISPATCHED THOSE BRIGANDS ONE AFTER ANOTHER!
IN THE BLINK OF AN EYE, THEY WERE VANQUISHED!
THAT WAS NATSU, TOO.

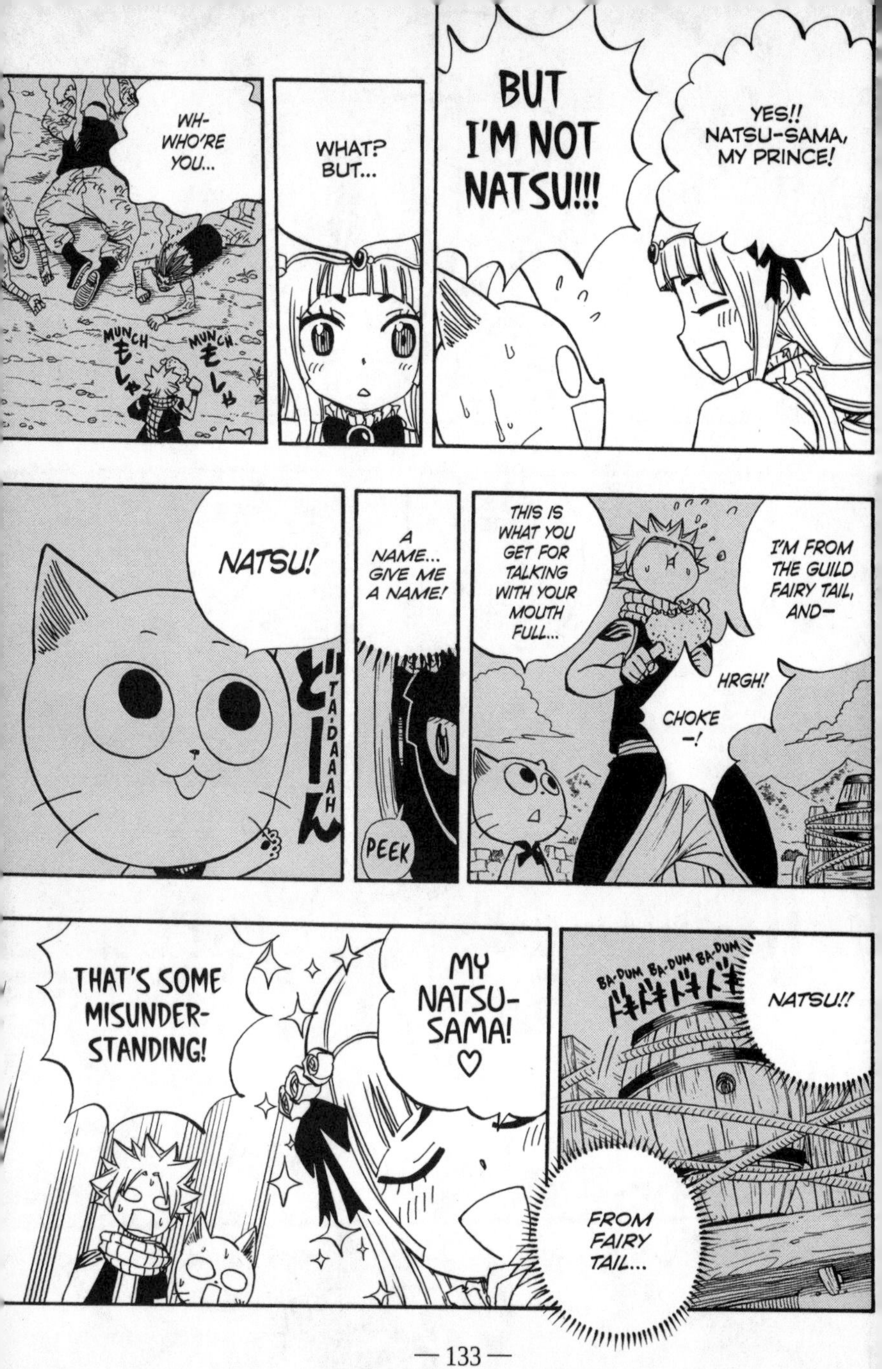
YES!! NATSU-SAMA, MY PRINCE!
BUT I'M NOT NATSU!!!
WHAT? BUT...
WH- WHO'RE YOU...
MUNCH
MUNCH
I'M FROM THE GUILD FAIRY TAIL, AND—
HRGH!
CHOKE —!
THIS IS WHAT YOU GET FOR TALKING WITH YOUR MOUTH FULL...
A NAME... GIVE ME A NAME!
PEEK
NATSU!
TA-DAAAAH
NATSU!!
BA-DUM BA-DUM BA-DUM
FROM FAIRY TAIL...
MY NATSU-SAMA! ♡
THAT'S SOME MISUNDER-STANDING!

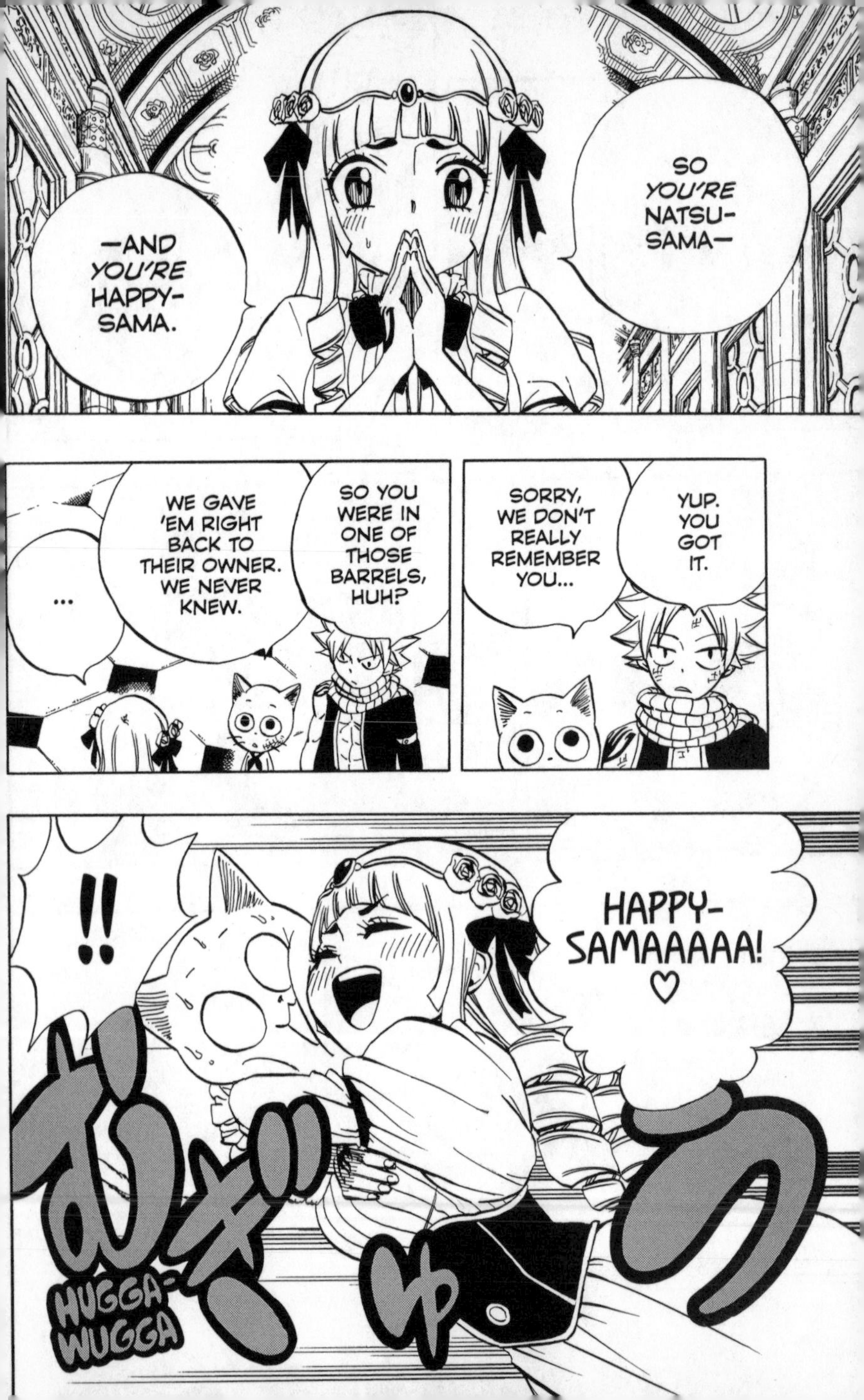
SO YOU'RE NATSU-SAMA—
—AND YOU'RE HAPPY-SAMA.
YUP. YOU GOT IT.
SORRY, WE DON'T REALLY REMEMBER YOU...
SO YOU WERE IN ONE OF THOSE BARRELS, HUH?
WE GAVE 'EM RIGHT BACK TO THEIR OWNER. WE NEVER KNEW.
...
HAPPY-SAMAAAAAA! ♡
!!
HUGGA-WUGGA

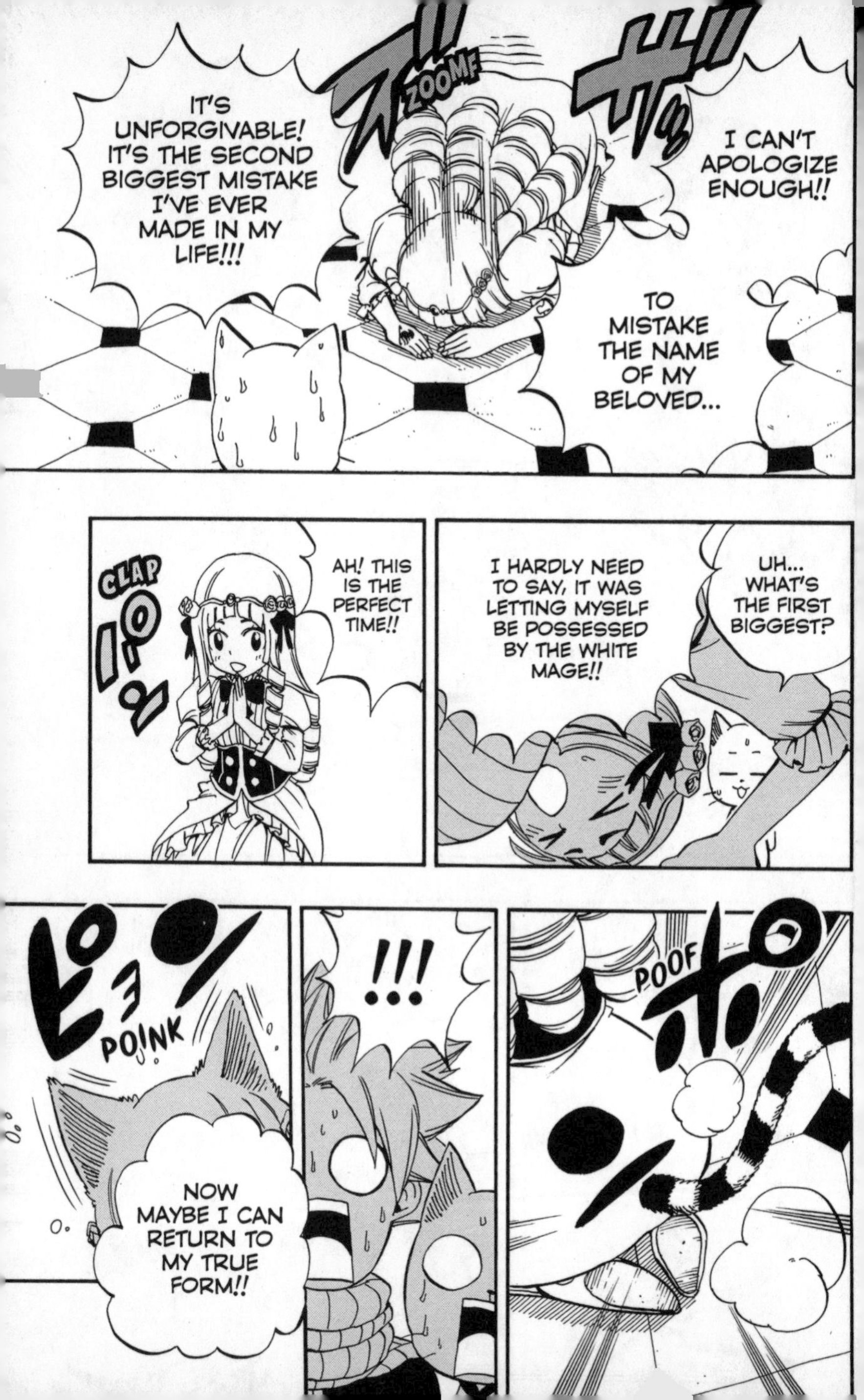
ZOOMF
I CAN'T APOLOGIZE ENOUGH!!
TO MISTAKE THE NAME OF MY BELOVED...
IT'S UNFORGIVABLE! IT'S THE SECOND BIGGEST MISTAKE I'VE EVER MADE IN MY LIFE!!!
UH... WHAT'S THE FIRST BIGGEST?
I HARDLY NEED TO SAY, IT WAS LETTING MYSELF BE POSSESSED BY THE WHITE MAGE!!
CLAP
AH! THIS IS THE PERFECT TIME!!
POOF
!!!
POINK
NOW MAYBE I CAN RETURN TO MY TRUE FORM!!

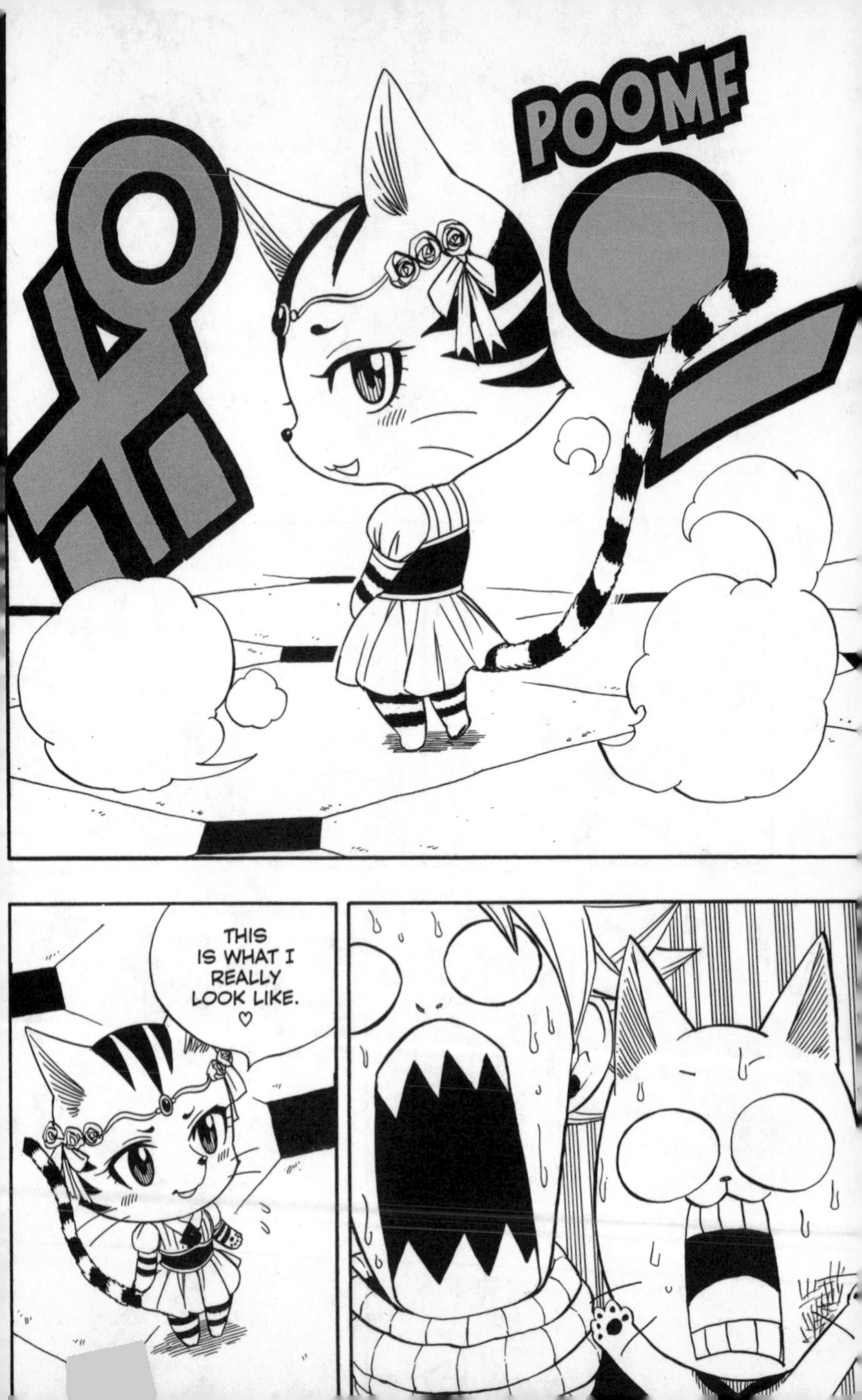
POOMF
THIS IS WHAT I REALLY LOOK LIKE. ♡

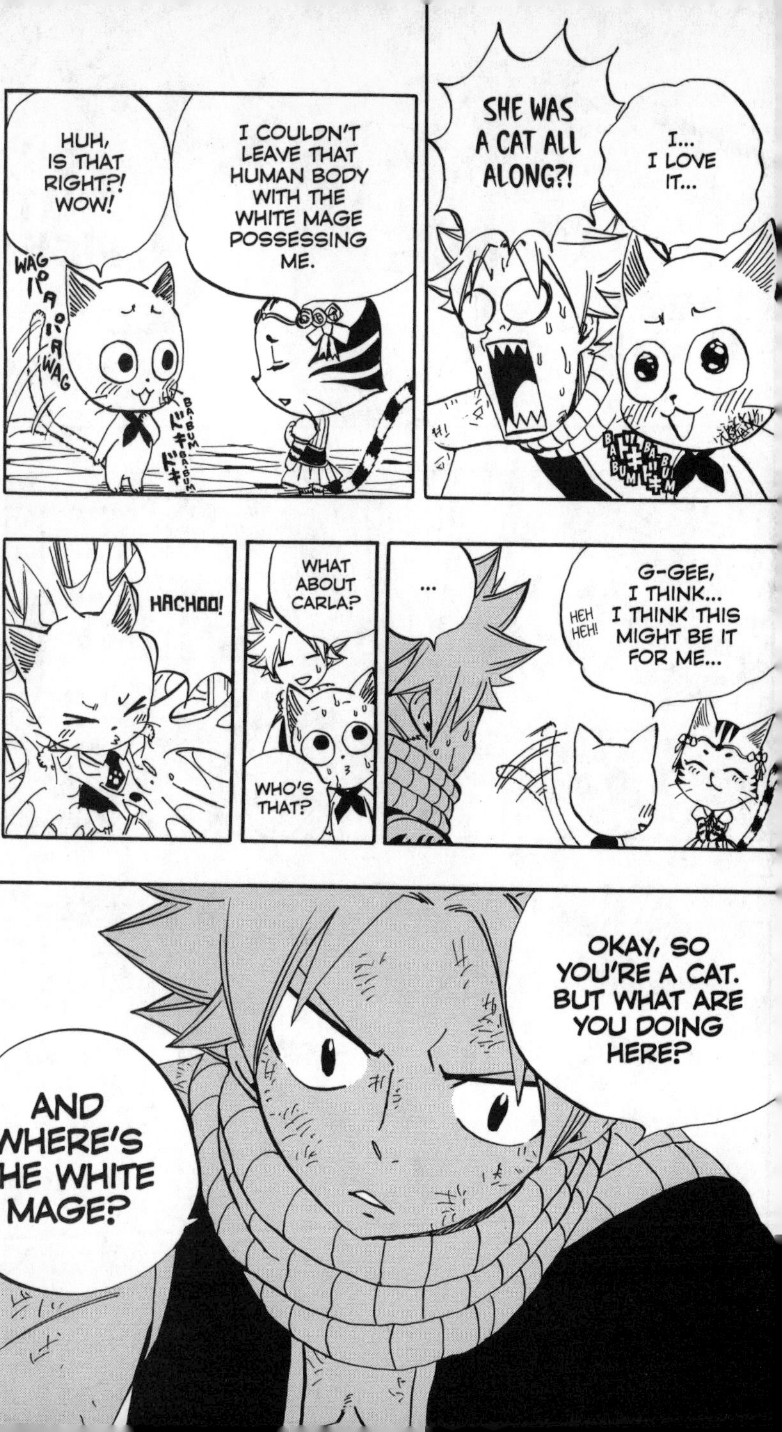
SHE WAS A CAT ALL ALONG?!
I... I LOVE IT...
BA-BUM BA-BUM
I COULDN'T LEAVE THAT HUMAN BODY WITH THE WHITE MAGE POSSESSING ME.
HUH, IS THAT RIGHT?! WOW!
WAG WAG
BA-BUM BA-BUM
G-GEE, I THINK... I THINK THIS MIGHT BE IT FOR ME...
HEH HEH!
...
WHAT ABOUT CARLA?
WHO'S THAT?
HACHOO!
OKAY, SO YOU'RE A CAT. BUT WHAT ARE YOU DOING HERE?
AND WHERE'S THE WHITE MAGE?

OH, THAT'S RIGHT!!

I HAVE TO HURRY!!!

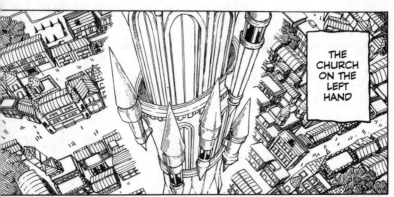

THE CHURCH ON THE LEFT HAND

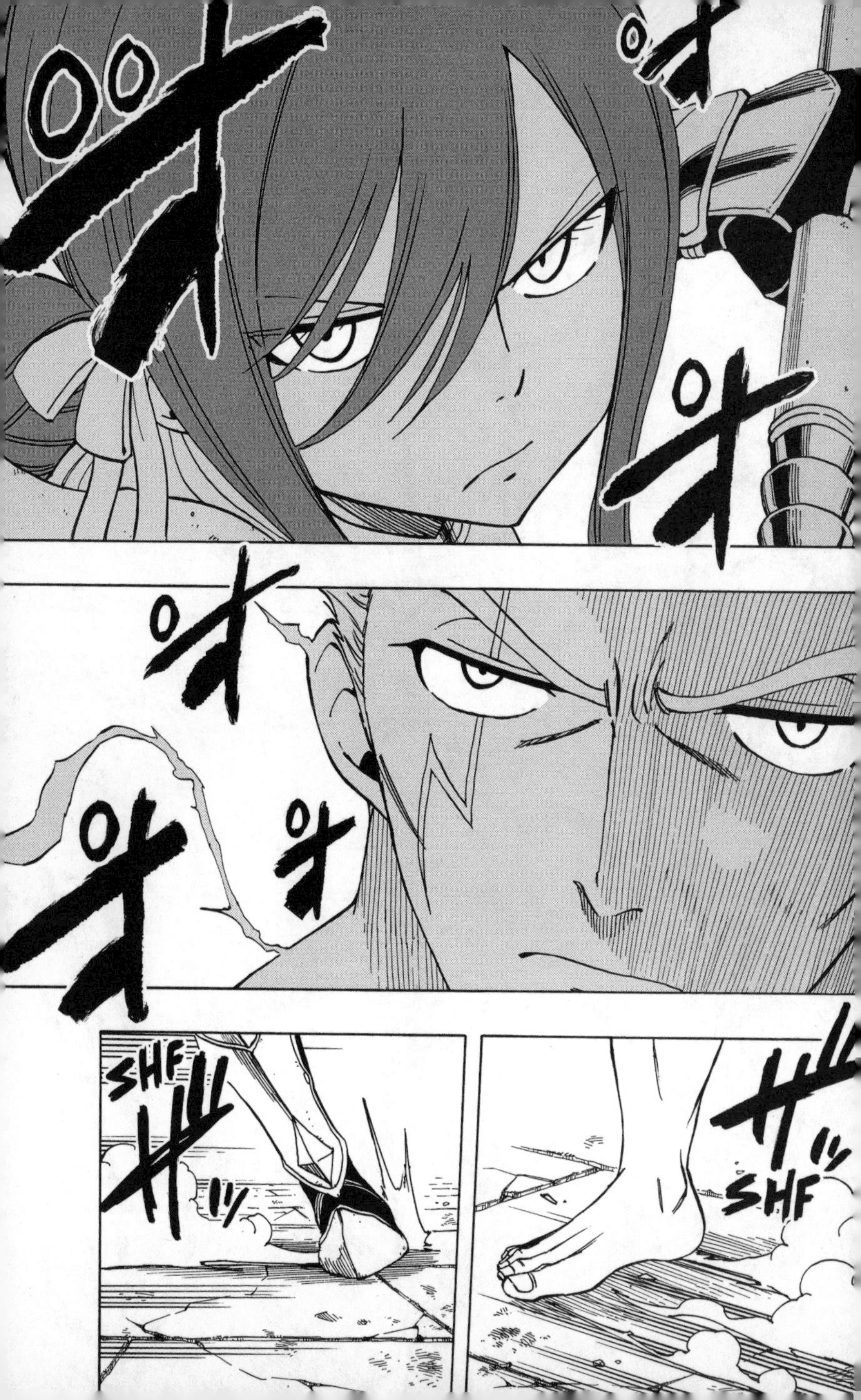
SHF
SHF

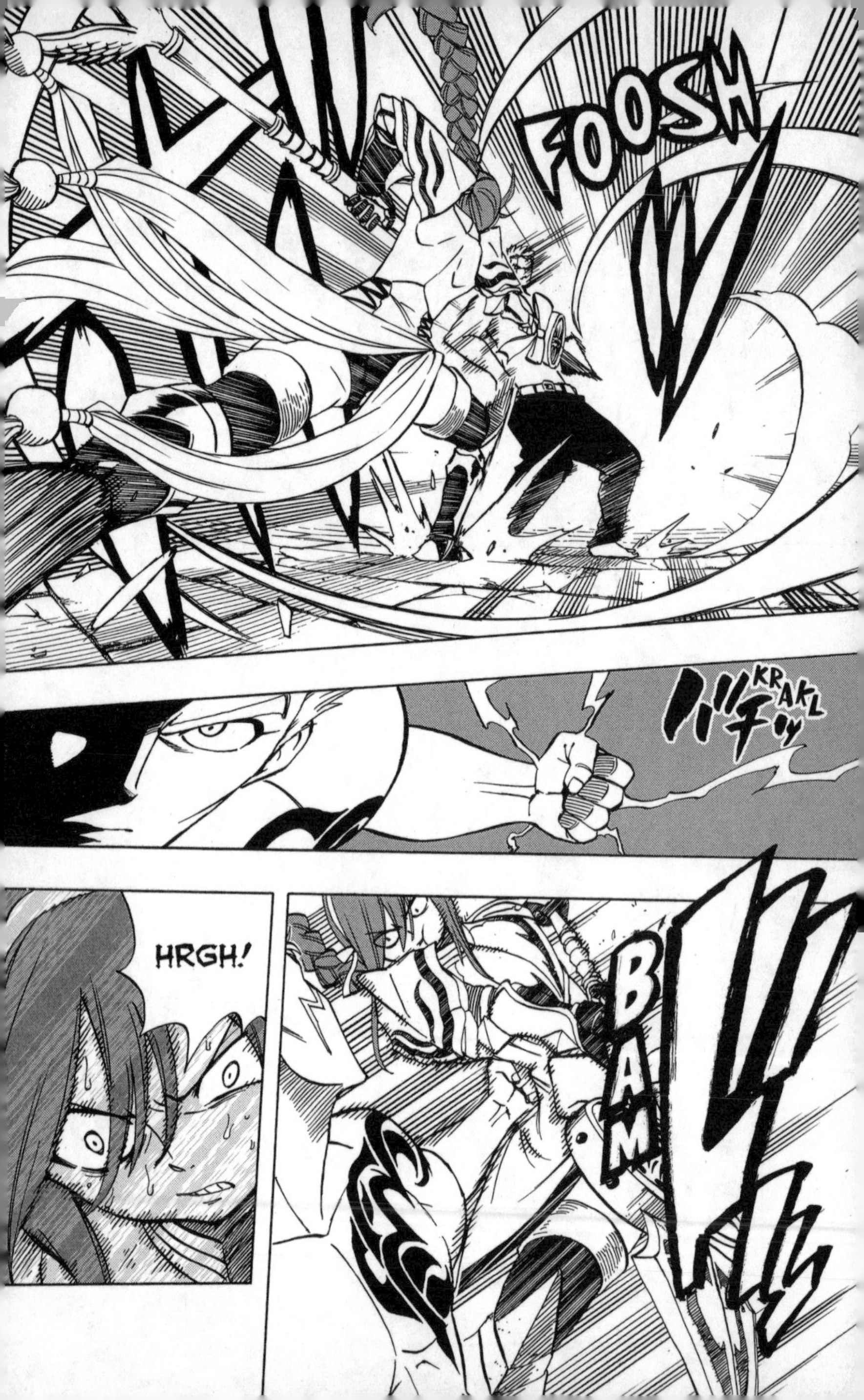
FOOSH
KRAKL
BAM
HRGH!

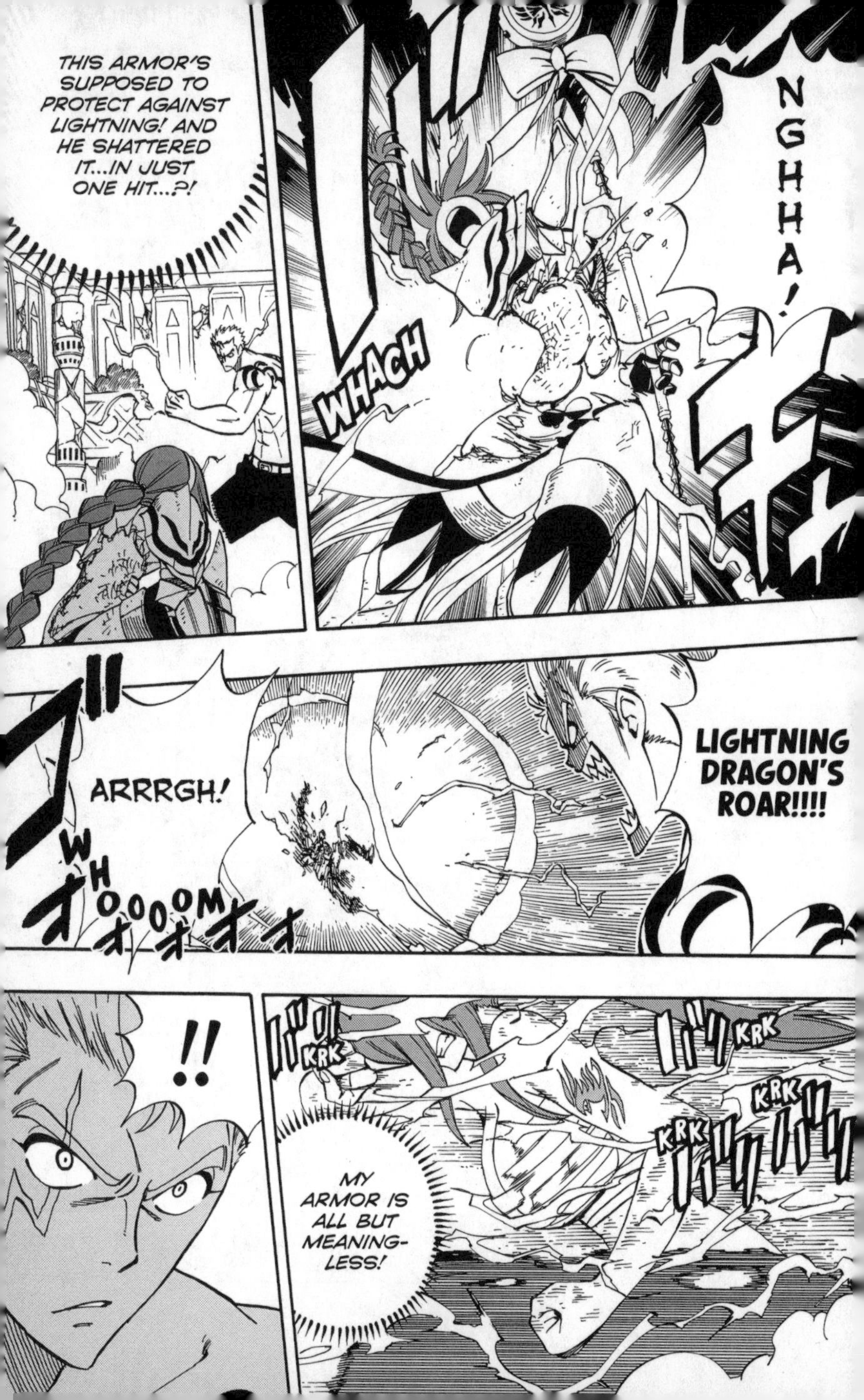
NGHHA!
WHACH
THIS ARMOR'S SUPPOSED TO PROTECT AGAINST LIGHTNING! AND HE SHATTERED IT...IN JUST ONE HIT...?!
LIGHTNING DRAGON'S ROAR!!!!
ARRRGH!
WHOOOOM
KRK
KRK
KRK
KRK
MY ARMOR IS ALL BUT MEANING-LESS!
!!

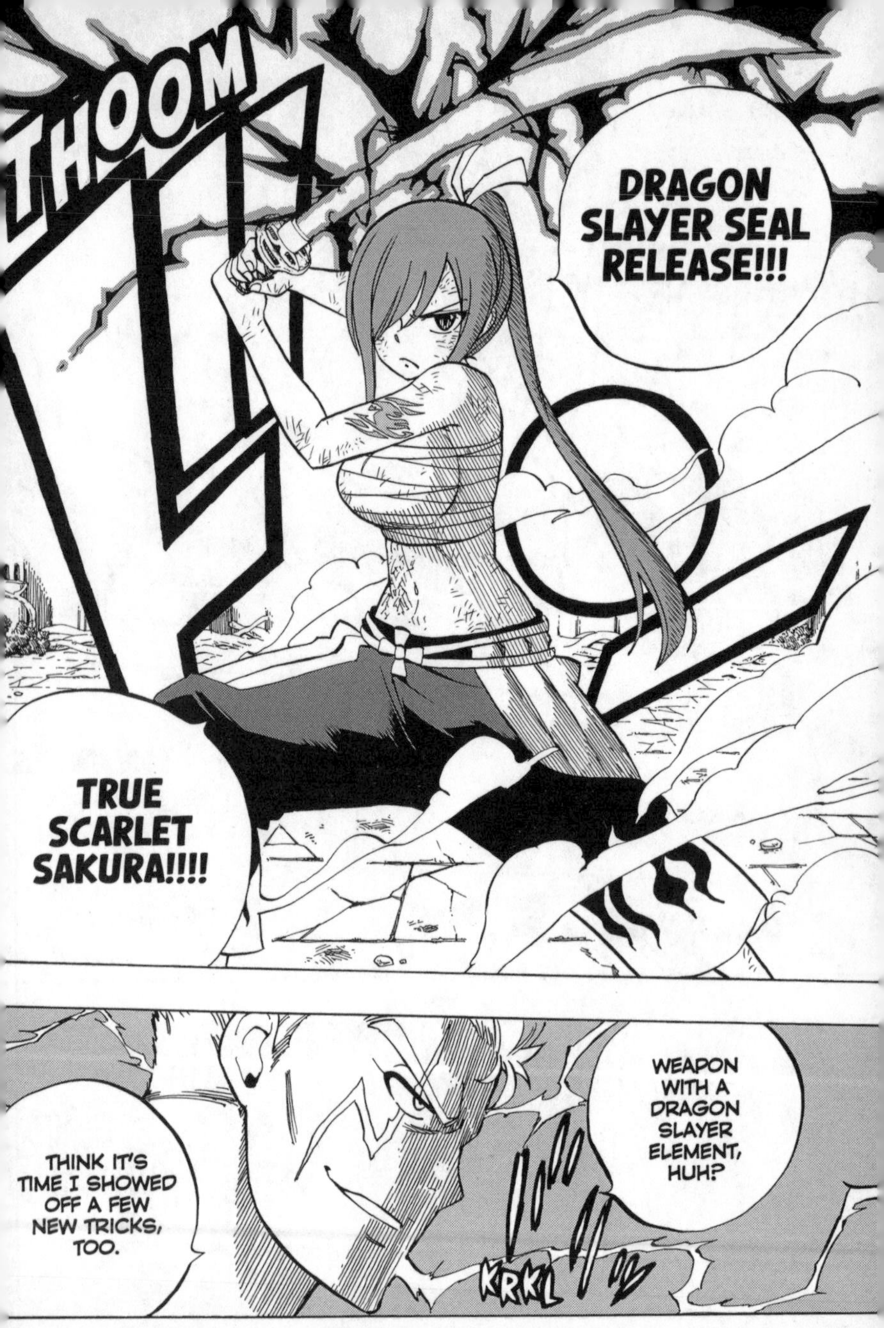
DRAGON SLAYER SEAL RELEASE!!!
THOOM
TRUE SCARLET SAKURA!!!!
WEAPON WITH A DRAGON SLAYER ELEMENT, HUH?
THINK IT'S TIME I SHOWED OFF A FEW NEW TRICKS, TOO.
KRKL

FAIRY TAIL 100 YEARS QUEST

Chapter 44: Scarlet Showdown

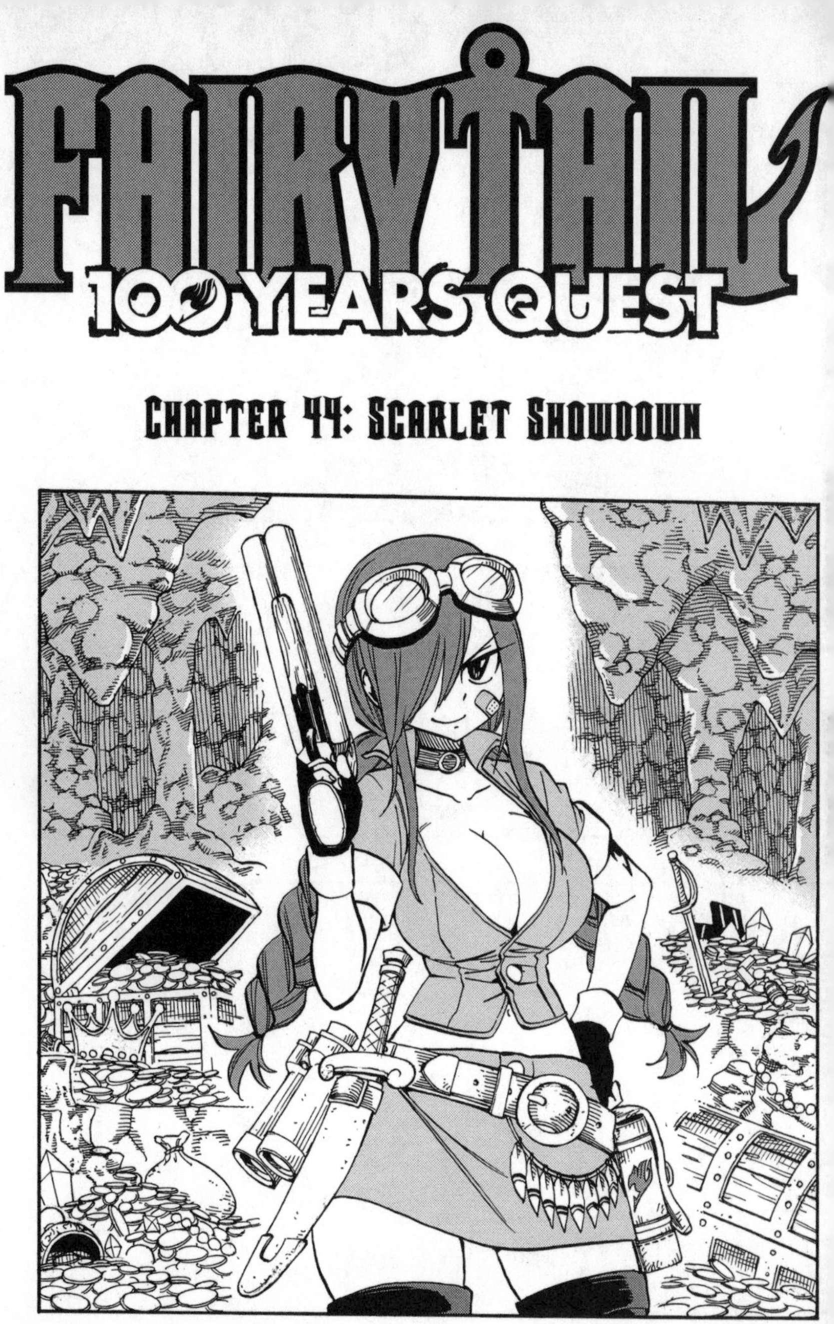

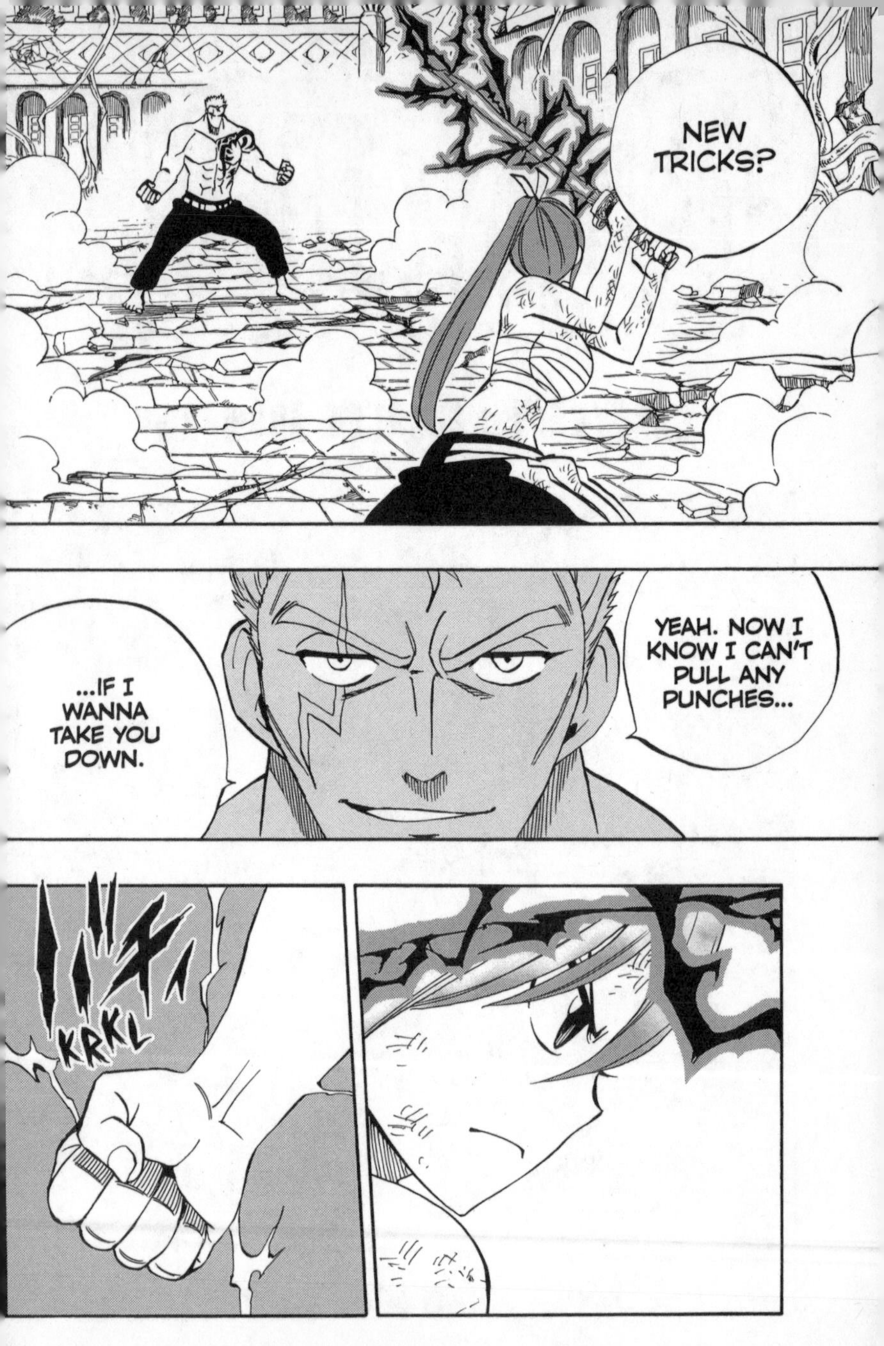
NEW TRICKS?
YEAH. NOW I KNOW I CAN'T PULL ANY PUNCHES...
...IF I WANNA TAKE YOU DOWN.
KRKL

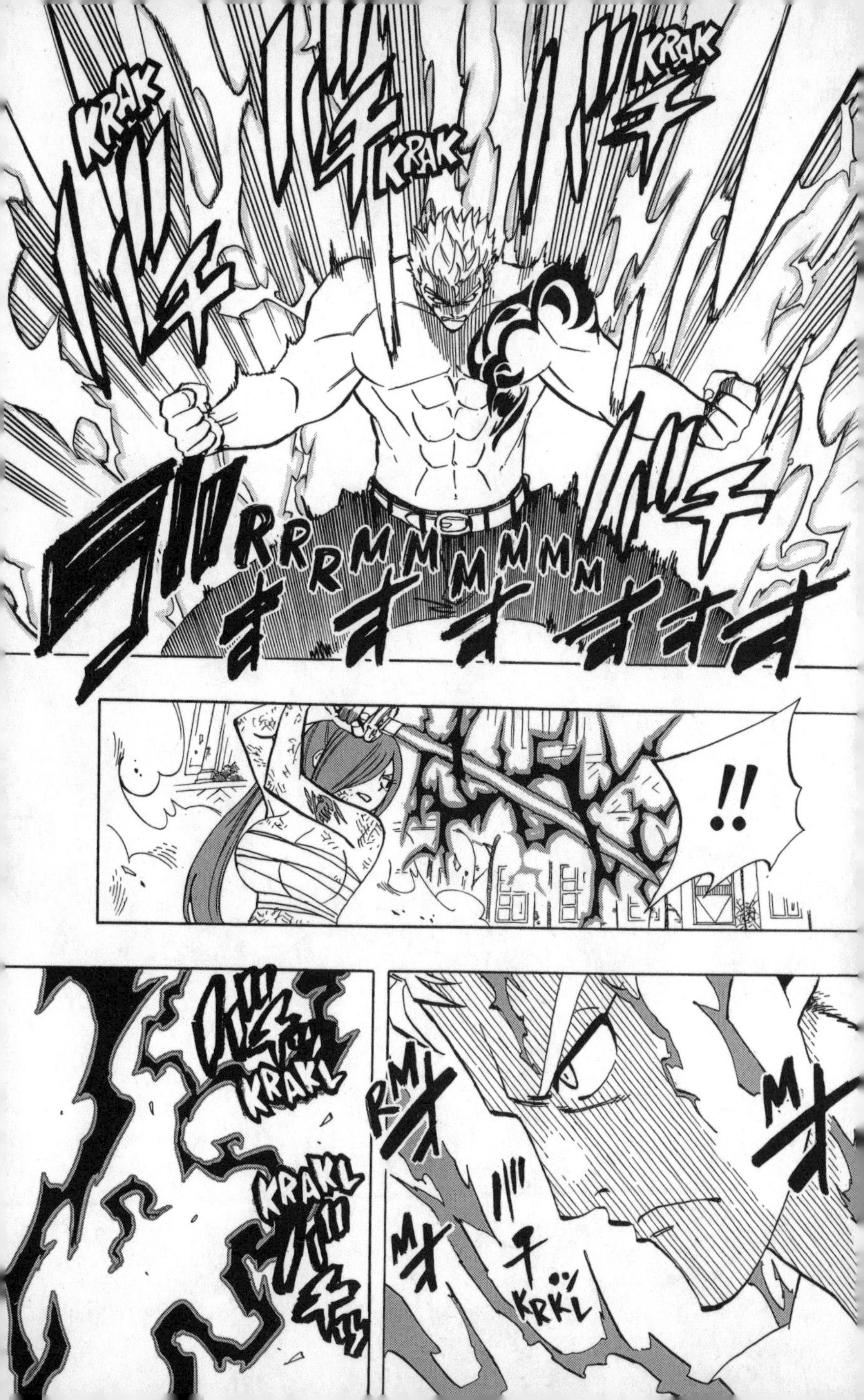
KRAK
KRAK
KRAK
RRRMMMMMMM
!!
M
RM
M
KRKL
KRAKL
KRAKL

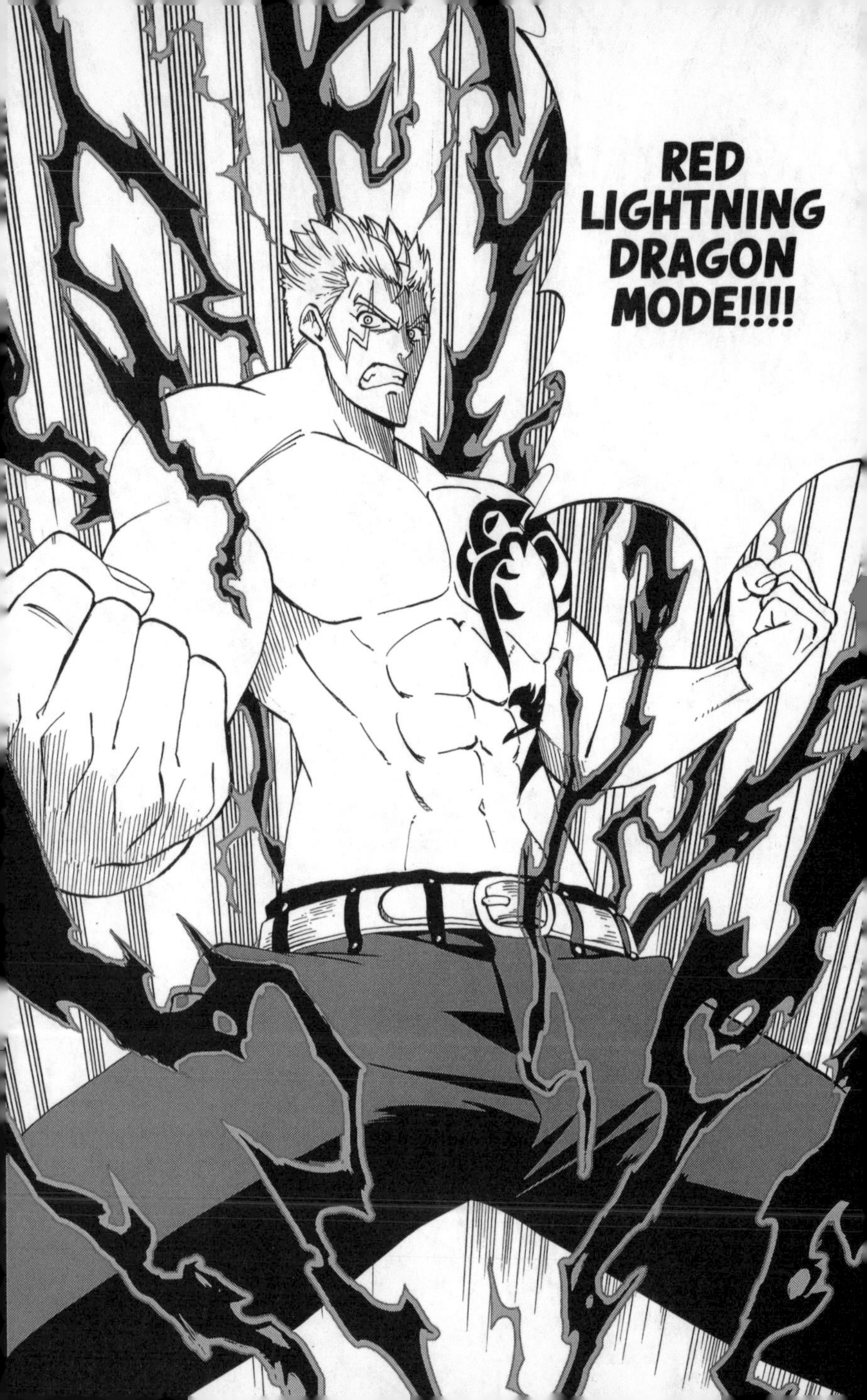
RED LIGHTNING DRAGON MODE!!!!

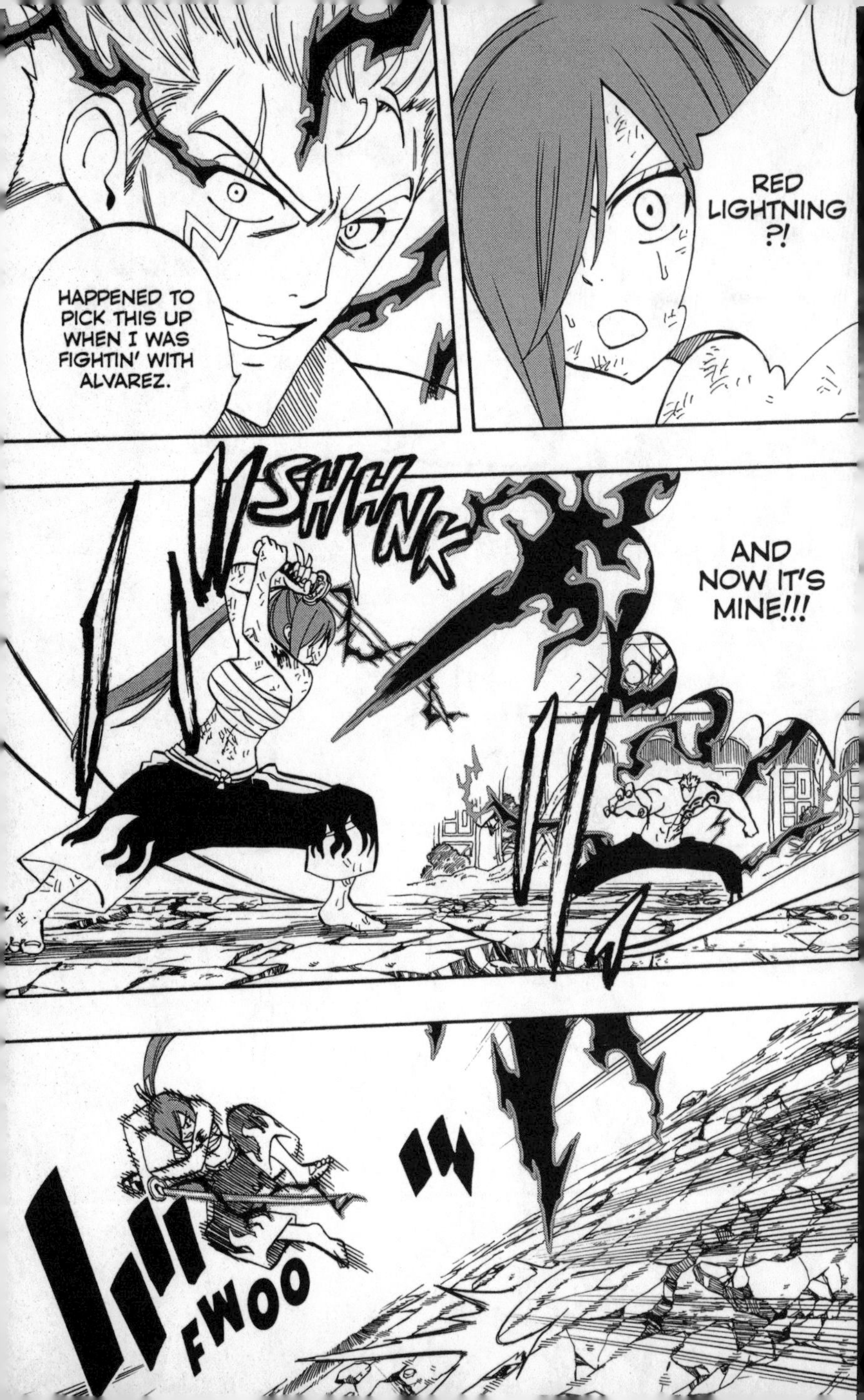
RED LIGHTNING ?!
HAPPENED TO PICK THIS UP WHEN I WAS FIGHTIN' WITH ALVAREZ.
SHHNK
AND NOW IT'S MINE!!!
FWOO

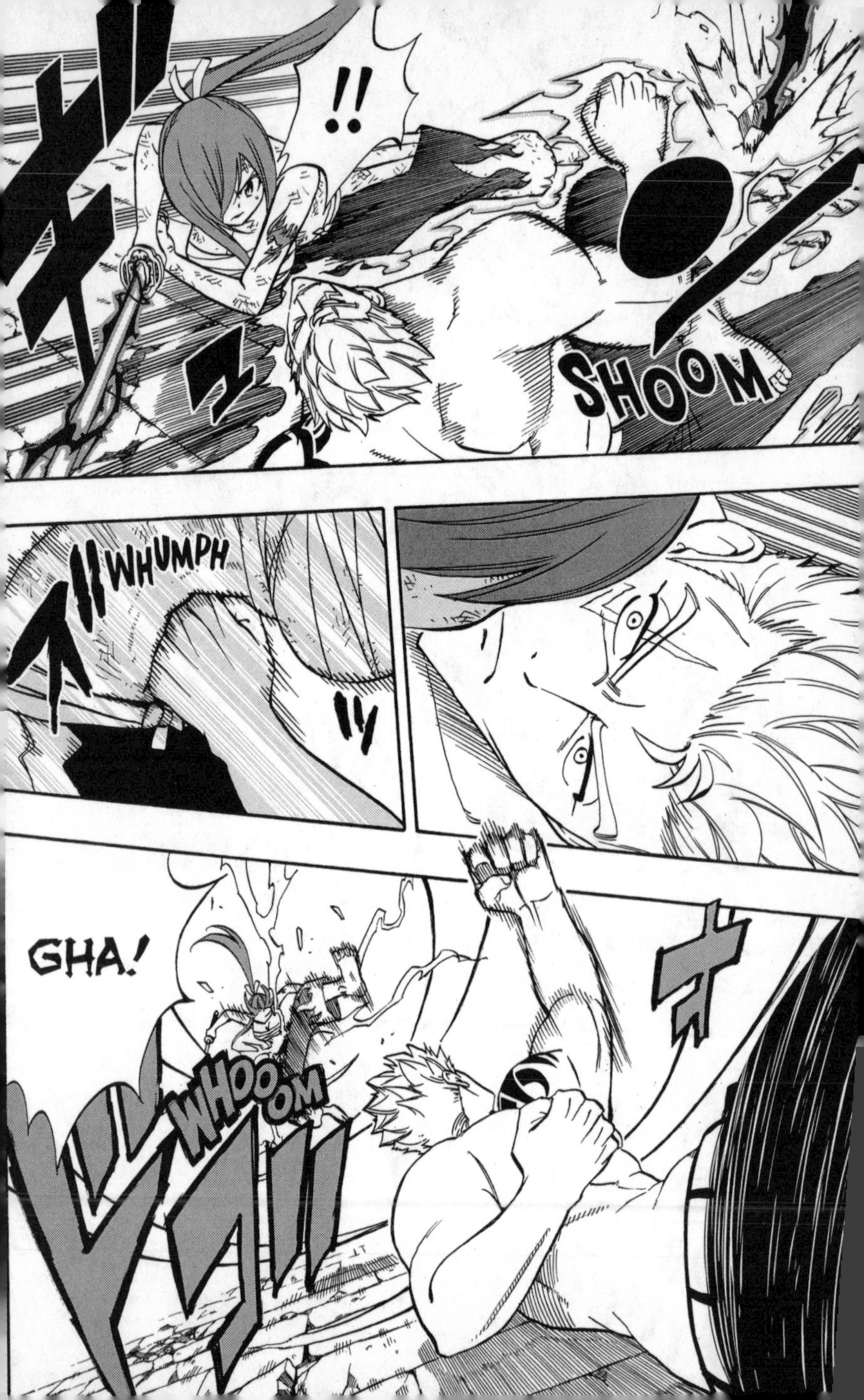
!!
SHOOM
WHUMPH
GHA!
WHOOOM

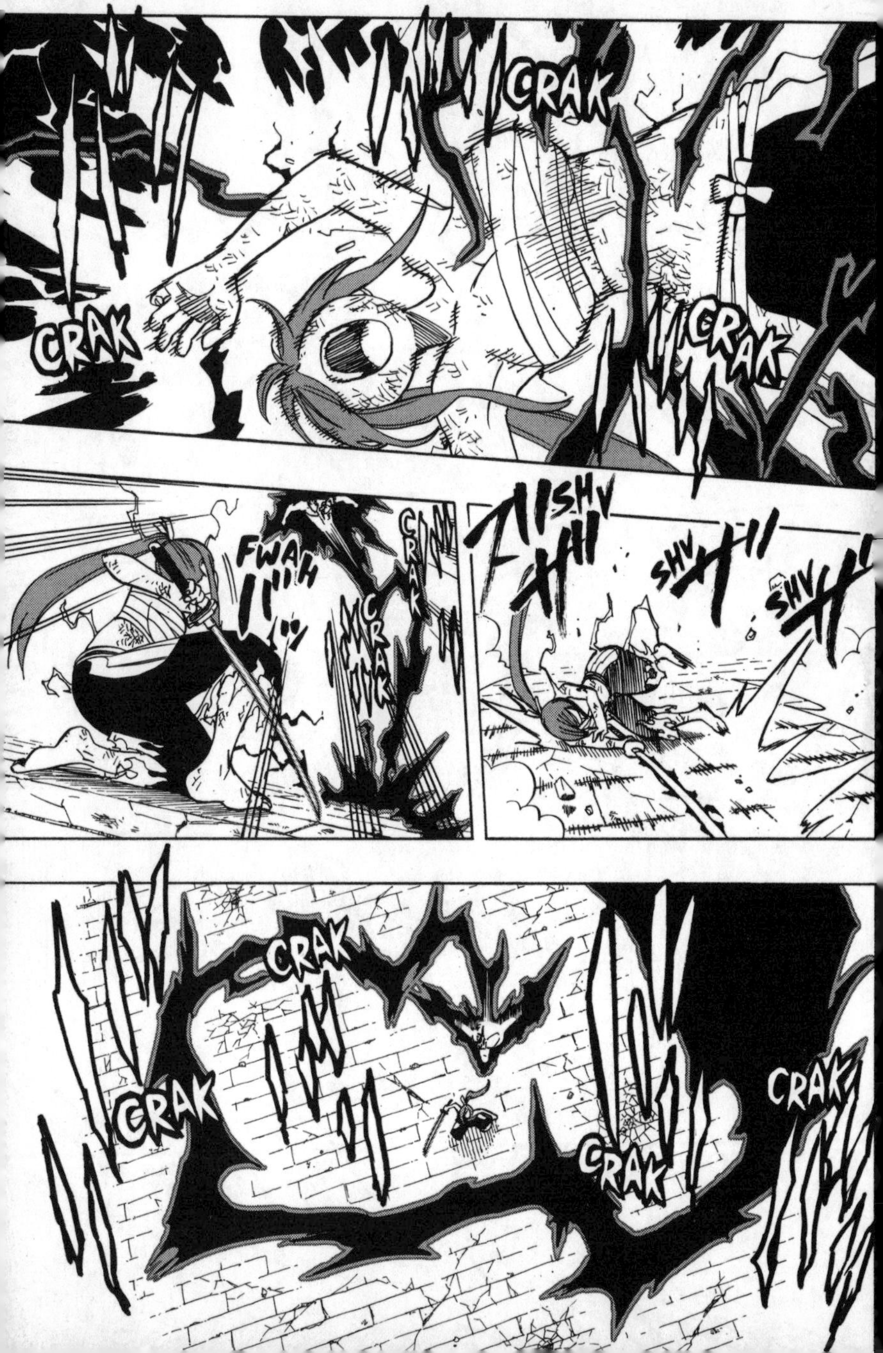

CRAK
CRAK
CRAK
SHV
SHV
SHV
CRAK
FWAH
CRAK
CRAK
CRAK
CRAK
CRAK
CRAK

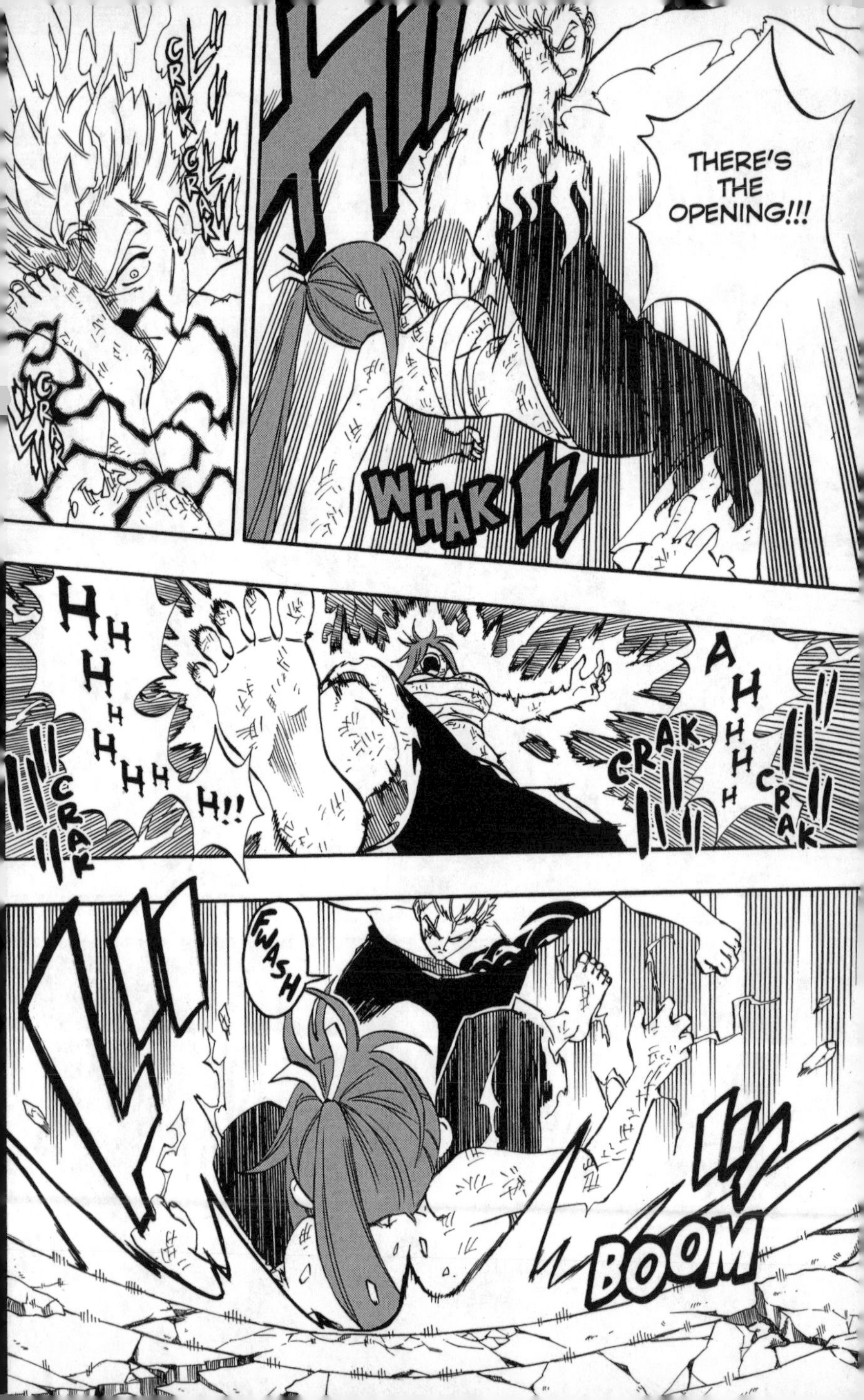
THERE'S THE OPENING!!!
WHAK!!
CRAK CRAK
CRAK
AHHHHH
CRAK
CRAK
HHHHHHHH!!
CRAK
FWASH
BOOM

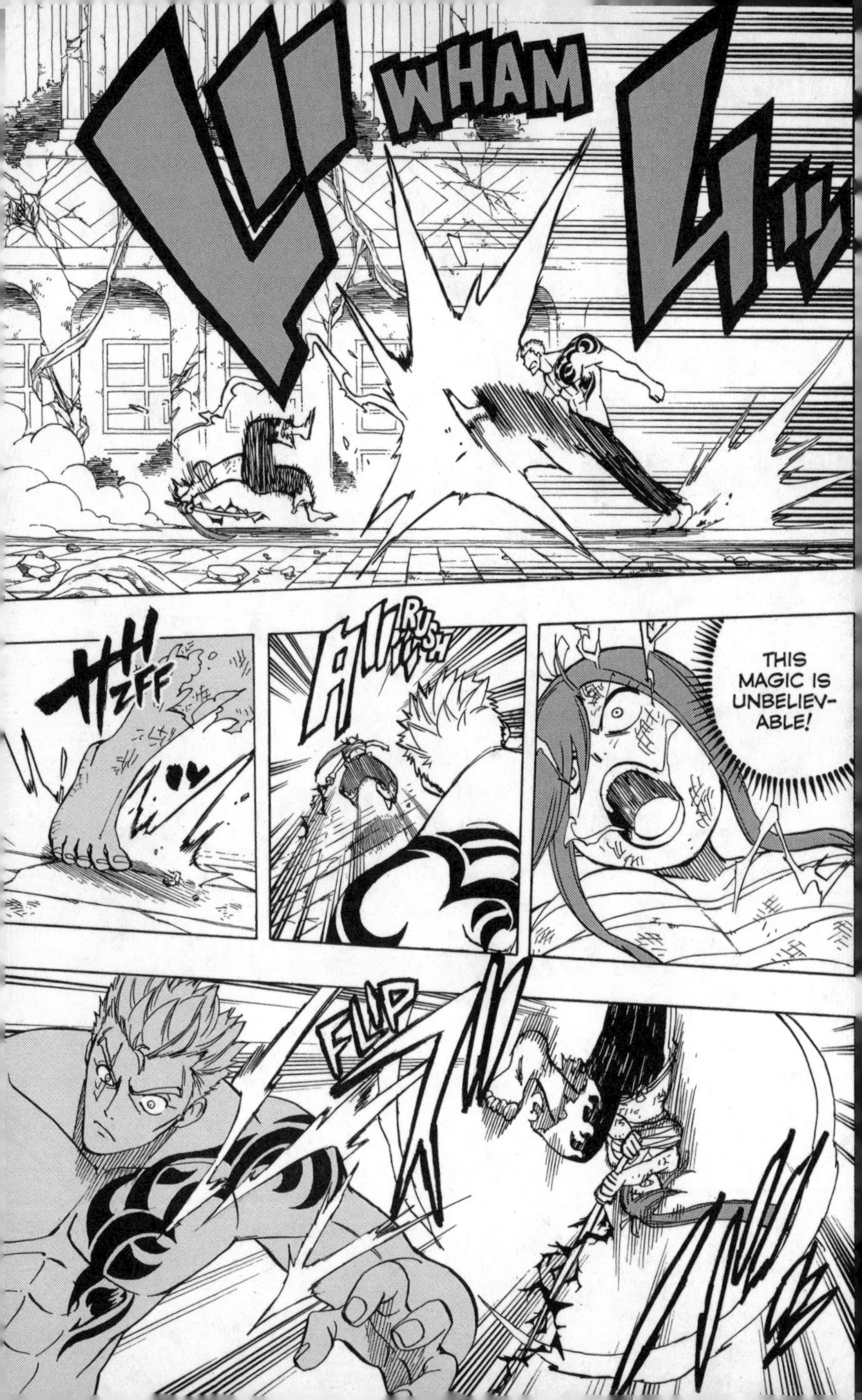
WHAM
THIS MAGIC IS UNBELIEV-ABLE!
RUSH
ZFF
FLIP

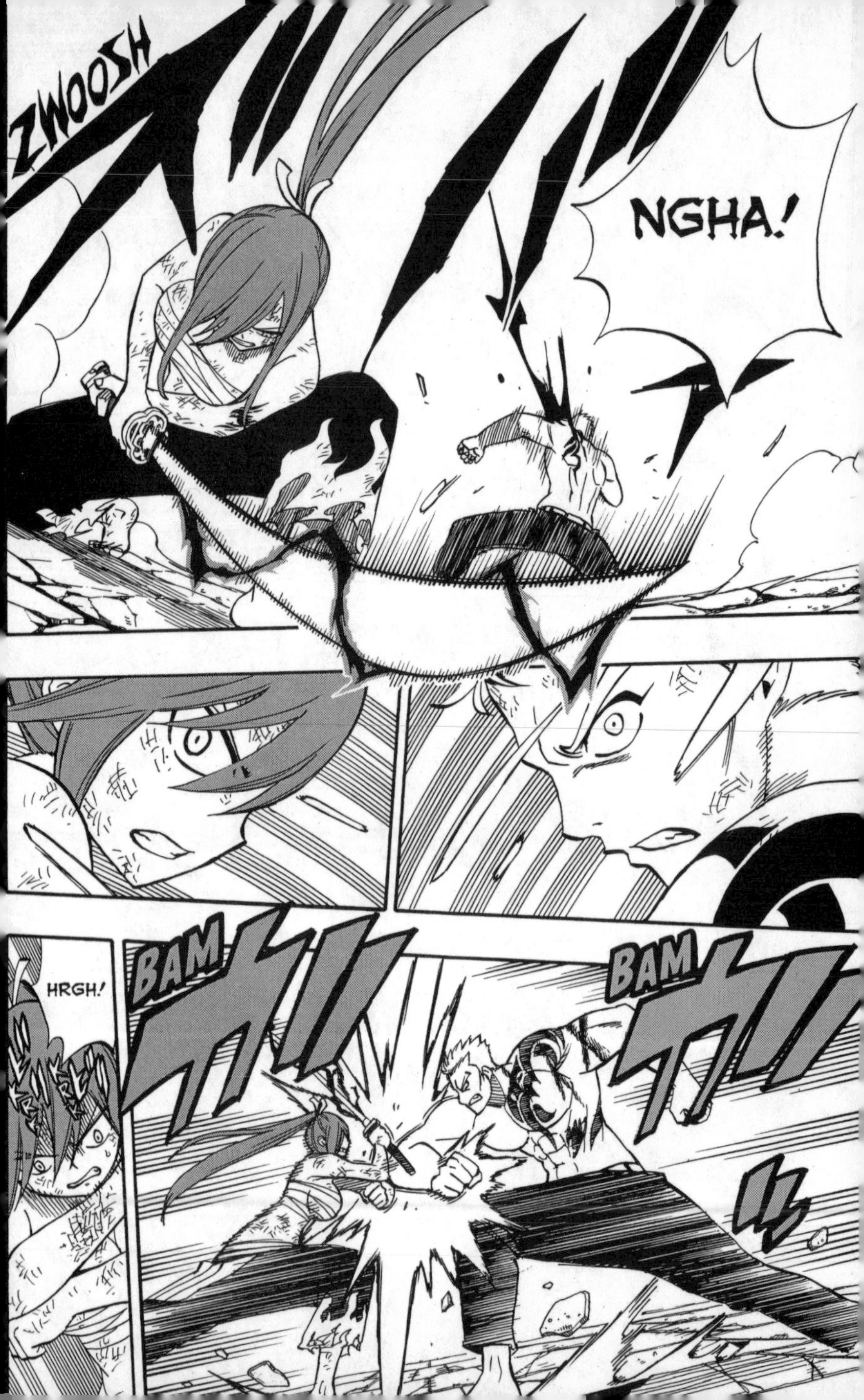
ZWOOSH
NGHA!
BAM
BAM
HRGH!

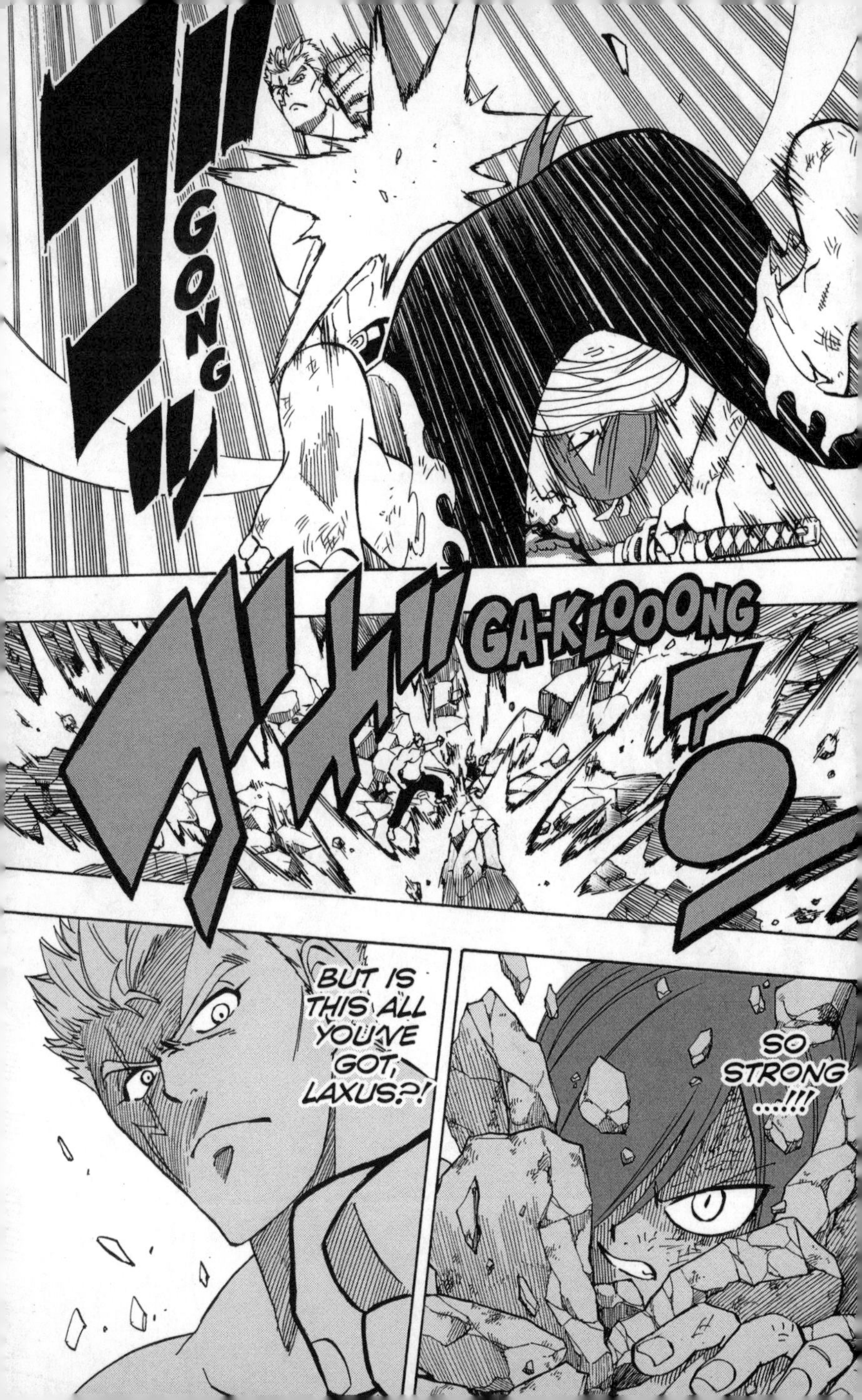
GONG
GA-KLOOONG
SO STRONG ...!!!
BUT IS THIS ALL YOU'VE GOT, LAXUS?!

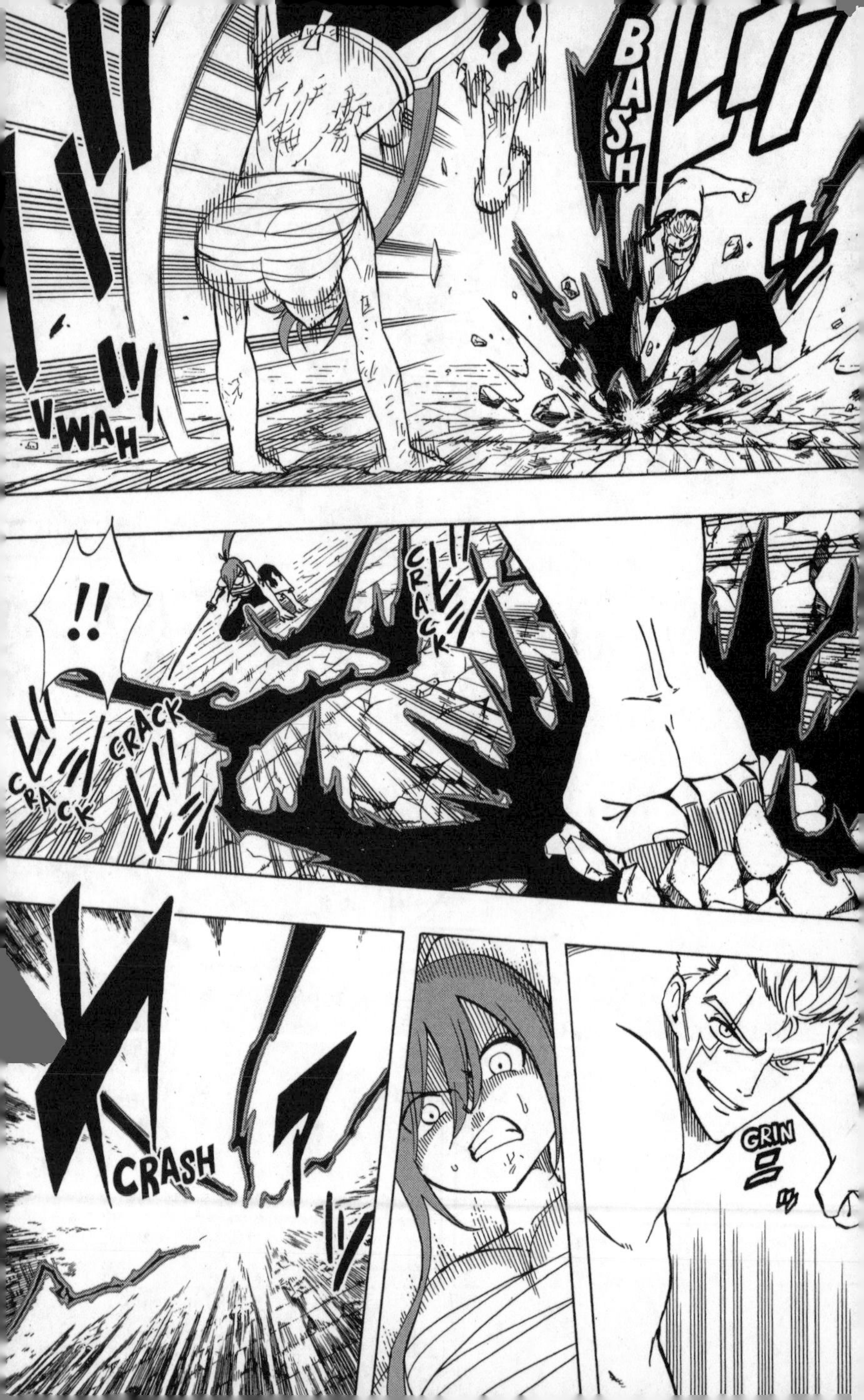
BASH
VWAH
CRACK
!!
CRACK
CRACK
GRIN
CRASH

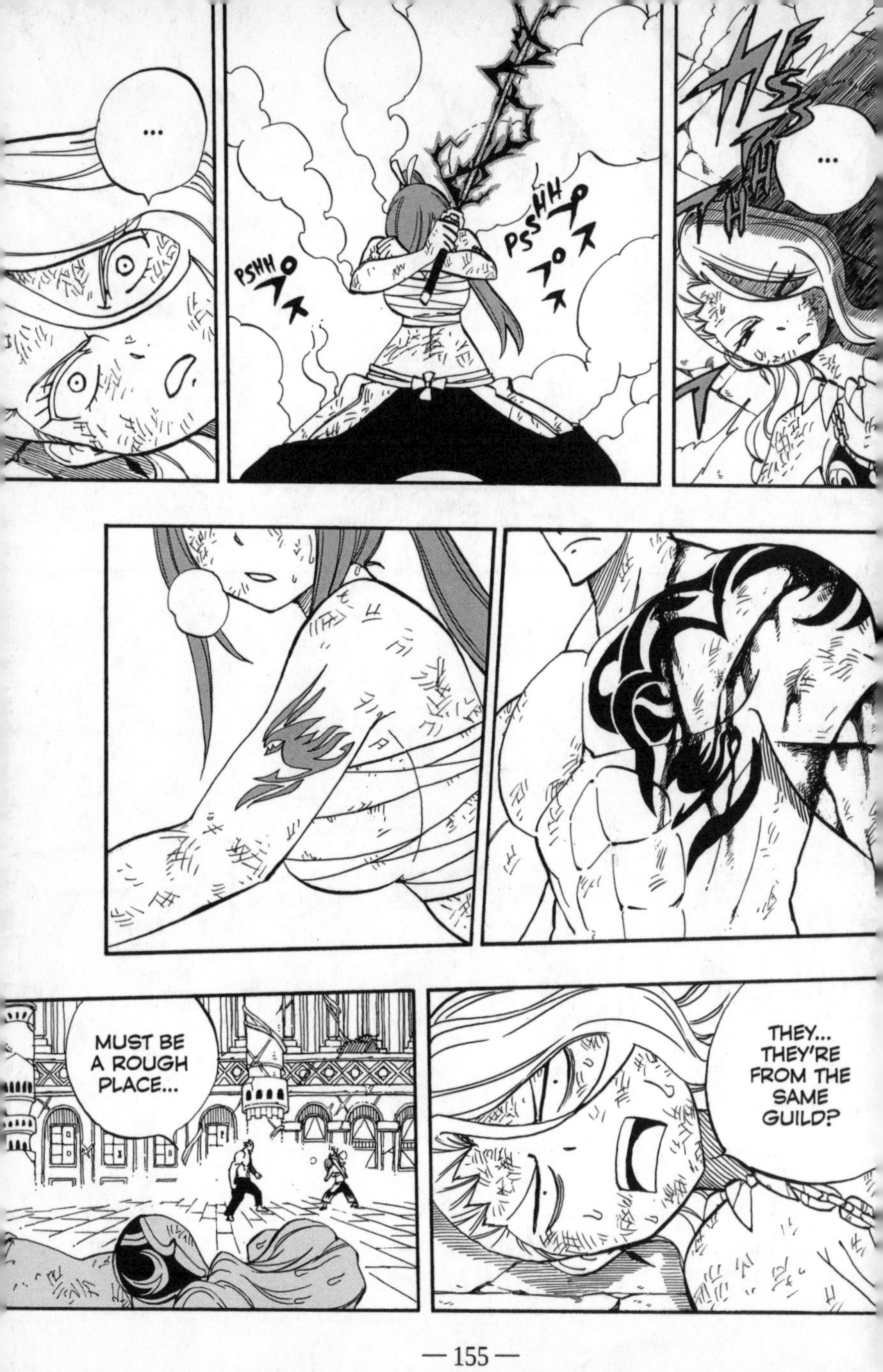
...
PSSHH
PSHH
...
THEY... THEY'RE FROM THE SAME GUILD?
MUST BE A ROUGH PLACE...

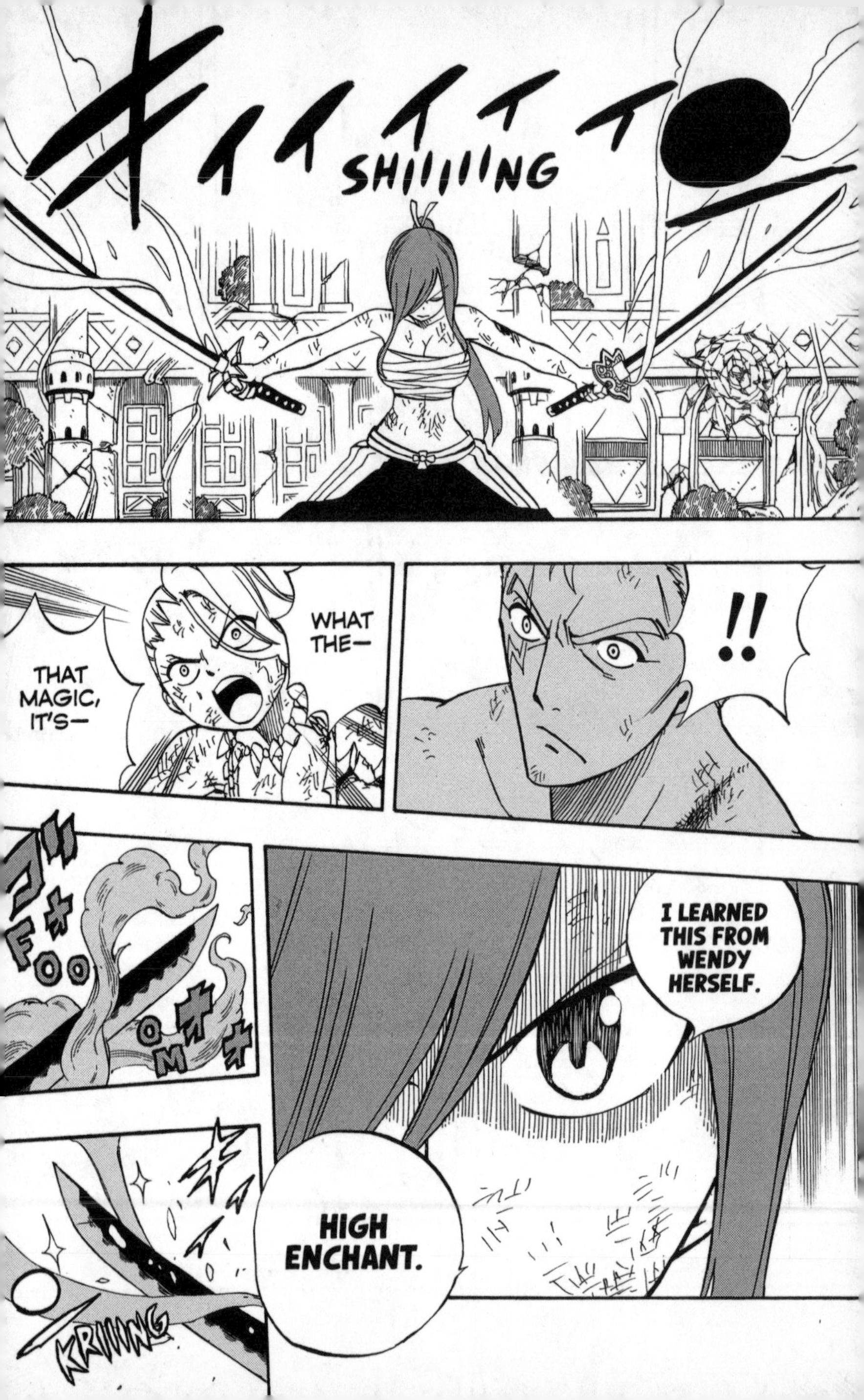
SHIIIING
!!
WHAT THE—
THAT MAGIC, IT'S—
I LEARNED THIS FROM WENDY HERSELF.
HIGH ENCHANT.
FOOOM
KRIIIING

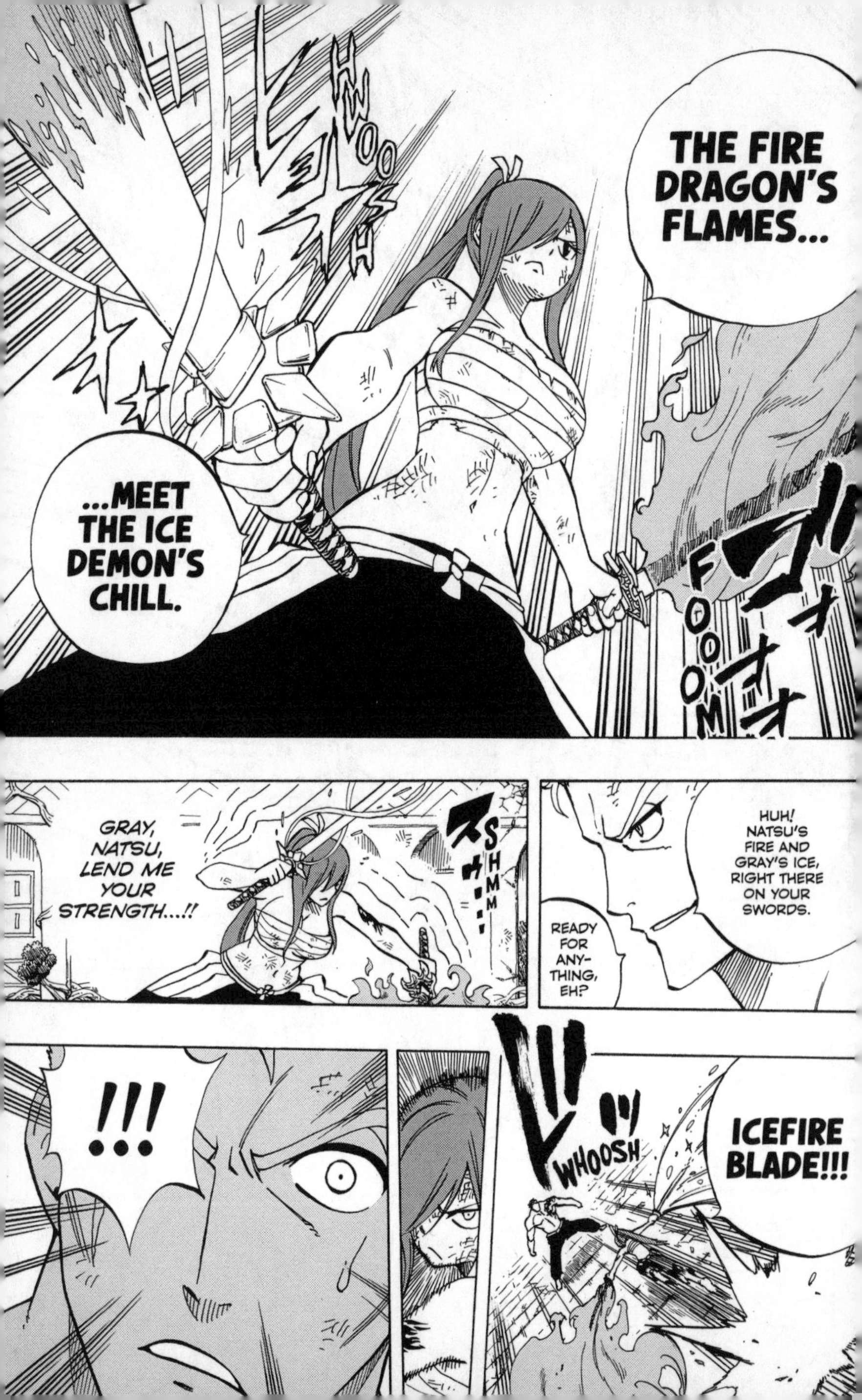
THE FIRE DRAGON'S FLAMES...
HWOOOSH
FOOOM
...MEET THE ICE DEMON'S CHILL.
HUH! NATSU'S FIRE AND GRAY'S ICE, RIGHT THERE ON YOUR SWORDS.
READY FOR ANY-THING, EH?
SHMM
GRAY, NATSU, LEND ME YOUR STRENGTH...!!
ICEFIRE BLADE!!!
WHOOSH
!!!

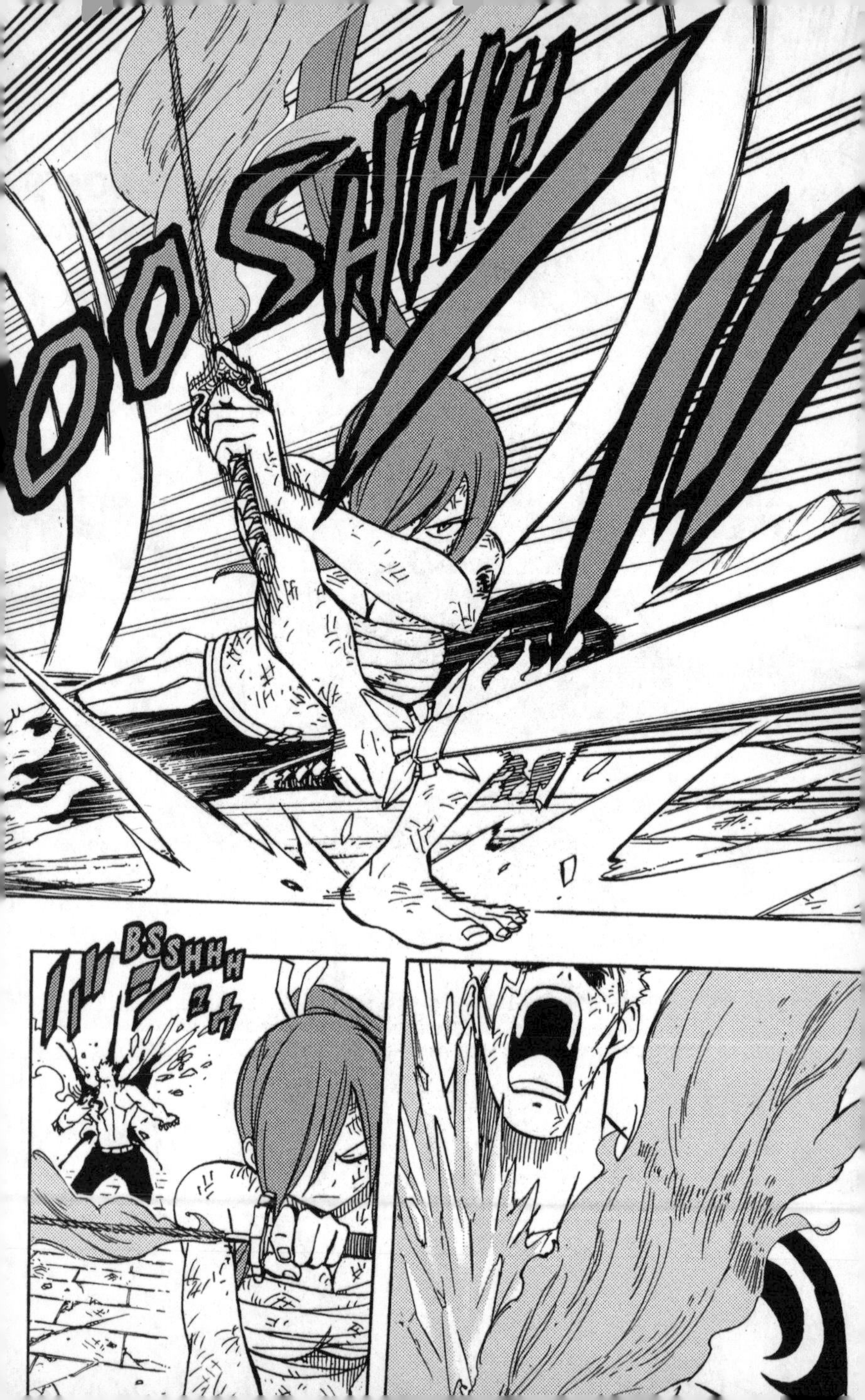
DOOSHHHH
BSSHHH

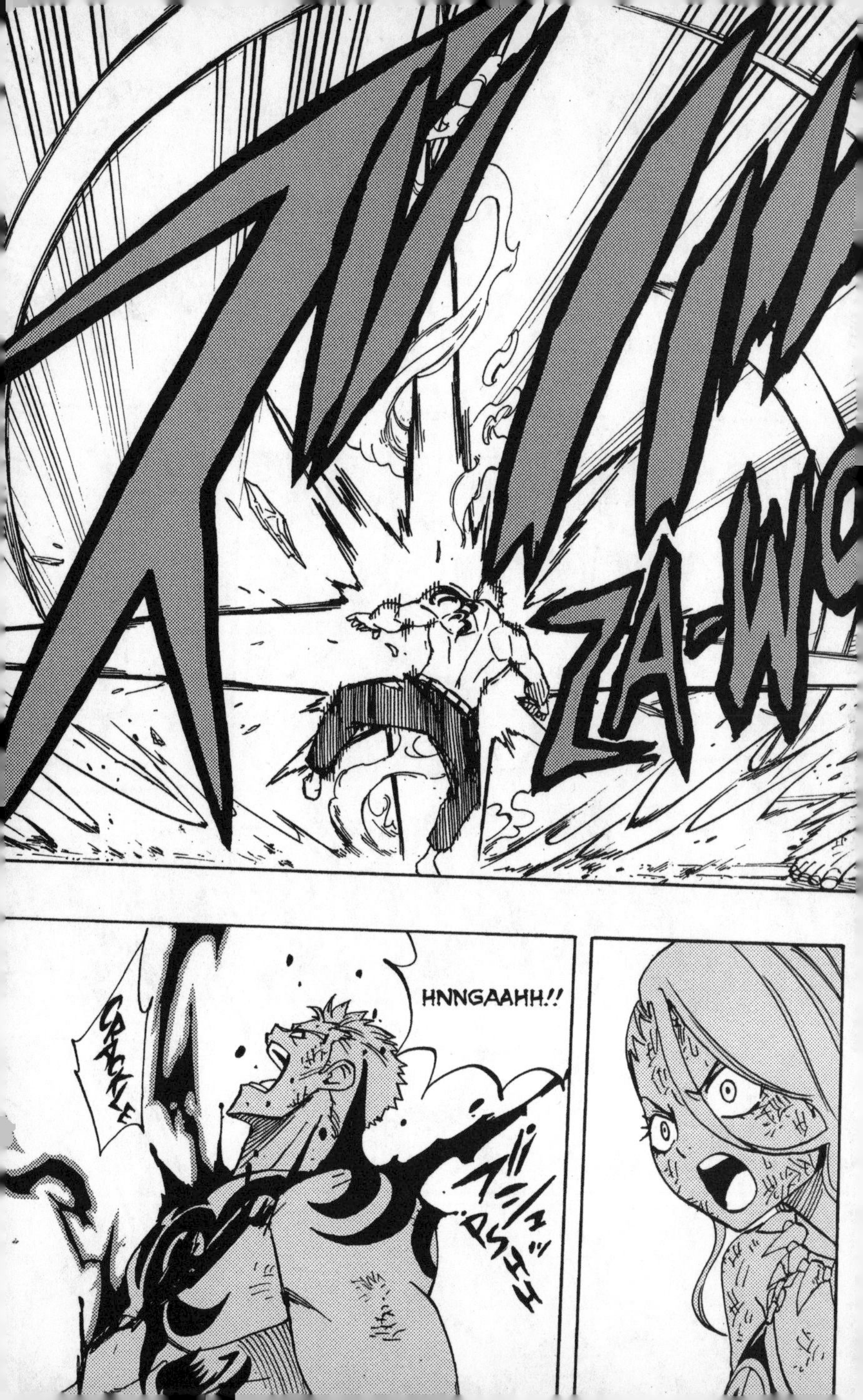
ZA-WO
HNNGAAHH!!
CRACKLE
PSHHH

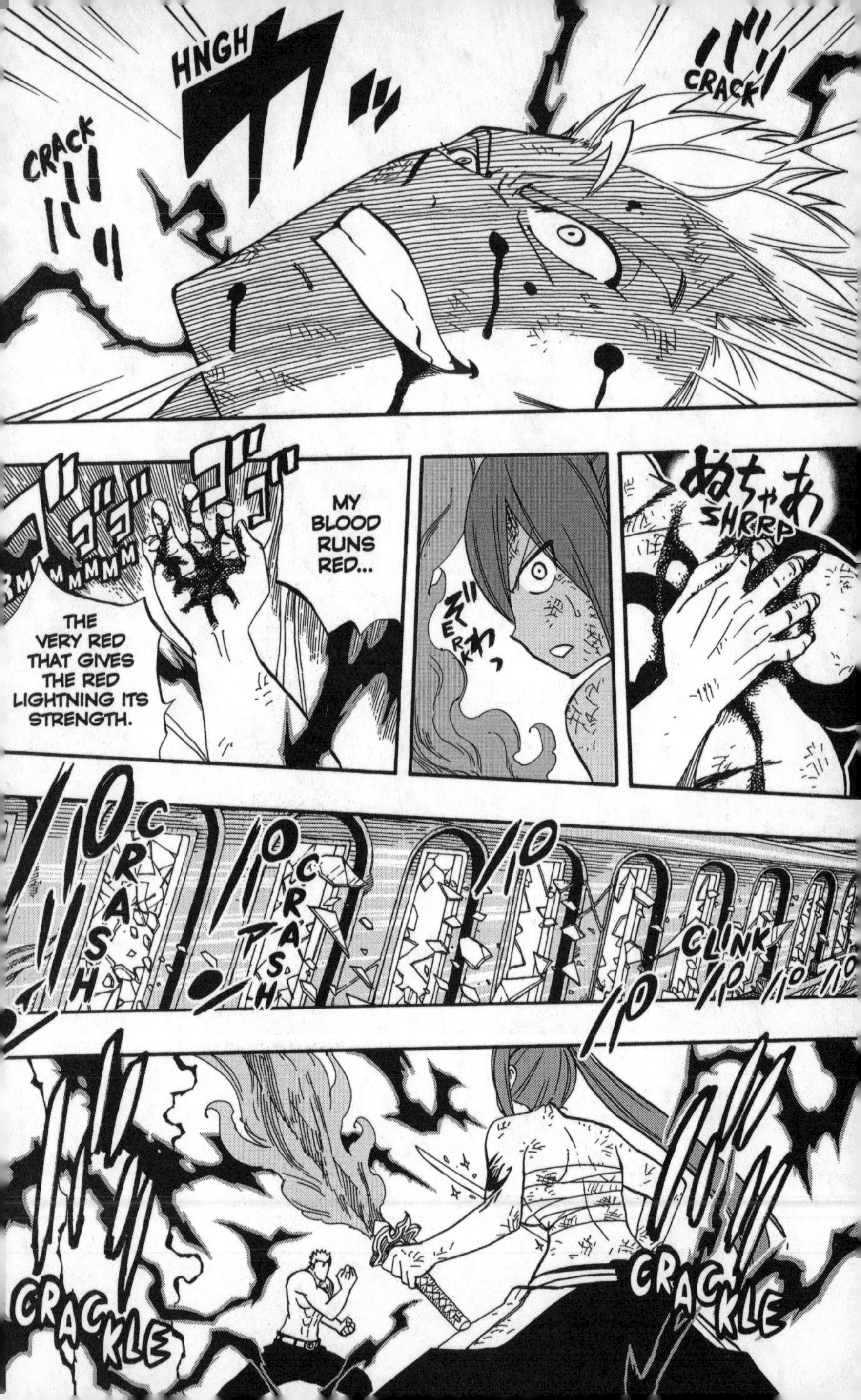

CRACK
HNGH
CRACK
ぬちゃあ
SHRRP
ぞわっ
ERK
MY BLOOD RUNS RED...
THE VERY RED THAT GIVES THE RED LIGHTNING ITS STRENGTH.
CLINK
CRASH
CRASH
CRACKLE
CRACKLE

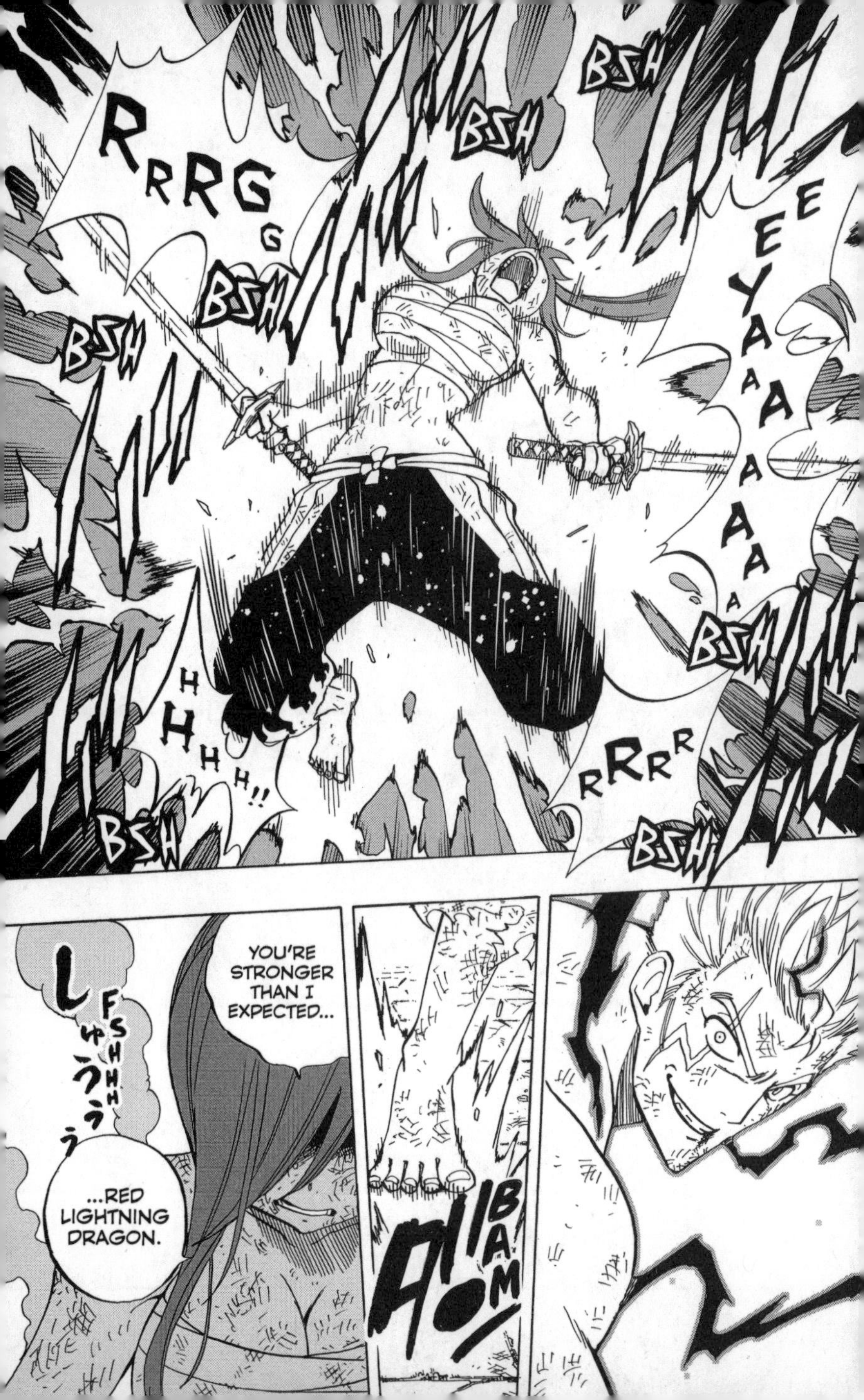
BSH
BSH
EEEYAAAAAAAAA
RRRGG
BSH
BSH
BSH
RRRRR
HHHHH!!
BSH
BAM
YOU'RE STRONGER THAN I EXPECTED...
FSHHH
しゅううう
...RED LIGHTNING DRAGON.

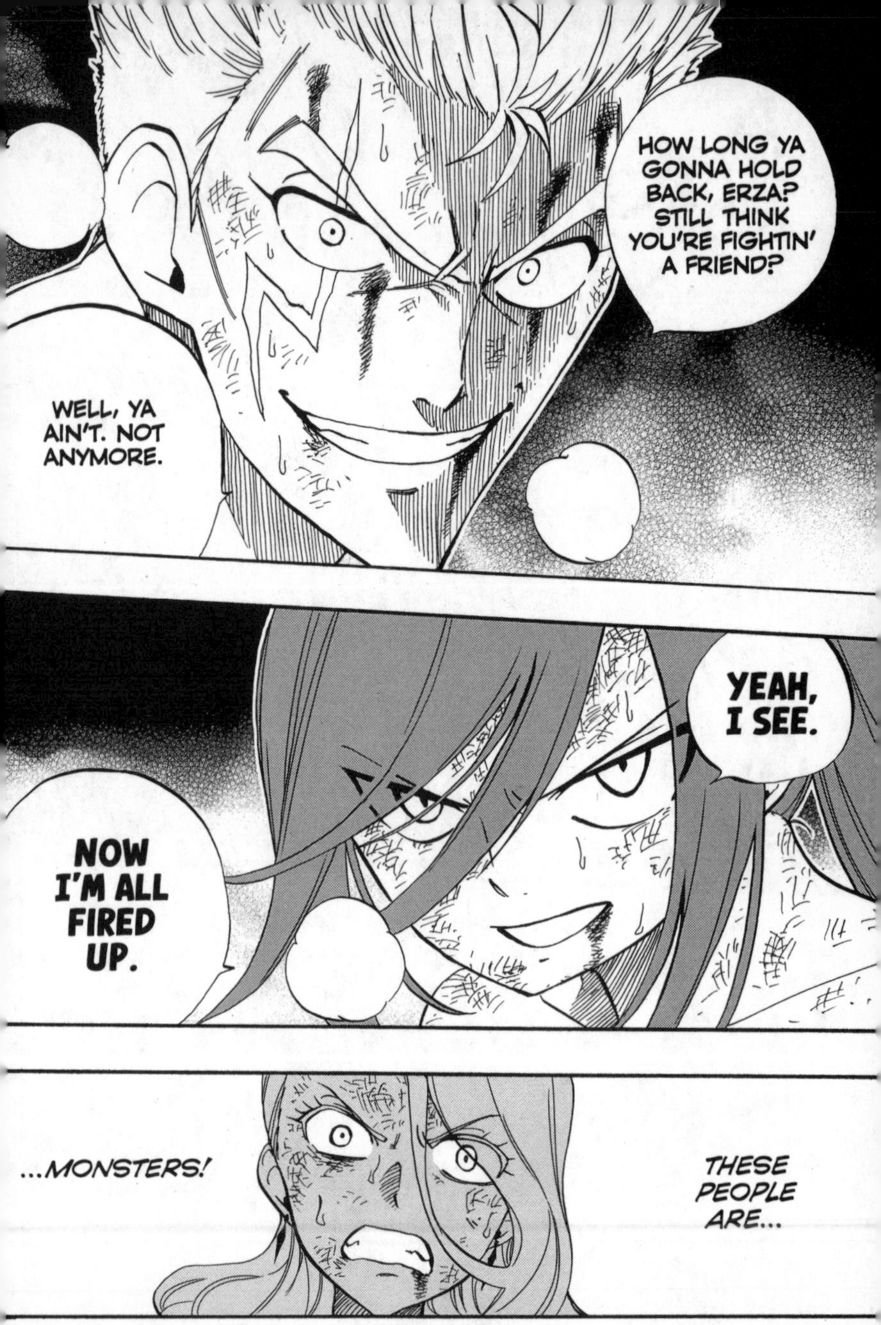
HOW LONG YA GONNA HOLD BACK, ERZA? STILL THINK YOU'RE FIGHTIN' A FRIEND?
WELL, YA AIN'T. NOT ANYMORE.
YEAH, I SEE.
NOW I'M ALL FIRED UP.
THESE PEOPLE ARE...
...MONSTERS!

FAIRY TAIL 100 YEARS QUEST

Chapter 45: Crimson Conclusion

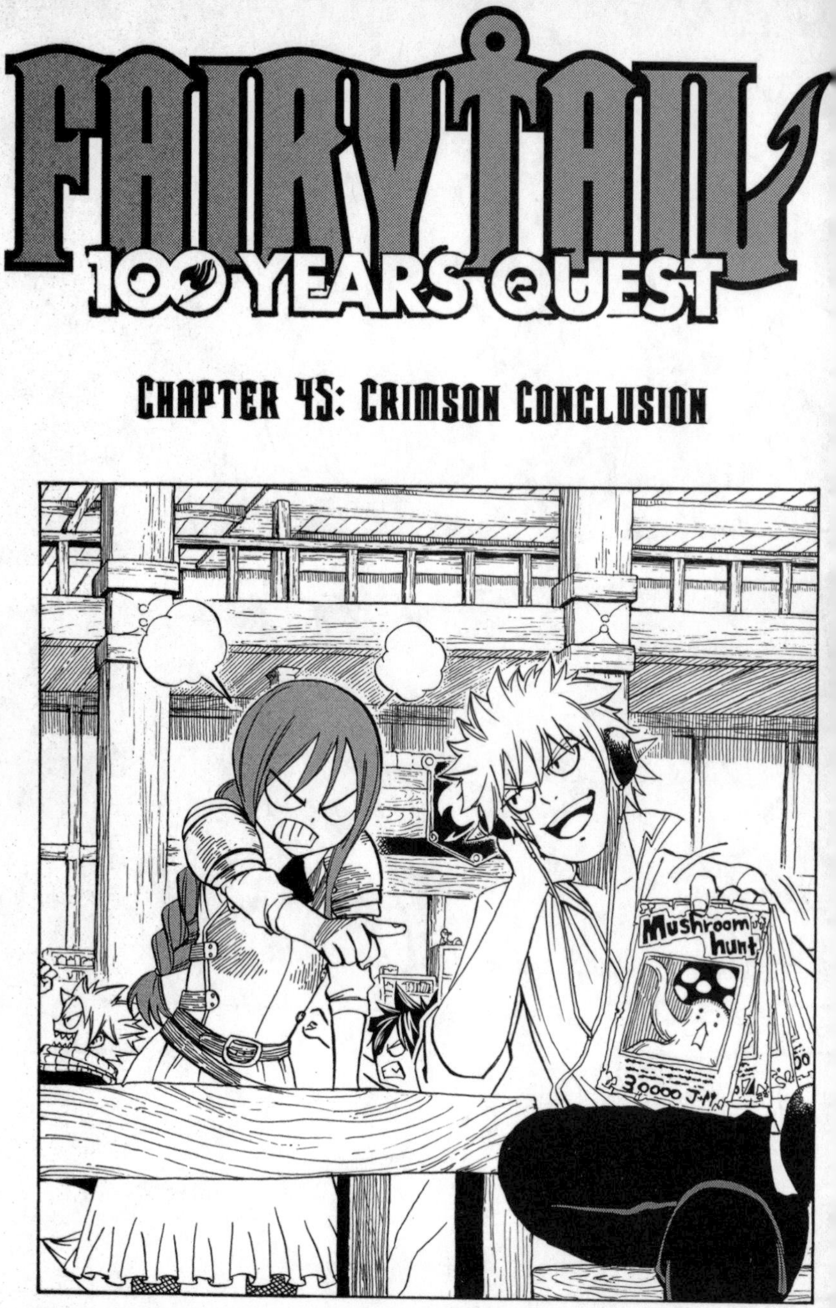
Mushroom hunt

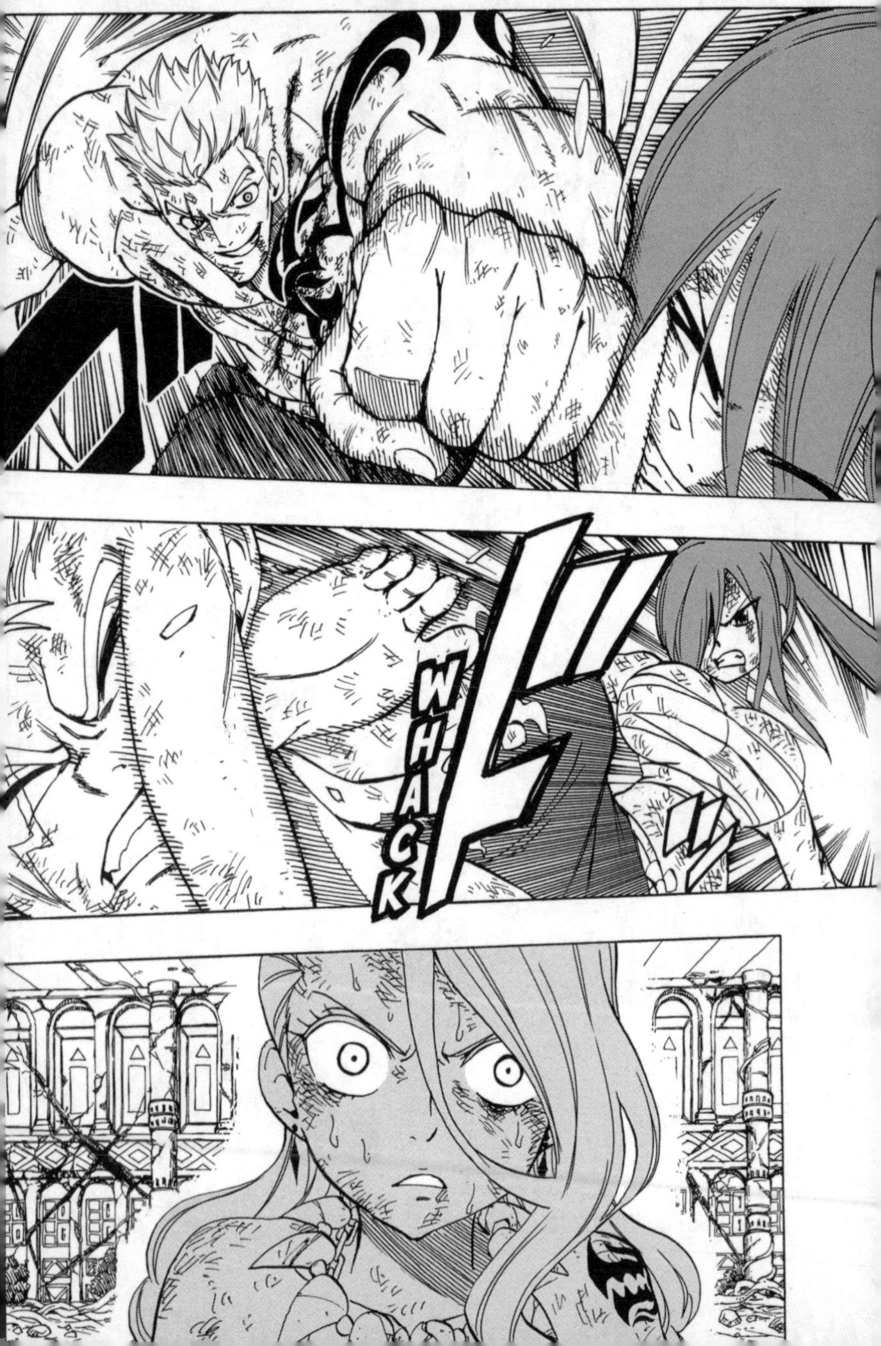
WHACK

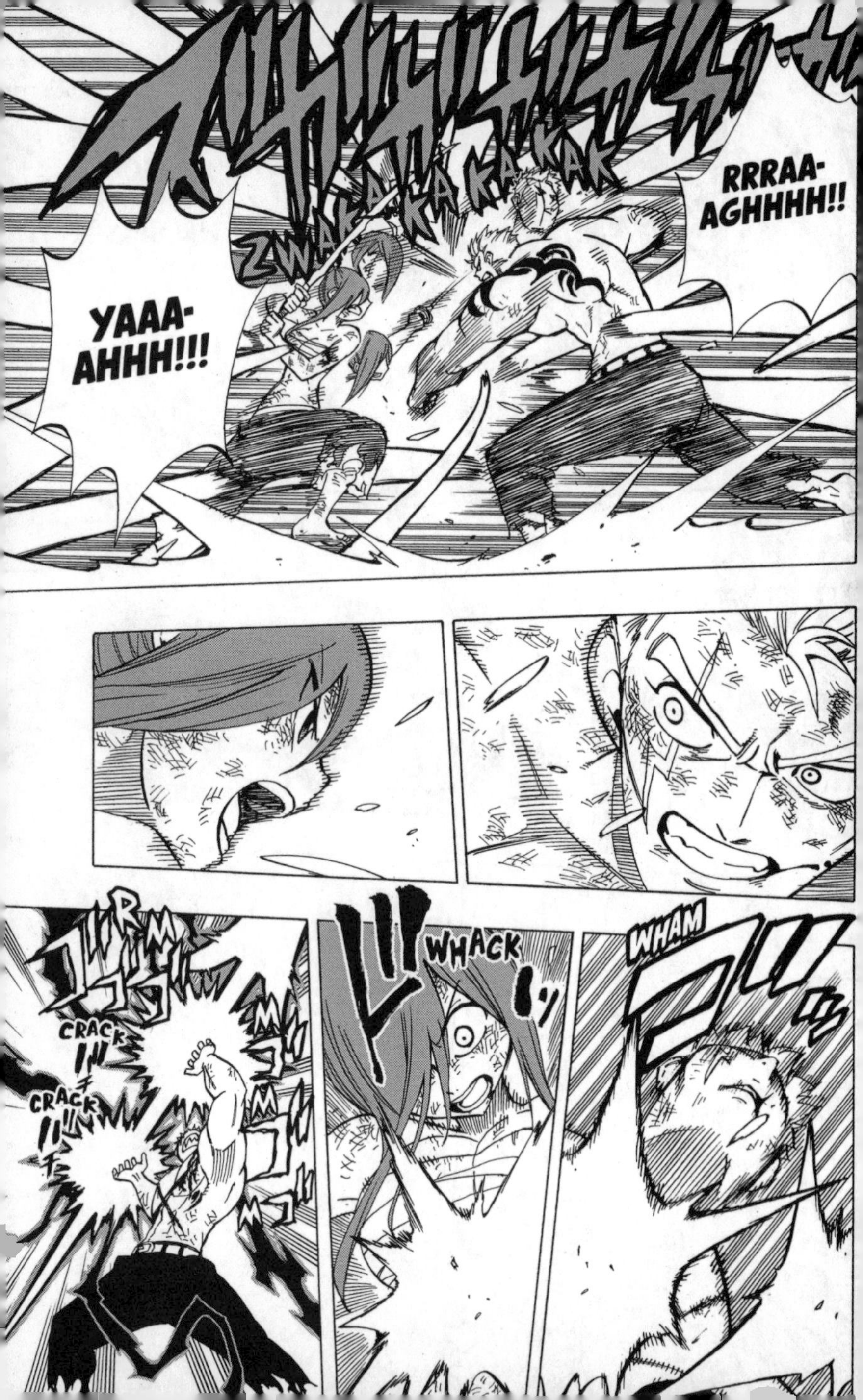
RRRAA-AGHHHH!!
ZWAKAKAKAKAK
YAAA-AHHH!!!
WHAM
WHACK
CRACK
CRACK

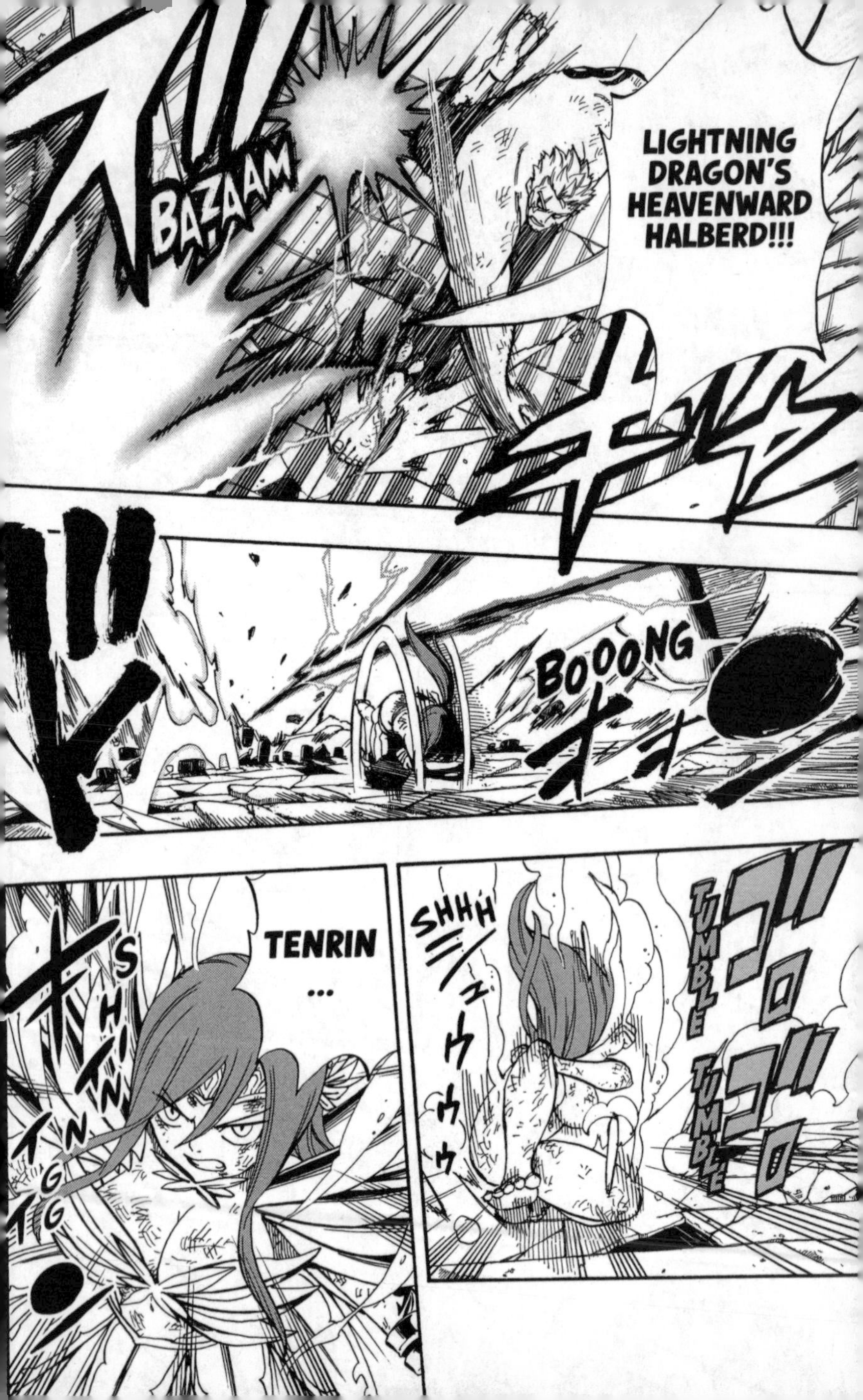
LIGHTNING DRAGON'S HEAVENWARD HALBERD!!!
BAZAAM
BOOONG
TUMBLE TUMBLE
SHHH
TENRIN
...
SHIIIN
TING
TING

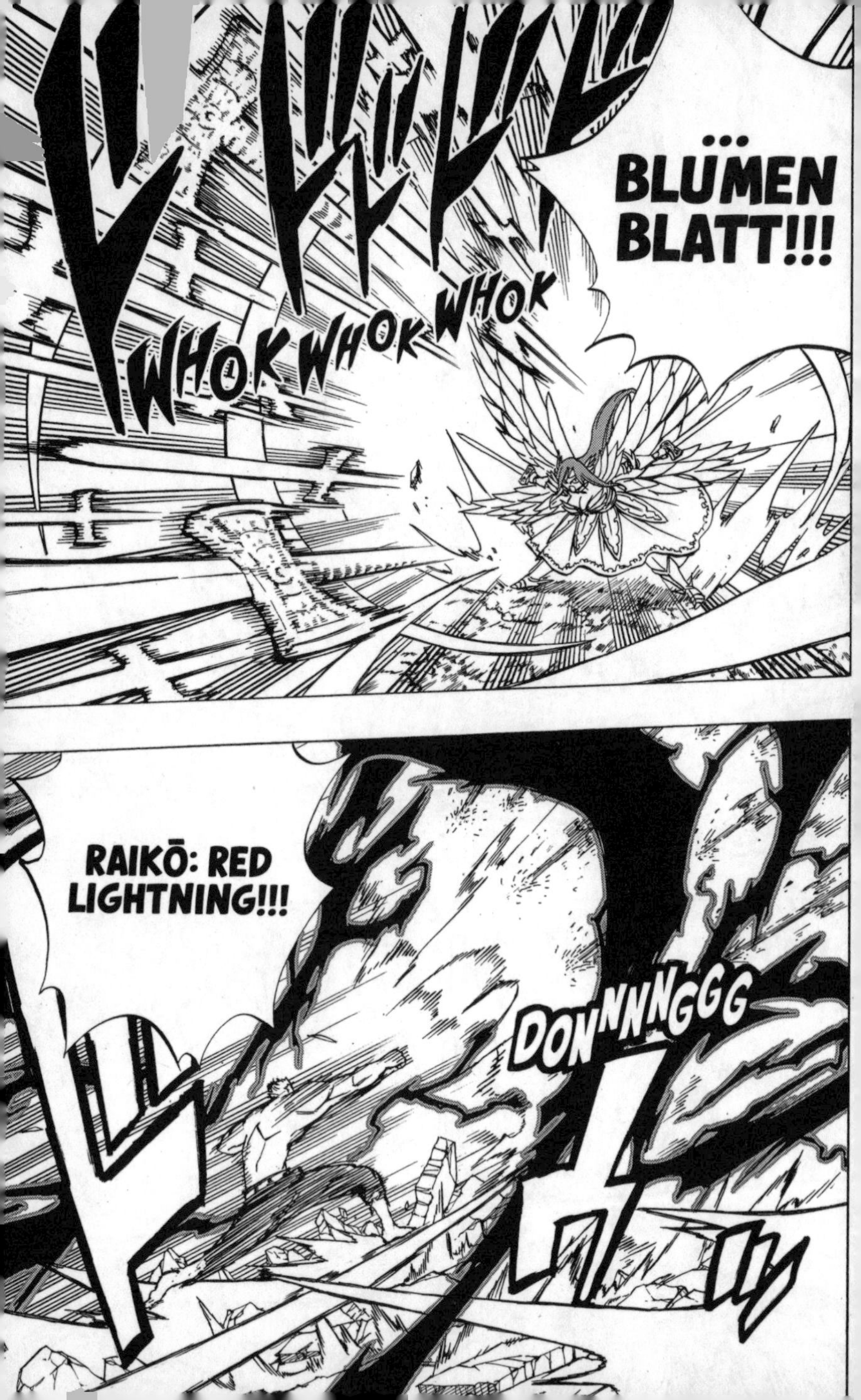
…BLÜMEN BLATT!!!
WHOK WHOK WHOK
RAIKŌ: RED LIGHTNING!!!
DONNNNGGG

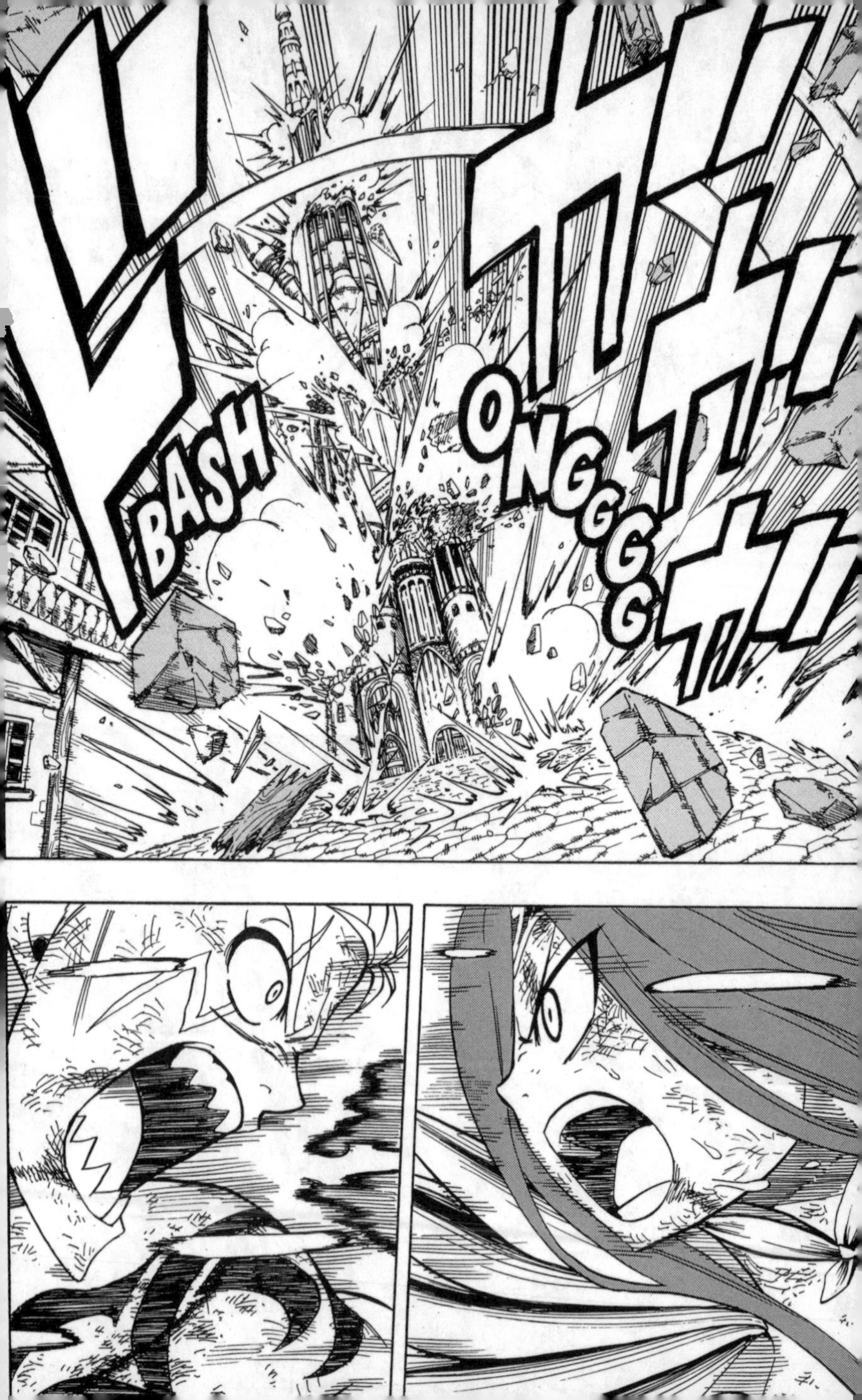

BASH
ONGGG

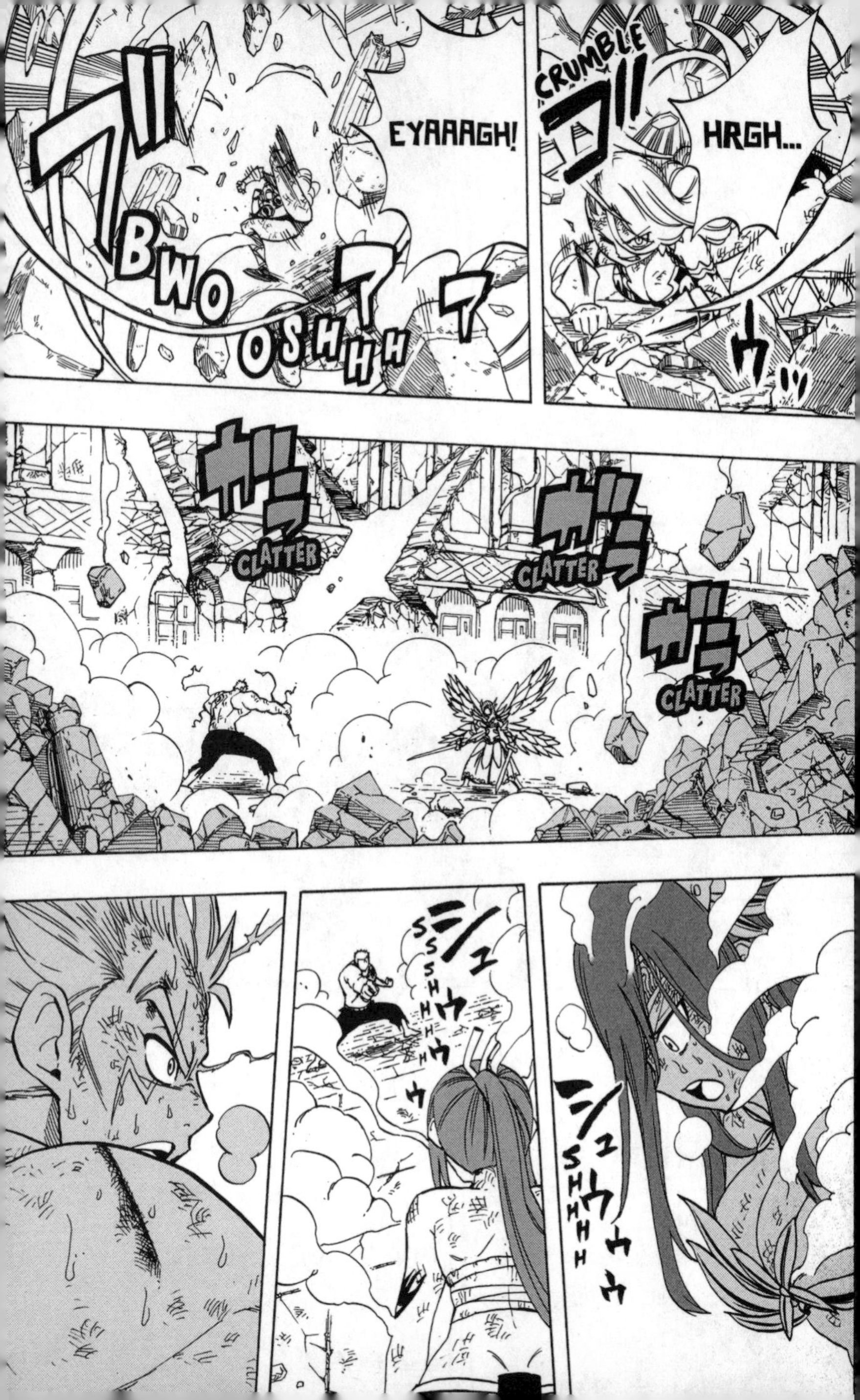
CRUMBLE
HRGH...
EYAAAGH!
BWOOSHHHH
CLATTER
CLATTER
CLATTER
SHHHHH
SSSHHHH

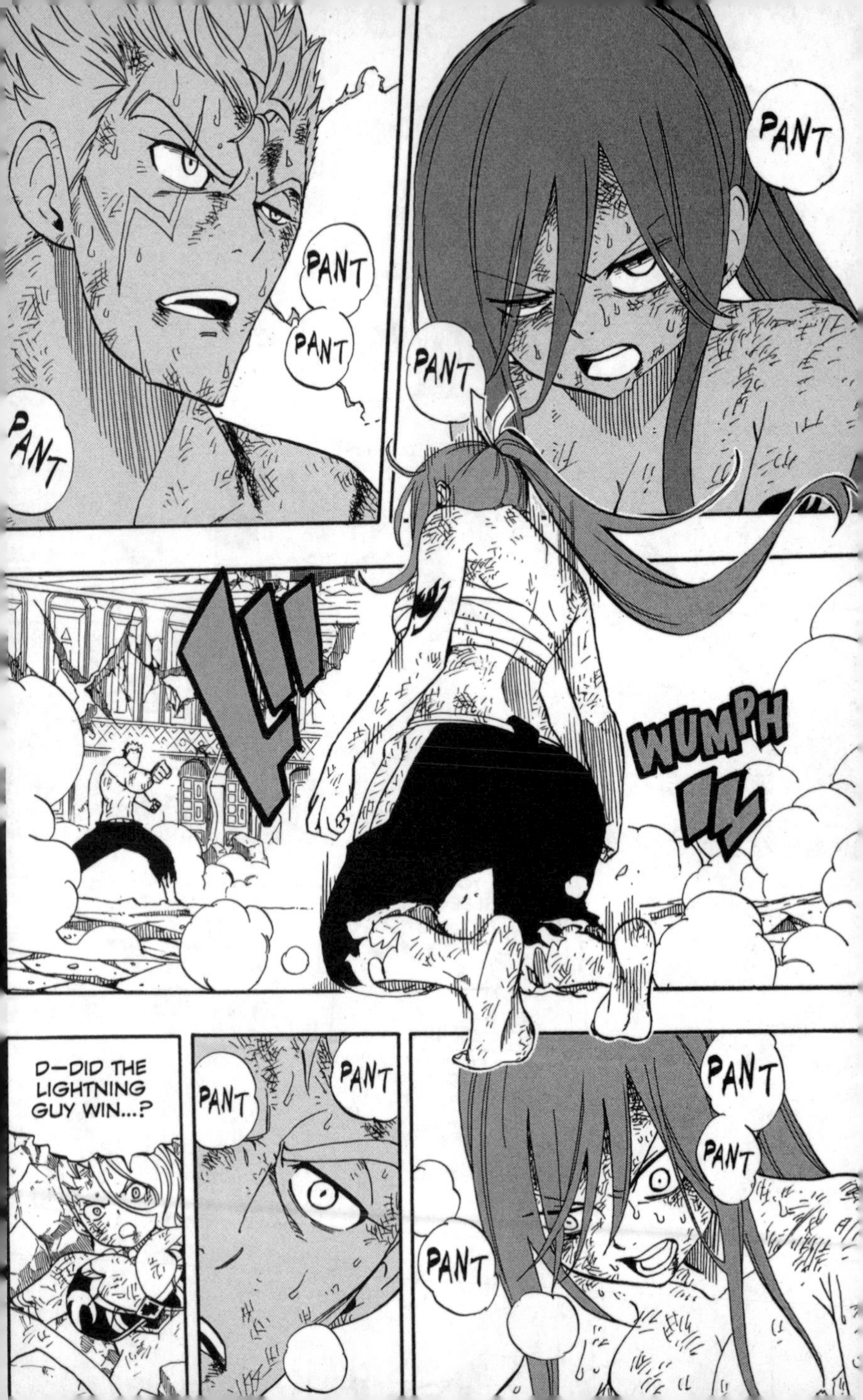
PANT
PANT
PANT
PANT
PANT
WUMPH
PANT
PANT
PANT
PANT
PANT
D—DID THE LIGHTNING GUY WIN...?

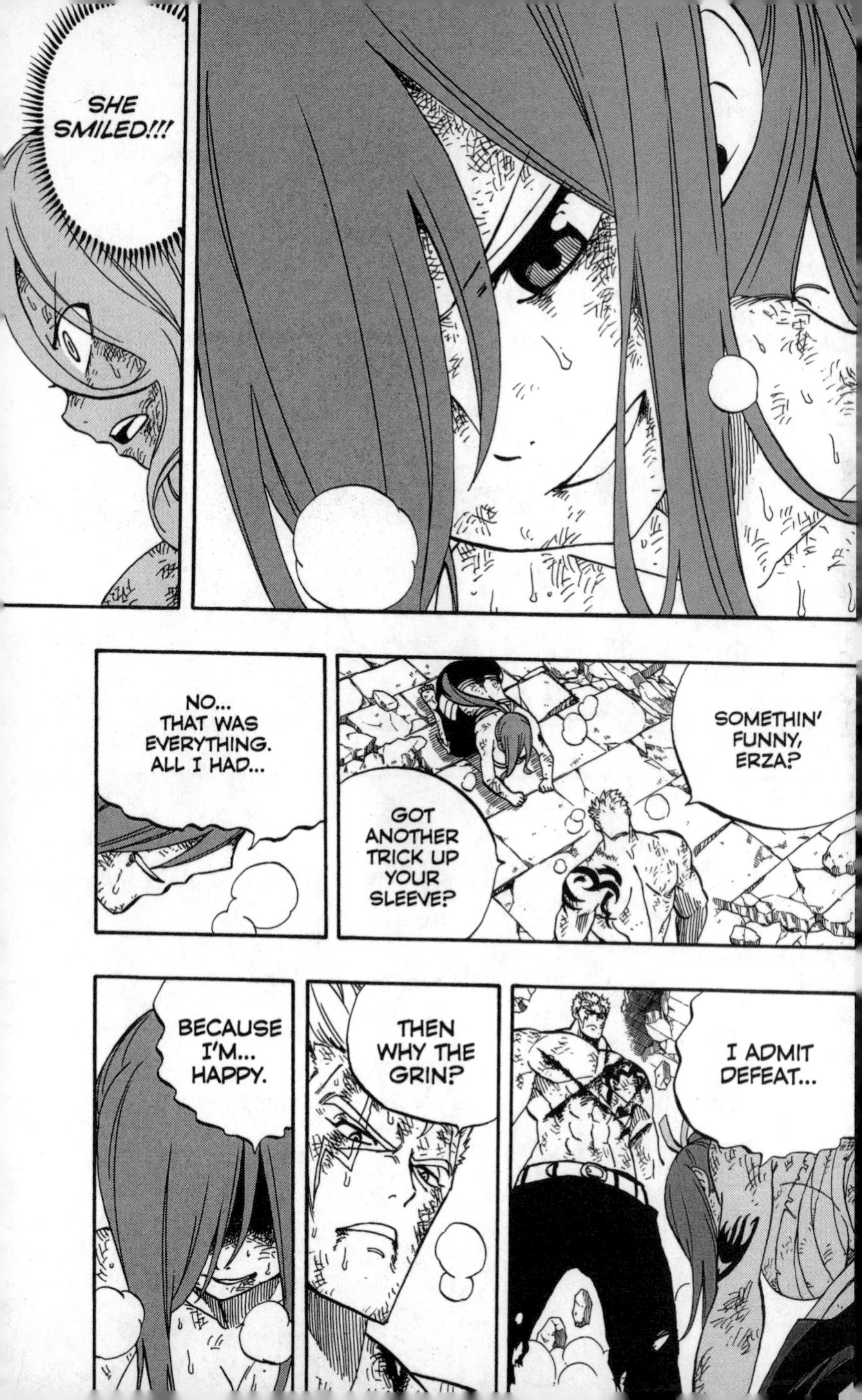
SHE SMILED!!!
SOMETHIN' FUNNY, ERZA?
GOT ANOTHER TRICK UP YOUR SLEEVE?
NO... THAT WAS EVERYTHING. ALL I HAD...
I ADMIT DEFEAT...
THEN WHY THE GRIN?
BECAUSE I'M... HAPPY.

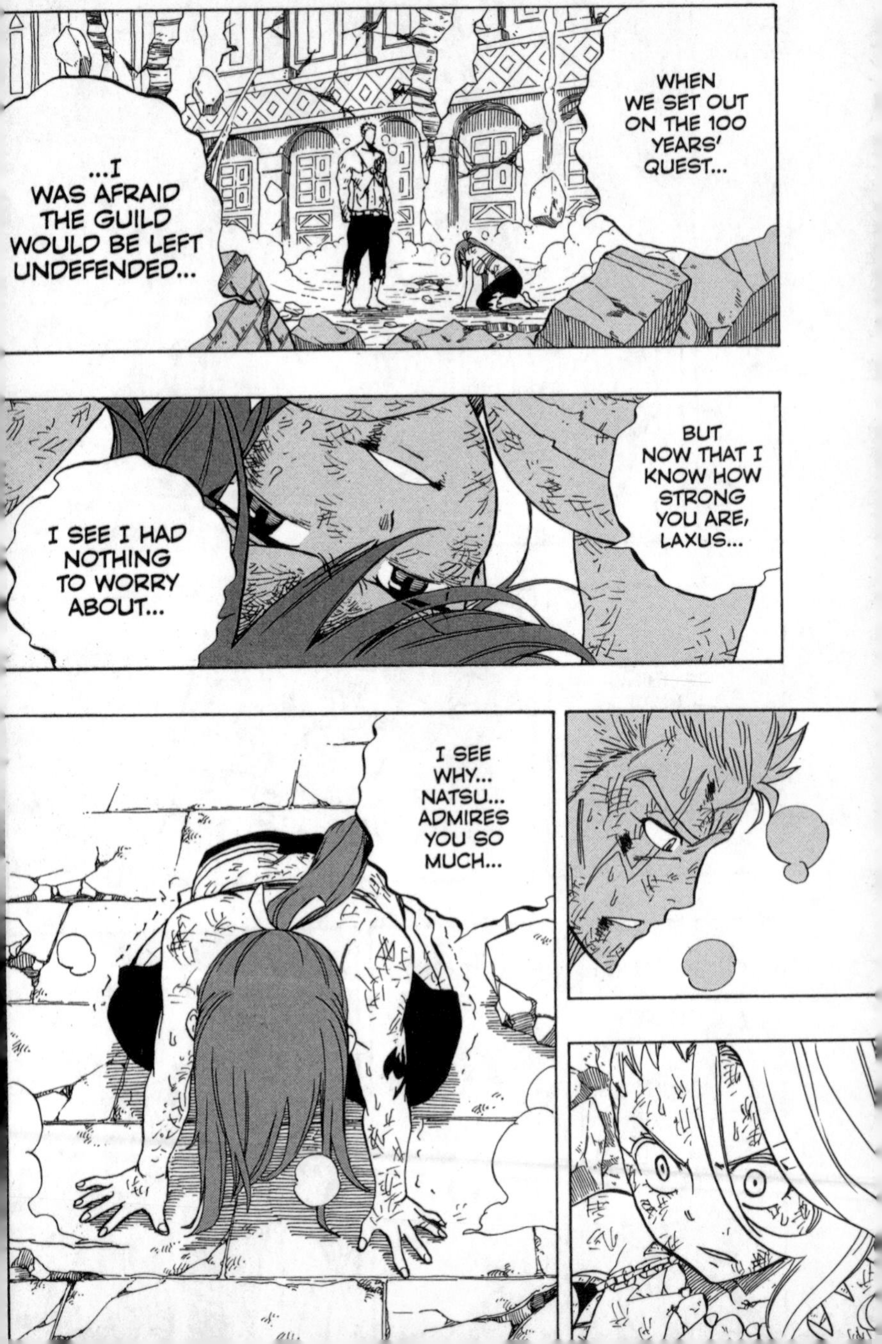
WHEN WE SET OUT ON THE 100 YEARS' QUEST...
...I WAS AFRAID THE GUILD WOULD BE LEFT UNDEFENDED...
BUT NOW THAT I KNOW HOW STRONG YOU ARE, LAXUS...
I SEE I HAD NOTHING TO WORRY ABOUT...
I SEE WHY... NATSU... ADMIRES YOU SO MUCH...

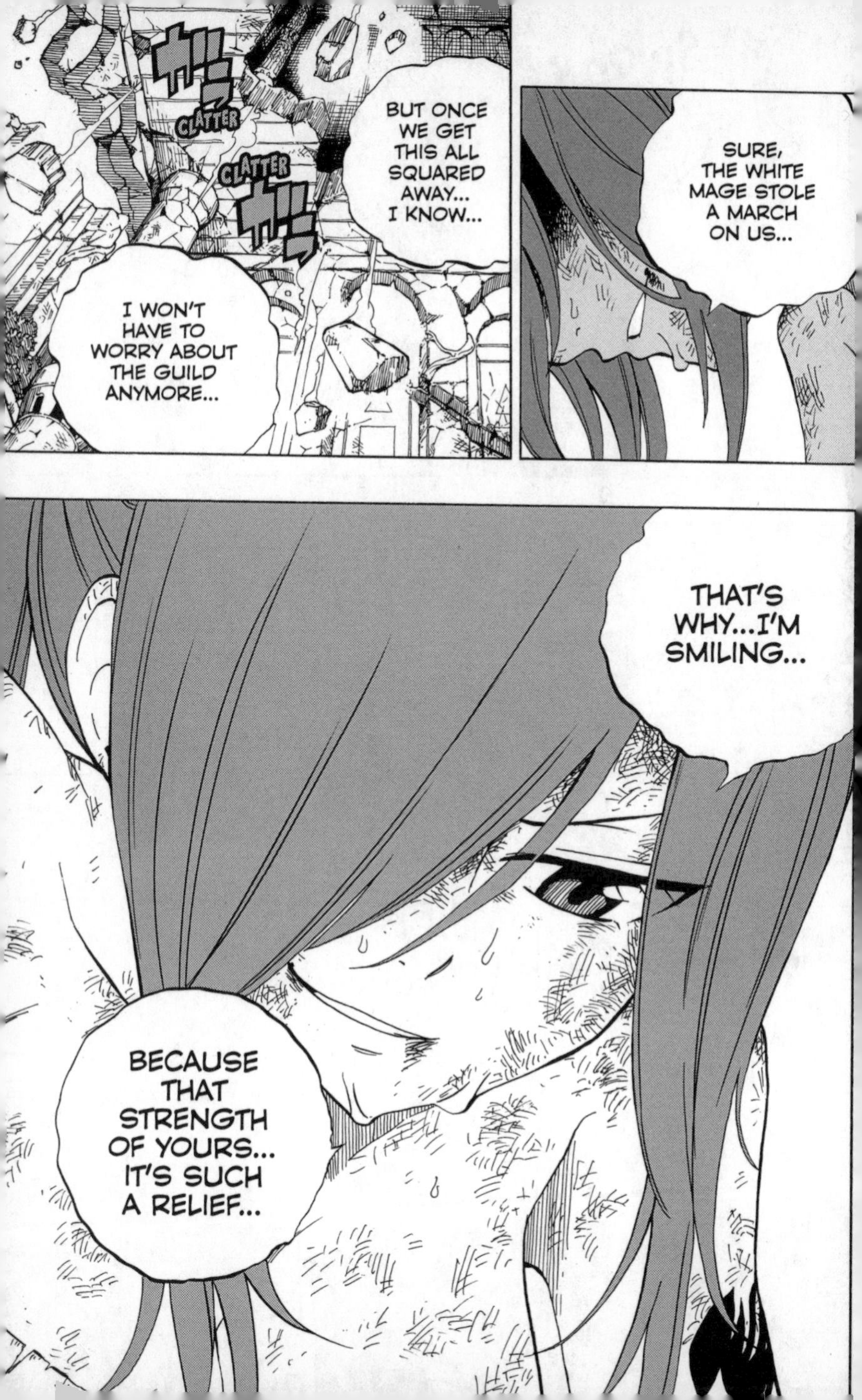
SURE, THE WHITE MAGE STOLE A MARCH ON US...
BUT ONCE WE GET THIS ALL SQUARED AWAY... I KNOW...
CLATTER
CLATTER
I WON'T HAVE TO WORRY ABOUT THE GUILD ANYMORE...
THAT'S WHY...I'M SMILING...
BECAUSE THAT STRENGTH OF YOURS... IT'S SUCH A RELIEF...

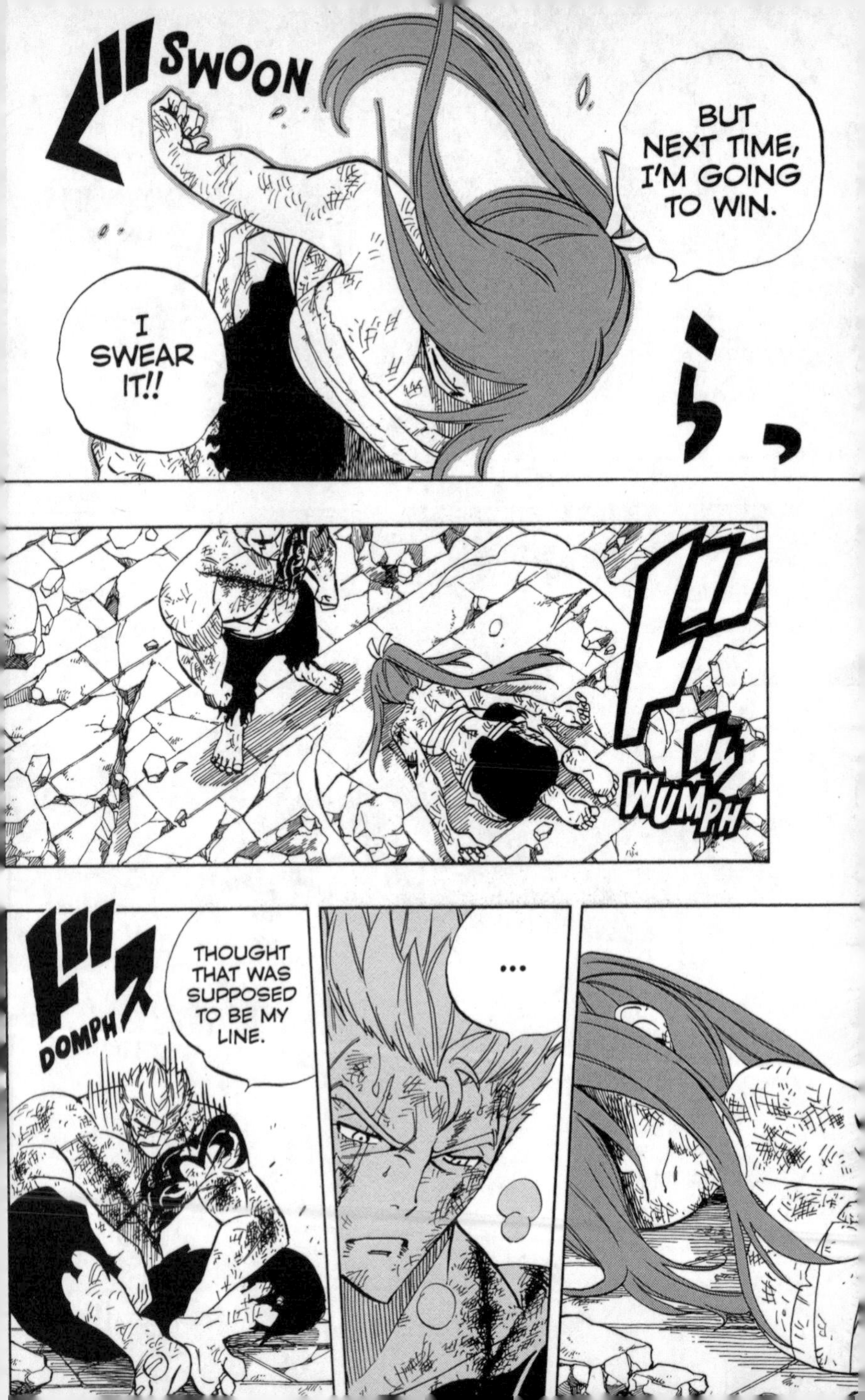
BUT NEXT TIME, I'M GOING TO WIN.
SWOON
I SWEAR IT!!
WUMPH
...
THOUGHT THAT WAS SUPPOSED TO BE MY LINE.
DOMPH

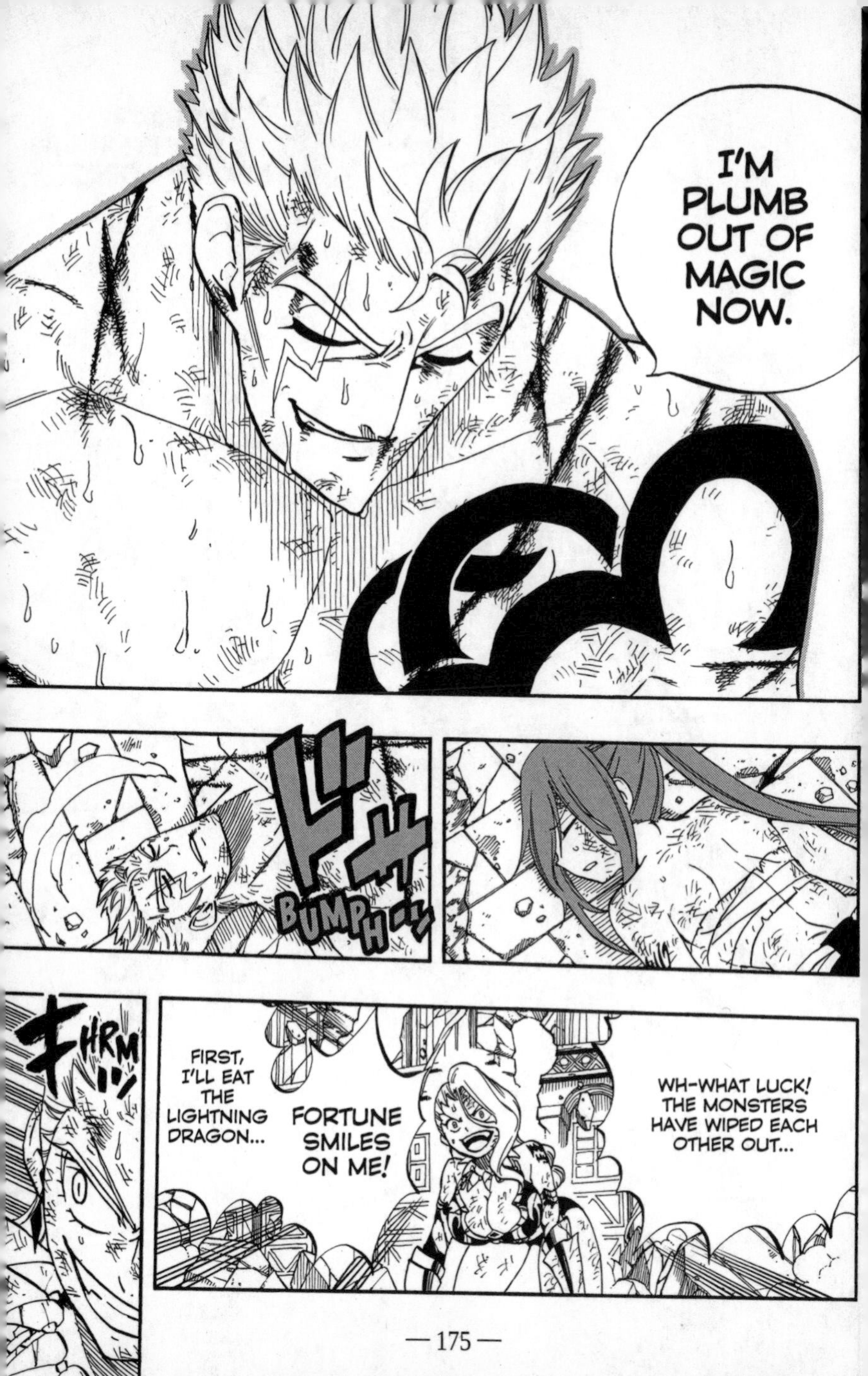
I'M PLUMB OUT OF MAGIC NOW.
BUMPH...
WH-WHAT LUCK! THE MONSTERS HAVE WIPED EACH OTHER OUT...
FORTUNE SMILES ON ME!
FIRST, I'LL EAT THE LIGHTNING DRAGON...
HRM

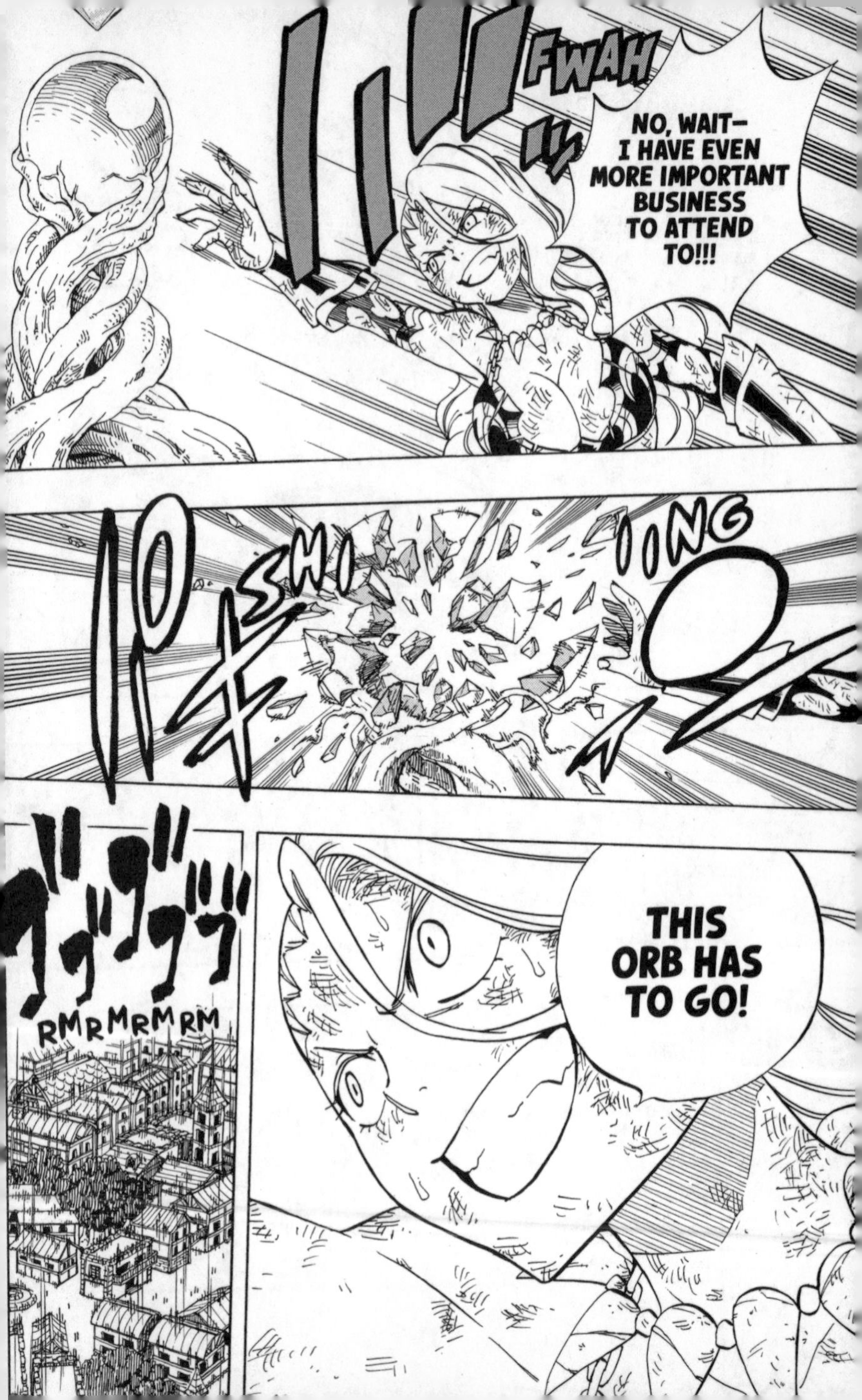
FWAH
NO, WAIT– I HAVE EVEN MORE IMPORTANT BUSINESS TO ATTEND TO!!!
SHIIING
THIS ORB HAS TO GO!
RMRMRMRM

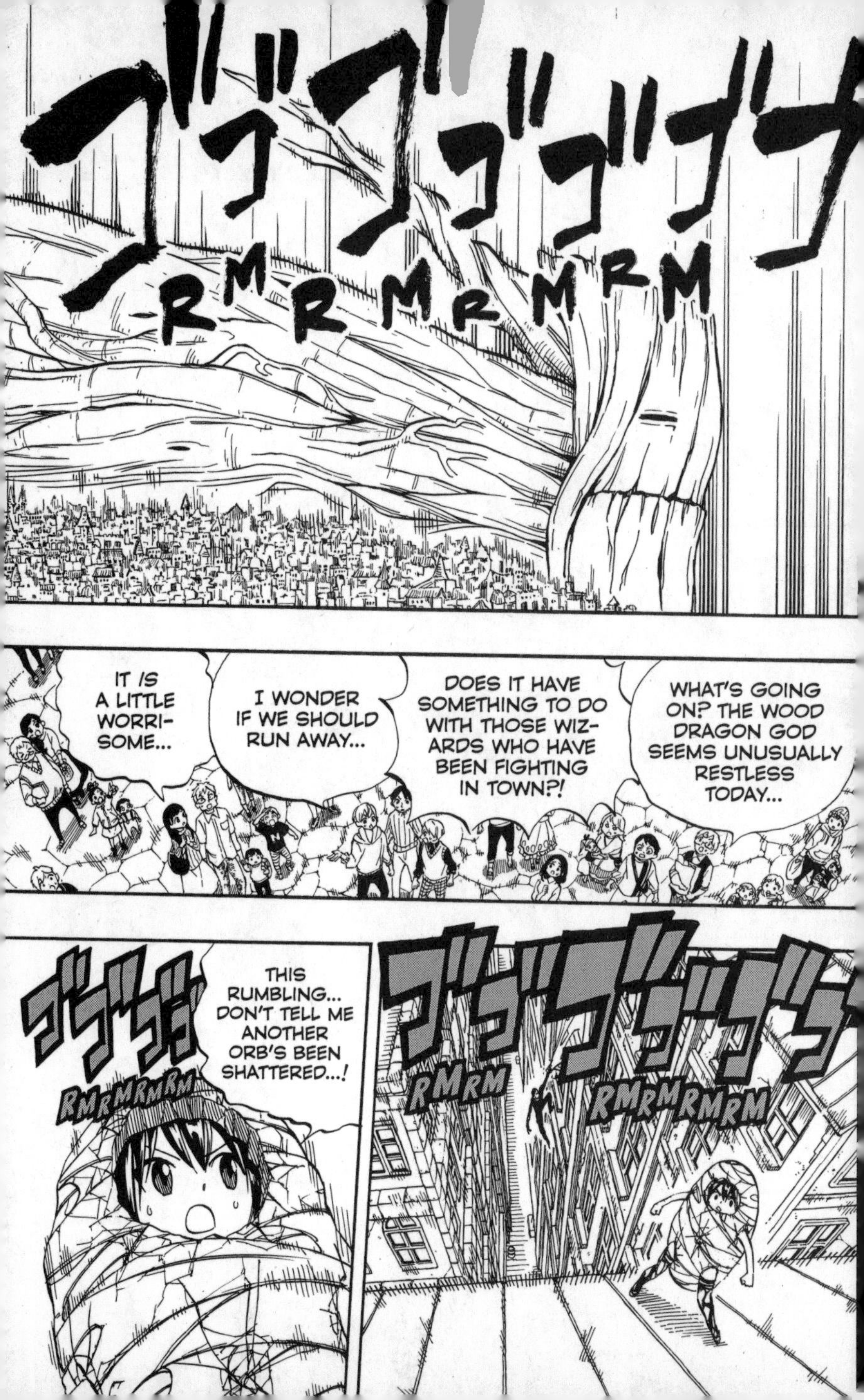
RMRMRMRM
WHAT'S GOING ON? THE WOOD DRAGON GOD SEEMS UNUSUALLY RESTLESS TODAY...
DOES IT HAVE SOMETHING TO DO WITH THOSE WIZ-ARDS WHO HAVE BEEN FIGHTING IN TOWN?!
I WONDER IF WE SHOULD RUN AWAY...
IT IS A LITTLE WORRI-SOME...
RMRM
RMRMRMRM
RMRMRMRM
THIS RUMBLING... DON'T TELL ME ANOTHER ORB'S BEEN SHATTERED...!

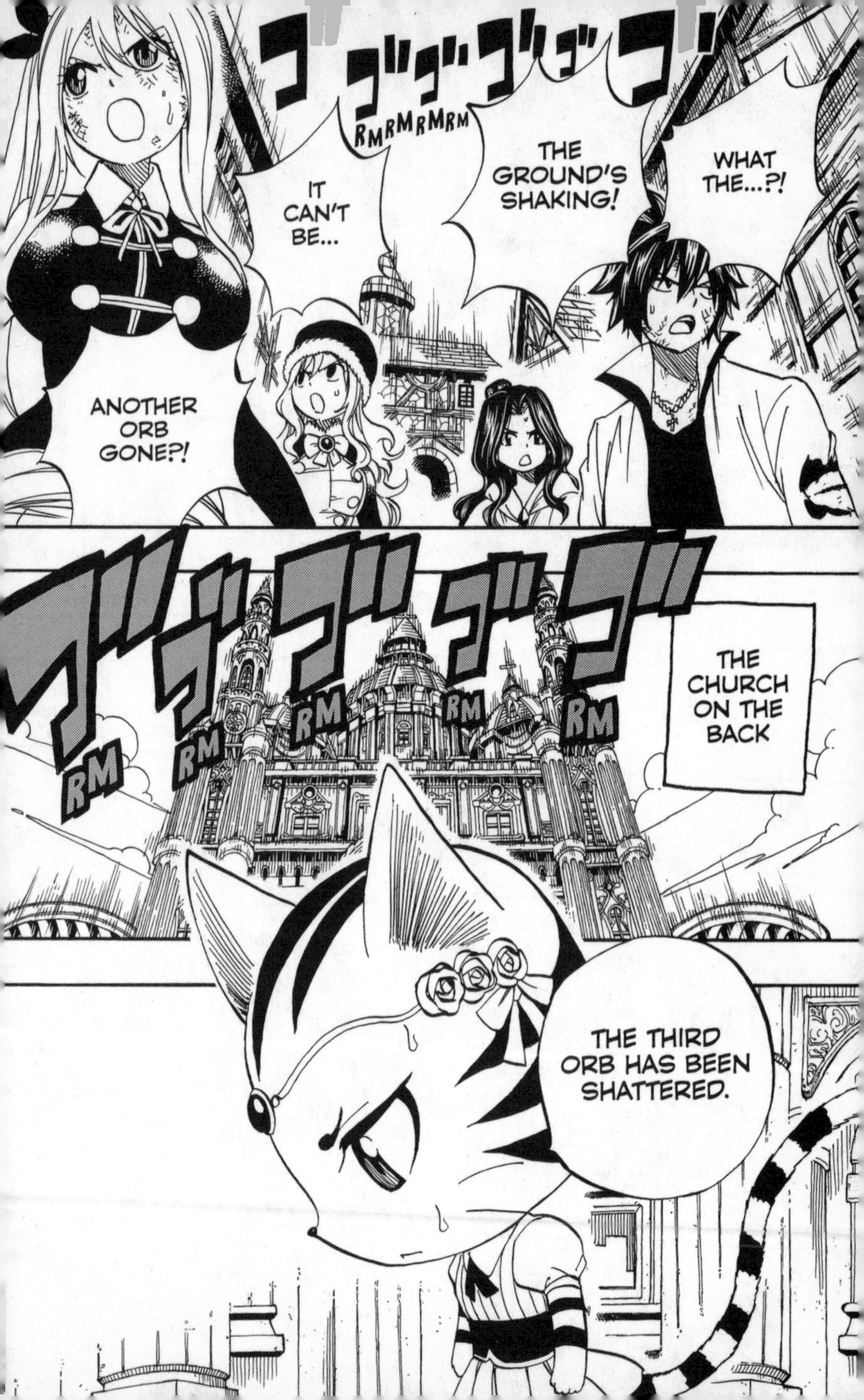
RMRMRMRM
WHAT THE...?!
THE GROUND'S SHAKING!
IT CAN'T BE...
ANOTHER ORB GONE?!
THE CHURCH ON THE BACK
RM RM RM RM RM
THE THIRD ORB HAS BEEN SHATTERED.

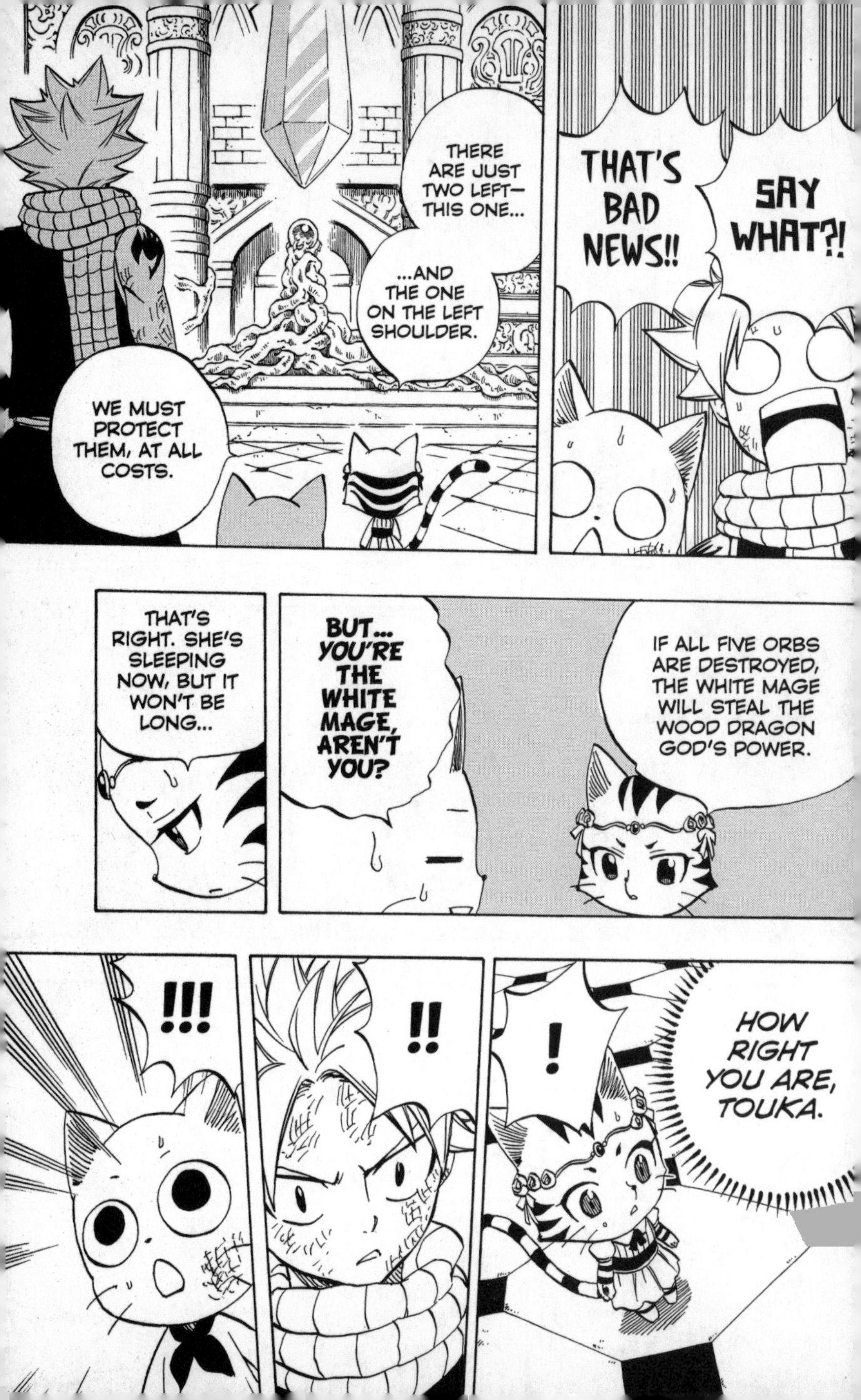
SAY WHAT?!
THAT'S BAD NEWS!!
THERE ARE JUST TWO LEFT— THIS ONE...
...AND THE ONE ON THE LEFT SHOULDER.
WE MUST PROTECT THEM, AT ALL COSTS.
IF ALL FIVE ORBS ARE DESTROYED, THE WHITE MAGE WILL STEAL THE WOOD DRAGON GOD'S POWER.
BUT... YOU'RE THE WHITE MAGE, AREN'T YOU?
THAT'S RIGHT. SHE'S SLEEPING NOW, BUT IT WON'T BE LONG...
HOW RIGHT YOU ARE, TOUKA.
!
!!
!!!

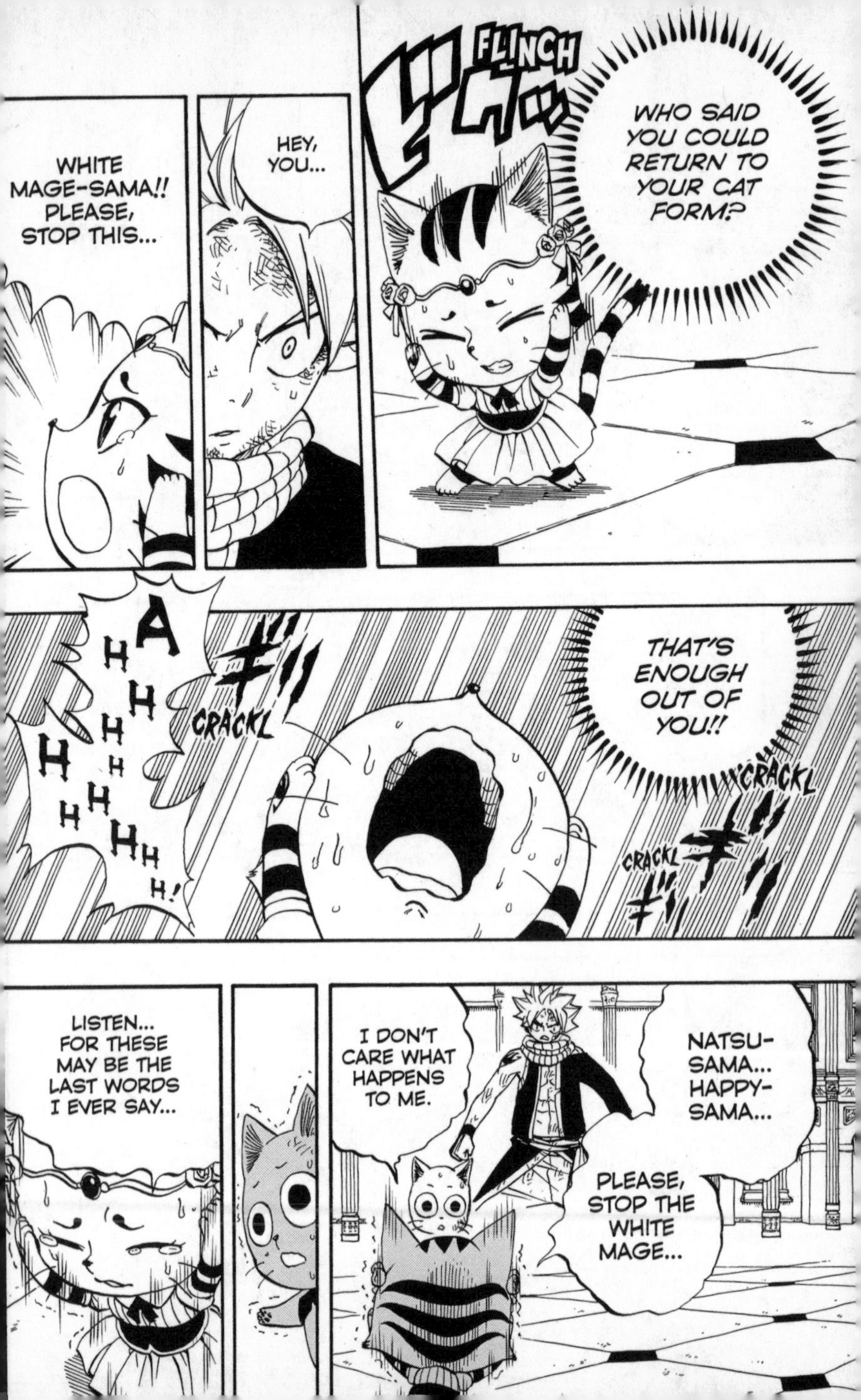
FLINCH
WHO SAID YOU COULD RETURN TO YOUR CAT FORM?
HEY, YOU...
WHITE MAGE-SAMA!! PLEASE, STOP THIS...
THAT'S ENOUGH OUT OF YOU!!
CRACKL
CRACKL
CRACKL
AHHHHHHHHHHHH!
NATSU-SAMA... HAPPY-SAMA...
PLEASE, STOP THE WHITE MAGE...
I DON'T CARE WHAT HAPPENS TO ME.
LISTEN... FOR THESE MAY BE THE LAST WORDS I EVER SAY...

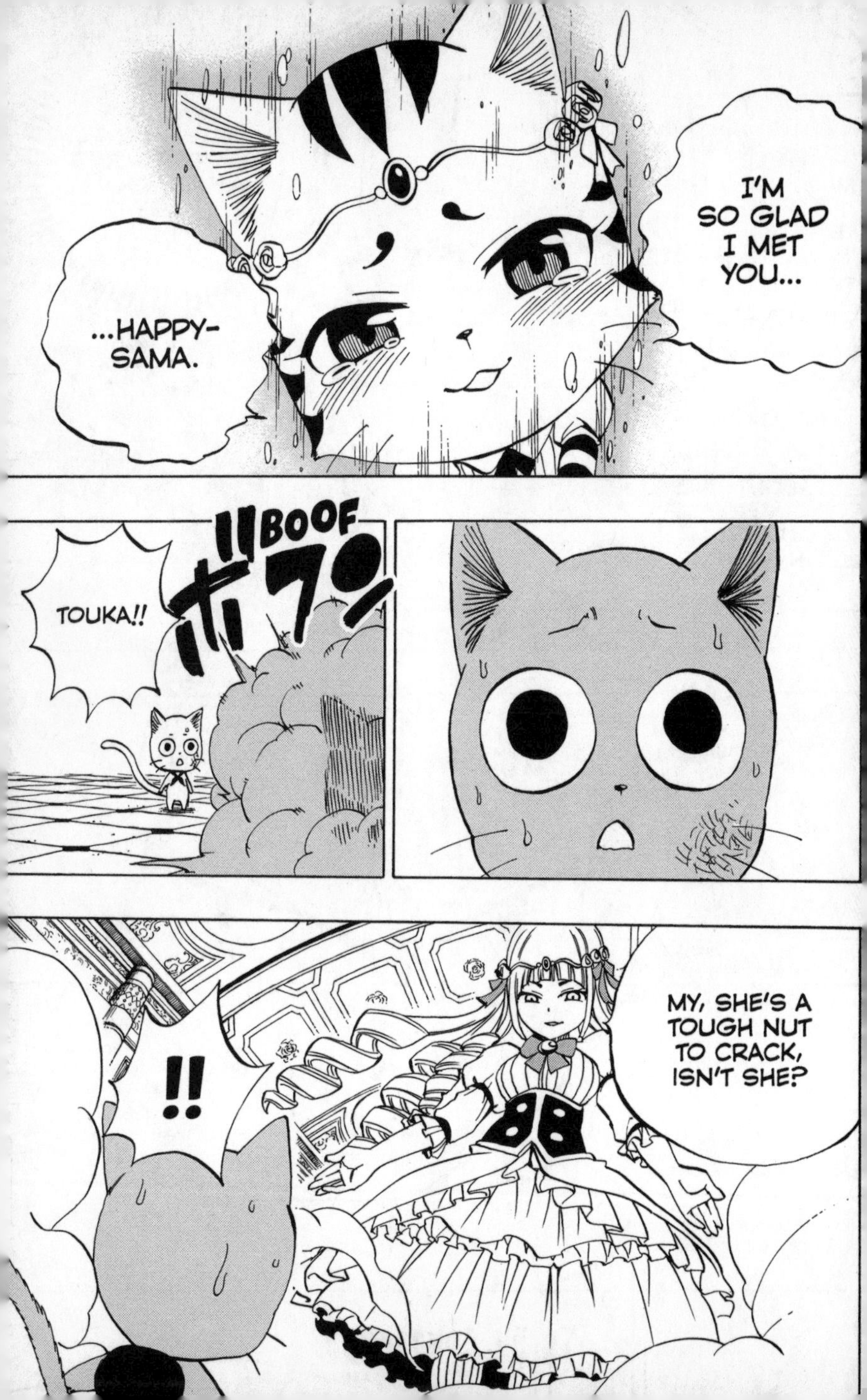
I'M SO GLAD I MET YOU...
...HAPPY-SAMA.
BOOF
ボフ
TOUKA!!
MY, SHE'S A TOUGH NUT TO CRACK, ISN'T SHE?
!!

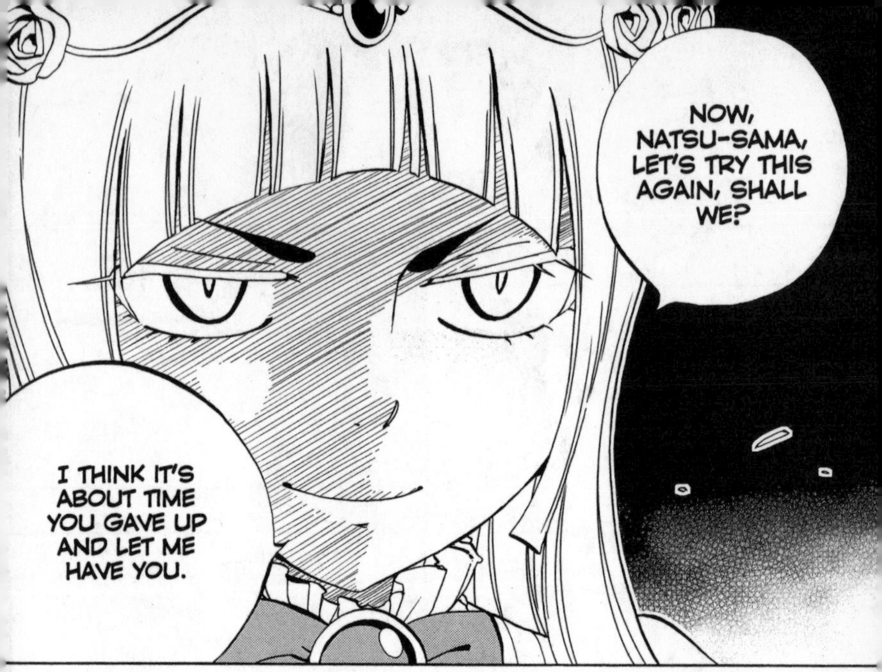
NOW, NATSU-SAMA, LET'S TRY THIS AGAIN, SHALL WE?
I THINK IT'S ABOUT TIME YOU GAVE UP AND LET ME HAVE YOU.

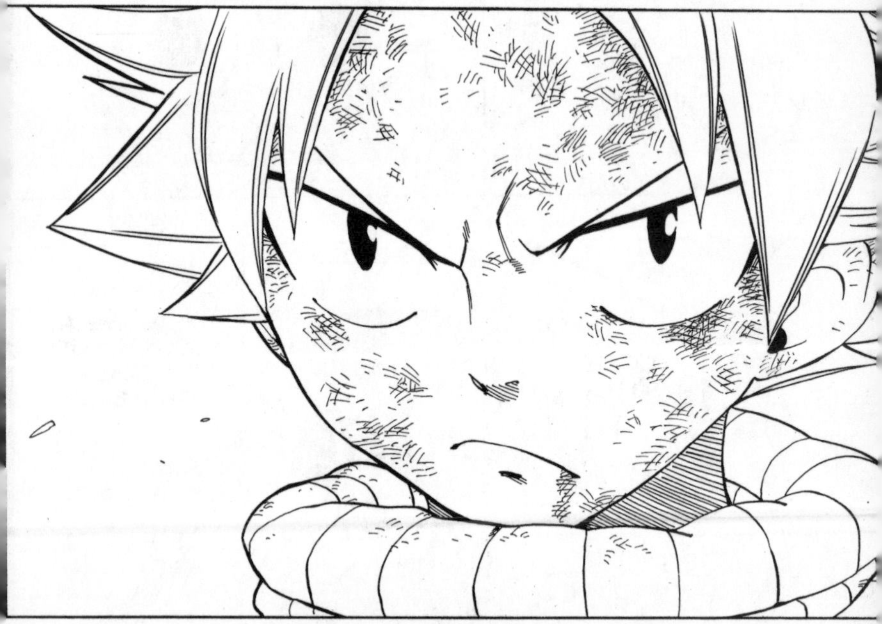

TO BE CONTINUED

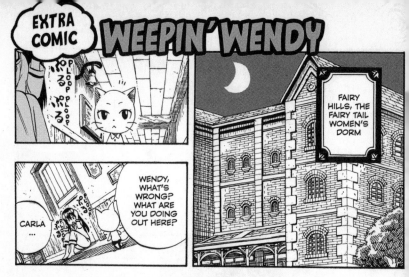

EXTRA COMIC WEEPIN' WENDY

FAIRY HILLS, THE FAIRY TAIL WOMEN'S DORM
ぷるぷる PLOOP PLOOP
WENDY, WHAT'S WRONG? WHAT ARE YOU DOING OUT HERE?
ぷるぷる PLOOP PLOOP
CARLA ...
CARLAAA!
ぷるぷる PLOOP PLOOP
ひぐっ HIC
ひぐっ HIC
ぷるぷる PLOOP PLOOP
OH MY GOD! YOU LOOK LIKE IT'S THE END OF THE WORLD. WHAT'S THE MATTER?
THERE'S A— A BUG...
IN MY ROOM...
ぐすっ SNIFF
ささっ ZIP ZIP ZIP

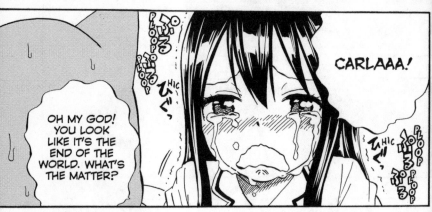

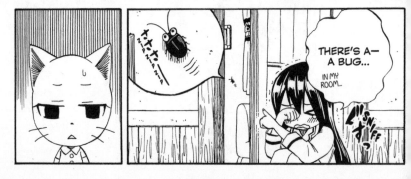

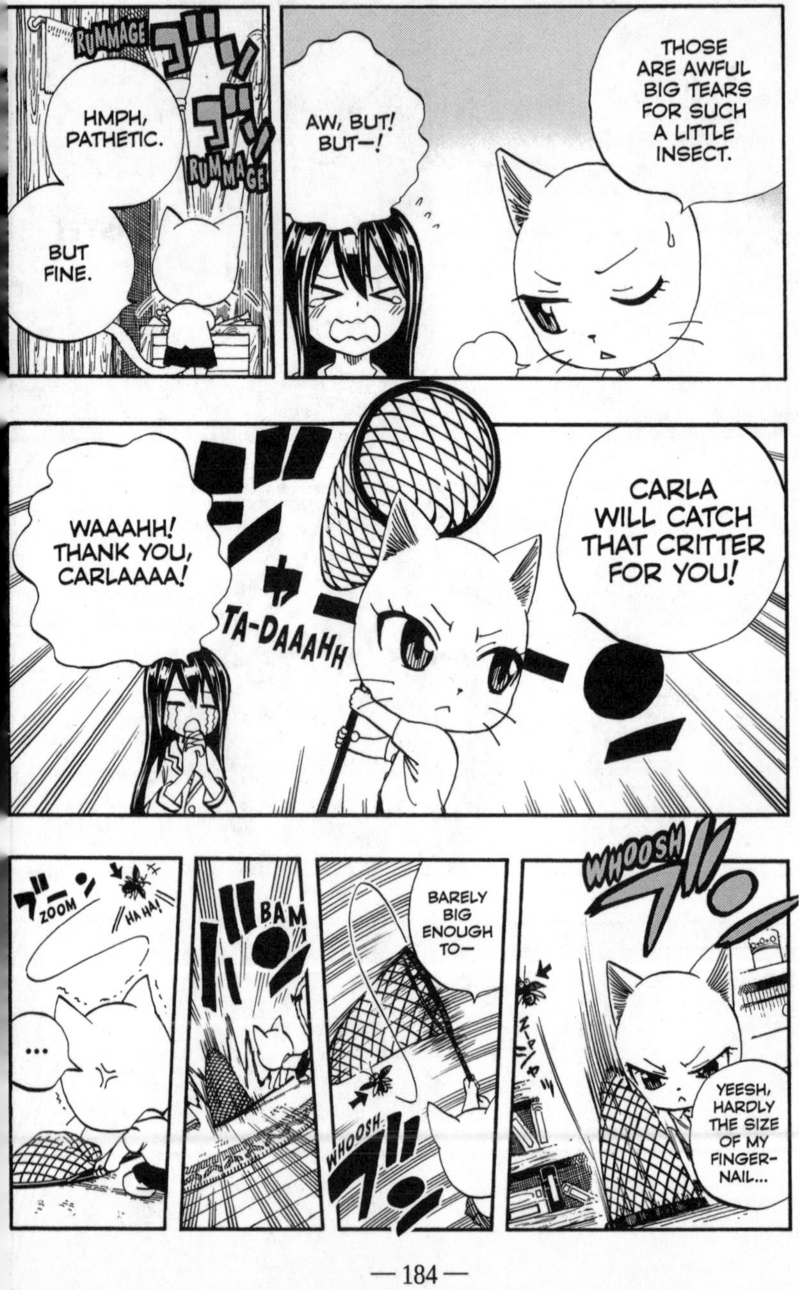
THOSE ARE AWFUL BIG TEARS FOR SUCH A LITTLE INSECT.
AW, BUT! BUT—!
RUMMAGE
RUMMAGE
HMPH, PATHETIC.
BUT FINE.
CARLA WILL CATCH THAT CRITTER FOR YOU!
TA-DAAAHH
WAAAHH! THANK YOU, CARLAAAA!
WHOOSH
YEESH, HARDLY THE SIZE OF MY FINGER-NAIL...
BARELY BIG ENOUGH TO—
WHOOSH
BAM
ZOOM
HA HA!
...

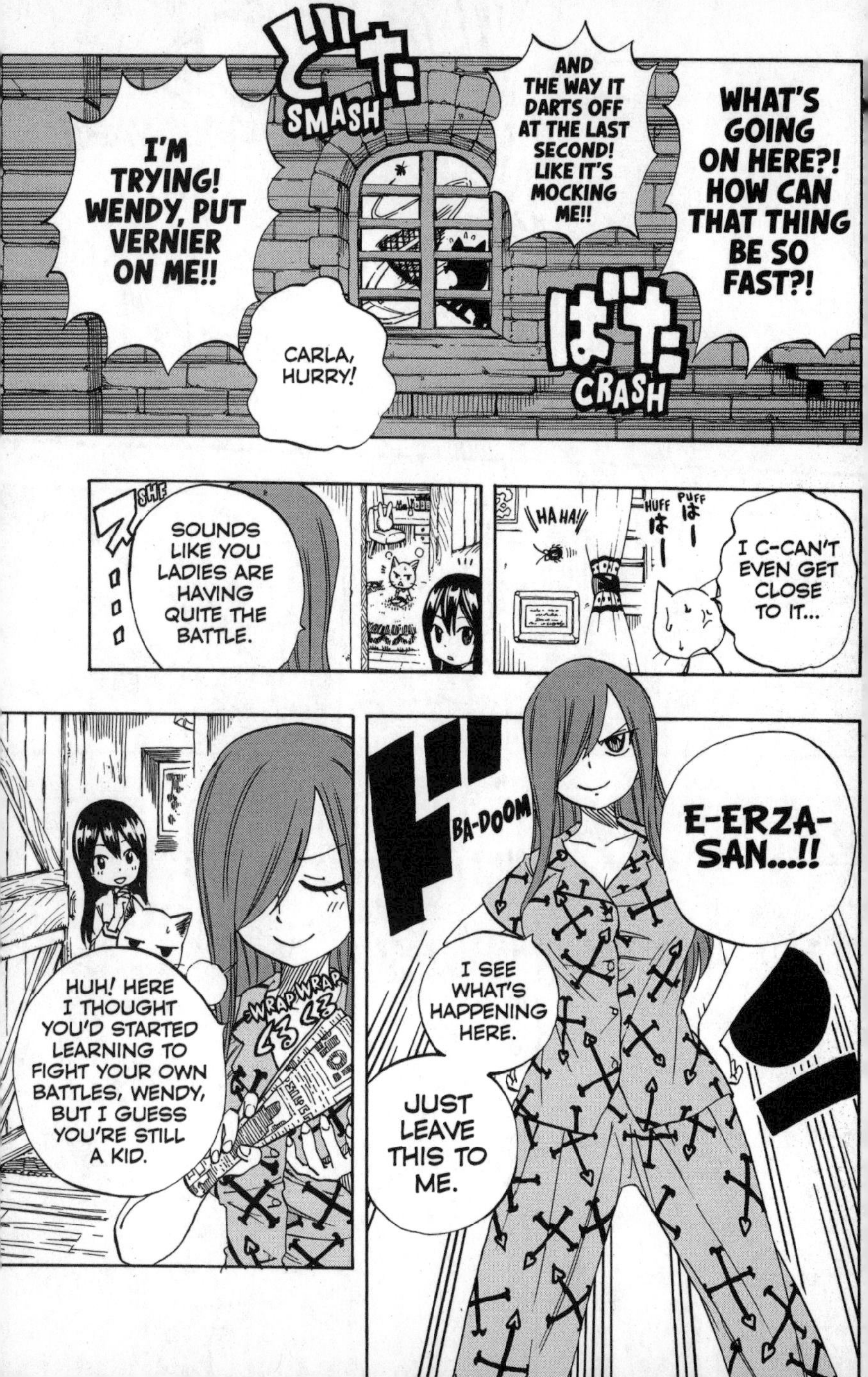
WHAT'S GOING ON HERE?! HOW CAN THAT THING BE SO FAST?!
AND THE WAY IT DARTS OFF AT THE LAST SECOND! LIKE IT'S MOCKING ME!!
SMASH
CRASH
I'M TRYING! WENDY, PUT VERNIER ON ME!!
CARLA, HURRY!
HUFF はー
PUFF はー
HA HA!
I C-CAN'T EVEN GET CLOSE TO IT...
SHF
SOUNDS LIKE YOU LADIES ARE HAVING QUITE THE BATTLE.
E-ERZA-SAN...!!
BA-DOOM
I SEE WHAT'S HAPPENING HERE.
JUST LEAVE THIS TO ME.
WRAP WRAP くるくる
HUH! HERE I THOUGHT YOU'D STARTED LEARNING TO FIGHT YOUR OWN BATTLES, WENDY, BUT I GUESS YOU'RE STILL A KID.

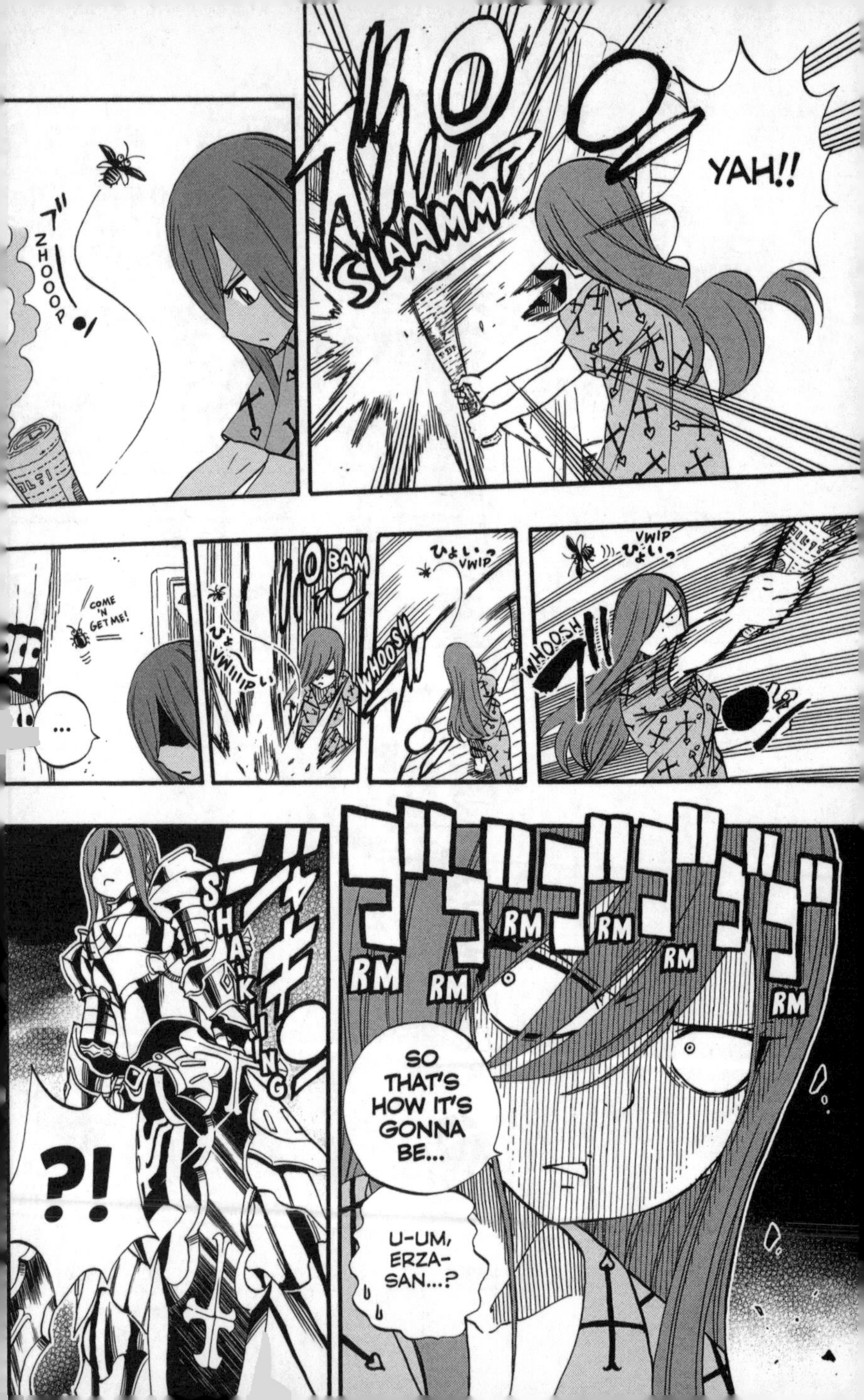
YAH!!
SLAAMM
ZHOOOOP
VWIP
WHOOSH
VWIP
BAM
WHOOSH
VWIIIIP
COME 'N GET ME!
...
RM RM RM RM RM RM
SO THAT'S HOW IT'S GONNA BE...
U-UM, ERZA-SAN...?
SHAKIIING
?!

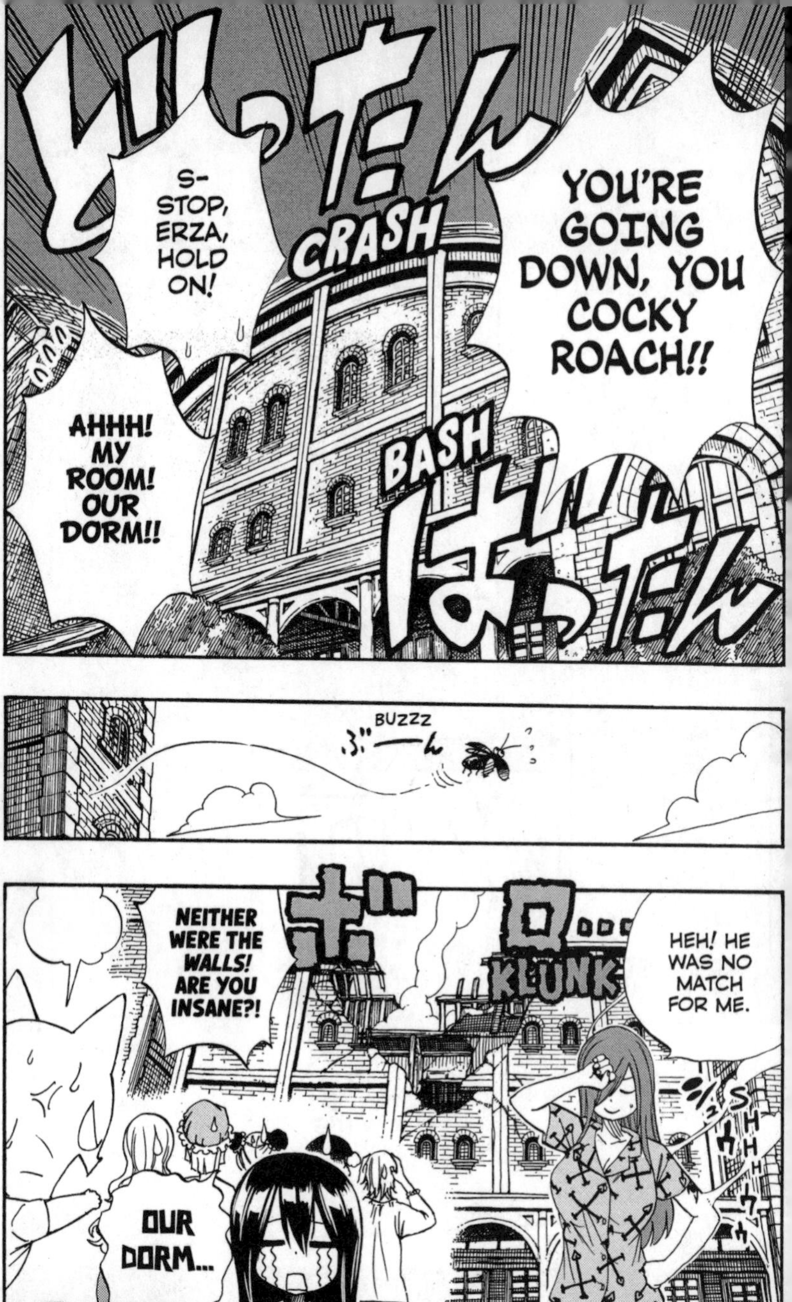
YOU'RE GOING DOWN, YOU COCKY ROACH!!
CRASH
S-STOP, ERZA, HOLD ON!
BASH
AHHH! MY ROOM! OUR DORM!!
BUZZZ
HEH! HE WAS NO MATCH FOR ME.
KLUNK
NEITHER WERE THE WALLS! ARE YOU INSANE?!
OUR DORM...

END

DE ART RETURNS

(MIYAGI PREFECTURE GAJI-LEVY LOVE)

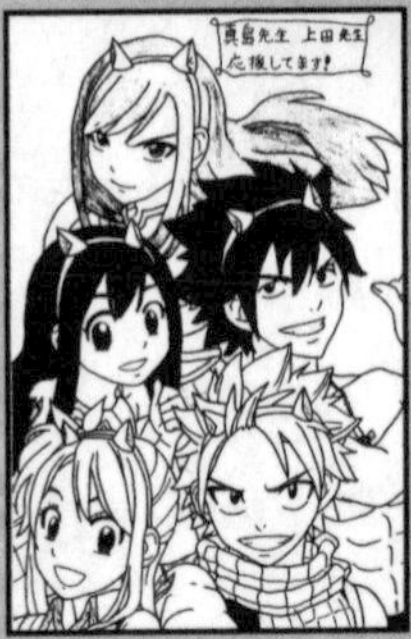

▼ CAT EARS ALL AROUND! HOW CUTE! I LOVE IT!

(KANAGAWA PREFECTURE SORA)

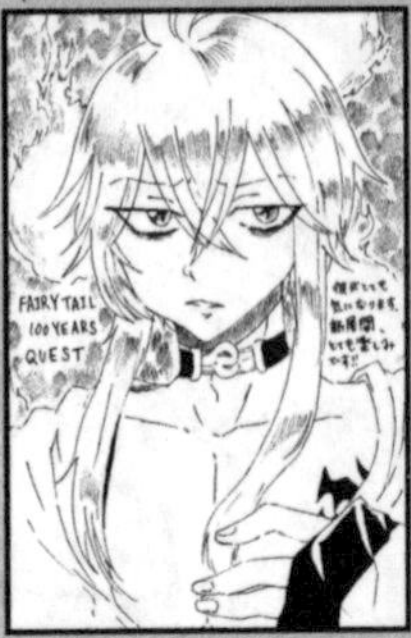
FAIRY TAIL
100 YEARS
QUEST

▲ WRAITH, VERY NICE.
I'M CURIOUS, TOO!

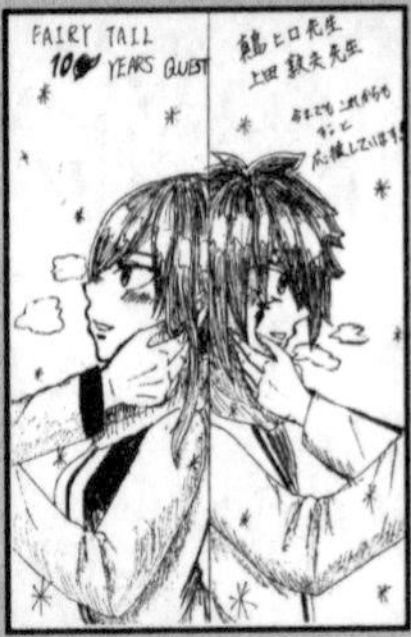
FAIRY TAIL
100 YEARS QUEST

▼ LOVE HOW THIS DESIGN USES THE TWO SIDES OF THE PAGE!

(AOMORI PREFECTURE KOSHU)

(HYOGO PREFECTURE NEKOSUZU)

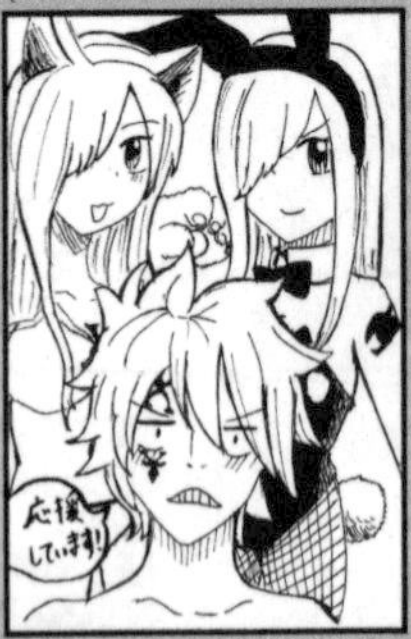

▲ JELLAL...
HOW DID THIS HAPPEN?

▼ HOW COULD I EVER REFUSE WENDY
WHEN SHE LOOKS LIKE THAT...?!

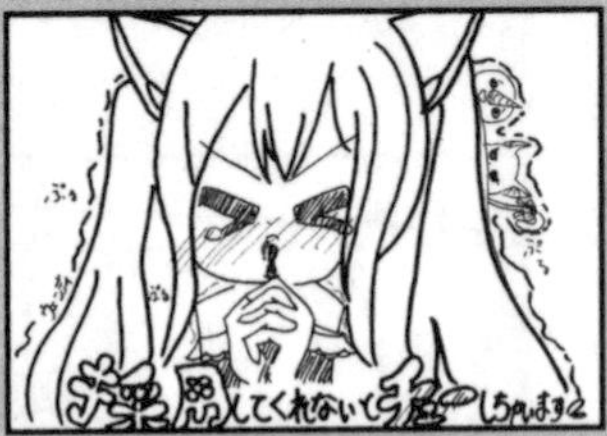

(AOMORI PREFECTURE KITSUNE)

(O!TA PREFECTURE ANNA SHIOZUKI)

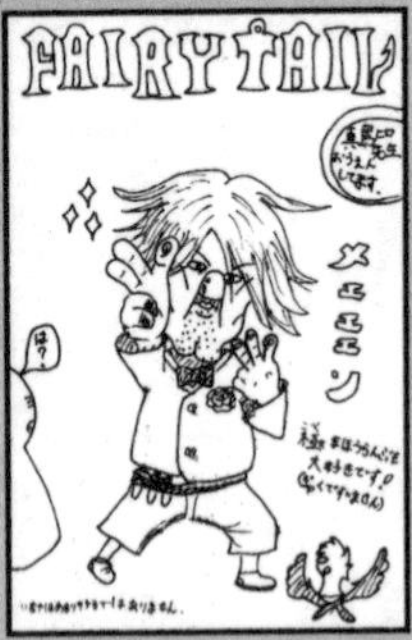
FAIRY TAIL

▲ HEY, DON'T I JUST LOVE IT!
(HEHE) THIS IS QUALITY ART.

FAIRY TAIL 100 YEARS QUEST GUILD

(CHIBA PREFECTURE NAGAO)

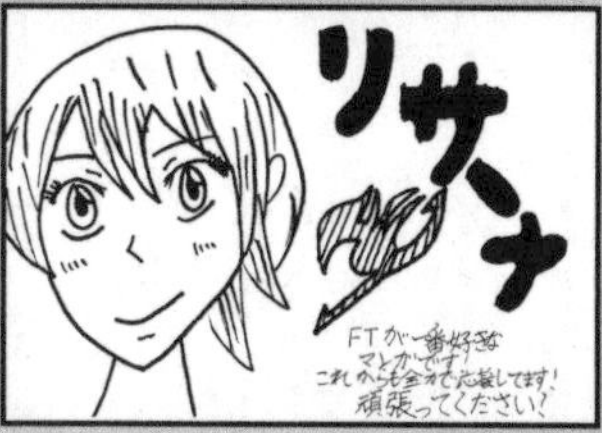
FTが一番好きなマンガです！これからも全力で応援してます！頑張ってください！

▼ OOH! LISANNA GETS A PICTURE ALL TO HERSELF! THANK YOU!

(AICHI PREFECTURE NONOKA YAMASHITA)

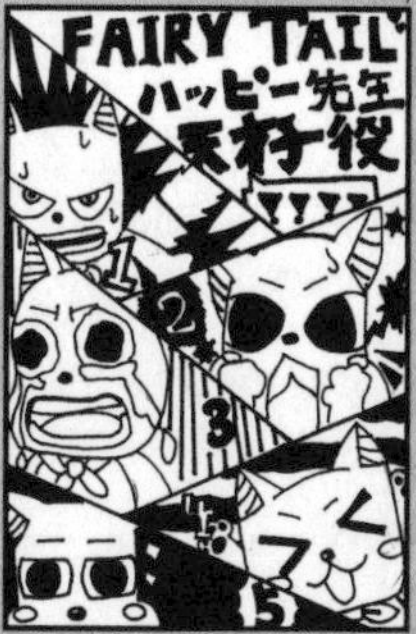
FAIRY TAIL

▼ THE MANY FACES OF HAPPY!

(KYOTO PREFECTURE HANA MORIKIYO)

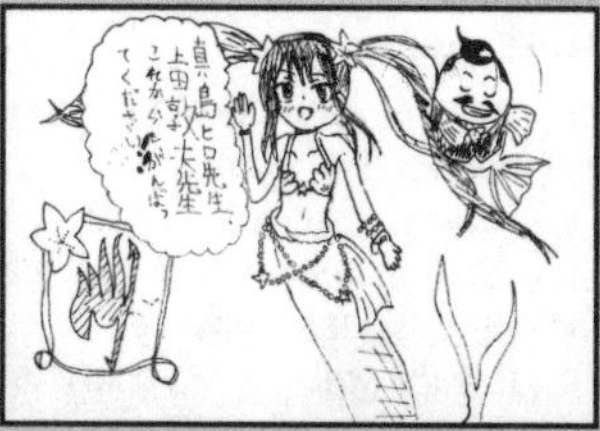

▼ I WISHED... I COULD HAVE LET HER BE A MERMAID...

(YAMAGUCHI PREFECTURE MAHIRON)

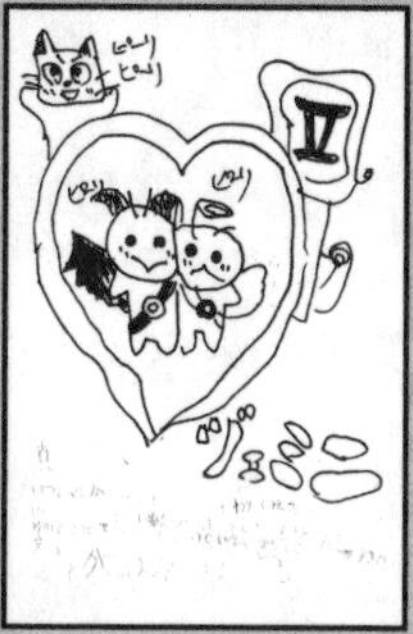

▲ CUTE~~!! LOVE HOW THE IDEA OF THE ANGEL/DEVIL VERSIONS WORKS!

FAIL CORNER

(TOKUSHIMA PREFECTURE TOSHIHIRO MIKI)

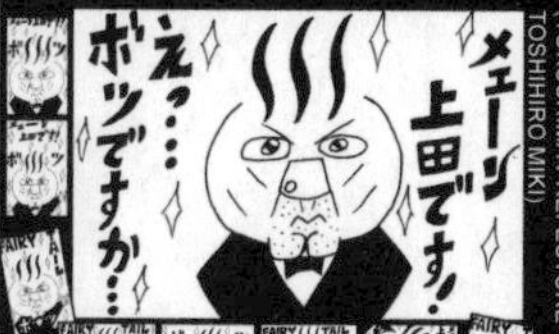
メェーン 上田です！
えっ…ボツですか…

▲ THEY ACTUALLY SENT ME 10 DIFFERENT PICTURES... (LOL) TRUST ME, I'M NOT THIS GOOD LOOKING! FAIL! (LOL)

(CHIBA PREFECTURE KANAKO NAGAO)

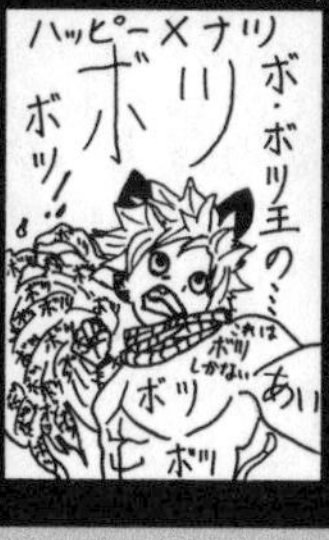
ハッピー×ナツ
ボ・ボツ王の…
ボツ!!
あい

▼ IT...IT'S A MONSTER! THIS CAN ONLY BE A FAIL! (LOL)

HERE'S OUR FOURTH BATCH OF FAN DRAWINGS! ENJOY!

EDITOR'S NOTE: DRAWING SUBMISSIONS LIMITED TO JAPAN.

TRANSLATION NOTES

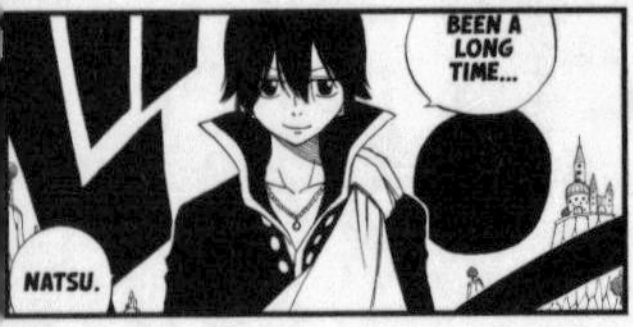
BEEN A LONG TIME...
NATSU.

Zeref's Outfit, page 8

Zeref appears to be wearing the robe of a Buddhist monk, or at least something meant to evoke one. That is, his outfit associates him with enlightenment, or perhaps with repose after death.

Hades, page 14

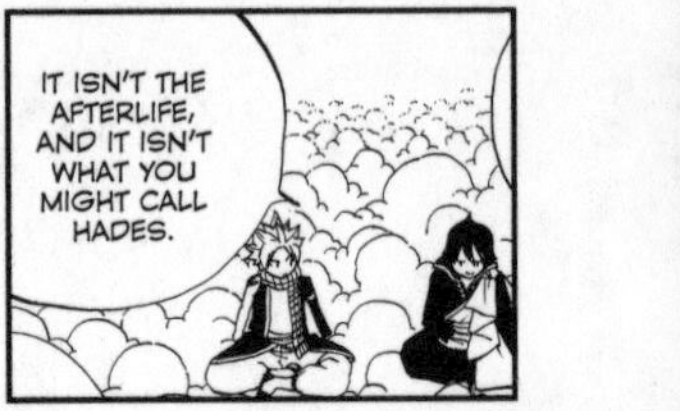
IT ISN'T THE AFTERLIFE, AND IT ISN'T WHAT YOU MIGHT CALL HADES.

In Japanese he says *yomi no kuni* (the land of Yomi), which is the traditional Japanese afterlife. Shinto mythology conceives this place not as a realm of reward and punishment for virtue and evil, but simply as a place where people continue to exist as shadowy spirits, very much like Hades or indeed Sheol ("the pit" of the Hebrew Bible).

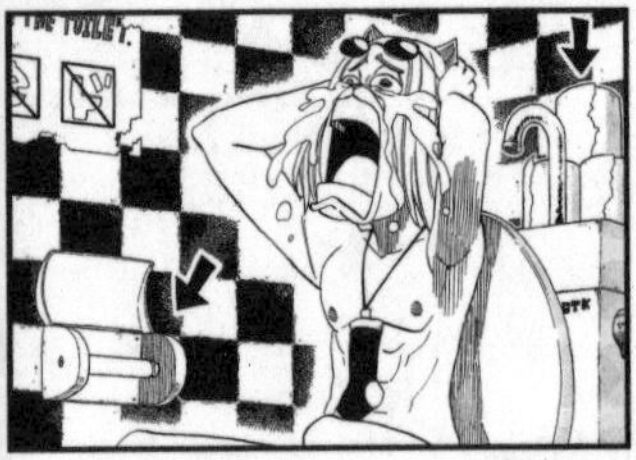

Toilet, page 43

Notice the faucet on the top of the toilet tank. This is standard equipment in Japan – the top of the toilet bowl is actually a little sink, and flushing the toilet automatically causes (clean) water to come out of the faucet as well. You can wash your hands, and the water flows down the drain of the sink and into the toilet tank.

Coo-Coo, page 45

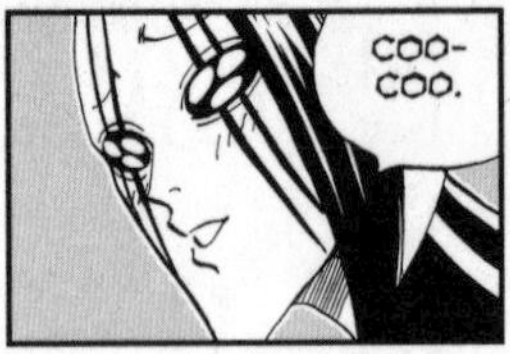
COO-COO.

Nebaru calls Wendy "*Mayu-mayu*," a simple play on the Japanese word for cocoon (*mayu*). We chose to localize it in the translation so that English readers would be able to immediately understand what the name was supposed to mean and why it seems to upset Wendy.

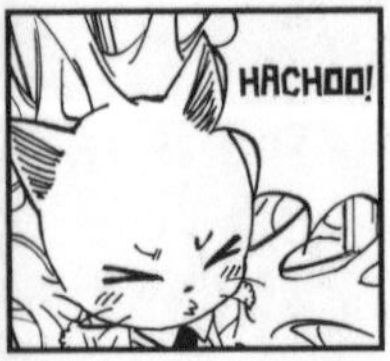
HACHOO!

Hachoo, page 137

A common Japanese belief holds that when you sneeze, it means someone's talking about you.

Magazine

The publication mentioned in Ueda-sensei's author blurb as simply *Magazine* is *Weekly Shonen Magazine* (*Shuukan Shounen Magajin*), a manga anthology published by Kodansha. It launched in 1959.

FAIRY TAIL
100 YEARS QUEST

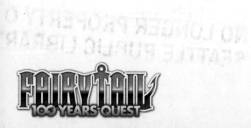

A Kodansha Comics Trade Paperback Original
FAIRY TAIL: 100 Years Quest 5 copyright © 2020 Hiro Mashima/Atsuo Ueda
English translation copyright © 2020 Hiro Mashima/Atsuo Ueda

Published in the United States by Kodansha Comics, an imprint of Kodansha USA Publishing, LLC, New York.

Publication rights for this English edition arranged through Kodansha Ltd., Tokyo.

First published in Japan in 2020 by Kodansha Ltd., Tokyo.

ISBN 978-1-63236-984-0

Original cover design by Hisao Ogawa (Blue in Green)

Printed in the United States of America.

www.kodanshacomics.com

9 8 7 6 5 4 3 2 1
Translation: Kevin Steinbach
Lettering: Phil Christie
Kodansha Comics edition cover design by Phil Balsman

Publisher: Kiichiro Sugawara

Director of publishing services: Ben Applegate
Associate director of operations: Stephen Pakula
Publishing services managing editor: Noelle Webster
Assistant production manager: Emi Lotto, Angela Zurlo